A829

$2.50

December 2, 1851

Contemporary
Writings on the
Coup d'Etat of
Louis Napoleon

Edited with
Introductions by
John B. Halsted

Commentary by
Alexis de Tocqueville
Walter Bagehot
Karl Marx
Pierre-Joseph Proudhon
Victor Hugo

DECEMBER 2, 1851

JOHN B. HALSTED is a Professor of History at Amherst College. He received his B.A. and M.A. from Wesleyan University and his Ph.D. from Columbia University. His masters thesis was a study of Tocqueville and his doctoral thesis was on Bagehot. He has also taught at Stevens Institute of Technology. A member of Phi Beta Kappa and the American Historical Association, he has previously edited *Romanticism: Problems in Definition, Explanation, and Evaluation* and *Romanticism*.

DECEMBER 2, 1851

CONTEMPORARY WRITINGS ON THE COUP D'ÉTAT OF LOUIS NAPOLEON

———

Edited with Introductions by John B. Halsted

ANCHOR BOOKS

DOUBLEDAY & COMPANY, INC.

GARDEN CITY, NEW YORK

1972

CONTENTS

PREFACE

THE CHIEF PURPOSE of this volume is to display the responses of five first-rate minds to a major political event. It is unusual that any event such as the coup d'état by means of which Louis Napoleon Bonaparte took over the control of the Second French Republic should have occasioned four significant works by major thinkers. Readers of Karl Marx's *The Eighteenth Brumaire of Louis Bonaparte* will readily recall two others, to which Marx refers in his preface: Victor Hugo's *Napoleon the Little,* and Pierre-Joseph Proudhon's *The Social Revolution Demonstrated by the Coup d'État.* The first is a scathing attack on the perpetrator of what Hugo considered the crime of the coup; the second is a paradoxical appeal by the great anarchist to the victorious Louis Napoleon to lead the "Revolution." All three studies had been finished within eight months after the date of the event, i.e., December 2, 1851. At the time the event occurred, a young Englishman who was to become one of England's most interesting political and social thinkers, Walter Bagehot, was in Paris. In the two months following, he was to send back to England his "Letters on the French *Coup d'État* of 1851," essays that anticipated many of the theories of his mature works. This constitutes the fourth major work emanating from the immediate time of the coup. I have added one further piece of contemporary comment, Alexis de Tocqueville's letter to the London *Times* of December 11, 1851. This is by no means a work of the stature or scope of the others—but it does allow the inclusion of the immediate reaction of the man whom I and many others feel was probably the most perceptive observer of his age and one who was himself deeply affected by the coup.

As introductory background for these works, there is a short narrative description of the salient events leading up to and surrounding the coup to provide context for the selections and to illuminate what might otherwise be puzzling references. The documents themselves are presented not as guides to "what really happened," but rather as expressions of the minds of their authors—I am therefore the more regretful that all except Tocqueville's letter have had to be cut significantly to fit into a single volume. The real interest here is in what such minds as those of Tocqueville, Bagehot, Marx, Proudhon, and Hugo could make of the coup and why they made what they did of it. There is an opportunity to assess how these men understood their present, how they connected it with the past and the future, and how they wanted others to understand these things. For example, they were especially concerned about the "meaning" of the event: as a commentary on the failure of the 1848 revolutions or as the temporary triumph of force or the bureaucratic state over the principles of the "Revolution" or of democracy. One of the most intriguing aspects of the conjunction of these readings is to display comparisons between, for example, the systematic way Marx was developing for looking at historical events and the very literary way in which Hugo confronted them. There is also an intriguing puzzle: all five men were immensely talented, and three—Tocqueville, Marx, and Proudhon—spent much effort on prediction, yet all of them were comparatively unsuccessful in predicting the long-run consequences of the coup d'état. We will return to some of these questions in a brief concluding chapter.

Another aspect that adds interest to the conjunction of these five pieces is the variety of interrelationships among the figures we study. It has for a couple of decades become nearly habitual for commentators to compare Tocqueville's and Marx's treatments of the Second French Republic; more recently the sociology and history of Marx and Tocqueville—their methods in general—have led to still further comparisons. Hugo and Proudhon knew one another, both sat on the left in the Assembly; Proudhon and Marx knew one another but were unable to collaborate; the similarities between Tocqueville's and Bagehot's thought are striking, but have never been explored. The purpose of the rather long introductory chapters preceding each author's study is to note some of these interrelationships, to sketch the author's career, especially in regard to his relationship to the coup d'état and Louis Napoleon, and to comment sufficiently upon his ideas so as to permit an informed reading of the selection.

I trust it is clear that the purpose of this volume is not to offer anything like a *sampling* of opinion, but instead to bring together in convenient form the views of some very great men. (Hence I feel quite free to dispense with all but a mention of lesser writers on the coup such as Louis Vieullot or Constantin Frantz.)

It is especially gratifying to have the opportunity to introduce readers to Proudhon's book, which has not before been translated into English.

I want particularly to express my appreciation for the assistance given me by Floyd S. Merritt and his staff at the Reference Desk at the Robert Frost Library at Amherst College.

J. B. H.

DECEMBER 2, 1851

INTRODUCTION

LOUIS NAPOLEON BONAPARTE had been President of the Second French Republic for eight days less than three years when he took full power into his own hands by means of a coup d'état. He chose December 2, 1851, the anniversary of his uncle's great victory at Austerlitz, as the moment to dissolve the National Legislative Assembly. He then prepared to inaugurate a new Constitution that would extend the presidential term beyond the four years (without re-election) allowed by the old Constitution. In the correct expectation of most contemporary observers, this was but a step toward the re-establishment of a Napoleonic Empire. The Empire was announced in 1852 and lasted until its defeat in 1870 in the Franco-Prussian War.

Three years earlier, Louis Napoleon had been elected President by an overwhelming majority. In December 1848, the Second French Republic's first presidential elections had culminated eight months of troubled existence for the new government which had been born in the revolution of the preceding February. Louis Napoleon drew 5,434,000 votes to 1,448,000 votes for his nearest rival, the staunch republican General Louis Cavaignac, who had controlled the executive power through the preceding summer. Other candidates, Alphonse de Lamartine, Alexandre Ledru-Rollin, and François Raspail, were weak also-rans.

Louis Napoleon had been active only briefly in French politics at the time of his election. The preceding regime, the July Monarchy, established in 1830 under Louis Philippe, had imprisoned and exiled him for two quite ludicrous attempted invasions of France. He had thereby obtained notoriety, but not the fame that accompanies success. His writings probably had a more useful effect. He had written his *Napoleonic Ideas*, outlining his views on the regime which would build a better France—clearly another Napoleonic Empire, making use of the highly centralized French bureaucratic machine—and his pamphlet on *The Extinction of Pauperism* suggesting vaguely socialist leanings. These may have begun to spread his appeal among that variety of interest groups that went to make up his immense majority in December 1848.

He returned from exile in England after the February revolution of 1848 had overthrown the July Monarchy, but the new Provisional Government nervously asked him to depart. He was none the less elected to the Assembly in June; but he resigned in the face of the uproar caused by his election. He was re-elected again in September, and thereafter began his successful presidential campaign.[1]

During the early days of the Second Republic there were not many avowed Bonapartists. There was, of course, the widespread Napoleonic legend and the latent Bonapartism that had survived—and been recurrently stimulated—through preceding regimes. To this was added the publicity produced by the press and the government over the return and election of Louis Napoleon, which raised the traditional problems of the proscription of the Bonapartes and Louis Napoleon's supposed role as pretender. Soon after his first election the Assembly withdrew his proscription. Two weeks later there were six Bonapartist newspapers, and his partisans were becoming a party with an active propaganda organization.

[1] A detailed treatment, with special attention to the press, is André-Jean Tudesq, *L'élection Présidentielle de Louis Napoleon Bonaparte, 10 December, 1848* (Paris, 1965).

A revival of Bonapartism had to contend against the dominant preferences of politically active Frenchmen. These fell into three major categories: first, the Legitimists, who sought a revival of the Bourbon monarchy which had been overthrown in 1789 and resuscitated after the fall of Napoleon, only to fall itself in the revolution of July 1830; second, the Orleanists, supporters of the restoration of the Orléans monarchy, which had succeeded to power in the July revolution of 1830, to fall in its turn in February 1848, as a major signal for the outbreak of liberal and nationalist revolutions throughout most of Europe; and third, a wide spectrum of republicans. These last included many whose constitutional and social views accorded closely with those of the monarchists, but who believed that the revival of monarchy itself was impossible; also among the republicans were many others who sought truly radical transformation of the entire social order, beginning with the use of the universal suffrage, which had been won by the February revolution, and ending only when property, and perhaps the relations of the sexes, had been totally remodeled. Socialists were still republicans in 1848, but by December their situation in France had changed significantly since the greatest crisis of the Second Republic, the June Days of 1848. Then the workers and artisans of Paris, fighting over the closing of the National Workshops and the "right to work," had gone down to bloody defeat before the combined forces of the bourgeois National Guard and troops of the line. Their defeat had greatly weakened their ties to the Second Republic; while the workers lost faith in the Republic, the socialist and radical republican politicians lost potential support and hence prestige.

Louis Napoleon's immense electoral victory is only partly explained by a propaganda organization on the one hand and the divisions between and within potentially opposing political groups on the other. It is important to note that he was misjudged and underestimated.

Louis Napoleon's abilities seemed trivial and the distance between his intentions in the fall of 1848 and the establishment of a Napoleonic regime truly formidable. The folly of his in-surrectionary failures served to mislead other politicians, who came to support him because they thought they could control him. Adolphe Thiers, a major figure in the opposition under the July Monarchy and later to be a founder of the Third Republic, is a leading example. He was one of the *notables*,[2] an important member of the Party of Order, which dominated the Republic after June. It was he who persuaded the monar-chist groups and the conservative republicans who opposed the candidature of General Cavaignac (joined together in the Comité de la rue de Poitiers) to put up no candidate of their own. In the course of the campaign, further support came from much of the monarchist and Catholic press. Among the mass of the population, it is evident that Louis Napoleon also re-ceived large-scale peasant support[3] and considerable support from workers who perhaps felt betrayed by the Republic after the June Days and hopeful that Louis Napoleon's brand of "socialism," as sketched in his early pamphlet on pauperism, might offer some benefit to them. T. A. B. Corley has explained his victory partly on the basis of possession of the Bonaparte name; but adds that his candidacy was also unique in other ways:

> Further, he had a definite programme which he had consist-ently proclaimed in terms that all could understand. Bona-partism represented the only realistic alternative to the various forms of government that France had had in recent years and had rejected. Only by this means could a progressive State above party be created, which would seek to foster the aspira-tions of the industrial and commercial bourgeoisie while recon-ciling its interests with those of the peasantry on the one hand and of the growing proletariat on the other. Most impor-tant of all, he had made his name and views known even

[2] The *notables* were Legitimists and Orleanists who had held leading positions in the Monarchy of July.
[3] Tudesq, p. 220. Tudesq views the election as the emergence of the peasantry into French political life.

4

in the remotest districts of France, not through the distrusted official channels, but by means of his own efforts. His opponents, especially the republicans, had been too fundamentally divided among themselves to make common cause or jointly to put forward any constructive policy. Cavaignac, the only man who might have defeated him, was suspected equally by left and right.[4]

Louis Napoleon's electoral success can also be understood as the crushing defeat of General Cavaignac, whose prestige in the early summer had been immense as the savior and defender of the Republic. The parties and their leaders on the Right, however, were offended by Cavaignac's consistent and stubborn republicanism. The Republic's repute had been in decline since February, as Parisian radicalism seemed to threaten the stability of provincial France. Frederick A. de Luna in his recent book on Cavaignac views the election as a vote against the February revolution and what were believed to be its consequences—the June Days—as a defeat for the victors in that revolution, the middle and lesser bourgeoisie.[5]

The very poor showing made by Lamartine (who had headed the Provisional Government from February to June) would clearly support such contentions, as would the similar fate of Ledru-Rollin and Raspail, a radical democrat and a socialist respectively. The inability of the parties on the Left to agree upon a candidate was in itself another factor contributing to Louis Napoleon's majority. There was obviously little numerical support for the radical Left, anyway, and the radical Left found it impossible to support Cavaignac, whom it viewed as the butcher of June and as implicated in all the subsequent repression, i.e., the state of siege instituted in June, the destruction of the autonomy of political clubs, the forbidding of secret societies, the tightened surveillance of political meetings, and increased restrictions on the radical press.

[4] T. A. B. Corley, *Democratic Despot* (London, 1961), p. 72.
[5] *The French Republic Under Cavaignac, 1848* (Princeton, 1969), ch. XV. See also Tudesq, p. 238.

The Constituent Assembly, which passed such repressive legislation under Cavaignac's leadership during the summer, had been elected in April. It had probably then contained a majority willing to support a republic, but as was increasingly to be demonstrated through the life of the Second Republic and the European revolutions of 1848, universal suffrage could have surprisingly conservative results. Provincial France had shocked Paris by returning moderates who were far from ready to satisfy the aspirations of Parisian radicals. Their major accomplishment was the Constitution under which Louis Napoleon was elected, a Constitution that on the one hand appeared liberal in restricting presidential powers by making the President ineligible for re-election, but on the other hand placed in his hands all the immense power of the strong centralized French civil service, police, and army, giving him great opportunity to subvert the Republic if he wished. The Constitution also provided that both the President and a new Legislative Assembly should derive their authority from the same source, i.e., be elected by universal suffrage. The possibility of conflict was to be feared, but given the muddled state of parties and powers in the winter of 1848, its outcome was not clearly predictable.

Louis Napoleon's overwhelming victory might suggest the contrary: that he was unchallengeable from the moment of his election, that in fact no other candidate could have opposed him successfully, and that he was in a position to effect a coup d'état on the morrow of his election. Contemporaries did not generally see matters in this light; they had not thought the outcome of the election a foregone conclusion, nor did they generally expect that the President would challenge the Assembly (some did expect a coup; Proudhon felt the coming of the Empire was inevitable). Most took Louis Napoleon too lightly at that time. It is only hindsight that allows us to regard the election of December 1848 as an obvious demonstration that the mass of Frenchmen were already disenchanted with the Republic.

The presidential election and the inauguration of the Constitution effected a stabilization of the Republic, marking a clear halt to any possible drift to the left, as was to be demonstrated by the ease with which later radical efforts were put down, especially in June 1849. This stabilization coincided in time with the weakening of the revolutionary impetus elsewhere in Europe; conversely, some of the success of the Right and of the old regime throughout Europe can be attributed to their revival of nerve which followed the defeat of the French lower classes in the June Days.[6]

The fate of the Second Republic was settled in an increasingly stable Europe, and settled without significant outside influence. The Republic's involvement in foreign affairs affected its life chiefly by affecting the strength of the parties competing for power within France. The major foreign imbroglio that warrants description here is the problem of the Roman expedition.

Reforms instituted by Pope Pius IX in 1848 had been deemed insufficient by Roman radicals in a year of revolution in Italy. In the uprising that occurred in January 1849—at the end of the wave of international revolutionary disturbances—the Pope fled from the Papal States, and a nationalist and anticlerical Roman Republic was formed, directed by a triumvirate whose leading figure was Giuseppe Mazzini. To preclude a papal restoration by reactionary Austria, in April 1849 Louis Napoleon obtained credits from the Assembly to send General Nicholas Oudinot and his troops on a campaign that finally overcame even the heroic resistance of Giuseppe Garibaldi, put down the Republic, and restored the Pope. The outcome of this action flew in the face of the republican Left in France, both within and without the Assembly, which asserted that the Constitution's pledge against any attack upon the liberties of other peoples had been violated. The consequence was a major demonstration on June 13, 1849, which ended in the flight of the leading political

[6] The defeat of the Viennese revolution in October 1848 is another vital moment in the international milieu in which the Second Republic lived out its life. By December the new Austrian Emperor was regaining authority in central Europe.

7

figures on the radical Left, including Ledru-Rollin, who a year before had been candidate for President.

While the defeat of the Roman Republic constituted another major defeat for the French Left, it consolidated the President's ties with the Right, especially and most obviously with all Catholic interests. In a less evident way, within the confines of government itself, the events enhanced Louis Napoleon's power. Through most of the Roman expedition, the President had governed with a ministry drawn from the parliamentary majority, including Alexis de Tocqueville as Minister of Foreign Affairs. The Roman issue started a major controversy between the French government and the Pope, centered upon the adequacy of the pledges offered by the restored Pius IX to institute reform. Louis Napoleon tried direct presidential intervention into diplomacy by means of a well-publicized letter to Colonel Edgar Ney, his friend and aide-de-camp to General Oudinot, asserting that the restoration had not been undertaken to reinstitute reaction. Lacking support from his ministers, Louis Napoleon succeeded in dismissing them and in appointing a ministry of his preference, his first truly presidential ministry drawn from groups outside the parliamentary majority—thereby increasing his independence of action.[7]

The link that was being forged with the Church was made stronger by the Falloux law of March 1850, granting vastly increased clerical authority in the public education system. This law was passed by the new and strongly conservative National Legislative Assembly, which after long delay was finally elected on May 13, 1849. The old Constituent Assembly, fearing its successor would be far less liberal than itself, had been slow to dissolve and to set the date for elections, but eventually the pressure from President, ministry, and public became too great. The results were just as anticipated. The Right, the so-called Party of Order, made up largely of monarchist factions, obtained some 500 seats; only some 75 moderate republicans were

[7] See also below, pp. 21–22, 317–18.

elected; while the numbers on the Left rose to about 180, the Social-Democrats who now called themselves a new "Mountain" (i.e., the *Montagne,* recalling the *Montagnards,* the radical deputies who gathered in the higher seats of the Assembly in the First Republic), to conservatives a surprising and frightening increase of radicalism at the expense of the center. The Legislative Assembly, however, was dominantly anti-republican; its influence over the ministry was weakened by the shake-up that followed the Roman affair, and the Social-Democrats were weakened after the July 13 demonstration. Little wonder Louis Napoleon felt safe in aligning himself with the Right on the question of suppressing the Left.

But the co-operation did not last long, for another conflict was building, between the Assembly majority of moderates and rightists, looking for some sort of monarchical restoration, and the President, hopeful of establishing an Empire. The issues they contested were largely connected with the control of the instruments of power; the central issue came to be the Constitution which disallowed the President's re-eligibility. What the other elements in the balance of forces were to be became clearer over the last two years of the Republic's life—in the long run the alignment of the army, the administration, and provincial opinion were to be of major importance.

Through the course of 1850–51 Louis Napoleon increased his popularity and influence with the army and with the population outside Paris, making an important contribution in the process to the success of his later coup d'état. He competed with the Assembly in granting raises in pay to the lower ranks of the army, held reviews, and praised the troops. Where he was able, he replaced unsympathetic (i.e., excessively republican) officers with more amenable personnel. By January 1851 he found himself able to dismiss General Nicholas Changarnier, the most powerful soldier in the nation. Changarnier, looked upon as the "sword of the Assembly," held simultaneously the posts of commander of the Paris garrison and director of the National

Guard; he was dismissed for his support of a junior officer who kept his troops from shouting "Vive l'Empereur" in a review. The Assembly found itself unable to do more than protest. A year before the coup d'état, then, Louis Napoleon was master of the army and had alienated a significant portion of its leadership from both the Assembly and the Republic.

He also obtained effective publicity in his continual conflict with the Assembly over the presidential allowance, which he kept finding insufficient, and a presidential party kept growing in the chamber. But especially effective were his tours and his speeches through which he came to be known to an ever-increasing number of provincial Frenchmen as a potential savior from the dangerous radicalism of Parisian politics.

He also had the skill and good fortune to avoid the implication that he was the sponsor of the reduction of the franchise which passed on May 31, 1850, without his opposition. By this measure, three million voters were disfranchised through tightened residency requirements. The antipathy of radical republicans and socialists against the conservative majority in the Assembly was thereby reinforced, and rightly, for it was such voters the measure sought to exclude. Its passage was a major evidence of the persisting fear of radicalism-socialism which was thought to have produced the June Days in 1848 and more recently to have elected "dangerous" radicals such as the novelist Eugène Sue in by-elections. Such fears continued to contribute significantly to the atmosphere surrounding the coup d'état of 1851. Louis Napoleon seems not to have shared this dread of universal suffrage; in fact, throughout his career he helped to teach Europe's conservatives about the conservatism of the masses.

A new Assembly was to be elected almost simultaneously with the presidential elections of May 1852 which set the terminus to Louis Napoleon's office. There was widespread and recurrent fear that the new Assembly might be "red," and every shift in the state of the economy (which had not recovered from the impact of 1848 and did not prosper again until after the coup d'état)[8] seemed to enhance such anticipations, even though the restriction of the suffrage might have been thought sufficient protection. There was fear, too, of the possibility of an uprising in the interregnum when neither newly elected authority would be in office—election results indicated a growth of radicalism in the provinces in the period since 1849 that might presage new unknown dangers. But the greatest concern was over the fate of the executive, for it was abundantly evident that a vast number of Frenchmen wanted to be able to re-elect Louis Napoleon. Following his tours of France in 1850, petitions for revision of the Constitution poured into the Assembly from fifty-two of eighty-six departmental assemblies, urged on by Bonapartist administrators, formally favoring revision. After the Assembly attempted revision and failed, seventy-nine departmental councils petitioned again, with strong business backing.

Within the Assembly the effort at revision was faced with the opposition of the convinced republicans and of Orleanist deputies who hoped an Orleanist President might be elected in May. Support came from the President's party, from most of the Party of Order (many of them monarchists),[9] as well as from moderates who hoped by a prolongation of the President's term to forestall both a red revolution and a rightist coup—there had been rumors aplenty of potential monarchist as well as Bonapartist coups as the royalist groups sought throughout the year some fusion of the Orleanist and Legitimist camps. But revision required the approval of three fourths of the sitting members obtained in three successive sessions; the necessary majority could not be obtained for the report submitted in July by the commission of which Alexis de Tocqueville served as *rapporteur* —the vote was 446 in favor, 278 against. Assembly and President seemed surely headed for collision in May 1852, if not before.

When Louis Napoleon opened the session on November 4,

[8] Rondo E. Cameron, *France and the Economic Development of Europe* (Princeton, 1961), p. 125.
[9] Some Legitimists favored "total" revision to bring an end to the Republic rather than merely to extend the President's term.

1851, he raised the red specter, anticipating a vast demagogic conspiracy planned for 1852. He sketched the manner in which fear of such a plot was depressing business conditions by inhibiting financiers from investing and as a result encouraging demagoguery through further depression of business conditions.[10] But the President also urged the abrogation of the May 31 suffrage restriction. Thus, while bidding for moderate support, he offered a hand to the Left minority and again emphasized how sharply he was by now opposed to the Assembly majority. The attempt at repeal barely lost.

The anticipated confrontation was foreshadowed once more, when on November 17, in the Quaestors' Bill, an effort was made to obtain for the Assembly the right to call out troops for its own protection. The Assembly was now so torn—and the President's bid to the Left on the suffrage bill had helped divide it further—that it could not even muster a majority to agree to protect itself. Nor did it act on the bill on presidential responsibility, which threatened the President's power. Too many of its members wished its end; even republicans had voted against the Quaestors' Bill, thinking it presaged a monarchist coup d'état.

Louis Napoleon had been planning his own coup for some time, rejecting one date after another, finally settling upon the night of December 1–2, the anniversary of the battle of Austerlitz. He arrived at his decision in consultation with his chief advisors and fellow plotters: his long-time friend the Duc de Persigny; his half-brother the Comte de Morny; General Armand Jacques de Saint-Arnaud whose reputation had been made in Algeria; and Charlemagne Emile Maupas, an ex-prefect. The plans were laid with great care and carried out, at the start at least, with great success. Through Morny they had control over the Ministry of the Interior, through Maupas, the police, and through Saint-Arnaud, the Ministry of War. They disarmed

---

[10] Clearly this speech was very influential; Bagehot's interpretation of the coup reflects its impact; Hugo and Proudhon make a special point of attacking the idea.

potentially disaffected troops and citizenry, breaking the drums that might beat the call to arms. They succeeded in wetting the powder the National Guard might have used against them and gained control of the presses of Paris to prevent the printing of opposition placards. The walls of Paris were covered with their own placards during the night, presenting decrees re-establishing universal suffrage, dissolving the Assembly, and setting up a plebiscite to approve or disapprove these acts within two weeks. Morny ordered seventy-eight potential leaders of resistance arrested during the night, including sixteen deputies, among them Cavaignac and Changarnier, plus other republican generals, journalists, etc. Efforts on the part of the remaining members of the Assembly to hold rump meetings were broken up by troops, with further mass arrests. The High Court met long enough to declare Louis Napoleon a traitor, before it, too, was dispersed.

In Paris there were minor risings on December 3 and significant fighting on December 4, besides some quite indiscriminate shooting on the part of troops with a total dead of several hundred. Those of the working classes who might have manned the barricades had been weakened since the June Days, their natural leaders imprisoned or exiled. Few followed the Republican deputies who remained free and tried to organize resistance; they had little love for the leadership of deputies to whom they attributed repression and who were notorious for having voted themselves a twenty-five-franc daily gratuity.

The government sent orders to prefects throughout France to put down potential opposition; the fighting was heavier in the country than in Paris and, especially in traditionally republican areas, continued for several days. Throughout France summary justice was in effect. Over 26,000 suspects were arrested; 9,581 were transported to Algeria, 239 to Guiana. The cases of 89 ex-representatives were quickly settled, 5 being among those transported, 66 expelled (including Victor Hugo), these including most of the leaders of the Left and of the feeble resistance generated on the two days after the coup d'état.[11] The plebiscite of December 20 supported the coup d'état by 7,439,-216 to 646,737 votes.

Louis Napoleon consolidated his position with a new Constitution which resembled the Consulate of his uncle and introduced a presidential term of ten years. No one was very surprised when the Empire was declared on December 2, 1852, again having been ratified by a plebiscitary victory.

Soon after attaining full power in 1851 he shocked public opinion by confiscating the property of the Orléans family, thereby lending his critics further grounds for attacks upon him, although he used the funds for charitable purposes and such social reforms as workmen's housing. He also introduced important economic changes such as initiation of the *Crédit foncier* to give agricultural credit, and the Bank of France lowered its interest rate, stimulating economic activity.[12]

The widespread reaction to his coup d'état was approval. Within France, prior to December, Louis Napoleon had gained increasing support. Important Catholic journalists and deputies were favoring the extension of his powers in the summer. Louis Vieullot, editor of the powerful Catholic organ *L'Univers*, expressed such support a week before the coup. And soon after the coup leading Catholic figures, including Vieullot, Charles de Montalembert,[13] and the Pope himself were urging Catholics to support the President. Foreign governments were almost universally favorable—the situation in France would now be stabilized—although they remained hesitant about the prospects of another French Empire.

Lord Palmerston, the British Foreign Secretary, was too vocal in his support of Louis Napoleon and was forced to resign from

[11] The figures are taken from Howard C. Payne, *The Police State of Napoleon III* (Seattle, 1967), pp. 43, 65.

[12] The new regime increasingly revealed the influence on its economic policy of Saint-Simonian support for economic development.

[13] Charles Forbes, Comte de Montalembert (1810–70), leading liberal Catholic, an Orleanist who supported the coup d'état.

the Cabinet. Lord Normanby, the British Ambassador to France, was, on the contrary, so outspoken an opponent of the coup that he had to be replaced. This suggests that English opinion was very mixed. The London *Times* was shocked, yet the business community was joyful. Palmerston's own words in his letter to Normanby on December 3 suggest some of the problems faced by moderate English Liberalism (as Bagehot's "Letters" do more incisively):

> As to respect for the law and Constitution, that respect belongs to just and equitable laws framed under a Constitution founded upon reason, consecrated by its antiquity and by the memory of long years of happiness which the nation has enjoyed under it. It is scarcely a proper application of those feelings to require them to be directed to the day-before-yesterday tom-foolery which the scatterbrained heads of Marrast[14] and Tocqueville invented for the torment and perplexity of the French nation. . . .
>
> (To Normanby, 3 December 1851)[15]

There was virtual unanimity of opposition and condemnation from the radical and republican Left, now defeated and mostly in exile, but no general consensus on the event's meaning. Our readings include three leftists—Marx, Hugo, and Proudhon— who show some of the variety of opinion. It is of interest to note that Mazzini, recently defeated at Rome, contended that the coup was the fault of the French socialists pursuing local selfish interests, failing to see the need for internationalizing their efforts and that his remarks were a major incitement to the publication of Proudhon's book. For many of the defeated exiles, by early 1852 the era of recriminations had arrived.

[14] Armand Marrast (1801–52), editor of *Le National*, member of the Provisional Government and president of the Constituent Assembly; served on committee on the Constitution.
[15] A. E. M. Ashley, *Life of Palmerston*, vol. 1 (London, 1879), p. 291.

The coup d'état prepared the way for the coming of the Second Empire. In one of the most interesting and controversial studies of the Empire, Albert Guérard has pointed out three characteristic interpretations that are usually offered of Louis Napoleon and his regime.[16] The first presents the Empire as a racket, the product of a band of adventurers (to this school he connects Victor Hugo). Guérard finds that this version omits the solid qualities of the regime and its leader. The second interpretation is based on the principle of Bonapartism which aims to save social order for the benefit of material prosperity (to this school *we* might tie Walter Bagehot). The third is concerned with Caesarism—the welfare state combined with liberal nationalism—which produced Guérard's own version of Napoleon III as a "reformer"—(here we may see some of Proudhon's hopes emerging). Marx and Tocqueville fit none of these categories so readily. Yet Guérard helps us to recognize how wide has been the range of interpretation of the regime that followed the Second Republic—and therefore how diverse have been the views of its origins. All of which, I suggest, lends more interest to the discovery that such a range of interpretation was already present when the regime was born.

SUGGESTED READINGS

René Arnaud, *Le Coup d'État du 2 Décembre*, Paris, 1926.

J. P. T. Bury, *Napoleon III and the Second Empire*, London, 1964.

T. A. B. Corley, *Democratic Despot*, London, 1961.

Adrian Dansette, *Louis Napoleon à la Conquète du pouvoir*, Paris, 1961.

Albert Guérard, *Napoleon III*, Cambridge, Mass., 1943.

Henry Guillemin, *Le Coup du 2 Décembre*, Paris, 1951.

The Earl of Kerry, ed., *The Secret of the Coup d'État*, New York, 1924.

[16] Albert Guérard, *Napoleon III* (Cambridge, Mass., 1943), pp. xv–xix.

Napoleon III, *Napoleonic Ideas*, ed. by Brison D. Gooch, New York, 1967.

Howard C. Payne, *The Police State of Louis Napoleon Bonaparte, 1851–1860*, Seattle, 1966.

Robert Sencourt, *Napoleon III, The Modern Emperor*, London, 1933.

F. A. Simpson, *Louis Napoleon and the Recovery of France, 1848–1856*, London, 1930.

J. M. Thompson, *Louis Napoleon and the Second Empire*, New York, 1955.

ALEXIS DE TOCQUEVILLE'S
DEFENSE OF THE ASSEMBLY

IN 1851, ALEXIS DE TOCQUEVILLE (1805–59) was a man of great eminence as a social and political philosopher both in his own homeland and in England. His fame faded after his death in 1859 and did not undergo a major resurgence until the 1940s. Since that time it has spread throughout the world. Tocqueville now ranks with Marx and John Stuart Mill as one of the three most significant social and political thinkers of nineteenth-century Europe.

Alexis de Tocqueville was no closet theorist; he was also an active politician until the coup d'état of Louis Napoleon marked the end of his career. He had first been elected to the Chamber of Deputies under the July Monarchy in 1839, was elected again to the Constituent Assembly following the February revolution of 1848, and subsequently to the Legislative Assembly of the Second Republic. His letter reprinted here appeared anonymously in the London *Times* on December 11, 1851. It describes the fate that befell him and 230 other moderate and conservative members of the Republic's Assembly on December 2.

Though Tocqueville had remained aloof from parties, his political importance had transcended that of the ordinary deputy, in part because he came to politics with his fame established as the author of *Democracy in America*.

He had been a magistrate under the Bourbon monarchy when the revolution of July 1830 occurred. His aristocratic forebears had suffered in the great Revolution, and his family was deeply disturbed at his taking the oath of allegiance to the new monarchy, even though he did so with reluctance. Faced with such disapproval, Tocqueville and his close friend and colleague Gustave de Beaumont visited the United States on the pretext of studying the American penal system for the new French government rather than continue their judicial duties. They produced such a study, but the most significant product of the trip was *Democracy in America*, volumes I and II of which appeared in 1835, volumes III and IV in 1840. Tocqueville became a famous man; he was elected to the Académie Française; he attained international celebrity. The great work on American character and institutions was clearly directed at a European audience, to suggest the nature of the problems European society would have to face as it inevitably entered a democratic age and to indicate ways in which Americans and Europeans might meet them. The central problem, as Tocqueville saw it, was the spread of equality and the likelihood that desire for equality would overcome the safeguards for freedom, those institutions that might encourage liberty. Tocqueville felt that liberty had developed in the aristocratic tradition and was still best preserved by the English. His ties with England were strong—he had married an Englishwoman—and he continually set before Frenchmen, in *Democracy* and elsewhere, the contrast of England, where the nobility still possessed civic virtue and local self-government trained the population to control its own affairs, against France, where all came increasingly to depend upon a centralized administration. He felt that France, with the decline and defeat of its own aristocracy, had established a situation most conducive to democratic tyranny, for a centralized egalitarian society could easily fall under a military despot. It was his steady but often despairing hope that forms and institutions might be developed in France that could counteract Frenchmen's inordinate love of equality over liberty.

In teaching such lessons to his contemporaries, he revealed striking insight while engaging in a remarkably sophisticated form of comparative sociological analysis and projection. It is not surprising that such a man was no ordinary politician, nor that he often found himself isolated from the parties and factions in the Chamber of Deputies. Nor is it surprising that his lessons remained largely unlearned.

But he was inevitably an active and important figure in the Chamber, and his pride, ambition, and sense of duty impelled him to seek a leading part. In the forties he was a major proponent of the law to abolish slavery in the French colonies; he visited Algeria as director of a commission on African affairs; and on the basis of the reputation he had established earlier by his famous visit to America he was a leader in efforts for prison reform.

He predicted the coming of the February days of the 1848 revolution; and as a representative of the Assembly he visited the barricades in the June Days to report its decisions. His standing as a political philosopher helped earn him a place on the committee charged with preparing the Constitution of the Second Republic—though his views, as we shall see, failed to dominate.

In June 1849 he attained his highest post, becoming Minister of Foreign Affairs in the ministry headed by Odilon Barrot which was established after the election of the Legislative Assembly. The ministry was made up largely of the old opposition of the July Monarchy, and in this it closely resembled its predecessor which had existed during the tenure of the Constituent Assembly, except that it now included Tocqueville and two others acceptable to the republicans who had recently shown new strength at the polls. It was a ministry dedicated none the less to repression, to saving freedom by restricting it. This policy had Tocqueville's approval; since February he had been pointing out the threat of socialism.

Tocqueville inherited the delicate and explosive Roman question as his most troublesome task, at the point where efforts at mediation were ended and General Oudinot attacked the Republic, taking Rome, and permitting the reinstallation of papal government. French policy (and Tocqueville's own preference) required liberal reforms at Rome; the cardinals serving on the governing commission introduced instead only a spurious amnesty for the Roman republicans. Louis Napoleon protested in a published letter to his personal friend Colonel Ney who was serving as aide-de-camp with Oudinot's troops; the Pope defended his policies in a *motu proprio*. The ministry sought to retain control of policy first by ignoring the President's letter, then by suggesting, as Tocqueville did in a speech in the Assembly, that papal policy actually was not far out of accord with the Ney letter. The conflict of President against ministry was blatant, and before long the ministry was dismissed.[1] Tocqueville thereafter increasingly withdrew from public life.

He retained his seat in the Assembly but ill health forced him to spend prolonged periods away from Paris. During this semiretirement he put together the record of his political life under the Second Republic in his *Recollections*. It is to be regretted that they did not cover the coup d'état, though they contain clear enough anticipations of it, especially in the sense they convey of the fragility of the Republic's institutions.

The *Recollections* are especially helpful in pointing up Tocqueville's early recognition of the problem inherent in the popular election of the President, which would set against one another two forces, President and Assembly, both claiming to be based upon popular favor. He had not, however, argued against such an arrangement in the committee on the Constitution, though he did work unsuccessfully for an upper house that

[1] For a discussion of Tocqueville's handling of the Roman affair, see E. T. Gargan, *Alexis de Tocqueville: The Critical Years, 1848–51* (Washington, 1951), pp. 132–37, 147 ff.

might balance contending parties.[2] He admitted that he and his colleagues had not recognized so early the dangers of popular election, although from the very first he greatly feared granting a President—in a nation with a monarchical tradition—the immense power of controlling the highly centralized French administrative machine. As he put it, "In such conditions who could be the president elected by the people unless he were a pretender to the throne?" (P. 177)

Despite his own aristocratic heritage and monarchist leanings, after February 1848 he had sincerely come to believe that the Republic was the only possible *free* government for France. As he said, "I wished to maintain it because I saw nothing either ready or fit to put in its place." (P. 201) After the June Days, one of his chief concerns was to maintain it against the threat of socialism. But he could not participate wholeheartedly with the Party of Order and its impulse to simple reaction, though he supported repressive measures against radicalism. He disagreed also with its presidential choice, supporting Cavaignac instead, although he expected Louis Napoleon's election. Louis Napoleon he looked on as "the *worst* of ends for the republic". (P. 278) His picture of the President is one of the most notable of many striking portraits in the *Recollections* and is worth quoting in full. He described him thus after having worked as his minister:

> Louis Napoleon will play such a large part in the rest of this story that I think he deserves a separate portrait, while sketches are enough for the rest of my contemporaries. I think that of all his Ministers, and perhaps of all the men who refused to take part in his conspiracy against the Republic, I was the one most in his good graces, who saw him closest and could judge him best.
>
> He was a great deal better than the impression of him one might fairly have formed from his earlier career and mad enterprises. That was my first impression as I got to know him.

[2] Alexis de Tocqueville, *Recollections* (New York, 1970), pp. 146 ff. (See also Gargan, ch. IV.) Parenthetical references are to this edition of the *Recollections*. Tocqueville also defended popular presidential election in the Assembly debate on the Constitution.

In this he disappointed his adversaries, but perhaps he disappointed his friends even more, if one can give that name to the politicians who supported his candidature. For most of them had chosen him, not for his worth, but for his presumed mediocrity. They thought he would be a tool for them to use at will and break any time they wanted. In this they were mightily deceived.

As a private individual, Louis Napoleon had some attractive qualities: a kindly, easy-going temperament; a humane character; a soul that was gentle and even rather tender, but without delicacy; great confidence in his relations with people; a perfect simplicity; an element of personal modesty mixed with immense pride in his ancestry; and a better memory for kindnesses than for resentment. He could feel affection, and he aroused it in those who came near him. He spoke little and poorly; he had not the art of making others talk and establishing intimacy with them, and no facility in expressing himself; he had the habits of a writer and something of an author's pride. His power of dissimulation, which, as one would expect from a man who had spent his life in conspiracies, was profound, and was peculiarly assisted by the immobility of his features and his want of expression; his eyes were lustreless and opaque like thick glass portholes that let light through but are not transparent. Careless of danger, his courage in moments of crisis was fine and cool, but, as is common enough, his plans were very vacillating. He was often noticed changing course, advancing, hesitating and drawing back, which greatly damaged his reputation. For the nation had chosen him to dare all and expected audacity, not prudence, from him. He was said to have been always much given to physical pleasures and not discriminating in his choice of them. This taste for vulgar enjoyments and comforts increased with the opportunities given by power. This was a daily drain on his energy, and it blunted and reduced his very ambition. His mind was incoherent and confused, being filled with great thoughts ill-clothed, some of them borrowed from Napoleon's example, some from socialist theories, and some from memories of England where he had lived for a time—those were very different and often contradictory sources. And they were the laborious result of solitary meditations far from men and affairs, for he was by nature a fantastic dreamer. But when forced to come down from these vast, vague regions and confine his attention within the limits of a definite matter, he could take a fair view of it, sometimes with subtlety and compass and occasionally even with a certain depth; but sure he never was, being always ready to put some fantastic idea beside a reasonable one.

One could not be in intimate contact with him for long without noticing a little vein of madness running through his good sense, which constantly brought the escapades of his youth to mind and served to explain them.

But yet, in the actual circumstances, he owed his success and strength more to his madness than to his sense, for the world's stage is a strange place. Sometimes the worst plays are the ones that come off best there. If Louis Napoleon had been a wise man, or a genius if you like, he would never have been President of the Republic.

He trusted his star, firmly believing himself the instrument of destiny and the necessary man. I have always thought that he was really convinced of his right, and I do not think Charles X[3] was more infatuated with his legitimism than he. He was also quite incapable of giving any reason for his faith, for while he had a sort of abstract adoration for the people, he had very little taste for liberty. In political matters, the basic characteristic of his mind was hate and contempt for assemblies. The rule of constitutional monarchy he found even more insupportable than that of the Republic. The pride he derived from his name, which knew no limit, would willingly bow before the nation but revolted at the idea of submitting to the influence of a parliament.

Before he came to power, he had had a long time in which to strengthen the taste that mediocre princes always have for lackeys, by the habits of twenty years spent in conspiracies with low-class adventurers, ruined men or men of blemished reputations, and young debauchees, the only persons who all the time would consent to serve him as go-betweens or accomplices. In him, too, for all his good manners, traces of the adventurer and prince of gamblers showed through. He con-

[3] King of France, 1824–30.

tinued to take pleasure in inferior company when he was no longer obliged to live in it. I think his difficulty in expressing his thoughts except in writing drew him to people who had long been familiar with his ideas and his dreams, and that his inferiority in discussion made the company of men of parts uncomfortable to him. Besides he desired above all devotion to himself and his cause (as if either he or his cause could inspire devotion); he felt hampered by merit when it was combined with any touch of independence. He wanted believers in his star and vulgar adorers of his fortune. So one couldn't reach him except through a group of intimate servants and personal friends, and I remember General Changarnier at that time using two rhyming words of abuse to describe the whole pack of sharpers and knaves. To conclude, nothing was worse than his familiars except his family, who were mostly good-for-nothings and hussies.

This was the man whom the need for a leader and the power of a memory had set at the head of France and with whom we were going to conduct the government.

(Pp. 202–5)

It is possible to trace how Tocqueville, like most of his colleagues, came increasingly to anticipate the crisis that led to December 2. While still his minister, Tocqueville had offered to support Louis Napoleon, not in overthrowing the Republic, but in seeking revision of the Constitution so as to allow reelection, and he had even hinted his belief that by governing well the President might be illegally re-elected with near unanimity. Thereafter, in January 1851, because of the Changarnier affair, he was genuinely pessimistic about the Republic's chances and expected a coup d'état. He argued again that constitutional revision to permit the prolongation of the President's term was the least objectionable of the possible ways out of the growing impasse, which might produce a coup d'état in May 1852. (He had by that time given up on the idea of near unanimous election, because of the antagonistic behavior of the President toward the Assembly.) Despite having played a part in writing the Constitution, he felt it was "detestable"; yet it remained a

25

necessary shelter against a dangerous interregnum, and hence he sought to preserve it. He even approved of the difficulties the Constitution placed in the way of revision, feeling they would give the republican experiment a chance. He said he would not have supported revision were a less dangerous alternative open, but seeing none and fearing that a legal solution was simply impossible, he became *rapporteur* for the commission that was directed to consider revision in November 1851. Even while proposing revision he feared the consequences of, for example, a Constituent Assembly elected by a restricted suffrage or of a "red" election. However, as we have noted in the introduction, the commission's proposals were voted down.[4]

Despite his ill health, he had preferred to be with the Assembly in the fall months of crisis. In October he was again anticipating a coup d'état; in November he once more wrote of the coming of catastrophe.[5] Having kept to his post, he was imprisoned with his colleagues on December 2. Tocqueville was at the meeting of deputies at the Tenth Arrondissement (and served as their *rapporteur*, sending their protest to the *Times*). He was taken with them to the Quai d'Orsay, and thence transferred to Vincennes. Though, like most others, he was held only two days, he suffered in health and dignity. Victor Hugo describes him in *The History of a Crime*, first at the meeting at the *Mairie* of the Tenth Arrondissement. He reports that Tocqueville indicated there that all through his ministry he and his colleagues had feared a coup; and later Hugo describes him, feeling unwell, accepting a soldier's bread and sharing it with

[4] For the foregoing paragraph, see *Correspondence and Conversations of Alexis de Tocqueville with Nassau William Senior, 1834–1859*, ed. by M. C. M. Simpson, 2 vols. (London, 1872), vol. 1, pp. 92–94, 209–12, 255–63, and Gargan, ch. VII.

[5] He wrote to N. W. Senior on November 28, 1851, "Our present condition . . . can only end by some great catastrophe. My clear view of the magnitude and of the proximity of the calamity is so bitterly painful, that I try as much as possible to divert it from my thoughts." (*Memoir, Letters, and Remains of Alexis de Tocqueville*, ed. by Gustave de Beaumont, Boston, 1862, vol. 2, p. 173.)

nother deputy, and again, still feeling ill, at the Quai d'Orsay
arracks.[6] Tocqueville's description of the events as he recounted
hem to Nassau William Senior, the English economist, gives a
lifferent flavor—one of hectic courage.

> Paris—December 31, 1851—
> The gayest time, that I ever passed was in the Quai d'Orsay.
> The *élite* of France in education, in birth, and in talents of
> society, was collected within the walls of that barrack.
> A long struggle was over, in which our part had not been
> timidly played; we had done our duty, gone through some
> perils, and had some to encounter, and we were all in the high
> spirits which excitement and dangers shared with others, when
> not too formidable, create. From the courtyard in which we
> had been penned for a couple of hours, where the Duc de
> Broglie and I tore our chicken with our hands and teeth, we
> were transferred to a long sort of gallery, or garret, running
> along through the higher part of the building, a spare dormi-
> tory for the soldiers when the better rooms are filled. Those
> who chose to take the trouble went below, hired palliasses
> from the soldiers, and carried them up for themselves. I was
> too idle and lay on the floor on my cloak. Instead of sleeping
> we spent the night shooting from palliasse to palliasse anec-
> dotes, repartees, jokes, and pleasantries.[7]

After the coup d'état, Tocqueville retired from public life,
unable to support a regime he despised. His letter to the *Times*
is his only formal comment on the coup, but in his letters and in
his recorded conversations we find many reflections suggesting a
more comprehensive interpretation. His immediate reaction was
that the army had bound and gagged France, and had done so
in response to the fear of socialism. (Edward Gargan makes the
insightful comment in this regard that Tocqueville was correct
in attributing Louis Napoleon's rise to an exaggerated fear of
socialism, but was quite unaware that he himself had played a

[6] Victor Hugo, *The History of a Crime*, vol. I, *Hugo's Works*,
Centenary Edition (Boston, 1892), pp. 89, 93, 112.
[7] *Correspondence and Conversations*, vol. 2, pp. 9–10.

role in generating that fear by his prophecies of the dangers of socialism and the coming of equality.)[8] Tocqueville believed the democrats had in this case, as they had in the spread of reaction across the Continent since 1849, aided the cause of absolutism, and the plebiscite supported his view. Tocqueville also shared the common belief that the possibility of a monarchist coup d'état had forced Louis Napoleon's hand, as had new Legitimist agitation for repeal of the suffrage law of May 31 which threatened his main weapon against the Assembly. Fears of violent action on both left and right were, he thought, involved in the final amalgam.[9] His fear of *mass tyranny*, which he shared with that other great contemporary liberal, John Stuart Mill, was ideally exemplified by the coup d'état and its aftermath.

His early reaction to the coup is presented in a letter sent to his close friend Gustave de Beaumont on the first of May, 1852:

. . . All work is for the present impossible. Being in Paris, I attribute my incapacity to the events that I see, and to the exciting conversations of every day. If I were in the country, I should attribute it to solitude. The truth is, that it arises from sickness at heart, and will not cease till this is cured, which can be the work only of time, the great healer of grief, as every one knows. I must try to wait patiently for the cure. And yet I cherish this grief as one does every real sorrow to which one has a right, bitter though it be. The sight of all that is going on, and especially of the way in which it is regarded, hurts every feeling of pride, honor and delicacy. I should be sorry to be less sad. In this respect, I ought to be thoroughly satisfied, for, indeed, I am sad unto death. I have reached my present age, and passed through all sorts of circumstances, advocating always the same cause—regulated liberty. Can this cause be lost forever? I began to fear it in 1848, I fear it now still more; not that I am convinced that this country will never possess again constitutional institutions, but will they last, or any others? It is a moving sand: the question is,

[8] Gargan, pp. 230–31.
[9] *Correspondence and Conversations*, vol. 2, pp. 6–7.

not whether it can be fixed, but what will be the winds that will toss it about.

Still I try to work. Every day I spend two or three hours in the library of the rue de Richelieu. In spite of my endeavors to turn my thoughts in another direction, a profound sadness sometimes steals over me; and if I allow it to seize upon me unawares, I am lost for the rest of the day. My life might be pleasant, but if I look aside from my book, I am cut to the heart.

Enclosed is the letter addressed to the electors of my canton, in which I resign my place as member of the *conseil général* . . . I could not take the oath . . . This result of the 2nd of December is, perhaps, the one which has most affected me individually. My position in the department was one of unmixed satisfaction. I had the moral inclination of every affair of importance: my empire over the minds of the people was founded upon personal regard, independently of political opinions. This portion of my public life shed a reflected light upon my private life, and made it all the happier. But these are only small miseries . . .[10]

As Tocqueville pondered longer on the coup d'état we find him suggesting that it could be seen as another phase of the Revolution, which he, with Proudhon and Hugo, believed was one continuing phenomenon. We also find him on occasion, in a justifiably pessimistic mood, wondering whether the nation might not have obtained the government it deserved. That government he in fact found detestable, and his concern in his retirement, as he devoted himself increasingly to scholarship, was whether and how long the regime would last. His views varied. In 1852 he concluded it might last quite a long time if it made no massive mistakes, but he remained sure France would not support an unpopular despot. In 1853 he sensed that disgust with the regime was increasing to the point where the first riot might produce its overturn; soon thereafter, he argued rather

10 *Memoir, Letters, and Remains*, vol. 2, pp. 198–99. *Conseil général*: elective departmental assembly.

differently that a brilliant success might establish Louis Napoleon, whereas a defeat would be fatal.[11]

With the passage of time, Tocqueville found he could work, and his attention and activity became increasingly centered on the production of his last great book, *The Old Régime and the French Revolution,* which began appropriately as a project on the *First* Empire.

Tocqueville succeeded in completing only the opening volume of his history in 1856; he never finished the study as he had envisioned it. It was to have been a work comparable in scope with *Democracy in America.* Many of the same themes recur in it; Tocqueville continued to teach basically the same lessons. In the *Old Régime,* however, his attachment to liberty had become perhaps even more unambiguous, his patriotism more evident, and also his despair.

Richard Herr has shown that the book should probably be taken to include Tocqueville's matured response to the Second Empire. The condition to which he felt the coup d'état and its aftermath had reduced his country comes through clearly in the following remarks from his Preface:

I hope and believe that I have written the present book without any *parti pris,* though it would be futile to deny that my own feelings were engaged. What Frenchman can write about his country and think about the age in which he lives in a spirit of complete detachment? Thus I confess that when studying our old social system under its infinitely various aspects I have never quite lost sight of present-day France. Moreover, I have tried not merely to diagnose the malady of which the sick man died but also to discover how he might have been saved. In fact, my method has been that of the anatomist who dissects each defunct organ with a view to eliciting the laws of life, and my aim has been to supply a picture that while scientifically accurate, may also be instructive. Whenever I found in our forefathers any of those virtues so vital to a nation but now well-nigh extinct—a spirit of healthy

[11] *Correspondence and Conversations,* vol. 2, pp. 40–41.

independence, high ambitions, faith in oneself and in a cause—
I have thrown them into relief. Similarly, wherever I found
traces of any of those vices which after destroying the old
order still affect the body politic, I have emphasized them; for
it is in the light of the evils to which they formerly gave rise
that we can gauge the harm they yet may do. . . .

. . . There may be some to accuse me of making overmuch
of liberty—that watchword of the past. Nowadays, so I am
told, no one in France sets any store on it. All I would say
(for what it is worth) in my defense is that my devotion to
freedom is of very long standing. Over twenty years have
passed since, apropos of another social group, I made the observations which are reproduced below almost verbatim.

Though there can be no certainty about the future, three
facts are plain to see in the light of past experience. First,
that all our contemporaries are driven on by a force that we
may hope to regulate or curb, but cannot overcome, and it is
a force impelling them, sometimes gently, sometimes at head-
long speed, to the destruction of aristocracy. Secondly, that
those peoples who are so constituted as to have the utmost
difficulty in getting rid of despotic government for any considerable period are the ones in which aristocracy has ceased
to exist and can no longer exist. Thirdly, that nowhere is
despotism calculated to produce such evil effects as in social
groups of this order; since, more than any other kind of régime,
it fosters the growth of all the vices to which they are con-
genitally prone and, indeed, incites them to go still farther on
the way to which their natural bent inclines them.

For in a community in which the ties of family, of caste,
of class, and craft fraternities no longer exist people are far
too much disposed to think exclusively of their own interests,
to become self-seekers practicing a narrow individualism and
caring nothing for the public good. Far from trying to counteract such tendencies despotism encourages them, depriving the
governed of any sense of solidarity and independence; of good-
neighborly feelings and a desire to further the welfare of the
community at large. It immures them, so to speak, each in his
private life and, taking advantage of the tendency they already

have to keep apart, it estranges them still more. Their feelings toward each other were already growing cold; despotism freezes them.

Since in such communities nothing is stable, each man is haunted by a fear of sinking to a lower social level and by a restless urge to better his condition. And since money has not only become the sole criterion of a man's social status but has also acquired an extreme mobility—that is to say it changes hands incessantly, raising or lowering the prestige of individuals and families—everybody is feverishly intent on making money, or, if already rich, on keeping his wealth intact. Love of gain, a fondness for business careers, the desire to get rich at all costs, a craving for material comfort and easy living quickly become ruling passions under a despotic government. They affect all classes, even those who hitherto have seemed allergic to them, and tend to lower the moral standards of the nation as a whole if no effort be made to check their growth. It is in the nature of despotism that it should foster such desires and propagate their havoc. Lowering as they do the national morale, they are despotism's safeguard, since they divert men's attention from public affairs and make them shudder at the mere thought of a revolution. Despotism alone can provide that atmosphere of secrecy which favors crooked dealings and enables the freebooters of finance to make illicit fortunes. Under other forms of government such propensities exist, undoubtedly; under a despotism they are given free rein.

Freedom and freedom alone can extirpate these vices, which indeed, are innate in communities of this order; it alone can call a halt to their pernicious influence. For only freedom can deliver the members of a community from that isolation which is the lot of the individual left to his own devices and, compelling them to get in touch with each other, promote an active sense of fellowship. In a community of free citizens every man is daily reminded of the need of meeting his fellow men, of hearing what they have to say, of exchanging ideas, and coming to an agreement as to the conduct of their common interests. Freedom alone is capable of lifting men's minds above mere mammon worship and the petty personal worries which crop up in the course of everyday life, and of making them aware at every moment that they belong each and all to a vaster entity, above and around them—their native land. It alone replaces at certain critical moments their natural love of material welfare by a loftier, more virile ideal; offers other objectives than that of getting rich; and sheds a light enabling all to see and appraise men's vices and their virtues as they truly are.

True, democratic societies which are not free may well be prosperous, cultured, pleasing to the eye, and even magnificent, such is the sense of power implicit in their massive uniformity; in them may flourish many private virtues, good fathers, honest merchants, exemplary landowners, and good Christians, too —since the patrimony of the Christian is not of this world and one of the glories of the Christian faith is that it has produced such men under the worst governments and in eras of the utmost depravity. There were many such in the Roman Empire in its decline. But, I make bold to say, never shall we find under such conditions a great citizen, still less a great nation; indeed, I would go so far as to maintain that where equality and tyranny coexist, a steady deterioration of the mental and moral standards of a nation is inevitable.

Such were my views and thus I wrote twenty years ago, and nothing that has taken place in the world since then has led me to change my mind. And, having proclaimed my love of freedom at a time when it was made much of, I can hardly be blamed for championing it today, when it is out of fashion.

Moreover, as regards my love of freedom, I differ less from those who disagree with me than they may imagine. Can there exist a man so mean-spirited that he would rather be at the mercy of a tyrant's whim than obedient to laws which he himself has helped to enact—provided of course that he believes his nation to have the qualities enabling it to make a proper use of freedom? Even despots do not deny the merits of freedom; only they wish to keep it for themselves, claiming that no one else is worthy of it. Thus our quarrel is not about the value of freedom *per se*, but stems from our opinion of our fellow men, high or low as the case may be; indeed, it is no exaggeration to say that a man's admiration of absolute government is proportionate to the contempt he feels for those around

33

him. I trust I may be allowed to wait a little longer before being converted to such a view of my fellow countrymen.[12]

The letter Tocqueville wrote to the *Times* is a forceful assertion of the same attachment to liberty. It is a striking document expressive of Tocqueville's fundamental moral stance. Tocqueville possessed immensely impressive analytical and theoretical skills to go with that set of values, but there is no question that the moral issue was for him always paramount, and that all the political and social analyses, which he was so eminently fitted to undertake, were secondary. He simply condemns the coup and its author for crime, immorality, the destruction of liberty and free institutions, and demeaning the dignity of Frenchmen. That these values stem from an aristocratic heritage need not be expanded upon.

It is important to emphasize that Tocqueville's is the earliest statement in this book. His letter gives a sense of real immediacy to the events of the coup.

SUGGESTED READINGS

Seymour Drescher, *Dilemmas of Democracy, Tocqueville and Modernization,* Pittsburgh, 1968.

E. T. Gargan, *Alexis de Tocqueville: The Critical Years, 1848–1851,* Washington, 1955.

Richard Herr, *Tocqueville and the Old Regime,* Princeton, 1962.

Jack Lively, *The Social and Political Thought of Alexis de Tocqueville,* Oxford, 1962.

J. P. Mayer, *Alexis de Tocqueville: A Biographical Study in Political Science,* New York, 1960.

Alexis de Tocqueville, *Recollections,* trans. by George Lawrence, New York, 1970.

Marvin Zetterbaum, *Tocqueville and the Problem of Democracy,* Stanford, 1967.

[12] Alexis de Tocqueville, *The Old Régime and the French Revolution,* trans. by Stuart Gilbert (Garden City, N.Y., 1955), pp. xi–xv.

TOCQUEVILLE'S LETTER OF

DECEMBER 11, 1851,

TO THE LONDON *TIMES*

TO THE EDITOR OF THE "TIMES."

Sɪʀ—The opinion expressed by certain organs of the English press on the events which have just occurred in France has caused a painful surprise to men who, like myself, preserve a steadfast attachment to the principles of regulated liberty and a fixed respect for legality. We are grieved to remark the purpose to which these observations of a portion of the English press are turned by the new Government, and that any English writers should seem to applaud what all honest Frenchmen condemn. It is for this reason that as a witness of these events, I wish to make them known to you in all sincerity, convinced as I am that when Englishmen approve violence and oppression, it is only because the truth is not yet before them.

Permit me to offer some general reflections before entering into details.

Sᴏᴜʀᴄᴇ: *Memoir, Letters, and Remains of Alexis de Tocqueville*, ed. by Gustave de Beaumont, Boston, 1862, vol. 2, pp. 173–79, 181–89. With corrections by the editor.

Louis Napoleon, in order to endeavor to palliate in Franc
and abroad the audacious violation of the laws which he ha
just committed, has caused a report to be circulated that he onl
anticipated the hostile measures of the Assembly, which wa
conspiring against himself, and that if he had not struck tha
body it would have struck him. This sort of defence is no novelt
to us in France. All our revolutionists have used it for thes
sixty years. The members of the convention, who sent each othe
to the scaffold, invariably treated their adversaries as conspira
tors. But in the present instance this accusation, as far as the
majority of the Assembly is concerned, is without a pretext, anc
can only pass current among strangers ignorant of the tru
course of events.

No doubt history will have weighty charges to bring agains
the Legislative Assembly, which has just been illegally and vio
lently dissolved. The parties of which that Assembly was com
posed failed to come to an understanding; this gave to the whole
body an uncertain and sometimes contradictory policy, and fi
nally discredited the Assembly, and rendered it incapable of de
fending either liberty or its own existence. History will record
thus much; but history will reject with contempt the accusation which Louis Napoleon has preferred against us. If you do
not believe my assurances, judge at least by the facts—not the
secret facts which I could disclose to you, but the public facts
printed in the *Moniteur*.[1]

In the month of August last, the Assembly voted the revision
of the Constitution by an immense majority. Why was the revision of the Constitution desired? Simply to legalize the re-
election of Louis Napoleon. Was that an act of conspiracy
against him?

The Assembly prorogued itself soon after this vote; the *Con-
seils Généraux*,[2] convoked immediately afterwards, and prin-
cipally consisting of representatives, also expressed an almost

[1] Official government daily which reported parliamentary debates.
[2] See above, p. 29, note 10.

unanimous desire for the revision of the Constitution. Was that an act of conspiracy against Louis Napoleon?

The Assembly met again on the 4th of November. There was an electoral law—that of the 31st of May—which the great majority of the Assembly had voted. This law was unpopular, and to catch the favor of the people, Louis Napoleon, who had been the first to propose and sanction the law of the 31st of May the year before, demands its abrogation, and proposes another law in a message insulting to the Assembly. The new electoral law proposed by him was, indeed, rejected, but by a majority of only two votes; and immediately afterwards the Chamber proceeded, in order to comply with the President's policy, to adopt in another form most of the changes which he had proposed.[3] Was that an act of conspiracy against Louis Napoleon?

Shortly afterwards a proposition was made by the Questors to enable us to place the Parliament in a state of defence, if attacked, and to call troops directly to our assistance. This proposition was, as nobody can deny, in strict conformity with the Constitution, and all that the proposed resolution did was to define the means of exercising a power which the Assembly incontestably possessed. Nevertheless, from fear of a collision with the Executive Power, the legislature dared not assert this incontestable right. The proposition of the Questors was rejected by a large majority. Was that an act of conspiracy against Louis Napoleon? What! the Assembly was conspiring, and it renounced the command of the troops which might have defended it, and made them over to the man who was compassing its ruin! And when did these things happen? A fortnight ago.

Lastly, a bill on the responsibility of the President and the different officers of state was sent up to the Assembly by the *Conseil d'État.* Observe, that this proposition did not emanate from the Assembly, that the Assembly had no right, by law, to refuse to entertain it. The bill was, therefore, brought up, but the

[3] Probably a reference to the liberalization of the law on municipal elections.

committee to which it was referred showed at once that its dis position was conciliatory. The provisions of the bill were rendered more mild, and the discussion was to be deferred, in order to avoid the displeasure of the Executive Power. Were these the actions of enemies and conspirators? And what was happening in the mean while? All the journals notoriously paid by the President, insulted the Assembly day by day in the coarsest manner, threatened it, and tried by every means to cover it with unpopularity.

This is history—the truth of history. The acts of which I speak are the last of the National Assembly of France, and I defy our adversaries to find any other facts to oppose to them. That an Assembly of 750 members may have included in that number certain conspirators, it would be absurd to deny. But the manifest truth, proved by its acts, is that the majority of this Assembly, instead of conspiring against Louis Napoleon, sought for nothing so much as to avoid a quarrel with him; that it carried its moderation towards him to the verge of weakness, and its desire of conciliation to a degree of pusillanimity. That is the truth. You may believe my assertions, for I participated in the passions of none of its parties, and I have no reason either to flatter or to hate them.

Let us now proceed to examine what the Assembly did on the 2d of December; and here I cease to express any opinion, I merely relate, as an actual witness, the things I saw with my eyes and heard with my ears.

When the representatives of the people learned, on waking that morning, that several of their colleagues were arrested, they ran to the Assembly. The doors were guarded by the Chasseurs de Vincennes, a corps of troops recently returned from Africa, and long accustomed to the violences of Algerine dominion, who, moreover, were stimulated by a donation of 5f. distributed to every soldier who was in Paris that day. The representatives, nevertheless, presented themselves to go in, having at their head one of their vice-presidents, M. Daru. This gentleman was violently struck by the soldiers, and the representatives who accompanied him were driven back at the point of the bayonet. Three of them, M. de Talhouet, Etienne, and Duparc, were slightly wounded. Several others had their clothes pierced. Such was the commencement.

Driven from the doors of the Assembly, the deputies retired to the *Mairie* of the 10th *arrondissement*. They were already assembled to the number of about three hundred, when the troops arrived, blocked up the approaches, and prevented a greater number of representatives from entering the apartment, though no one was at that time prevented from leaving it.

Who, then, were those representatives assembled at the *Mairie* of the 10th *arrondissement*, and what did they do there? Every shade of opinion was represented in this extemporaneous Assembly. But eight tenths of its members belonged to the different conservative parties which had constituted the majority. This Assembly was presided over by two of its vice-presidents, M. Vitet and M. Benoist d'Azy. M. Daru was arrested in his own house; the fourth vice-president, the illustrious General Bedeau, had been seized that morning in his bed, and handcuffed like a robber. As for the president, M. Dupin,[4] he was absent, which surprised no one as his cowardice was known. Besides its vice-presidents, the Assembly was accompanied by its secretaries, its ushers, and even its short hand writer, who will preserve for posterity the records of this last and memorable sitting. The Assembly, thus constituted, began by voting a decree in the following terms:—

"In pursuance of Article 68 of the Constitution—viz.: the President of the Republic, the Ministers, the agents, and depositaries of public authority are responsible, each in what concerns themselves respectively, for all the acts of the government and the administration—any measure by which the President of the Republic dissolves the National Assembly, prorogues it, or

---

[4] André Marie J.-J. Dupin (1783–1865) was one of the first deputies to support the President at the time of the coup d'état. His behavior is treated very harshly in Hugo's works on the coup, where he is also portrayed as simply pusillanimous.

places obstacles in the exercise of its powers, is a crime of high-treason.

"By this act merely the President is deprived of all authority the citizens are bound to withhold their obedience, the executive power passes in full right to the National Assembly. The Judges of the High Court of Justice will meet immediately under pain of forfeiture; they will convoke the juries in the place which they will select to proceed to the judgment of the President and his accomplices; they will nominate the magistrates charged to fulfil the duties of public ministers.

"And seeing that the National Assembly is prevented by violence from exercising its powers, it decrees as follows, viz.:—

"*Louis Napoleon Bonaparte is deprived of all authority as President of the Republic.* The citizens are enjoined to withhold their obedience. The executive power has passed in full right to the National Assembly. The Judges of the High Court of Justice are enjoined to meet immediately, under pain of forfeiture, to proceed to the judgment of the President and his accomplices; consequently, all the officers and functionaries of power and of public authority are bound to obey all requisitions made in the name of the National Assembly, under pain of forfeiture and of high treason.

"Done and decreed unanimously in public sitting, this 2d of December, 1851.

(Signed) BENOIST D'AZY, *President.*
VITET, *Vice President.*
MOULIN,
CHAPOT, } *Secretaries.*

[Tocqueville then lists the names of 230 representatives]"

All the members whose names I have here given were arrested. Several others having left the room after having signed, could not be taken. Among these, the best known are M. de Tracy, M. de Malleville, Ferdinand de Lasteyrie, and General Rulhière.

After having voted this first decree, another was unanimously passed, naming General Oudinot commander of the public forces, and M. Tamisier was joined with him as chief of the staff. The choice of these two officers from distinct shades of political opinion showed that the Assembly was animated by one common spirit.

These decrees had scarcely been signed by all the members present, and deposited in a place of safety, when a band of soldiers, headed by their officers, sword in hand, appeared at the door, without, however, daring to enter the apartment. The Assembly awaited them in perfect silence. The president alone raised his voice, read the decrees which had just been passed to the soldiers, and ordered them to retire. The poor fellows, ashamed of the part they were compelled to play, hesitated. The officers, pale and undecided, declared that they should go for further orders. They retired, contenting themselves with blockading the passages leading to the apartment. The Assembly, not being able to go out, ordered the windows to be opened, and caused the decrees to be read to the people and the troops in the street below, especially that decree which, in pursuance of the 68th Article of the Constitution, pronounced the deposition and impeachment of Louis Napoleon.

Soon, however, the soldiers reappeared at the door, preceded this time by two *commissaires de police*. These men entered the room, and, amid the unbroken silence and total immobility of the Assembly, summoned the representatives to disperse. The president ordered them to retire themselves. One of the *commissaires* was agitated, and faltered; the other broke out in invectives. The President said to him, "Sir, we are here the lawful authority, and sole representatives of law and of right. We know that we cannot oppose to you material force, but we will only leave this chamber under constraint. We will not disperse. Seize us, and convey us to prison." "All, all!" exclaimed the members of the Assembly. After much hesitation, the *commissaires de police* decided to act. They caused the two presidents to be seized by the collar. The whole body then rose, and, arm-in-arm, two-and-two, they followed the presidents, who were led off. In this order we reached the street, and were marched across the city, without knowing whither we were going.

Care had been taken to circulate a report among the crowd and the troops that a meeting of Socialist and Red Republican deputies had been arrested. But when the people beheld among those who were thus dragged through the mud of Paris on foot, like a gang of malefactors, men the most illustrious by their talents and their virtues, ex-ministers, ex-ambassadors, generals, admirals, great orators, great writers, surrounded by the bayonets of the line, a shout was raised, *"Vive l'Assemblée Nationale."* The representatives were attended by these shouts until they reached the barracks of the Quai d'Orsay, where they were shut up. Night was coming on, and it was wet and cold. Yet the Assembly was left two hours in the open air, as if the Government did not deign to remember its existence. The representatives here made their last roll-call in presence of their short hand writer, who had followed them. The number present was 218, to whom were added about twenty more in the course of the evening, consisting of members who had voluntarily caused themselves to be arrested. Almost all the men known to France and to Europe who formed the majority of the Legislative Assembly were gathered together in this place. Few were wanting, except those who, like M. Molé, had not been suffered to reach their colleagues. There were present, among others, the Duke de Broglie, who had come, though ill; the father of the house, the venerable Keratry, whose physical strength was inferior to his moral courage, and whom it was necessary to seat in a straw chair in the barrack-yard; Odilon Barrot, Dufaure, Berryer, Rémusant, Duvergier de Hauranne, Gustave de Beaumont, De Tocqueville, De Falloux, Lanjuinais, Admiral Lainé and Admiral Cécille, Generals Oudinot and Lauriston, the Duke de Luynes, the Duke de Montebello; twelve ex-ministers, nine of whom had served under Louis Napoleon himself; eight members of the Institute; all men who had struggled for three years to defend society and to resist the demagogic faction.

When two hours had elapsed this assemblage was driven into barrack-rooms up-stairs, where most of them spent the night, without fire, and almost without food, stretched upon the boards. It only remained to carry off to prison these honorable men, guilty of no crime but the defence of the laws of their country. For this purpose the most distressing and ignominious means were selected. The cellular vans, in which convicts are conveyed to the prison, were brought up. In these vehicles were shut up the men who had served and honored their country, and they were conveyed like three bands of criminals, some to the fortress of Mont Valerien, some to the Prison Mazas in Paris, and the remainder to Vincennes. The indignation of the public compelled the Government two days afterwards to release the greater number of them; some are still in confinement, unable to obtain either their liberty or their trial.

The treatment inflicted on the generals arrested in the morning of the 2d December was still more disgraceful. Cavaignac, Lamoricière, Bedeau, Changarnier—the conquerors of Africa, were shut up in these infamous cellular vans, which are always inconvenient, and become almost intolerable on a lengthened journey. In this manner they were conveyed to Ham—that is, they were made to perform upwards of a day's journey. Cavaignac, who had saved Paris and France in the days of June—Cavaignac, the competitor of Louis Napoleon at the last elections, shut up for a day and a night in the cell of a felon! I leave it to every honest man and every generous heart to comment on such facts. Can it be that indignities which surpass the actions of the King of Naples find a defender in England? No; England knows but a small portion of what is taking place. I appeal to her better judgment when these facts are known to the world.

Such are the indignities offered to persons. Let me now review the series of general crimes. The liberty of the press is destroyed to an extent unheard of even in the time of the Empire. Most of the journals are suppressed; those which appear cannot say a word on politics or even publish any news. But this is by no means all. The Government has stuck up a list of persons who are formed into a "Consultative Commission." Its object is to induce France to believe that the Executive is not abandoned by every man of respectability and consideration among us. More than half the persons on this list have refused to belong to the commission; most of them regard the insertion of their names as dishonor. I may quote, among others, M. Léon Faucher, M. Portalis, First President of the Court of Cassation, and the Duke of Albuféra, as those best known. Not only does the Government decline to publish the letters in which these gentlemen refuse their consent, but even their names are not withdrawn from a list which dishonors them. The names are still retained, in spite of their repeated remonstrances. A day or two ago, one of them, M. Joseph Périer, driven to desperation by this excess of tyranny, rushed into the street to strike out his own name with his own hands from the public placards, taking the passers-by to witness that it had been placed there by a lie.

Such is the state of the public journals. Let us now see the condition of personal liberty. I say, again, that personal liberty is more trampled on than ever it was in the time of the Empire. A decree of the new Power gives the *prefets* the right to arrest, in their respective departments, whomsoever they please; and the *prefets,* in their turn, send blank warrants of arrest, which are literally *lettres de cachet,*[5] to the *sous-prefets* under their orders. The Provisional Government of the Republic never went so far. Human life is as little respected as human liberty. I know that war has its dreadful necessities, but the disturbances which have recently occurred in Paris have been put down with a barbarity unprecedented in our civil contests; and when we remember that this torrent of blood has been shed to consummate the violation of all laws, we cannot but think that sooner or later it will fall back upon the heads of those who shed it. As for the appeal to the people, to which Louis Napoleon affects to submit his claims, never was a more odious mockery offered

[5] Under the old regime, a private, sealed communication from the King; often used to notify of imprisonment or exile, it became a symbol of tyranny.

to a nation. The people is called upon to express its opinion, yet not only is public discussion suppressed, but even the knowledge of facts. The people is asked its opinion, but the first measure taken to obtain it is to establish military terrorism throughout the country, and to threaten with deprivation every public agent who does not approve in writing what has been done.

Such, Sir, is the condition in which we stand. Force overturning law, trampling on the liberty of the press and of the person, deriding the popular will, in whose name the Government pretends to act—France torn from the alliance of free nations to be yoked to the despotic monarchies of the Continent —such is the result of this *coup d'état*. If the judgment of the people of England can approve these military saturnalia, and if the facts I have related, and which I pledge myself are accurately true, did not rouse its censures, I should mourn for you and for ourselves, and for the sacred cause of legal liberty throughout the world; for the public opinion of England is the grand jury of mankind in the cause of freedom, and if its verdict were to acquit the oppressor, the oppressed would have no other resource but in God.

One word more, to record a fact which does honor to the magistracy of France, and which will be remembered in its annals. The army refused to submit to the decree of the captive Assembly impeaching the President of the Republic; but the high court of justice obeyed it. These five judges, sitting in the midst of Paris enslaved, and in the face of martial law, dared to assemble at the palace of justice, and to issue process commencing criminal proceedings against Louis Napoleon, charged with high treason by the law, though already triumphant in the streets. I subjoin the text of this memorable edict:—

"THE HIGH COURT OF JUSTICE,

"Considering the 68th Article of the Constitution, considering that printed placards commencing with the words 'the President of the Republic,' and bearing at the end the signatures of Louis Napoleon Bonaparte and De Morny, Minister of the Interior, which placards announce, among other things, the dissolution of the National Assembly, have this day been affixed to the walls of Paris; that this fact of the dissolution of the Assembly by the President of the Republic would fall under the case provided for by the 68th Article of the Constitution, and render the convocation of the High Court of Justice imperative, by the terms of that article declares, that the High Court is constituted, and names M. Renouard, counsellor of the Court of Cassation, to fill the duties of public accuser, and to fill those of Greffier M. Bernard, Greffier in Chief of the Court of Cassation; and, to proceed further in pursuance of the terms of the said 68th Article of the Constitution, adjourns until to-morrow, the 3d of December at the hour of noon.

"Done and deliberated in the Council Chamber. Present, M. Hardouin, president, M. Pataille, M. Moreau, M. de la Palme, and M. Cauchy, judges, this 2d day of December, 1851."

After this textual extract from the minutes of the high court of justice there is the following entry—

"1. A *procès-verbal* stating the arrival of a *Commissaire de Police,* who called upon the High Court to separate.

"2. A *procès-verbal* of a second sitting held on the morrow, the 3d day of December (when the Assembly was in prison), at which M. Renouard accepts the functions of public prosecutor, charged to proceed against Louis Napoleon, after which the High Court, being no longer able to sit, adjourned to a day to be fixed hereafter."

With these extracts from the judicial records I terminate this communication.

WALTER BAGEHOT'S
DEFENSE OF THE COUP D'ÉTAT

LIKE TOCQUEVILLE, Walter Bagehot (1826–77) was in Paris
when the coup occurred. He came to Paris in October, at the
age of twenty-five, to make a career decision that was soon to
lead him to join his father in banking in the town of Langport,
in Somerset. Bagehot had attended University College, London,
where he completed his B.A. in 1846 and obtained his M.A. in
1848, winning with the latter a gold medal in philosophy. He
had attended that new institution because of his father's Uni-
tarianism—University College had been founded to provide
non-Anglicans with an alternative to Oxford or Cambridge,
and it offered in those years an education equal or superior
to that available at the great universities. He had pursued his
degree in moral philosophy, and in one of his first publications
(1847) had revealed the impact of this course of study by criticising the poet Philip James Bailey for failing to reveal the force
of retribution in the moral economy of the universe.

He had published two other major essay-reviews prior to his
visit to Paris in 1851, both on economic subjects. He wrote on
"The Currency Monopoly" (a largely theoretical discussion of
currency questions directed at the government's handling of
the problem in the crisis of 1847) and a review of John Stuart

Mill's *Principles of Political Economy* (which included a good deal of social and political comment), both for the *Prospective Review* in 1848. It is an impressive commentary upon his formal education and his informal association with his father's banking concerns that he was prepared to write these essays at so early an age. The essays help make clearer why his political analysis of the coup is grounded in economic concerns, important among which is the question of financial confidence.

The preparation he had obtained was of a diversity and a quality sufficient to allow him to pursue the wide-ranging career he was subsequently to follow as a banker; a steady contributor to *The Economist* after 1859 and its editor from 1861 till his death; editor of *The National Review;* author of two major books on politics, *The English Constitution* (1867) and *Physics and Politics* (1872), and another, *Lombard Street* (1873) on the money market, plus a steady stream of essays on subjects literary, philosophical and religious, historical, political and economic; and an unofficial advisor to Liberal governments on economic questions.

Had he been aware that such a splendid and diverse career was possible to a banker, the decision he sought to make when he went to the Continent would have been easier. It was not a simple question of matching his abilities to a task. He had gone on from his M.A. to the study of law, which he was finding increasingly uncongenial; yet law was the career which his father preferred for him. His mother, on the other hand, preferred to have him at home, and she and her wishes constituted a special problem and a special need.

Since Bagehot's infancy, his family had been disrupted by his mother's periodic bouts of insanity, and he felt he should be near his father to help in any way he could. Adding to the problem was a mentally defective half-brother. It is quite conceivable that Bagehot was troubled by fear that the disease was heritable. It is certain that he made the trip to Paris in a very troubled state of mind.

The alternative to a legal career was unpromising. He was

not much attracted by what appeared to him the humdrum aspects of a country banker's life—only later was he to find he could successfully compartmentalize his activities and become banker, writer, and editor simultaneously.

He arrived in Paris in the fall of 1851 when political agitation and rumor were rife, and he immersed himself in the excitement of the events leading up to and surrounding the coup d'état. These proved a healthy tonic, taking him out of himself, turning his attention to public affairs, and providing him, by the publication of his "Letters" in *The Inquirer*, with an enhancement of his self-esteem.

His improving mood and his interest in the mounting French crisis were already evident in a letter of October 20 to his mother, in which he expressed his view that the Republic's Constitution should be revised to allow for the President's re-election.[1] The "Letters" he sent to *The Inquirer* after the coup show him jauntily in command of himself and full of high spirits.

Bagehot seemed to have been in such a mood throughout the three crucial days of December 2–4. He described his doings in letters to his father and to his friend Richard Holt Hutton. The latter reported:

> . . . He climbed over the rails of the Palais Royal on the morning of 2nd December to breakfast, and used to say that he was the only person who did breakfast there on that day.[2]

And to his father, Bagehot wrote on December 5:

> My Dearest Father:
> I forgot the electric telegraph and thought that my note would be the first or about the first intelligence that you would receive of the new Revolution. Wednesday was extremely quiet, unnaturally so almost, and everybody seemed

[1] Mrs. Russell Barrington, *The Life of Walter Bagehot,* vol. 10 in *The Life and Works of Walter Bagehot,* ed. by Mrs. Barrington (London, 1918), pp. 190–91.

[2] "Memoir," in Barrington, *Works,* vol. 1, p. 2.

to stand in the streets to know as soon as might be what would turn up; however, no one seemed to like to stay still in any place for fear that something of great importance might have happened or be happening somewhere else. I assisted in the evening at a great gathering in the Boulevards, and a man whose name I could not learn read a paper announcing the *déchéance* of the President, but the appearance of a very few soldiers sent the swarm in all directions, for they were mere peaceful citizens or curious foreigners, and had no fighting aptitude. Altogether the characteristic of that day was exactly what Lord Byron in some letter calls *"quiet* inquietude."

Yesterday, Thursday, the *Coup d'État* you will remember was on Tuesday, was much more disturbed, the Paris [sic] Royal was closed, and a formidable notice was affixed to all the walls informing all persons that the *"*enemies of order*"* had begun their operations. Being curious to see their tactics, I immediately hied to the Boulevard St. Martin which I fancied would be the centre of operations, for it is in the narrow streets leading out of that great thoroughfare that the most "exalted" of the *ouvriers* are said to reside. I had not been misinformed, for as soon as I got on the ground, the preparations for barricades were immediately visible. It is a simple process, though there being no paving stones on the Boulevards was a difficulty, but the stones of a half-built house supplied the place excellently well for the one where I was. These with palings, iron rails, planks, etc., and three overturned omnibuses and two upset cabs completed the bulwark. It took about half an hour to make mine, as the Boulevards are about there very wide, but others especially in the side streets were run up much more rapidly. The people making them were of two very unlike sorts. Immensely the greater number were mere boys or lads, *gamins* is the technical word, the lower sort of shopboys and sons of the better artisans, not bad-looking young fellows at all, liking the fair, and in general quite unarmed. Besides these and directing them were a few old stagers who have been at it these twenty years—men whose faces I do not like to *think* of—yellow, sour, angry, fanatical, who would rather shoot you than not. Each barricade that I saw was constructed under the eye of one or two, not more, of such

fellows; the most of them do not, I was told, show until the
building is over and the fighting begins. They were implicitly
obeyed; indeed, a man must have a great deal of pluck not to
do as they said, for they were armed, and a trifle bigoted in
their temper. These (Montagnards[3] is their name technically)
I very studiously avoided, but I asked a question or two of
some of the young fellows, and found that they thought that
all the *troups* [sic] were out of Paris, that the provinces—
Lyons especially—were rising, and that all the military would
be wanted to prevent their march on the capital. It was likely
enough that there was a row at Lyons, but not likely from
the distance that they could yet be at the gates of Paris. Why
the *troups* did not come I do not know, but for I suppose a
couple of hours the barricade-people had it all their own way,
and erected I think five in that part of the Boulevards, one
after another, with about a hundred yards between them. I
scrambled over two and got as far as I dared towards the
centre. The silence was curious: on the frontier a raging
though industrious multitude, within the kingdom no one, a
woman hurrying home, an old man shrugging his shoulders,
all as quiet as the grave. I did not stay long in the inside, as
I feared the *troups* would come and I might be shot that
Napoleon might rule the French or some Montagnard might
be so kind as to do it just to keep his hand in. The moment
the barricades were done, they began to break into the shops
and houses, not to rob but for arms. As soon as they were
satisfied there was no more weapons to be had, they chalked
"death to robbers" or something of that sort on the shutters
and went away. I should not think they stole sixpenny worth
of any matter except powder and guns. The Montagnards
would have shot any young fellow that tried it on. I tried
hard to hire a window to see the capture of the fortress as
well as its erection but this was not to be, for everybody said
they meant to shut their windows and indeed it would not
have been very safe to look out on them firing. I therefore
retired, though not too quickly. It is a bad habit to run in a
Revolution, somebody may think you are the "other side" and
shoot at you, but if you go calmly and look English, there is

3 See above, p. 9.

no particular danger. As I retired I met the *troups* at some distance, slowly and cautiously hemming in the insurgents. Anybody might go out who would but no one come in. The whole operation reminded me very much of the description of the Porteous mob in the *Heart of Midlothian*. If you will read over that again you will have the best idea of the thoroughbred Parisian *émeute* that I know. There is the same discipline, order, absence of plunder, and in the leaders the same deep hatred and fanaticism.[4] I am pleased to have had an opportunity of seeing it *once* but once is enough, as there is, I take it, a touch of sameness in this kind of sight, and I shall not go again into the citadel of operation. In no other part is there any danger for a decently careful person. To-day is much quieter. The *troups* soon cleared my barricade, though I heard cannon and musketry, the latter in plenty, and there was blood and a good deal of it in the approachable parts of the Boulevards; the field of the hardest battle was not to be approached for soldiers. I have not got time for a word more. You will have better accounts in the English papers than we have here. Only those of the Government are allowed to appear and these I know from the description of what I saw are written to tranquillise the provinces and diminish the disorder much. However, my notion is that the President will hold his own. Many thanks to my Mother for her note and also for your letter—I will write in a day or two.

Yours ever,

W. Bagehot.[5]

These remarks reveal much the same mood as do his "Letters on the French *Coup d'État* of 1851." The "Letters" appear rather a *jeu d'esprit*, full of wit and zest, perhaps a little too consciously aimed at outraging the sentiments of staid readers of the Unitarian periodical in which his friend Hutton arranged to have them published. That they were outrageous enough is

[4] Readers interested in Bagehot's perceptions here might compare his comments with George Rudé's recent brilliant study, *The Crowd in History* (New York, 1964).

[5] Barrington, vol. 10, pp. 193–96.

evidenced by the fact that the editor of *The Inquirer* found it necessary to introduce the first two with disclaimers of any editorial agreement with the sentiments they expressed. The sentiments, supporting the coup, were similar to those Lord Palmerston had voiced, and he in consequence was forced to resign his post in the Cabinet, an indication of how unpopular the coup d'état and its author were in liberal circles in England.

Taking advantage of our historical perspective, we need not react as violently as did his first readers to the apparent immorality of Bagehot's approval of the coup. We can enjoy his light touch of wit while listening for the deeper tones as well, premonitions of the mature political philosophy which was to inform his major works of the 1860s. It is this developing political philosophy that makes Bagehot's interpretation of the coup so memorable. It allowed him, young as he was and even in a flippant tone, to say important things about the outcome of the 1848 revolutions, the political and temperamental differences between England and France, and about the political process in the middle of the nineteenth century.

The framework of his interpretation is grounded in his profound conviction of fundamental human irrationality. His personal family experience certainly inclined him to such a view—an experience much on his mind as he wrote the "Letters." We find very clear expression of this idea in the centrality he gives to the unreasoning fears of the business community as both cause and justification of the coup—a recollection of his already developed sense of businessmen's behavior in financial panics.

Such a conviction is scarcely surprising in a disciple of Edmund Burke, though it is not a point of dependence to which Bagehot makes explicit reference as he does to others, such as the idea of national character. A view of irrationality such as Bagehot was developing leads to an expectation of an ever-imminent eruption of violence, to a view that the social and political order is a frighteningly fragile thing, dependent for its maintenance to a major degree on irrationality itself in the form of custom, habit, and unreasoning faith and obedience. Bagehot became, with Burke, a critic of revolutionaries' and reformers' excessive faith in rationality—a naïve faith because it fails to take account of man's basically irrational character. Worse, it is a real danger, likely to lead men to tamper with arrangements that might work only because of their very irrationality— to threaten social and political traditions that, however apparently offensive to logic and reason, might be truly requisite to provide the framework for society. Again, naïve rationalism could combine casual destructiveness with the belief that it is easy to *construct* politics to suit men's ideals.[6]

Bagehot drew from Burke his historically based relativism, his view that institutions, like customs, grow almost insensibly in accord with the national traits of the people possessing them. Both opposed the attempt at generalized application of universal abstract standards, and like Burke, Bagehot also opposed what seemed to him the unreasoning, misguided, and dangerous expectation that institutions might be transferred from one nation to another. One of his main arguments in the "Letters" is against this latter opinion, widespread among his contemporaries in England. In this context, political morality takes on a new and different coloration; it becomes relativized.

Both Tocqueville and Bagehot were Burkeans, and a comparison of Bagehot with Tocqueville is illuminating, despite the radical difference in their judgments of the coup. Ideas Bagehot and Tocqueville had in common—as Bagehot revealed in the "Letters" and in his later writings—indicate a similar style of moderate liberalism. Bagehot shared Tocqueville's view of the dangers of socialism and socialist theorists—as is evidenced by his surprising quotation from Proudhon. More centrally, we find both Bagehot and Tocqueville fearing the tyranny of the majority, a Caesarist elected despot, and the removal of intermediary

[6] Many of the themes Bagehot pursued are to be found in Constantin Frantz's essay *Louis Napoleon*, written in 1852, where he stressed the need of the French for strong leadership to prevent anarchy, showing how the coup d'état had saved France from the evils of a parliamentarism for which it was unsuited.

powers that might cushion the operation of government upon the governed. Here Bagehot echoes the characteristic liberal concern Tocqueville emphasized in his discussion of American institutions, i.e., the problem of local control versus the tendency toward centralization; neither had much hope for French local government in the near future. For both, Louis Napoleon became the symbol of a new *democratic* despotism, militarist and bureaucratized, peculiarly French in origin. They shared with all the authors included here a recognition of the power of the French bureaucracy.

In the "Letters" we also find that Bagehot was trying his hand at one of Tocqueville's great skills, comparative analysis, illuminating French behavior by means of his understanding of English affairs. Both described versions of the English and French "national characters" which echo Burke and even John Stuart Mill, and, in fact, had already begun to take on the flavor of clichés—yet which in the hands of Tocqueville and Bagehot acquired new sharpness.[7] These were images of, on the one hand, the deductive, logical French, pursuing political abstractions at the expense of social stability and, on the other, the pragmatic, untheoretical Englishmen, muddling through without principle or guiding purpose.

Their views are by no means identical, however. Bagehot certainly saw Frenchmen as more volatile and changeable than did Tocqueville. Tocqueville attended particularly to the practical wisdom of an experienced political class, the English aristocracy—a social element his nation had not acquired (for the nobility of the old regime had lacked the governing experience of the English) and could not seemingly any longer obtain. He was no admirer of the bourgeoisie. Bagehot's main work (in the

[7] Woodrow Wilson noted this similarity; see "A Wit and a Seer," *Atlantic Monthly*, vol. 82 (1898), p. 532. (We find a hint of the same idea in Proudhon's remarks on subjectivism in French politics. Proudhon also offers a very brief sketch of the French national character which, not surprisingly, has some echoes of those versions we have noted.)

sixties) was as interpreter of England and sometimes of France of a generation later than Tocqueville. He was the interpreter of an era wherein the middle class was ascendant, and its rule and role were his special concern. He had considerable praise for the qualities of businessmen, something not to be readily found in the works of Tocqueville, and he was interested in the dignified, "impressive" functions of an aristocracy rather than being dedicated to aristocratic values.

Bagehot's conception of "national character" was still relatively unsophisticated in 1852. When he began to publish *Physics and Politics* as a series of articles in 1865, he was able to draw the intriguing analogy between the growth of a national character and that of a literary style; in 1852 he had not yet so fully refined the notion, which was already widespread and usually associated with some quite unscientific stereotypes. His remarks include some of these stereotypes, revealing their racist implications. But what Bagehot came to discuss seems clearly to be a political style, set by French politicians and journalists,[8] evident in their behavior and in their speech and writing, and that of upper-class Parisian Frenchmen as well. It appears in the Assembly and in the press and its final results are the barricades. These are the clever, inconsistent, impatient Frenchmen, with their tendency to abstract and deductive manipulation of universal principles.[9] The result in France was a recurrent unsettling of the political and social fabric in revolutionary upheavals, requiring the intervention of temporary military despotism to restore social stability. It is notable that Bagehot's comments on Benjamin Disraeli often suggest a fear that this very un-English politician was introducing the same sort of unsettling tendency into English politics.

In contrast to this French political type, Bagehot sets the

[8] Although by no means unique in expressing such a concern, Bagehot will strike present-day readers as very modern in his remarks about journalists' need to create sensation.

[9] In contrast, Bagehot feels that Englishmen expect the universalization of English *practice,* as noted above.

"stupid" unimaginative, stolid, custom-ridden Englishman. And a question is posed for us by his doing so. For the Frenchmen who favored the coup, who desired stability, sound in some passages strikingly like the "stupid" Englishmen—Bagehot even refers in his "Letters" to the stupidity of the French bourgeoisie. In much of his later writing, Bagehot made evident that he felt the mass of mankind to be politically opaque—and much alike in its political behavior. He seemed to believe that on the lower levels of society the characteristics that linked ignorance and lack of culture were similar in all "advanced" nations.

Two points might be made here. First, I believe something of the same difficulty occurs as that which John Stuart Mill attributed to Tocqueville when he reviewed the concluding portion of *Democracy in America,* which appeared in 1840. Mill argued that what Tocqueville regarded as characteristically American, he, Mill, from his English vantage point saw as rather characteristically commercial—forms of behavior likely to be widespread in an age or nation dominated by its middle class.[10] Similarly, traits Bagehot refers to as uniquely English share something with Tocqueville's idea of the American character. Bagehot may have been approaching a description such as Mill offered of middle-class forms of behavior that transcended national lines. Secondly, he was of course dealing with more than one class, for the working class was of major importance in the politics of 1848 and the June Days, and its volatility constituted a very special problem.[11] I think it fair to suggest that while the young Bagehot was working with the idea of national character producing a national political style, he was confronting along with his contemporaries the evidences of class behavior as well. The mid-century revolutionary years made increasingly clear to those concerned with politics that there were similarities that transcended national lines, but they were faced

[10] J. S. Mill, "Tocqueville on Democracy in America," *Essays on Politics and Culture,* ed. by Gertrude Himmelfarb (Garden City, N.Y., 1963), pp. 257 ff.

[11] As Proudhon also notes.

with a real poverty of conceptual tools for their serious treatment. The coup d'état was to spur Karl Marx to one of the most important statements of the mid-century on just this subject.

That Bagehot turned first to national character should be no surprise. Mill, in 1843, in his *System of Logic*, had argued that a science of the subject, to be called "political ethology," was the next most needed step in the study of social affairs. And the Revolutions of 1848 had kept the national issue before the European public for almost three years. Bagehot's relativist argument from national character, his assertion to his English readers of the fragility of French politics and the political need for a temporary despotism, constitute the primary lessons he sought to instill to alleviate the "stupidity" of his English readers. For, despite his admiring remarks about stupidity, his "Letters," like all his other writings, are clear enough evidence that he wanted to have Englishmen better informed, their stupidity animated by some principle and theory.[12]

Despite his approval of the coup d'état, the principles Bagehot taught were thoroughly Liberal. A careful reading of the "Letters" points up his attachment to local control against centralized administration, a reflection of the characteristic Liberal belief in the educational effect of participation in politics. Bagehot remained a believer in the potentially civilizing consequences

[12] This was an objective he shared with his great Liberal contemporary John Stuart Mill, who also hoped to introduce some share of such "French" qualities into English public life. But their emphases were different. Mill's theoretical bent obviously far outshone Bagehot's and his faith in theory did too. Bagehot, far more than Mill, emphasized the dangers both of too much theory and of too sudden action—he had none of Mill's radicalism. Bagehot really appreciated the value of English "stupidity." He was always far more closely in touch with and sympathetic to the dominant middle class. Bagehot might be understood in much of his political writing as adopting a kind of middle ground between Burke and Mill (or as performing more amusingly the conservative role Gertrude Himmelfarb attributes to Mill in his middle years), i.e., preserving the values and institutions of England's past, while subjecting them to informed practical and theoretical criticism. See Himmelfarb, Introduction, *passim*.

of parliamentary government and a free press, given, of course, the basic requirement of fundamental social stability. He was, besides, a warm advocate of toleration, of free "government of discussion" which might offer the "teaching apparatus" whereby the mass of men might be civilized. The "Letters" never advocated the continuance of despotism. In 1865, in one of the many articles he wrote for *The Economist* upon the Empire Louis Napoleon established after the coup, Bagehot still repeated essentially the same comment we find in the "Letters." "It is an admirable government for present and coarse purposes, but a detestable government for future and refined purposes."[13]

We have noted above that Bagehot's interpretation of the coup pointed up the importance of the economic fears of the business community as a political factor. In this regard, again like Mill and like Marx and Proudhon, Bagehot differed from many contemporaries who had real difficulty bridging economic and political categories. Bagehot remained predominantly a laissez-faire economic Liberal, but he always viewed economic affairs in their full social context and used psychological insights to link politics and economics. And for all his emphasis upon politics here, it is clear that economic affairs form the basis upon which they rest.

We may conclude by wondering whether the "Letters" might be taken as symptomatic of what Benedetto Croce called "a change in the public spirit of Europe,"[14] a new realism, later to be epitomized in the Machiavellianism of Cavour and Bismarck. The shift from the older exclusive stress on politics and politicians seems part of such a change; to an even greater extent the apparent amorality of the "Letters" might be taken to provide evidence of a new attitude. Bagehot speaks of the disillusioned and to those who still had illusions, who had lost so much after their dreams had seemed briefly to come to fruition

---

[13] "Caesarism as It now Exists," reprinted in Bagehot, *Works*, vol. 4, ed. by N. St. John-Stevas (Cambridge, Mass., 1968), p. 113.
[14] In his *History of Europe in the Nineteenth Century* (London, 1934), ch. VIII.

in 1848–49 all over the Continent.[15] But Bagehot himself was not disillusioned for the illusions had not been his, and he wrote with youthful disdain for the vision of universal liberation his elders had held. In this his tone differs little from that of Marx. It is salutary, I think, to keep in mind that if after 1851 an identifiably different attitude toward society and politics existed than the dominant one in 1848, it was not simply that the old Right, chastened and newly enlightened by its experience, returned to power, but that a new generation, which had scarcely been involved, was growing up—and as always seems to be the case, had seen what a mess its elders of all parties in the revolutionary years had made of things.

SUGGESTED READINGS

Alistair Buchan, *The Spare Chancellor*, London, 1959.

Mrs. Russell Barrington, *The Life of Walter Bagehot*, vol. 10, in *The Life and Works of Walter Bagehot*, ed. by Mrs. Barrington, London, 1918.

Jacques Barzun, Introduction to Bagehot's *Physics and Politics*, New York, 1948.

William Irvine, *Walter Bagehot*, London, 1939.

Norman St. John-Stevas, *Walter Bagehot*, London, 1959.

———, *The Collected Works of Walter Bagehot*, vols. 1, 3, 4 (vol. 1 contains a biographical essay, vol. 3 an essay by Jacques Barzun on Bagehot as historian, vol. 4 the "Letters," plus an essay by Stevas on Bagehot and Napoleon III), Cambridge, Mass., 1965–68.

[15] Proudhon and Hugo, like Marx, saw the dispelling of illusions as a significant potential lesson or consequence of the coup: see pp. 138, 232, 328, 404.

SELECTIONS FROM BAGEHOT'S

"Letters on the French *Coup d'État* of 1851"

————————

LETTER I—THE DICTATORSHIP OF LOUIS NAPOLEON

Paris, January 8, 1852.

MY DEAR SIR—You have asked me to tell you what I think of
French affairs. I shall be pleased to do so; but I ought perhaps
to begin by cautioning you against believing, or too much heed-
ing, what I say. However, I do not imagine that I need do so;
for with your experience of the public journals, you will be
quite aware that it is not difficult to be an "occasional correspond-
ent." Have your boots polished in a blacking-shop, and call the
interesting officiator an intelligent *ouvrier*; be shaved, and cite
the *coiffeur* as "a person in rather a superior station"; call your
best acquaintance "a well-informed person," and all others "persons whom I have found to be occasionally not in error," and—
abroad, at least—you will soon have matter for a newspaper let-

SOURCE: Reprinted, by permission of the publishers, from Norman St.
John-Stevas, editor, *The Collected Works of Walter Bagehot*, volume
4. Cambridge, Mass.: Harvard University Press. Copyright © 1968,
by *The Economist*. Pp. 29–37, 39–43, 45–46, 48–58, 60–61, 63–70,
71–84.

ter. I should quite deceive you if I professed to have made these profound researches. . . . I only know what a person who is in a foreign country during an important political catastrophe cannot avoid knowing, what he runs against, what is beaten into him, what he can hardly help hearing, seeing, and reflecting.

That Louis Napoleon has gone to Notre Dame to return thanks to God for the seven millions and odd suffrages of the French people—that he has taken up his abode at the Tuileries, and that he has had new Napoleons coined in his name—that he has broken up the trees of liberty for firewood—that he has erased, or is erasing (for they are many), *Liberté, Egalité,* and *Fraternité* from the National buildings—all these things are so easy and so un-English that I am pretty sure with you they will be thought signs of pompous impotence. . . .

I am inclined, however, to imagine that this idea would be utterly erroneous; that, on the contrary, the President is just now, at least, really strong and really popular, that the act of 2nd of December did succeed and is succeeding, that many, that most, of the inferior people do really and sincerely pray *Domine Salvum fac Napoleonem.*

In what I have seen of the comments of the English press upon recent events here, two things are not quite enough kept apart—I mean the temporary dictatorship of Louis Napoleon to meet and cope with the expected crisis of '52, and the continuance of that dictatorship hereafter—the new, or as it is called, the *Bas*-Empire—in a word, the coming Constitution and questionable political machinery with which "the nephew of my uncle" is now proposing to endow France. Of course in reality these two things *are* separate. It is one thing to hold that a military rule is required to meet an urgent and temporary difficulty: another to advocate the continuance of such a system, when so critical a necessity no longer exists.

It seems to me, or would seem, if I did not know that I was contradicted both by much English writing and opinion, and also by many most competent judges here, that the first point, the temporary dictatorship, is a tolerably clear case; that it is not to be complicated with the perplexing inquiry what form of government will permanently suit the French people;—that the President was, under the actual facts of the case, quite justified in assuming the responsibility, though of course I allow that responsibility to be tremendous. My reasons for so believing I shall in this letter endeavour to explain, except that I shall not, I fancy, have room to say much on the moral defensibility or indefensibility of the *coup d'état*; nor do I imagine that you want from me any ethical speculation;—that is manufactured in Printing-house-square; but I shall give the best account I can of the matter-of-fact consequences and antecedents of the New Revolution, of which, in some sense, a resident in France may feel without presumption that he knows something hardly so well known to those at home.

The political justification of Louis Napoleon is, as I apprehend, to be found in the state of the public mind which immediately preceded the *coup d'état*. It is very rarely that a country expects a revolution at a given time; indeed it is perhaps not common for ordinary persons in any country to anticipate a revolution at all; though profound people may speculate, the mass will ever expect to-morrow to be as this day at least, if not more abundant. But once name the day, and all this is quite altered. As a general rule the very people who would be most likely to neglect general anticipation are exactly those most likely to exaggerate the proximate consequences of a certain impending event. At any rate, in France five weeks ago, the tradespeople talked of May '52, as if it were the end of the world. Civilisation and socialism might probably endure, but buying and selling would surely come to an end; in fact, they anticipated a worse era than February '48, when trade was at a standstill so long that it has hardly yet recovered, and when the government stocks fell 40 per cent. It is hardly to be imagined upon what petty details the dread of political dissolution at a fixed and not distant time will condescend to intrude itself. I was present when a huge *Flamande*,[1] in appearance so

[1] A Flemish woman.

intrepid that I respectfully pitied her husband, came to ask the character of a *bonne*. I was amazed to hear her say, "I hope the girl is strong, for when the revolution comes next May, and I have to turn off my helper, she will have enough to do." It seemed to me that a political apprehension must be pretty general when it affected that most non-speculative of speculations, the *reckoning* of a housewife. With this feeling, everybody saved their money: who would spend in luxuries that which might so soon be necessary and invaluable! This economy made commerce—especially the peculiarly Parisian trade, which is almost wholly in articles that *can* be spared—worse and worse; the more depressed trade became, the more the traders feared, and the more they feared, the worse all trade inevitably grew.

I apprehend that this feeling extended very generally among all the classes who do not find or make a livelihood by literature or by politics. Among the clever people, who understood the subject, very likely the expectation was extremely different; but among the stupid ones who mind their business, and have a business to mind, there was a universal and excessive tremour. The only notion of '52 was "on se battra dans la rue." Their dread was especially of socialism; they expected that the followers of M. Proudhon, who advisedly and expressly maintains "anarchy" to be the best form of government, would attempt to carry out their theories in action, and that the division between the legislative and executive power would so cripple the party of order as to make their means of resistance for the moment feeble and difficult to use. The more sensible did not, I own, expect the annihilation of mankind: civilisation dies hard; the organised sense in all countries is strong; but they expected vaguely and crudely that the party which in '93 ruled for many months, and which in June '48 fought so fanatically against the infant republic, would certainly make a desperate attack—*might* for some short time obtain the upper hand. Of course it is now matter of mere argument whether the danger was real or unreal, and it is in some quarters rather the fashion to quiz the past fear, and to deny that any socialists anywhere exist. In spite

of the literary exertions of Proudhon and Louis Blanc, in spite
of the prison quarrels of Blanqui and Barbès[2]—there are certainly found people that question whether anybody buys the
books of the two former, or cares for the incarcerated dissen-
sions of the two latter. But however this may be, it is certain
that two days after the *coup d'état* a mass of persons thought it
worth while to erect some dozen barricades, and among these,
and superintending and directing their every movement there
certainly were, for I saw them myself, men whose physiognomy
and accoutrements exactly resembled the traditional Montagnard, sallow, stern, compressed, with much marked features,
which expressed but resisted suffering, and brooding one-idea'd
thought, that from their youth upward had for ever imagined,
like Jonah, that they did well—immensely well, to be angry—
armed to the teeth, and ready, like the soldiers of the first Republic, to use their arms savagely and well in defence of theories broached by a Robespierre, a Blanqui, or a Barbès, gloomy
fanatics, *over*-principled ruffians. I may perhaps be mistaken in
reading on their features the characters of such men, but I
know that when one of them disturbed my superintendence of
barricade-making with a stern *allez vous en* it was not too slowly
that I departed, for I *felt* that he would rather shoot me than
not. Having seen these people, I conceive that they exist. But
supposing that they were all simply fabulous, it would not less
be certain that they were believed to be, and to be active; nor
would it impair the fact that the quiet classes awaited their
onslaught in morbid apprehension, with miserable and craven,
and I fear we ought to say, *commercial* disquietude.

You will not be misled by any highflown speculations about

2 Louis Blanc (1811–82), socialist member of the Provisional Government, proponent of National Workshops, and historian; Louis
Auguste Blanqui (1805–81), radical revolutionary, advocate of violent revolution and conspiratorial tactics, spent much of his life in
prison; Armand Barbès (1809–70), leading figure among radical revolutionaries in the early days of the Second Republic, was imprisoned after an uprising in support of Poland on May 15, 1848.

liberty or equality. You will, I imagine, concede to me that the first duty of a government is to ensure the security of that industry which is the condition of social life and civilised cultivation;—that especially in so excitable a country as France it is necessary that the dangerous classes should be saved from the strong temptation of long idleness; and that no danger could be more formidable than six months' beggary among the revolutionary *ouvriers*, immediately preceding the exact period fixed by European as well as French opinion for an apprehended convulsion. It is from this state of things, whether by fair means or foul, that Louis Napoleon has delivered France. The effect was magical, like people who have nearly died because it was prophecied they would die at a specified time, and instantly recovered when they found or thought that the time was gone and past. So France, so timorously anticipating the fated revolution, in a moment revived when she found or fancied that it was come and over. Commerce instantly improved; New Year's Day, when all the boulevards are one continued fair, has not (as I am told) been for some years so gay and splendid. . . . Clever people may now prove that the dreaded peril was a simple chimera, but they can't deny that the fear of it was very real or painful, nor can they dispute that in a week after the *coup d'état* it had at once, and apparently for ever, passed away.

I fear it must be said that no legal or constitutional act could have given an equal confidence. What was wanted was the assurance of an audacious government, which would stop at nothing, scruple at nothing, to secure its own power and the tranquillity of the country. That assurance all now have; a man who will in this manner dare to dissolve an assembly constitutionally his superiors, then prevent their meeting by armed force; so well and so sternly repress the first beginning of an outbreak, with so little misgiving assume and exercise sole power —may have enormous other defects, but is certainly a bold ruler—most probably an unscrupulous one—little likely to flinch from any inferior trial.

Of Louis Napoleon, whose personal qualities are, for the

moment, so important, I cannot now speak at length. But I may say that, with whatever other deficiencies, he has one excellent advantage over other French statesmen—he has never been a professor, nor a journalist, nor a promising barrister, nor, by taste, a *littérateur*. He has not confused himself with history; he does not think in leading articles, in long speeches, or in agreeable essays. But he is capable of observing facts rightly, of reflecting on them simply, and acting on them discreetly. And his motto is Danton's *De l'audace et toujours de l'audace*, and this you know, according to Bacon, in time of revolution, will carry a man far, perhaps even to ultimate victory, and that ever-future millennium *"la consolidation de la France."*

But on these distant questions I must not touch. I have endeavoured to show you what was the crisis, how strong the remedy, and what the need of a dictatorship. I hope to have convinced you that the first was imminent, the second effectual, and the last expedient. I remain yours,

AMICUS.

LETTER II—THE MORALITY OF THE COUP D'ÉTAT

Paris, January 15, 1852.

My DEAR SIR—I know quite well what will be said about, or in answer to, my last letter. It will be alleged that I think everything in France is to be postponed to the Parisian commerce— that a Constitution, Equality, Liberty, a Representative Government, are all to be set aside if they interfere even for a moment with the sale of *étrennes*[3] or the manufacture of gimcracks.

I, as you know, hold no such opinions: it would not be necessary for me to undeceive you, who would, I rather hope, never

[3] Gifts.

suspect me of *that* sort of folly. But as St. Athanasius aptly observes, "for the sake of the women who may be led astray, I will this very instant explain my sentiments."

Contrary to Sheridan's rule, I commence by a concession. I certainly admit, indeed I would, upon occasion, maintain *boutons* and bracelets to be things less important than common law and constitutional action. A *coup d'état* would, I may allow, be mischievously superogatory if it only promoted the enjoyment of what a lady in the highest circles is said to call "bigotry and virtue." But the real question is not to be so disposed of. The Parisian trade, the jewellery, the baubles, the silks, the luxuries, which the Exhibition showed us to be the characteristic industry of France, are very dust in the balance if weighed against the hands and arms which their manufacture employs —the industrial habits which their regular sale rewards—the hunger and idle weariness which the certain demand for them prevents. For this is the odd peculiarity of commercial civilisation. The life, the welfare, the existence of thousands depend on their being paid for doing what seems nothing when done. That gorgeous dandies should wear gorgeous studs—that pretty girls should be prettily dressed—that pleasant drawing-rooms should be pleasantly attired—may seem, to people of our age, sad trifling. But grave as we are, we must become graver still when we reflect on the horrid suffering the sudden cessation of large luxurious consumption would certainly create, if we imagine such a city as Lyons to be, without warning, turned out of work, and the population feelingly told "to cry in the streets when no man regardeth."

The first duty of society is the preservation of society. By the sound work of old-fashioned generations—by the singular painstaking of the slumberers in churchyards—by dull care—by stupid industry, a certain social fabric somehow exists—people contrive to go out to their work, and to find work to employ them actually until the evening, body and soul are kept together, and this is what mankind have to show for their six thousand years of toil and trouble.

To keep up this system we must sacrifice everything. Parliaments, liberty, leading articles, essays, eloquence—all are good, but they are secondary; at all hazards, and if we can, mankind must be kept alive. And observe, as time goes on, this fabric becomes a tenderer and a tenderer thing. Civilisation can't bivouac; dangers, hardships, sufferings, lightly borne by the coarse muscle of earlier times, are soon fatal to noble and cultivated organisation. Women in early ages are masculine, and, as a return match, the men of late years are becoming women. The strong apprehension of a Napoleonic invasion has, perhaps, now caused more substantial misery in England than once the Wars of the Roses.

To apply this "screed of doctrine" to the condition of France. I do not at all say that, but for the late *coup d'état,* French civilisation would certainly have soon come to a final end. *Some* people might have continued to take their meals. Even socialism would hardly abolish *eau sucrée.* But I do assert that, according to the common belief of the common people, their common comforts were in considerable danger. The debasing torture of acute apprehension was eating into the crude pleasure of stupid lives. No man liked to take a long bill; no one could imagine to himself what was coming. Fear was paralysing life and labour, and as I said at length, in my last, fear, so intense, whether at first reasonable or unreasonable, will, ere long, invincibly justify itself. May, 1852, would, in all likelihood, have been an evil and bloody time if it had been preceded by six months' famine among the starvable classes.

At present all is changed. Six weeks ago society was living from hand to mouth: now she feels sure of her next meal. And this, in a dozen words, is the real case—the political excuse for Prince Louis Napoleon. You ask me, or I should not do so, to say a word or two on the moral question and the oath. You are aware how limited my means of doing so are. I have forgotten Paley, and have never read the casuists. But it certainly does not seem to me proved or clear, that a man who has sworn, even in the most solemn manner, to see another drown, is therefore quite bound, or even at liberty, to stand placidly on the bank. What ethical philosopher has demonstrated this? Coleridge said it was difficult to advance a new error in morals—yet this, I think, would be one; and the keeping of oaths is peculiarly a point of mere science, for Christianity in terms, at least, only forbids them all. And supposing I am right, such certainly was the exact position of Louis Napoleon. He saw society, I will not say dying or perishing—for I hate unnecessarily to overstate any point—in danger of incurring extreme and perhaps lasting calamities—and calamities, likely not only to impair the happiness, but moreover to debase the character of the French nation, and these calamities he could prevent. Now who has shown that ethics require of him to have held his hand?

The severity with which the riot was put down on the first Thursday in December has, I observe, produced an extreme effect in England; with our happy exemption from martial bloodshed, it must, of course, do so. But better one *émeute* now than many in May, be it ever remembered. There are things more demoralising than death, and among these is the sickly-apprehensive suffering for long months of an entire people.

Of course you understand that I am not holding up Louis Napoleon as a complete standard either of ethical scrupulosity or disinterested devotédness; veracity has never been the family failing—for the great Emperor was a still greater liar. And he has been long playing what, morality apart, is the greatest political misfortune to any statesman—a visibly selfish game. Very likely, too, the very high heroes of history—a Washington, an Aristides, by Carlyle profanely called "favourites of Dryasdust," would have extricated the country more easily, and perhaps more completely, from its scrape. Their ennobling rectitude would have kept M. de Girardin[4] consistent, and induced

---

[4] Émile de Girardin (1806–81), journalist and politician, edited several papers during the July Monarchy and later; a Republican who turned Bonapartist.

M. Thiers[5] to vote for the revision of the Constitution; and
even though, as of old, the mountain were deafer than the un-
charmed adder, a sufficient number of self-seeking Conservatives
might have been induced by perfect confidence in a perfect
president, to mend a crotchety performance, that was visibly
ruining, what the poet calls, "The ever-ought-to-be-conserved-
thing," their country.

. . . I have but one last point to make about this *coup d'état*,
and then I will release you from my writing. I do not know
whether you in England rightly realise the French socialism.
Take, for instance, M. Proudhon, who is perhaps their ideal
and perfect type. He was *représentant de la Seine* in the late
Assembly, elected, what is not unimportant, after the publication
of his books and on account of his opinions. In his "Confessions
d'un Révolutionnaire," a very curious book—for he writes extremely well—after maintaining that our well-known but, as
we imagine, advanced friends, Ledru Rollin, and Louis Blanc,
and Barbès, and Blanqui are all *réactionnaires,* and clearly showing, to the grief of mankind, that once the legislator of the
Luxembourg wished to preserve "equilibrium," and the author
of the provincial circulars to maintain the "tranquillity," he
gives the following *bona fide* and amusing account of his own
investigations:—"I commenced my task of solitary conspiracy by
the study of the socialisms of antiquity, necessary, in my judgment, to determine the law, whether practical or theoretical, of
progress. These socialisms I found in the Bible. A memoir on the
institution of the Sabbath—considered with regard to morals, to
health, and in its relation to the family and the city—procured
for me a bronze medal from my academy. From the faith in
which I had been reared, I had precipitated myself head-long,
head-foremost, into the pure reason, and already, what was wonderful and a good omen, when I made Moses a philosopher and

5 Louis-Adolphe Thiers (1797–1877), historian and politician,
played a leading role in French politics from 1830 on; leading figure
in the July Monarchy; later, he became a founder of the Third Republic.

a socialist, I was greeted with applause. If I am now in error, the fault is not merely mine. Was there ever a similar seduction?

"But I studied, above all, with a view to action. I cared little for academical laurels. I had no leisure to become *savant*, yet less a *litterateur* or an archæologist. I began immediately upon political economy.

"I had assumed as the rule of my investigations that every principle which, pushed to its consequences, should end in a contradiction, must be considered false and null; and that if this principle had been developed into an institution, the institution itself must be considered as factitious, as utopian.

"Furnished with this criterion, I chose for the subject of investigation what I found in society the most ancient, the most respectable, the most universal, the least controverted—property. Everybody knows what happened; after a long, a minute, and, above all, an impartial analysis, I arrived, as an algebraist, guided by his equations, to this surprising conclusion. Property, consider it as you will—refer it to what principle you may, is a contradictory idea; and as the denial of property carries with it of necessity that of authority, I deduced immediately from my first axiom also this corollary, not less paradoxical, the true form of government is *anarchy*. Lastly, finding by a mathematical demonstration that no amelioration in the economy of society could be arrived at by its natural constitution, or without the concurrence and reflective adhesion of its members; observing, also, that there is a definite epoch in the life of societies, in which their progress, at first unreflecting, requires the intervention of the free reason of man, I concluded that this spontaneous and impulsive force (*cette force d'impulsion spontanée*), which we call Providence, is not everything in the affairs of this world: from that moment, without being an Atheist, I ceased to worship God. He'll get on without your so doing, said to me one day the *Constitutionnel*. Well; perhaps he may." These theories have been expanded into many and weary volumes, and condensed into the famous phrase, "La Proprieté c'est le vol"; and have procured their author, in his own sect, reputation and authority.

The *Constitutionnel* had another hit against M. Proudhon, a day or two ago. They presented their readers with two decrees in due official form (the walls were at the moment covered with those of the 2nd of December), as the last ideal of what the straitest sect of the socialists particularly desire. It was as follows:—"Nothing any longer exists. Nobody is charged with the execution of the aforesaid decree. Signed, Vacuum."

Such is the speculation of the new reformers—what their practice would be I can hardly tell you. My feeble income does not allow me to travel to the Basses Alpes and really investigate the subject; but if one quarter of the stories in circulation are in the least to be believed (we are quite dependent on oral information, for the government papers deal in asterisks and "details unfit for publication," and the rest are devoted to the state of the navy, and say nothing) the atrocities rival the nauseous corruption of what our liberal essayist calls "Jacobin carrion," the old days of Carrier and Barère. This is what people here are afraid of; and that is why I write such things—and not to horrify you, or amuse you, or bore you—anything rather than that; and they think themselves happy in finding a man who, with or without whatever other qualities or defects, will keep them from the vaunted millennium, and much-expected *Jacquerie*. I hope you think so too—and that I am not, as they say in my native Tipperary, "Whistling jigs to a milestone." I am, my dear sir, yours truly,

AMICUS.

P.S.—You will perhaps wish me to say something on the great event of this week, the exile of the more dangerous members of the late Assembly, and the transportation of the socialists to Cayenne. Both measures were here expected; though I think that both lists are more numerous than was anticipated; but no one really knew what would be done by this silent government. You will laugh at me when I tell you that both measures have been well received; but, properly limited and understood, I am

73

persuaded that the fact is so. Of course among the friends of exiled *Représentants,* among the *littérateurs* throughout whose ranks these measures are intended to "strike terror and inspire respect," you would hear that there never was such tyranny since the beginning of mankind. But among the mass of the industrious classes—between whom and the politicians there is internecine war—I fancy that on turning the conversations to either of the most recent events, you would hear something of this sort:—"*Ça ne m'occupe pas*" "What is that *to me.*" "*Je suis pour la tranquillité, moi.*" "I sold four brooches yesterday." The socialists who have been removed from prison to the colony, it is agreed were "pestilent fellows perverting the nation," and forbidding to pay tribute to M. Bonaparte. Indeed they can hardly expect commercial sympathy. "Our national honour rose —our stocks fell" is Louis Blanc's perpetual comment on his favourite events, and it is difficult to say which of its two clauses he dwells upon with the intenser relish. It is generally thought by those who think about the matter, that both the transportation, and, in all cases, certainly, the exile will only be a temporary measure, and that the great mass of the people in both lists will be allowed to return to their homes when the present season of extreme excitement has passed over. Still I am not prepared to defend the *number* of the transportations. That strong measures of the sort were necessary I make no doubt. If socialism exist, and the fear of it exist, something must be done to re-assure the people. You will understand that it is not a judicial proceeding either in essence or in form; it is not to be considered as a punishment for what men have done, but as a perfect precaution against what they may do. Certainly it is to be regretted that the cause of order is so weak as to need such measures; but if it *is* so weak, the government must no doubt take them. Of course however "our brethren" who are retained in such numbers to write down Prince Louis, are quite right to use without stint or stopping this most un-English proceeding; it is their case, and you and I from old misdeeds know pretty well how it is to be managed. There will be no imputation of reasonable or humane motives to the government, and no examination of the existing state of France;—let both these come from the other side—but elegiac eloquence is inexhaustibly exuded—the cruel corners of history are ransacked for petrifying precedents—and I observe much excellent weeping on the Cromwellian deportations and the ten years' exile of Madame de Staël.[6] But after all they have missed the tempting parallel—I mean the "rather long" proscription-list which Octavius—*"l'ancien neveu de l'ancien oncle"*—concocted with Mark Antony in the marshes of Bononia, and whereby they thoroughly purged old Rome of its turbulent and revolutionary elements. I suspect our estimable contemporaries regret to remember of how much good order, long tranquillity, *"beata pleno copia cornu"* and other many "little comforts" to the civilised world that very "strong" proceeding, whether in ethics justifiable or not, certainly was in fact the beginning and foundation. . . .

LETTER III—ON THE NEW CONSTITUTION OF FRANCE, AND THE APTITUDE OF THE FRENCH CHARACTER FOR NATIONAL FREEDOM

Paris, January 20, 1852.

MY DEAR SIR—We have now got our Constitution. The Napoleonic era has commenced; the term of the dictatorship is fixed, and the consolidation of France is begun. . . .

The details of the new institutions you will have long ago learnt from the daily papers. I believe they may be fairly and nearly accurately described as the Constitution of the Consulate, *minus* the ideas of the man that made it. You will remember

---

[6] Germaine de Staël (1766–1817), author of important works of comparative literature, novels, etc.; exiled by Napoleon I for her opposition to his regime.

that, besides the First Magistrate, the Senate, the House of Representatives, the Council of State, (which we may call, in legal language, the "common form" of continental constitution), the ingenious Abbé Sieyès had devised some four principal peculiarities, which were to be remembered to all time as masterpieces of political invention. These were the utter inaction of the First Magistrate, copied, as I believe, from the English Constitution—the subordination to him of two Consuls, one to administer peace and the other war, who were intended to be the real hands and arms of the government—the silence of the Senate—the double and very peculiar election of the House of Representatives. Napoleon the Great, as we are now to speak, struck out the first of these, being at the moment working some fifteen hours a day at the reorganisation of France. . . . Napoleon the Little, as I fear the Parisian multitude may learn to call him, has effaced the other three "strokes of statesmanship." The new Constitution of France is exactly the "common form" of political conveyancing, *plus* the *Idée Napoléonienne* of an all-suggesting and all-administering mind.

. . . I fancy—for I have no data on which to found real knowledge of so delicate a point—the new Constitution is regarded merely as what Father Newman[7] would call a "preservative addition" or a "necessary development," essential to the "chronic continuance" of the Napoleonic system; for the moment the mass of the people wish the President to govern them, but they don't seem to me to care how. The political people, I suppose, hate it, because for some time it will enable him, if not shot, to govern effectually. I say if not shot—for people are habitually recounting under their breath some new story of an attempt at assassination, which the papers suppress. I am inclined to think that these rumours are pure lies; but they show the feeling. You know, according to the Constitution of 1848, the President would now be a mere outlaw, and whoever finds

[7] John Henry Newman (1801–90), English theologian, leader of the Oxford Movement; turned Catholic in 1845, became a priest, made a cardinal in 1879.

him may slay him if he can. It is true that the elaborate master-piece of M. Marrast is already fallen into utter oblivion, (it is no more remembered than yesterday's *Times,* or the political institutions of Saxon Mercia); but nevertheless such, according to the antediluvian *régime,* would be the law, and it is possible that a mindful Montagnard may upon occasion recall even so insignificant a circumstance. . . .

In discussing any Constitution, there are two ideas to be first got rid of. The first is the idea of our barbarous ancestors—now happily banished from all civilised society, but still prevailing in old manor-houses, in rural parsonages, and other curious repositories of mouldering ignorance, and which in such arid solitudes is thus expressed "Why can't they have Kings, Lords and Commons *like we have?* What fools foreigners are." The second pernicious mistake is, like the former, seldom now held upon system, but so many hold it in bits and fragments, and without system, that it is still rather formidable. I allude to the old idea which still here creeps out in conversation, and some-times in writing—that politics are simply a subdivision of im-mutable ethics; that there are certain rights of men in all places and all times, which are the sole and sufficient foundation of all government, and that accordingly a single stereotype govern-ment is to make the tour of the world—and you have no more right to deprive a Dyak of his vote in a "possible" Polynesian parliament, than you have to steal his mat.

Burke first taught the world at large, in opposition to both, and especially to the latter of these notions, that politics are made of time and place—that institutions are shifting things, to be tried by and adjusted to the shifting conditions of a mutable world—that, in fact, politics are but a piece of business—to be determined in every case by the exact exigencies of that case: in plain English—by sense and circumstances.

This was a great step in political philosophy—though it *now* seems the events of 1848 have taught thinking persons (I think) further. They have enabled us to say that of all these circum-stances so affecting political problems, by far and out of all

77

question the most important is *national character*. In that year the same experiment—the experiment, as its friends say, of Liberal and Constitutional Government—as its enemies say of Anarchy and Revolution—was tried in every nation of Europe— with what varying futures and differing results! The effect has been to teach men—not only speculatively to know, but practically to feel, that no absurdity is so great as to imagine the same species of institutions suitable or possible for Scotchmen and Sicilians, for Germans and Frenchmen, for the English and the Neapolitans. With a well-balanced national character (we now know) liberty is a stable thing. A really practical people will work in political business, as in private business, almost the absurdest, the feeblest, the most inconsistent set of imaginable regulations. Similarly, or rather reversely, the best institutions will not keep right a nation that *will* go wrong. Paper is but paper, and no virtue is to be discovered in it to retain within due boundaries the undisciplined passions of those who have never set themselves seriously to restrain them. In a word—as people of "large roundabout common sense" will (as a rule) somehow get on in life—(no matter what their circumstances or their fortunes)—so a nation which applies good judgment, forbearance, a rational and compromising habit to the management of free institutions, will certainly succeed; while the more eminently gifted national character will but be a source and germ of endless and disastrous failure, if, with whatever other eminent qualities, it be deficient in these plain, solid, and essential requisites.

The formation of *this* character is one of the most secret of marvellous mysteries. Why nations have the character we see them to have is, speaking generally, as little explicable to our shallow perspicacity, as why individuals, our friends or our enemies, for good or for evil, have the character which they have; why one man is stupid and another clever—why another volatile and a fourth consistent—this man by instinct generous, that man by instinct niggardly. I am not speaking of actions, you observe, but of tendencies and temptations. These and other similar problems daily crowd on our observation in millions and millions, and only do not puzzle us because we are too familiar with their difficulty to dream of attempting their solution. Only this much is most certain, all men and all nations have a character, and that character, when once taken, is, I do not say unchangeable—religion modifies it, catastrophe annihilates it —but the least changeable thing in this ever-varying and changeful world. Take the soft mind of the boy, and (strong and exceptional aptitudes and tendencies excepted) you may make him merchant, barrister, butcher, baker, surgeon, or apothecary. But once make him an apothecary, and he will never afterwards bake wholesome bread—make him a butcher, and he will kill too extensively, even for a surgeon—make him a barrister, and he will be dim on double entry, and crass on bills of lading. Once conclusively form him to one thing, and no art and no science will ever twist him to another. Nature, says the philosopher, has no Delphic daggers!—no men or maids of all work— she keeps one being to one pursuit—to each is a single choice afforded, but no more again thereafter for ever. And it is the same with nations. The Jews of to-day are the Jews in face and form of the Egyptian sculptures; in character they are the Jews of Moses—the negro is the negro of a thousand years—the Chinese, by his own account, is the mummy of a million. "Races and their varieties," says the historian, "seem to have been created with an inward *nisus* diminishing with the age of the world." The people of the South are yet the people of the South, fierce and angry as their summer sun—the people of the North are still cold and stubborn like their own North wind—the people of the East "mark not, but are still"—the people of the West "are going through the ends of the earth, and walking up and down in it." The fact is certain, the cause beyond us. The subtle system of obscure causes, whereby sons and daughters resemble not only their fathers and mothers, but even their great-great-grandfathers and their great-great-grandmothers, may very likely be destined to be very inscrutable. But, as the fact is so, so moreover, in history, nations have one character, one set of talents, one list of temptations, and one duty, to use the one and get the better of the other. There are breeds in the animal man just as in the animal dog. When you hunt with greyhounds and course with beagles, then, and not till then, may you expect the inbred habits of a thousand years to pass away, that Hindoos can be free, or that Englishmen will be slaves.

I need not prove to you that the French *have* a national character. Nor need I try your patience with a likeness of it. I have only to examine whether it be a fit basis for national freedom. I fear you will laugh when I tell you what I conceive to be about the most essential mental quality for a free people, whose liberty is to be progressive, permanent, and on a large scale; it is much *stupidity*. I see you are surprised—you are going to say to me, as Socrates did to Polus, "My young friend, *of course* you are right; but will you explain what you mean—as yet you are not intelligible." I will do so as well as I can, or endeavour to make good what I say—not by an *a priori* demonstration of my own, but from the details of the present, and the facts of history. Not to begin by wounding any present susceptibilities, let me take the Roman character—for, with one great exception—I need not say to whom I allude—they are the great political people of history. Now, is not a certain dullness their most visible characteristic? What is the history of their speculative mind?—a blank. What their literature?—a copy. They have left not a single discovery in any abstract science; not a single perfect or well-formed work of high imagination. The Greeks, the perfection of narrow and accomplished genius, bequeathed to mankind the ideal forms of self-idolising art—the Romans imitated and admired; the Greeks explained the laws of nature—the Romans wondered and despised; the Greeks invented a system of numerals second only to that now in use—the Romans counted to the end of their days with the clumsy apparatus which we still call by their name; the Greeks made a capital and scientific calendar —the Romans began their month when the Pontifex Maximus happened to spy out the new moon. Throughout Latin literature, this is the perpetual puzzle—Why are we free and they slaves? we prætors and they barbers? Why do the stupid people always win, and the clever people always lose? I need not say that, in real sound stupidity, the English are unrivalled. You'll hear more wit, and better wit, in an Irish street row than would keep Westminster Hall in humour for five weeks. Or take Sir Robert Peel—our last great statesman, the greatest member of parliament that ever lived, an absolutely perfect transacter of public business—the type of the nineteenth century Englishman as Sir Robert Walpole was of the eighteenth. Was there ever such a dull man? Can any one, without horror, foresee the reading of his memoirs? A *clairvoyante*, with the book shut, may get on; but who now, in the flesh, will ever endure the open *vision* of endless recapitulation of interminable Hansard. Or take Mr. Tennyson's inimitable description:—

> No little lily-handed baronet he,
> A great broad-shouldered genial Englishman,
> A lord of fat prize oxen and of sheep,
> A raiser of huge melons and of pine
> A patron of some thirty charities
> A pamphleteer on guano and on grain,
> A quarter-sessions chairman, abler none.

Whose company so soporific? His talk is of truisms and bullocks; his head replete with rustic visions of mutton and turnips, and a cerebral edition of Burn's "Justice!" Notwithstanding, he is the salt of the earth, the best of the English breed. Who is like him for sound sense? But I must restrain my enthusiasm. You don't want me to tell you that a Frenchman—a real Frenchman —can't be stupid; *esprit* is his essence, wit is to him as water, *bons-mots* as *bon-bons*. He reads and he learns by reading; levity and literature are essentially his line. Observe the consequence. The outbreak of 1848 was accepted in every province in France; the decrees of the Parisian mob were received and registered in all the municipalities of a hundred cities; the Revolution ran like the fluid of the telegraph down the *Chemin de fer du Nord*; it stopped at the Belgian frontier. Once brought into contact with the dull phlegm of the stupid Fleming, the poison was powerless. . . . *Les braves Belges,* I make no doubt, were quite pleased to observe what folly was being exhibited by those very clever French, whose tongue they want to speak, and whose literature they try to imitate. In fact, what we opprobriously call stupidity, though not an enlivening quality in common society, is nature's favourite resource for preserving steadiness of conduct and consistency of opinion. It enforces concentration; people who learn slowly, learn only what they must. The best security for people's doing their duty is that they should not know anything else to do; the best security for fixedness of opinion is that people should be incapable of comprehending what is to be said on the other side. These valuable truths are no discoveries of mine. They are familiar enough to people whose business it is to know them. Hear what a dense and aged attorney says of your peculiarly promising barrister:—"Sharp! oh yes, yes! he's too sharp by half. He is not *safe;* not a minute, isn't that young man." "What style sir," asked of an East India Director some youthful aspirant for literary renown, "is most to be preferred in the composition of official dispatches?" "My good fellow," responded the ruler of Hindostan, "the style *as we* like is the Humdrum." I extend this, and advisedly maintain that nations, just as individuals, may be too clever to be practical, and not dull enough to be free.

How far this is true of the French, and how far the gross deficiency I have indicated is modified by their many excellent qualities, I hope at a future time to inquire.

I am, my dear sir, yours truly,

AMICUS.

LETTER IV—ON THE APTITUDE OF THE FRENCH
CHARACTER FOR NATIONAL SELF-GOVERNMENT

Paris, January 29, 1852.

MY DEAR SIR—There is a simple view of the subject on which I
wrote to you last week that I wish to bring under your notice.
The experiment (as it is called) of establishing political freedom
in France is now sixty years old; and the best that we can say of
it is, that it is an experiment still. There have been perhaps
half-a-dozen new beginnings—half-a-dozen complete failures. I
am aware that each of these failures can be excellently explained
—each beginning shown to be quite necessary. But there are
certain reasonings which, though outwardly irrefragable, the
crude human mind is always most unwilling to accept. Among
these are different and subtle explications of several apparently
similar facts. Thus, to choose an example suited to the dignity
of my subject, when a gentleman from town takes a day's shooting in the country, and should chance (as has happened) at
first going off, to miss some six times running, how luminously
soever he may "explain" each failure as it occurs, "however
expanded a view" he may take of the whole series, whatever
popular illustrations of projectile philosophy he may propound
to the bird-slaying agriculturists—the impression on the crass
intelligence of the gamekeeper will quite clearly be "He beint
noo shot homsoever—aint thickeer." Similarly, to compare small
things with great, when I myself read in Thiers and the many
other philosophic historians of this literary country, various and
excellent explanations of their many mischances;—of the failure
of the Constitution of 1791—of the Constitution of the year 3

83

—of the Constitution of the year 5—of the *charte*[8]—of the system of 1830—and now we may add, of the second republic—the annotated constitution of M. Dupin—I can't help feeling a suspicion lingering in my crude and uncultivated intellect—that some common principle is at work in all and each of these several cases—that over and above all odd mischances, so many bankruptcies a little suggest an unfitness for the trade; that besides the ingenious reasons of ingenious gentlemen—there is some lurking quality, or want of a quality, in the national character of the French nation which renders them but poorly adapted for the form of freedom and constitution which they have so often, with such zeal and so vainly, attempted to establish.

In my last letter I suggested that this might be what I ventured to call a "want of stupidity." I will now try to describe what I mean in more accurate, though not, perhaps, more intelligible words.

I believe that I am but speaking what is agreed on by competent observers, when I say that the essence of the French character is a certain mobility; that is, as it has been defined, a certain "excessive sensibility to *present* impressions," which is sometimes "levity"—for it issues in a postponement of seemingly fixed principles to a momentary temptation or a transient whim; sometimes "impatience"—as leading to an exaggerated sense of existing evils; often "excitement"—a total absorption in existing emotion; oftener "inconsistency"—the sacrifice of old habits to present emergencies; and yet other unfavourable qualities. But it has also its favourable side. The same man who is drawn aside from old principles by small pleasures, who can't bear pain, who forgets his old friends when he ceases to see them, who is liable in time of excitement to be a one-idea-being, with no conception of anything but the one exciting object; yet who nevertheless is apt to have one idea to-day and quite another to-morrow (and this, and more than this, may I fancy be said of the ideal Frenchman) may and will have the subtlest perception of

[8] Constitution granted by Louis XVIII upon his return to power in 1814 after the Napoleonic Wars.

existing niceties, the finest susceptibility to social pleasure, the keenest tact in social politeness, the most consummate skilfulness in the details of action and administration—may in short be the best companion, the neatest man of business, the lightest *homme de salon*, the acutest diplomat of the existing world. . . .

I will not say that the quality which I have been trying to delineate is exactly the same thing as "cleverness." But I do allege that it is sufficiently near it for the rough purposes of popular writing. For this *quickness* in taking in—so to speak— the present, gives a corresponding celerity of intellectual apprehension, an amazing readiness in catching new ideas and maintaining new theories, a versatility of mind which enters into and comprehends everything as it passes, a concentration in what occurs, so as to use it for every purpose of illustration, and consequently, (if it happen to be combined with the least fancy), quick repartee on the subject of the moment, and *bonmots* also without stint and without end—and these qualities are rather like what we style cleverness. And what I call a proper stupidity keeps a man from all the defects of this character; it chains the gifted possessor mainly to his old ideas; it takes him seven weeks to comprehend an atom of a new one; it keeps him from being led away by new theories—for there is nothing which bores him so much; it restrains him within his old pursuits, his well-known habits, his tried expedients, his verified conclusions, his traditional beliefs. He is not tempted to "levity," or "impatience," for he does not see the joke, and is thick-skinned to present evils. Inconsistency puts him out—"What I says is this here, as I was a saying yesterday," is his notion of historical eloquence and habitual discretion. He is very slow indeed to be "excited"—his passions, his feelings, and his affections are dull and tardy strong things, falling in a certain known direction, fixing on certain known objects, and for the most part acting in a moderate degree, and at a sluggish pace. You always know where to find his mind.

Now this is exactly what, in politics at least, you do not know about a Frenchman. I like—I have heard a good judge say—to hear a Frenchman talk. He strikes a light, but what light he will strike it is impossible to predict. I think he doesn't know himself. Now, I know you see at once how this would operate on a parliamentary government, but I give you a gentle illustration. All England knows Mr. Disraeli, the witty orator, the exceedingly clever *littérateur*, the versatile politician; and all England has made up its mind that the stupidest country gentleman would be a better Home Secretary than the accomplished descendant of the "Caucasian race." Now suppose, if you only can, a House of Commons all Disraelis, and do you imagine that Parliament would work? It would be what M. Proudhon said of some French assemblies, "a box of matches."

The same quality acts in another way, and produces to English ideas a most marvellous puzzle, both in their philosophical literature and their political discussion. I mean their passion for logical deduction. Their habitual mode of argument is to get hold of some large principle or principles; to begin to deduce immediately; and to reason down from them to the most trivial details of common action. *Il faut être conséquent avec soi-même* —is their fundamental maxim; and in a world, the essence of which is compromise, they could not well have a worse. I hold, metaphysically perhaps, that this is a consequence of that same impatience of disposition to which I have before alluded. Nothing is such a bore as looking for your principles—nothing so pleasant as working them out. People who have thought, know that enquiry is suffering. A child a-stumbling timidly in the dark is not more different from the same child playing on a sunny lawn, than is the philosopher groping, hesitating, doubting and blundering about his primitive postulates, from the same philosopher proudly deducing and commenting on the certain consequences of his established convictions. On this account mathematics have been called the paradise of the mind. In Euclid at least, you have your principles, and all that is required is acuteness in working them out. The long annals of science are one continued commentary on this text. Read in Bacon, the beginner of intellectual philosophy in England, and every page of the "Advancement of Learning" is but a continued warning against the tendency of the human mind to start at once to the last generalities from a few and imperfectly observed particulars. Read in the "Méditations" of Descartes, the beginner of intellectual philosophy in France, and in every page (once I read five) you will find nothing but the strictest, the best, the most lucid, the most logical deduction of all things actual and possible, from a few principles obtained without evidence, and retained in defiance of probability. Deduction is a game, and induction a grievance. Besides, clever impatient people want not only to learn, but to teach. And instruction expresses at least the alleged possession of knowledge. The obvious way is to shorten the painful, the slow, the tedious, the wearisome process of preliminary inquiry—to assume something pretty —to establish its consequences—discuss their beauty—exemplify their importance—extenuate their absurdities. A little vanity helps all this. Life is short—art is long—truth lies deep—take some side—found your school—open your lecture-rooms—tuition is dignified—learning is low. . . .

. . . It is as necessary for a public writer to have a system as it is for him to have a pen. His course is obvious; he assumes some grand principle—the principle of Legitimacy, or the principle of Equality, or the principle of Fraternity—and thence he reasons down without fear or favour to the details of every-day politics. Events are judged of, not by their relation to simple causes, but by their bearing on a remote axiom. Nor are these speculations mere exercises of philosophic ingenuity. Four months ago, hundreds of able writers were debating with the keenest ability and the most ample array of generalities, whether the country should be governed by a Legitimate Monarchy, or an illegitimate; by a Social, or an old-fashioned Republic, by a two-chambered Constitution, or a one-chambered Constitution; on "Revision" or Non-revision; on the claims of Louis Napoleon, or the divine right of the national representation. Can any intellectual food be conceived more dangerous or more stimulating for an over-excitable population? It is the same in parliament.

The description of the Church of Corinth may stand for a description of the late Assembly: every one had a psalm, had a doctrine, had a tongue, had a revelation, had an interpretation. Each member of the Mountain had his scheme for the regeneration of mankind; each member of the vaunted majority had his scheme for newly consolidating the government; Orleanist hated Legitimist, Legitimist Orleanist; moderate Republican detested undiluted Republican; scheme was set against scheme, and theory against theory. No two Conservatives would agree what to conserve; no Socialist could practically associate with any other. No deliberative assembly can exist with every member wishing to lead, and no one wishing to follow. Not the meanest Act of Parliament could be carried without more compromise than even the best French statesmen were willing to use on the most important and critical affairs of their country. Rigorous reasoning would not manage a parish-vestry, much less a great nation. In England to carry half your own crotchets, you must be always and everywhere willing to carry half another man's. Practical men must submit as well as rule; concede as well as assume. Popular government has many forms, a thousand good modes of procedure; but no one of those modes can be worked, no one of those forms will endure, unless by the continual application of sensible heads and pliable judgments, to the systematic criticism of stiff axioms, rigid principles, and incarnated propositions.

I am, &c.,

Amicus.

LETTER V—ON THE CONSTITUTION OF THE PRINCE-PRESIDENT

[Undated]

My Dear Sir—The many failures of the French in the attempt to establish a predominantly parliamentary government, have a strong family likeness. Speaking a little roughly, I shall be right in saying that the constitutions of France have perished, both lately and formerly, either in a street-row or under the violence of a military power, aided and abetted by a diffused dread of impending street-rows, and a painful experience of the effects of past ones. Thus the constitution of 1791 (the first of the old series) perished, on the 10 of August, amid the exultation of the brewer Santerre.[9] The last of the old series fell on the 18th Brumaire, under the hands of Napoleon, when the 5 per cents. were at 12, the whole country in disorder, and all ruinable persons ruined. The Monarchy of 1830 began in the riot of the three days, and ended in the riot of the 24 of February; the Republic of February perished but yesterday, mainly from the terror that Paris might again see such days as the "days of June."

I think all sensible Englishmen who review this history (the history of more than sixty years), will not be slow to divine a conclusion peculiarly agreeable to our orderly national habits, viz., that the first want of the French is somebody or something able and willing to keep down street-rows, to repress the frightful elements of revolution and disorder which, every now and then, astonish Europe; capable of maintaining, and desirous to maintain, the order and tranquillity which are (all agree) the essential and primary pre-requisites of industry and civilisation. If any one seriously and calmly doubts this, I am afraid nothing that I can further say will go far in convincing him. But let him read the account of any scene in any French revolution, old or new, or better let him come here and learn how people look back to the time I have mentioned (to June, 1848), when the socialists—not under speculative philosophers like Proudhon or Louis Blanc, but under practical rascals and energetic mur-

[9] Antoine-Joseph Santerre (1752–1809); French Revolutionist who helped storm the Bastille; became commander of the National Guard and warden of Louis XVI; imprisoned as an Orleanist and not released until after the Terror, when he returned to private life.

derers, like Sobrier and Caussidière[10]—made their last and final stand, and against them, on the other side, the National Guard (mostly solid shopkeepers, three-parts ruined by the events of February) fought (I will not say bravely or valiantly, but) furiously, frantically, savagely, as one reads in old books that half-starved burgesses in beleaguered towns have sometimes fought, for the food of their children; let any sceptic hear of the atrocities of the friends of order, and the atrocities of the advocates of disorder, and he will, I imagine, no longer be sceptical on two points—he will hope that if he ever have to fight it will not be with a fanatic socialist, nor against a demi-bankrupt, fighting for "his shop"; and he will admit, that in a country subject to collisions between two such excited and excitable combatants, no earthly blessing is in any degree comparable to a power which will stave off, long delay, or permanently prevent the actual advent and ever-ready apprehension of such bloodshed. I therefore assume that the first condition of good government in this country is a really strong, a reputedly strong, a continually strong, executive power.

Now, on the face of matters, it is certainly true that such a power is perfectly consistent with the most perfect, the most ideal type of parliamentary government. Rather I should say, such and so strong an executive is a certain consequence of the existence of that ideal and rarely found type. If there is among the people, and among their representatives, a strong, a decided, an unflinching preference for particular ministers, or a particular course of policy, that course of policy can be carried out, and will be carried out, as certainly as by the Czar Nicholas, whose ministers can do exactly what they will. . . .

. . . But the case is (as we know by experience of what passes under our daily observation) immensely altered, when there is no longer this strong, compact, irrefragable, "following;" no distinctly divided, definite faction, no regular opposition to

[10] Marc Caussidière (1808–61), radical republican, Prefect of Police in Paris after February 1848; Marie-Joseph Sobrier, extreme radical Republican, aide to Caussidière on the police.

be daily beaten, no regular official party to be always victorious —but, instead, a mere aggregate of "independent members," each thinking for himself, propounding, as the case may be, his own sense or his own nonsense—one, profound ideas applicable to all time; another, something meritorious from the Eton Latin grammar, and a mangled republication of the morning's newspaper. . . . Again, divide a political [assembly] into three parties, any two of which are greater than the third, and it will be always possible for an adroit and dexterous intriguer (M. Thiers has his type in most assemblies) to combine, three or four times a fortnight, the two opposition parties into a majority on some interesting questions, on some matter of importance. The best government possible under the existing circumstances will be continually, and, in a hazardous state of society, even desperately and fatally weakened. . . .

Nor am I drawing a French Assembly from mere history, or from my own imagination. In the late chamber, the great subject of the very last *Annual Register,* there were not only three parties but four. There was a perpetually shifting element of 200 members, calling itself the Mountain, which had in its hands the real casting vote between the President's government and the constitutional opposition. In the very last days of the constitution they voted against, and thereby negatived, the proposition of the questors for arming the Assembly; partly because they disliked General Changarnier, and detested General Cavaignac; partly because, being extreme socialists, they would not arm anybody who was likely to use his arms against their friends on the barricades. The same party was preparing to vote for the Bill on the Responsibility of the President, actually, and according to the design of its promoters, in the nature of a bill of indictment against him, because they feared his rigour and efficiency in repressing the anticipated convulsion. The question, the critical question, *Who* shall prevent a new revolution? was thus actually, and owing to the lamentable divisions of the friends of order, in the hands of the parliamentary representatives, of the very men who wished to effect that revolution, was determined, I may say, ultimately, and in the last resort by the party of disorder.

Nor on lesser questions was there any steady majority, any distinctive deciding faction, any administering phalanx, anybody regularly voting with anybody else, often enough, or in number enough, to make the legislative decision regular, consistent, or respectable. Their very debates were unseemly. On anything not pleasing to them, the Mountain (as I said) a yellow and fanatical generation—had (I am told) an engaging knack of rising *en masse* and screaming until they were tired. It will be the same, I do not say in degree, (for the Mountain would certainly lose several votes now, and the numbers of the late Chamber were unreasonably and injudiciously large), but, in a measure, you will be always subject to the same disorder. A fluctuating majority, and a minority, often a ruling minority, favourable to rebellion. The cause, as I believe, is to be sought in the peculiarities of the French character, on which I dwelt, prolixly, I fear, and *ad nauseam,* in my last two letters. If you have to deal with a *mobile,* a clever, a versatile, an intellectual, a dogmatic nation, inevitably, and by necessary consequence, you will have conflicting systems—every man speaking his own words, and always giving his own suffrage to what seems good in his own eyes—many holding to-day what they will regret to-morrow—a crowd of crotchety theories and a heavy percentage of philosophical nonsense—a great opportunity for subtle stratagem, and intriguing selfishness—a miserable division among the friends of tranquillity, and a great power thrown into the hands of those who, though often with the very best intentions, are practically, and in matter of fact, opposed both to society and civilisation. And, moreover, beside minor inconveniences and lesser hardships, you will indisputably have periodically—say three or four times in fifty years—a great crisis; the public mind much excited, the people in the streets swaying to and fro with the breath of every breeze, the discontented *ouvriers* meeting in a hundred knots, discussing their real sufferings and their imagined grievances with lean features and angry gesticulations;

the parliament, all the while in permanence, very ably and eloquently expounding the whole subject, one man proposing this scheme, and another that; the opposition expecting to oust the Ministers, and ride in on the popular commotion; the Ministers fearing to take the odium of severe or adequate repressive measures, lest they should lose their salary, their places and their majority: finally, a great crash, a disgusted people, overwhelmed by revolutionary violence, or seeking a precarious, a pernicious, but after all a precious protection from the bayonets of military despotism. Louis Philippe met these dangers and difficulties in a thoroughly characteristic manner. He bought his majority. . . . Of course, on the face of it, this system worked, as far as business went, excellently well. For eighteen years the tranquillity was maintained. France, it may be, has never enjoyed so much calm civilisation, so much private happiness; and yet, after all such and so long blessings, it fell in a mere riot—it fell unregretted. It is a system which no wise man can wish to see restored; it was a system of regulated corruption.

But it does not at all follow, nor I am sure will you be apt so to deduce, that because I imagine that France is unfit for a government in which a House of Commons is, as with us, the sovereign power in the state, I therefore believe that it is fit for no freedom at all. Our own constitutional history is the completest answer to any such idea. For centuries, the House of Commons was habitually, we know, but a third-rate power in the state. First the Crown, then the House of Lords enjoyed the ordinary and supreme dominion; and down almost to our own times the Crown and House of Lords, taken together, were much more than a sufficient match for the people's house; but yet we do not cease to proclaim, daily and hourly, in season and out of season, that the English people never have been slaves. It may, therefore, well be that our own country having been free under a constitution in which the representative element was but third-rate in power and dignity, France and other nations may contrive to enjoy that advantage from institutions in which it is only second-rate.

Now, of this sort is the Constitution of Louis Napoleon. I am not going now, after prefacing so much to discuss its details; indeed, I do not feel competent to do so. What should we say to a Frenchman's notion of a £5 householder, or the 4th and 5th clauses of the New Reform Bill? and I quite admit that a paper building of this sort can hardly be safely criticised till it is carried out on *terra firma,* till we see not only the theoretic ground-plan, but the actual inhabited structure. The life of a constitution is in the spirit and disposition of those who work it; and we can't yet say in the least what that, in this case, will be; but so far as the constitution shows its meaning on the face of it, it clearly belongs to the class which I have named. The *Corps Législatif* is not the administering body, it is not even what perhaps it might with advantage have been, a petitioning and remonstrating body; but it possesses the legislative veto, and the power of stopping *en masse* the supplies. They are not a working, a ruling, or an initiative, or supremely decisive, but an immense checking power. They will be unable to change ministers, or aggravate the course of revolutions, but they could arrest an unpopular war—they could reject an unpopular law —they are, at least in theory, a powerful and important drag-chain. Out of the mouths of its adversaries this system possesses what I have proved, or conjectured, or assumed to be the prime want of the French nation—a strong executive. The objection to it is that the objectors find nothing else in it. We confess there is no doubt now of a power adequate to repress street rows and revolutions.

At the same time, I guard myself against intimating any opinion on the particular minutiæ of this last effort of institutional invention. I do not know enough to form a judgment; I sedulously, at present, confine myself to this one remark, that the new government of France belongs, in theory at least, to the right class of Constitutions—the class that is most exactly suited to French habits, French nature, French social advantages,

French social dangers—the class, I mean, in which the representative body has a consultative, a deliberative, a checking and a minatory; not as with us a supreme, nearly an omnipotent, and exclusively initiatory function.

I am, yours, &c.

AMICUS.

P.S.—You may like five words on a French invasion. I can't myself imagine, and what is more to the point, I do not observe that anybody has here any notion of any such inroad into England as was contemplated and proposed by General Changarnier. No one in the actual conduct of affairs, with actual responsibility of affairs, not, as the event proved, even Ledru Rollin could, according to me, encounter the risk and odium of such a hateful and horribly dangerous attempt. But, I regret to add, there is a contingency which sensible people here (so far as I have had the means of judging) do not seem to regard as at all beyond the limits of rational probability, by which a war between England and France would most likely be superinduced; that is, a French invasion of Belgium. I do not mean to assure you that this week or next the Prince-President will make a razzia in Brussels. But I do mean that it is thought not improbable that somehow or other, on some wolf-and-the-lamb pretext, he may pick a quarrel with King Leopold, and endeavour to restore to the French the "natural limit" of the Rhine. Now, I have never seen the terms of the guarantee which the shrewd and cautious Leopold exacted from England before he would take the throne of Belgium; but as the only real risk was a French aggression upon that tempting territory, I do not make any doubt that the expressions of that instrument bind us to go to war in defence of the country whose limits and independence we have guaranteed. And in this case an invasion of England would be as admissible a military movement as an invasion of France. I hope, therefore, you will use your

best rhetoric to induce people to put our pleasant country in a
state of adequate and tolerable defence. . . .

LETTER VI—THE FRENCH NEWSPAPER PRESS

Paris, February 10 [1852]

MY DEAR SIR—We learn from an oriental narrative in considerable circulation, that the ancient Athenians were fond of
news. Of course they were. It is in the nature of a mass of clever
and intellectual people living together to want something to
talk about. Old ideas—common ascertained truths—are good
things enough to live by, but are very rare, and soon sufficiently
discussed. Something else—true or false, rational or nonsensical
—is quite essential; and, therefore, in the old literary world
men gathered round the travelling sophist, to learn from him
some thought, crotchet, or speculation. And what the vagabond
speculators were once, that, pretty exactly, is the newspaper
now. To it the people of this intellectual capital look for that
daily mental bread, which is as essential to them as the less
ethereal sustenance of ordinary mortals. With the spread of
education this habit travels downward. Not the literary man
only, but the *ouvrier* and the *bourgeois,* live and did live on
the same food. This day's *Siècle* is discussed not only in gorgeous drawing-rooms, but in humble reading-rooms, and still
humbler workshops. According to the printed notions of us
journalists, this is a matter of pure rejoicing. The influence of
the Press, if you believe writers and printers, is the one sufficient
condition of social well-being. Yet there are many considerations
which make very much against this idea: I can't go into several
of them now, but those that I shall mention are suggested at
once by matters before me. First, newspaper people are the
only traders that thrive upon convulsion. In quiet times, who

cares for the paper? In times of tumult, who does not? Commonly, the *Patrie* (the *Globe* of this country), sells, I think, for three sous: the evening of the *coup d'état*, itinerant ladies were crying under my window, "Demandez la *Patrie*—Journal du soir—trente sous—Journal du soir"; and I remember witnessing, even in our sober London, in February, '48, how bald fathers of families paid large sums, and encountered bareheaded the unknown inclemencies of the night air, that they might learn the last news of Louis Philippe, and, if possible, be in at the death of the revolutionary Parisians. "Happy," says the sage, "for the people whose annals are vacant"; but "woe! woe! woe!" he might add, "to the wretched journalists that have to compose and sell leading articles therein."

I am constrained to say, that even in England this is not without its unfavourable influence on literary morals. Take in *The Times*, and you will see it assumed that every year ought to be an era. "The Government does nothing," is the indignant cry, and simple people in the country don't know that this is merely a civilized *façon de parler* for "I have nothing to say." Lord John[11] must alter the suffrage, that we may have something pleasant in our columns.

I am afraid matters are worse here. The leading French journalist is, as you know, the celebrated Émile de Girardin, and, so far as I can learn anything about him, he is one of the most unprincipled politicians in existence. Since I have read the *Presse* regularly, it has veered from every point of the compass, well-nigh to every other—now for, now against, the revision of the constitution—now lauding Louis Napoleon to the skies—now calling him plain M. Bonaparte, and insinuating that he had not two ideas, and was incapable of moral self-government—now connected with the red party, now praising the majority; but all and each of these veerings and shiftings

11 Lord John Russell, 1st Earl Russell, (1792–1878) English Liberal statesman, Prime Minister 1846–52, 1865–66, forced Palmerston's resignation from the Cabinet in 1851 for his recognizing the coup d'état without approval.

determined by one most simple and certain principle—to keep up the popular excitement, to maintain the gifted M. de Girardin at the head of it.

Now a man who spends his life in stimulating excitement and convulsion is really an incendiary; and however innocent and laudable his brother exiles may be, the old editor and founder of the *Presse* is, as I believe, now only paying the legitimate penalty of systematic *arson*.

When a foreigner—at least an Englishman—begins to read the French papers, his first idea is "How well these fellows write? Why, every one of them has a style, and a good style too. Really, how clear, how acute, how clever, how perspicuous; I wish our journalists would learn to write like this"; but a little experience will modify this idea, at least I have found it so. I read for a considerable time in these witty periodicals with pleasure and admiration; after a little while I felt somehow that I took them up with an effort, but I fancied, knowing my disposition, that this was laziness; when on a sudden, in the waste of *Galignani*, I came across an article of the *Morning Herald*. Now you'll laugh at me, if I tell you that it was a real enjoyment. There was no toil, no sharp theory, no pointed expression, no fatiguing brilliancy, in fact, what the man in Lord Byron desired, "no nothing," but a dull creeping satisfactory sensation that now, at least, there was nothing to admire. As long walking in picture galleries makes you appreciate a mere wall, so I felt that I understood for the first time that really dulness had its interest. I found a pure refreshment in coming across what possibly might be latent sense, but was certainly superficial stupidity.

I think there is nothing we English hate like a clever but prolonged controversy. Now this is the life and soul of the Parisian press. Everybody writes against everybody. It is not mere sly hate or solemn invective, nothing like what we occasionally indulge in, about the misdemeanours of a morning contemporary. But they take the other side's article piece by piece, and comment on him, and, as they say in libel cases, *innuendo* him, and satisfactorily show that, according to his arithmetic, two and two make five—useful knowledge that. It is really good for us to know that some fellow (you never heard of him) it rather seems can't add up. But it interests people here—*c'est logique* they tell you, and if you are trustful enough to answer, "*Mon Dieu, c'est ennuyeux, je n'en sais rien,*" they look as if you sneered at the Parthenon.

It is out of these controversies that M. de Girardin has attained his power and his fame. His articles (according to me at least) have no facts and no sense. He gives one all pure reasoning—little scrappy syllogisms; as some one said most unjustly of old Hazlitt, he "writes pimples." But let an unfortunate writer in the *Assemblée Nationale,* or anywhere else, make a little refreshing blunder in his logic, and next morning small punning sentences (one to each paragraph like an equation) come rattling down on him: it is clear as noonday that somebody said "something followed," and it does *not* follow, and it is so agreed in all the million *Cabinets de Lecture* after due gesticulation; and, moreover, that M. de Girardin is the man to expose it, and what clever fellows they are to appreciate him, but what the truth is who cares? The subject is forgotten.

Now all this, in my notion, does great harm. Nothing destroys common-place like the habit of arguing for arguing's sake; nothing is so bad for public matters as that they should be treated, not as the data for the careful formation of a sound judgment, but as a topic or background for displaying the shining qualities of public writers. It is no light thing that. M. de Girardin for many years has gained more power, more reputation, more money, than any of his rivals; not because he shows more knowledge—he shows much less; not because he has a wiser judgment—he has no fixed judgment at all; but because he has a more pointed sharp way of exposing blunders, intrinsically paltry, obvious to all educated men; and does not care enough for any subject to be diverted from this logical trifling by a serious desire to convince anybody of anything.

Don't think I wish to be hard on this accomplished gentleman. I am not going to require of hack-writers to write only on what they understand—if that were the law, what a life for the sub-editor; I should not be writing these letters, and how seldom and how timidly would the morning journals creep into the world. Nor do I expect, though I may still, in sentimental moods, desire—middle-aged journals often buoyed up by chimerical visions of improving mankind.

. . . I am not going to require supernatural excellence from writers. Yet there are limits. If I were a chemist, I should not mind, I suppose, selling, now and then, a deleterious drug on a due affidavit of rats, then and there filed before me; yet I don't feel as if I could live comfortably on the sale of mere arsenic. I fancy I should like to sell something wholesome occasionally. So, though one might, upon occasion, edge on a riot, or excite to a breach of the peace, I should not like to be every day feeding on revolutionary excitement. Nor should I like to be exclusively selling diminutive acute quibbling leaders (what they call in the Temple special demurrers), certain to occupy people with small fallacies, and lead away their minds from the great questions actually at issue.

Sometimes I might like to feel as if I understood what I wrote on, but of course with me this indulgence must be very rare. You know in France journalism is not only an occupation, it is a career. As in far off Newcastle a coalfitter's son looks wistfully to the bar, in the notion that he too may emulate the fame and fortune of Lord Eldon or Lord Stowell,[12] so in fair Provence, a pale young aspirant packs up his little bundle in the hope of rivalling the luck and fame of M. Thiers; he comes to Paris—he begins, like the great historian, by dining for thirty sous in the Palais Royal, in the hope that after long years of labour and jealousy he, too, may end by sleeping amid curtains of white muslin, lined with pink damask. Just consider for a moment what a difference this one fact shows between France

[12] John Scott, Lord Eldon (1751–1838), became Lord High Chancellor of England after 1801; Lord Stowell (1745–1836) was a famous judge.

and England. Here a man who begins life by writing in the newspapers, has an appreciable chance of arriving to be Minister of Foreign Affairs. The class of public writers is the class from which the representative of Lord Aberdeen, Lord Palmerston, or Lord Granville will most likely be chosen. Well, well, under that *régime* you and I might have been important people; we might have handled a red box, we might have known what it was to have a reception, to dine with the Queen, to be respectfully mystified by the *corps diplomatique*. But angry Jove forbade—of course we can hardly deny that he was wrong—and yet if the revolutions of '48 have clearly brought out any fact, it is the utter failure of newspaper statesmen. Everywhere they have been tried: everywhere they have shown great talents for intrigue, eloquence, and agitation—how rarely have they shown even fair aptitude for ordinary administration; how frequently have they gained a disreputable renown by a laxity of principle, surpassing the laxity of their aristocratic and courtly adversaries. Such being my imperfect account of my imperfect notions of the French press, I can't altogether sympathise in the extreme despondency of many excellent persons at its temporary silence since the *coup d'état*. I might even rejoice at it, if I thought that the Parisian public could in any manner be broken of their dependence on the morning's article. But I have no such hope; the taste has got down too deep into the habits of the people: some new thing will still be necessary; and every government will find some of its most formidable difficulties in their taste for political disputation and controversial excitement. The ban must sooner or later be taken off; the President sooner or later must submit to censure and ridicule, and whatever laws he may propose about the press, there is none which scores of ingenious men—now animated by the keenest hatred, will not try every hazard to evade. What he may do to avoid this is as yet unknown. One thing, however, I suppose is pretty sure, and I fancy quite wise. The press will be restrained from discussing the principles of the government. Socialists will not be allowed to advocate a democratic republic. Legitimists will not be allowed to advocate the cause of Henri Cinq: nor Orleanists the cause of the Comte de Paris. Such indulgence might be tolerable in more temperate countries, but experience shows that it is not safe now and here.

A really sensible press, arguing temperately after a clear and satisfactory exposition of the facts, is a great blessing in any country. It would be still more a blessing in a country where, as I tried to explain formerly, the representative element must play (if the public security is to be maintained), a rather secondary part. It would then be a real stimulus to deliberate inquiry and rational judgment upon public affairs; to the formation of common-sense views upon the great outlines of public business; to the cultivation of sound moral opinions and convictions on the internal and international duties of the state. Even the actual press, which we may expect to see here may not be pernicious. It will doubtless stimulate to many factious proceedings, and many interruptions of the public prosperity; it may very likely conduce to drive the President (contrary, if not to his inclination, at least to his personal interest) into foreign hostilities and international aggression; but it may be, notwithstanding, useful in preventing private tyranny, in exposing wanton oppression, in checking long-suffering revenge; it may prevent acts of spoliation like what they call here *le premier vol de l'aigle*—the seizure of the Orleans property;— in a word, being certain to oppose the executive, where the latter is unjust its enemy will be just.

I had hopes that this letter would be the last with which I should tease you; but I find I must ask you to be so kind as to find room for one, and only for one, more.

I am, yours, &c.,

AMICUS.

LETTER VII—CONCLUDING LETTER

Paris, February 19, 1852.

MY DEAR SIR—There is a story of some Swedish Abbé, in the last century, who wrote an elaborate work to prove the then constitution of his country to be immortal and indestructible. While he was correcting the proof sheets, a friend brought him word that—behold! the King had already destroyed the said polity. "Sir," replied the gratified author, "our sovereign, the illustrious Gustavus, may certainly overthrow the constitution, but never *my book.*" I beg to parody this sensible remark; for I wish to observe to you, that even though Louis Napoleon turn out a bad and mischievous ruler, he won't in the least refute these letters.

What I mean is as follows. Above all things, I have designed to prove to you that the French are by character unfit for a solely and predominantly parliamentary government; that so many and so great elements of convulsion here exist, that it will be clearly necessary that a strong, vigorous, anti-barricade executive should, at whatever risk and cost, be established and maintained; that such an Assembly as the last is irreconcilable with this; in a word, that riots and revolutions must, if possible, come to an end, and only such a degree of liberty and democracy be granted to the French nation, as is consistent with the consolidated existence of the order and tranquillity which are equally essential to rational freedom and civilised society.

In order to combine the maintenance of order and tranquillity with the maximum of possible liberty, I hope that it may in the end be found possible to admit into a political system a representative and sufficiently democratic Assembly, without that Assembly assuming and arrogating to itself those nearly omnipotent powers, which in our country it properly and rightfully possesses, but which in the history of the last sixty years, we have, as it seems to me, so many and so cogent illustrations that a French chamber is, by genius and constitution, radically incapable to hold and exercise. I hope that some checking, consultative, petitioning Assembly—some βουλή, in the real sense of the term—some *Council,* some provision by which all grave and deliberate public opinion (I do not speak more definitely, for an elaborate constitution, from a foreigner, must be an absurdity) may organise and express itself—yet at the same time, without utterly hampering and directing—and directing amiss—those more simple elements of national polity, on which we must, after all, rely for the prompt and steady repression of barricade-making and bloodshed.

I earnestly desire to believe that some such system as this may be found in practice possible; for otherwise, unless I quite misread history, and altogether mistake what is under my eyes, after many more calamities, many more changes, many more great Assemblies abounding in Vergniauds and Berryers, the essential deficiencies of debating Girondin statesmen will become manifest, the uncompact, unpractical, over-volatile, over-logical indecisive, ineffectual rule of Gallican parliaments will be unequivocally manifest (it is *now* plain, I imagine, but a truth so humiliating must be written large in letters of blood before those that run will read it), and no medium being held or conceived to be possible, the nation will sink back, not contented but discontented, not trustfully but distrustfully, under the rule of a military despot; and if they yield to this, it will be from no faith, no loyalty, no credulity; it will be from a sense—a hated sense—of unqualified failure, a miserable scepticism in the probable success and the possible advantages of long-tried and ill-tried rebellion.

Now whether the constitution of Louis Napoleon is calculated to realise this ideal and intermediate system is, till we see it at work, doubtful and disputable. It is not the question so much of what it may be at this moment, as of what it may become in a brief period, when things have begun to assume a more normal state, and the public mind be relaxed from its present and painful tension. However, I should be deceiving you, if I did not inform you that the state of men's minds towards the Prince-President is not, so far as I can make it out, what it was the day after the *coup d'état*. The measures taken against the socialists are felt to have been several degrees too severe, the list of exiles too numerous; the confiscation of the Orleans' property could not but be attended with the worst effect; the law announced by the government organs respecting or rather against the Press, is justly (though you know from my last letter I have no partiality for French newspapers) considered to be absurdly severe, and likely to countenance much tyranny and gross injustice; above all, instead of maintaining mere calm and order, the excessive rigour, and sometimes the injustice, of the President's measures, have produced a breathless pause (if I may so speak) in public opinion;—political conversation is a whispered question, what will he do next? Firstly, the government is dull, and the French want to be amused; secondly, it is going to spoil the journals (depreciate newspapers to a Frenchman, disparage nuts to a monkey); thirdly, it is producing (I do not say it has yet produced, but it has made a beginning in producing), a habit of apprehension. . . . Yet it is, I imagine, a great mistake to suppose that the present constitution, if it work at all, will permanently work as a despotism, or that the *Corps Législatif* will be without a measure of popular influence; the much more helpless *Tribunal* was not so in the much more troublesome times of the Consulate. And the source of such influence, and the manner of its operation may be, I imagine, well enough traced in the nature of the forces whereby Louis Napoleon holds his power.

A truly estimable writer says, I know "that the legislative body cannot have, by possibility, any analogy with the consultative and petitioning senate of the Plantagenets," nor can any one deny that the likeness is extremely faint (no illustration ever yet ran on all fours), the practical differences clear and convincing. But yet, according to the light which is given me now,

I affirm that for one vital purpose—the resisting and criticising
any highly unpopular acts of a highly unpopular government
—the *corps législatif* of Louis Napoleon must, and will, inevitably possess a power compared with which the forty-day followers of the feudal *noblesse* seem as impotent as a congregation
of Quakers; a force the peculiarity of which is that you can't
imprison, can't dissolve, can't annihilate it—I mean, of course,
the moral power of civilised opinion. You may put down newspapers, dissolve parliaments, imprison agitators, almost stop conversation, but you can't stop thought. You can't prevent the
silent, slow, creeping, stealthy progress of hatred, and scorn,
and shame. You can't attenuate easily the stern justice of a re-
tarded retaliation. These influences affect the great reservoir
of physical force—they act on the army. A body of men enlisted
daily from the people, take to the barracks the notions of the
people; in spite of new associations, the first impressions are
apt to be retained; you overlay them but they remain. What is
believed elsewhere and out of doors gives them weight. Each
soldier has relations, friends, a family—he knows what they
think. Much more with the officers. These are men moving in
Parisian society, accessible to its influences, responsible to its
opinion, apt to imbibe its sentiments. Certainly *esprit de corps*
—the habit of obedience, the instinct of discipline, are strong,
and will carry men far; but certainly, also, they have natural
limits. Men won't stand being cut, being ridiculed, being detested, being despised, daily and for ever, and that for measures
which their own understandings disapprove of. Remember there
is not here any question of barbarous bands overawing a civilised
and imperial city; no question of ugly Croats keeping down
cultivated Italians; it is but a question of French gentlemen
and French peasantry in uniform acting in opposition to other
French gentlemen and other French peasants without uniform.
Already there has been talk, (I do not say well-founded, but
still the matter was named) of breaking a couple or three hundred officers, for speaking against the Orleans decrees. Do you
fancy that can be done every day? Do you imagine that a parlia-

ment, whatever its nominal functions may be (remember those of the old *régime*), speaking the sense of the people about the question of the day, in a time of convulsion, and in a critical hour, would not be attended to, or at any rate thought of and considered, by an army taken from the people, in a few years to return to the people—commanded by men selected from and every day mixing with common society and very ordinary mankind. The 2nd of December showed how readily such troops will support a decided and popular President, against an intriguing, divided, impotent chamber. But such hard blows won't bear repetition. Soldiers—French soldiers, I take it especially from their quickness and intelligence, are neither deaf nor blind. If there be truth in history or speculation, national forces can't long be used against the nation; they are unmerciful, and often cruel to feeble minorities; they are ready now for a terrible onslaught on mere socialists, just as of old they turned out cheerfully for awful dragonnades on the ill-starred Protestants; but once let them know and feel that everybody is against them— that they are alone, that their acts are contemned and their persons despised—and gradually, or all at once, discipline and habit surely fail, men murmur or desert, officers hesitate or disobey, one regiment is dismissed to the Cabyles, another relegated to rural solitudes; at last, most likely in the decisive moment of the whole history, the rulers, who relied only on their troops, are afraid to call them out; they hesitate, send spies and commissioners to inquire, *"Vive le Gouvernement Provisoire!"* —the black and roaring multitude rises and comes on; but two seconds, and the obnoxious institutions are lost in the flood; nothing is heard but the cry of the hour, sounding shrill and angry over the waste of Revolution—*"Vive le Diable!"* With such a force behind them, a French parliament, of whatever nature, with whatever written duties, is, if at the head of the movement, in the critical hour, apt to be stronger than the strongest of the barons. . . .

I therefore fall back on what I told you before—my essential view or crotchet about the mental aptitudes and deficiencies of the French people. The French, said Napoleon, are *des machines nerveuses.*

The point is, can their excitable, volatile, superficial, overlogical, uncompromising character be managed and manipulated as to fit them for entering on a practically uncontrolled system of parliamentary government? Will not any large and omnipotent Assembly resemble the stormy constituent and the late chamber, rather than the business-like formal ennui-diffusing parliament to which in our free and dull country we are felicitously accustomed? Can one be so improved as to keep down a riot? I foresee a single and but a single objection. I fancy, indeed I know, that there is a school of political thinkers not yet in possession of any great influence, but, perhaps, a little on the way thereto, which has improved or invented a capital panacea, whereby all nations are, within very moderate limits of time, to be surely and certainly fitted for political freedom; and that no matter how formed—how seemingly stable—how long ago cast and constructed be the type of popular character to which the said remedy is sought to be applied. This panacea is the foundation or restoration of provincial municipalities. Now, I am myself prepared to go a considerable length with the school in question. I do myself think, that a due and regular consideration of the knotty points of paving and lighting, and the deciding in the last resort upon them is a valuable discipline of national character. It exercises people's minds on points they know, in things of which there is a test. Very few people are good judges of a good constitution; but everybody's eyes are excellent judges of good light; every man's feet are profound in the theory of agreeable stones. Yet I can't altogether admit, nevertheless, that municipalities are the sufficient and sole, though they may be very likely an essential prerequisite of political freedom. There is the great instance of Hindostan to the contrary. . . . The business of life through that whole vast territory, has always been practically determined by potails[13] and parish-vestries, and yet

[13] Mayors of villages.

nevertheless and in spite of this capital and immemorial municipal system, our subjects, the Hindoos, are still slaves and still likely to be slaves; still essentially slavish, and likely, I much fear, very long indeed to remain so. It is therefore quite certain that rural and provincial institutions won't so alter and adapt all national characters, as to fit all nations for a parliamentary constitution; consequently the *onus probandi* is on those who assert that it will so alter and mould the French. Again, I assure you the French do think of paving and lighting; not enough, perhaps, but still they have begun. The country is, as you know, divided into departments, arrondissements, and communes; in each of these there is a council, variously elected, but, in all cases, popularly and from the district, which has the sole control over the expenditure of the particular locality for every special and local purpose, and which, if I am rightly informed, have, in theory at least, the sole initiative in every local improvement. The defect, I fancy, is that in the exercise of these, considerable bodies are hampered and controlled by the veto and supervision of the central authority. The rural councils discuss and decide what in their judgment should be then done and what money shall be so spent; the better sort of the agricultural population have much more voice in the latter, than have the corresponding class in England, in the determination and imposition of our own country rate;—but it is the central authority which decides whether such proposals and recommendations shall in fact be carried out. In a word, the provinces have to *ask leave* of the Parisian Ministry of the Interior. Now I admit this is an abuse. I should maintain that elderly gentlemen with bald heads and local influence, ought to feel that they in the final resort, settle and determine all truly local matters. Human nature likes its own road, its own bridge, its own lapidary obstacles, its own deceptive luminosity. But I ask again, can you fancy that these little luxuries, to whatever degree indulged in, alter and modify in any essential particular, the levity and volatility of the French character. How much light to how much logic? How many paving stones, to how much mobility? I can't foresee any such change. And even if so, what in the meantime?

We are left then, I think, to deal with the French character pretty much as we find it. What stealthy, secret, unknown, excellent, forces may, in the wisdom of Providence, be even now modifying this most curious intellectual fabric, neither you nor I can know or tell. Let us hope they may be many. But if we indulge, and from the immense records of revolutionary history, I think, if with due distrust, we may legitimately and even beneficially in system-building and speculation, we must take the *data* which we have, and not those which we desire or imagine. Louis Napoleon has proposed a system: English writers by the thousand (if I was in harness instead of holiday-making I should be most likely among them) proclaim his system an evil one. What then? Do you know what Father Newman says to the religious reformers, rather sharply, but still well, "make out first of all where you stand—draw up your creed—write down your catechism." So I answer to the English eloquence, "State first of all what you would have—draw up your novel system for the French government—write down your political constitution." Don't criticise but produce—do not find fault but propose—and when you have proposed upon theory and have created upon paper, let us see whether the system be such an one as will work, in fact, and be accepted by a wilful nation in reality —otherwise your work is nought.

And mind, too, that the system to be sketched out must be fit to protect the hearths and homes of men. It is easy to compose policies if you do but neglect this one essential condition. Four years ago, Europe was in a ferment with the newest ideas, the best theories, the most elaborate, the most artistic constitutions. There was the labour, and toil, and trouble, of a million intellects, as good, taken on the whole, perhaps, as the world is likely to see—of old statesmen, and literary gentlemen, and youthful enthusiasts, all over Europe, from the Baltic Sea to the Mediterranean, from the frontiers of Russia to the Atlantic Ocean. Well, what have we gained? A parliament in Sardinia!

Surely this is a lesson against proposing polities which won't work, convening assemblies that can't legislate, constructing executives that aren't able to keep the peace, founding constitutions inaugurated with tears and eloquence, soon abandoned with tears and shame; beginning a course of fair auguries and liberal hopes, but from whose real dangers and actual sufferings a frightened and terrified people, in the end, flee for a temporary, or may be a permanent, refuge under a military and absolute ruler.

Mazzini sneers at the selfishness of shopkeepers—I am for the shopkeepers against him. There are people who think because they are republican there shall be no more "cakes and ale." Aye, verily, but there will though; or else stiffish ginger will be hot in the mouth. Legislative assemblies, leading articles, essay eloquence—such are good—very good—useful—very useful. Yet they can be done without. We can want them. Not so with all things. The selling of figs, the cobbling of shoes, the manufacturing of nails—these are the essence of life. And let whoso frameth a constitution for his country think on these things.

I conclude, as I ought, with my best thanks for the insertion of these letters; otherwise I were so full of the subject that I might have committed what Disraeli calls "the extreme act of human fatuity," I might have published a pamphlet: from this your kindness has preserved me, and I am proportionably grateful.

I am, yours,

AMICUS.

KARL MARX'S ANALYSIS
OF THE COUP D'ÉTAT IN TERMS
OF CLASS STRUGGLE

KARL MARX (1818–83) had already worked out the main lines of his philosophy of history before he wrote *The Eighteenth Brumaire of Louis Bonaparte* in the winter of 1852. In the chief statement of his theoretical position, *The Communist Manifesto*, written at end of 1847, he had revealed his basic techniques of social analysis, as well as his theories of social classes, class struggle, and the state. The full economic underpinnings of the theory, the analysis of capitalist society, still had to wait until he wrote *Das Kapital*, of which he completed only the first volume, published in 1867. Friedrich Engels, in his preface to the third German edition of *The Eighteenth Brumaire* (1885), corroborates the conclusion that the book put a fully formulated historical analytical system to the test, though his praise is rather fulsome.

> It was precisely Marx who had first discovered the great law of motion of history, the law according to which all historical struggles, whether they proceed in the political, religious, philosophical or some other ideological domain, are in fact only the more or less clear expression of struggles of social classes, and

that the existence and thereby the collisions, too, between these classes are in turn conditioned by the degree of development of their economic position, by the mode of their production and of their exchange determined by it. This law, which has the same significance for history as the law of the transformation of energy has for natural science—this law gave him here, too, the key to an understanding of the history of the Second French Republic. He put his law to the test on these historical events, and even after thirty-three years we must still say that it has stood the test brilliantly.[1]

We will have occasion to note that the book is far more than a test of an already formulated theory—it also introduced major refinements into that theory, and perhaps also contradictions or deviations, which were not accommodated in later Marxian writings. Specifically, we find material of special pertinence to his theories of ideology and social classes and of the state and revolution.

Marx had already written an immense amount prior to the publication of *The Eighteenth Brumaire*. A large part of his writing had been in formal philosophy, such as his doctoral thesis on Democritus and Epicurus (1841), or in philosophical polemics such as *The Holy Family* (1844) and the *German Ideology* (1845–46), books written in collaboration with Engels. The latter book went unpublished in Marx's lifetime. Another philosophical work, later titled *Economic and Philosophic Manuscripts of 1844* (published in 1927 in an incomplete Russian translation, then in German in 1932), has since led scholars to major reinterpretations of the youthful Marx, to a new stress upon his humanism and to re-evaluation of his ties to the philosophy of Georg W. F. Hegel. Marx's other major work of this period was *The Poverty of Philosophy* (1847), his destructive treatment of Proudhon's *The System of Economic Contradictions, or the Philosophy of Poverty*. Much of this early work was heavily academic, devoted to intellectual

[1] Karl Marx and Friedrich Engels, *Selected Works*, Foreign Language Publishing House (Moscow, 1951), vol. 1, pp. 223–24.

battles against his former allies or mentors, particularly those in the Young Hegelian philosophic school, as Marx worked out his own independent position through the process of assimilation and rejection. Marx's major essays on "The Jewish Question" and on Hegel's *Philosophy of Law*, written in Paris in 1844, were also part of the same process.

Marx gave some lectures to working men while he was in Brussels in 1847; *Wage Labor and Capital*, published in 1849 was based on these. His chief pursuit, however, after his early academic ventures, was journalism, wherein he became increasingly adept and where he could put to good use his skill at polemic—as he reveals in *The Eighteenth Brumaire*. By 1842 he was a contributor to the *Rheinische Zeitung*, and soon became an editor. For much of the remainder of his career he continued to rely on journalism as a means of support.

Marx first tried combining reportage with sustained historical analysis in his *Class Struggles in France* (1850), which treated the early life of the Second Republic. *The Eighteenth Brumaire* is the successor to this work; it uses less narrative and more theoretical structure to bring intelligibility to the muddled course of contemporary history. It is presented in prose of striking force and clarity which carries a heavy load of impressive imagery without much strain.[2] It is one of Marx's most attractive

[2] See, for example, Stanley Edgar Hyman, *The Tangled Bank: Darwin, Marx, Frazer and Freud as Imaginative Writers* (New York, 1966), pp. 106 ff.; and here are the comments of Marx's friend and colleague Wilhelm Liebknecht on *The Eighteenth Brumaire*:

Is the *Eighteenth Brumaire* unintelligible? Is the dart incomprehensible that flies straight at his target and pierces the flesh? Is the spear unintelligible that, hurled by a steady hand, penetrates the heart of the enemy? The words of the *Brumaire* are darts, are spears—they are a style that stigmatizes, kills. If hate, if scorn, if burning love of freedom ever found expression in flaming, annihilating, elevating words, then it is surely in the *Eighteenth Brumaire*, in which the aroused seriousness of Tacitus is united to the deadly satire of Juvenal and the holy wrath of Dante. The style is here what it—the stylus—originally was in the hands of the Ro-

and accessible writings, avoiding most of the heavy antithesis and wordplay of the early philosophic works and among his works probably ranks stylistically second only to his propaganda masterpiece, *The Communist Manifesto.*

Edmund Wilson, not a friendly critic, wrote of *The Class Struggles in France* and *The Eighteenth Brumaire:*

> These writings of Marx are electrical. Nowhere perhaps in the history of thought is the reader so made to feel the excitement of a new intellectual discovery. Marx is here at his most vivid and his most vigorous—in the closeness and the exactitude of political observation; in the energy of the faculty that combines, articulating at the same time that it compresses; in the wit and the metaphorical phantasmagoria that transfigures the prosaic phenomena of politics, and in the pulse of the tragic invective—we have heard its echo in Bernard Shaw—which can turn the collapse of an incompetent parliament, divided between contradictory tendencies, into the downfall of a damned soul of Shakespeare.[3]

Marx wrote *The Eighteenth Brumaire* in German between December and March of 1852 and sent the essays to his friend Joseph Weydemeyer in the United States. Marx described the preparation of the book in the Preface to the first German reprint in 1869:

> My friend *Joseph Weydemeyer,* whose death was so untimely, intended to publish a political weekly in New York starting from January 1, 1852. He invited me to provide this weekly with a history of the *coup d'état.* Down to the middle of February, I accordingly wrote him weekly articles under the title: *The Eighteenth Brumaire of Louis Bonaparte.* Meanwhile Weydemeyer's original plan had fallen through. Instead,

---

mans—a sharp-pointed steel pencil for writing and for stabbing. The style is the dagger used for a well-aimed thrust at the heart. . . . *Biographical Memoirs,* trans. by Ernest Unterman (Chicago, 1908), p. 76.

[3] Edmund Wilson, *To the Finland Station* (Garden City, N.Y., 1953), p. 201.

in the spring of 1852 he published a monthly, *Die Revolution*, the first number of which consists of my *Eighteenth Brumaire*. A few hundred copies of this found their way into Germany at that time, without, however, getting into the actual book trade. A German publisher of extremely radical pretensions to whom I offered the sale of my book was most virtuously horrified at a "presumption" so "contrary to the times."[4]

From the above facts it will be seen that the present work took shape under the immediate pressure of events and its historical material does not extend beyond the month of February (1852).[5]

The work was published in April, as the whole of *Die Revolution*'s first number (it had only two). Marx was at that time one of many revolutionary exiles living in London,[6] the chief place of refuge for continental radicals after the defeat of the 1848 revolutions.

Marx's early training had been far from revolutionary. His upbringing was in the bourgeois milieu wherein his father moved as a lawyer in the Rhineland town of Trier, which after the Napoleonic wars became part of Prussian territory. The Marx family had converted from Judaism to Christianity in 1816—at a time when the new liberties which had been granted to Jews during the French Revolutionary era were being withdrawn. The young Marx, born two years thereafter, never seems to have held deep religious beliefs. His father was a Voltairian, an Enlightenment skeptic; Karl Marx grew up to become a bitter opponent of all religion, of churches as supports of the exist-

---

[4] Paul LaFargue, in "Personal Recollections of Karl Marx," notes that there was virtually no mention of the book in the bourgeois press; see R. Ryazanov, ed., *Karl Marx: Man, Thinker and Revolutionist, a Symposium* (New York, 1927), p. 203.

[5] Marx and Engels, *Selected Works*, Foreign Language Publishing House, (Moscow, 1951), vol. 1, p. 221.

[6] Marx's daughter Eleanor recalled that in the flat in Camberwell, where *The Eighteenth Brumaire* was composed, Marx, a dedicated family man, worked surrounded by his children, even writing while playing "horsie" with them. Hyman, p. 83.

ing power arrangements and of faith as the opium of the masses.

After his early education in Trier, in 1835 Marx was sent to the University of Bonn where he was expected to study law, probably heading for an official career; but he does not seem to have studied very seriously. In 1836 he went on to the University of Berlin, then dominated by the heritage of the philosopher, G. W. F. Hegel, who had died five years before. There Marx turned his attention to philosophy and history, mixing with the group which came to be called the "Young Hegelians," immersing himself in Hegelian thought, and making a reputation for himself in academic circles as a radical philosopher.

The Young Hegelians were for the most part a full decade older than Marx. Marx came to know well Bruno Bauer, Moses Hess, and Arnold Ruge. Others of note were Max Stirner, the philosophical anarchist, and Ludwig Feuerbach, whose anthropological interpretation of religion was immensely influential in the forties (*The Essence of Christianity*, 1841).[7] All found it necessary to wrestle with the massive and impressive system of the master, which conservative circles—like Hegel himself—tended to view as a support for the social and political status quo in Prussia. They adopted Hegel's idea of the central importance of philosophy—Hegel had contended that the meaning of history is the realization of reason in human affairs—and hence of the importance of criticism—Hegel had argued that progress occurs dialectically through the negation of dominant ideas and their supercession; but the Young Hegelians differed from the conservatives and from their master in contending that the role of philosophy had not ended with the demonstration of its past accomplishments and argued that more remained to be done. They did not share Hegel's view that existing institutional and social arrangements constituted a satisfactory realization of Uni-

---

[7] Feuerbach's contention was that the whole religious realm constituted a projection of essential human qualities which man had alienated from himself and then set up to worship. His anthropological view of religion and his version of alienation seem both to have influenced Marx significantly.

versal Reason. The prevailing censorship, and their own idealist bias, served to inhibit them from broaching political issues. Instead, they first made their attack upon contemporary religion, in the belief that all else was implicated therein. Marx shared in their general atheism. He became closely associated with Bruno Bauer, one of the most vehement of these critics, and when Bauer lost his teaching post in consequence of his writings, the possibility of an academic career for Marx virtually ended.

Marx began to break with the Young Hegelians after he took his next step toward an independent career, working with the *Rheinische Zeitung* in Cologne in 1842. In the course of the succeeding year he concluded that his former fellow disciples were excessively conservative, for they tended, he believed, to remain in the realm of philosophy when increasingly the problems that needed to be dealt with were in the area of German reality and material conditions.

Conversely, however, some of Marx's old colleagues tended to think that by this time Marx himself had become too conservative. He rejected some of their sweeping proposals of a socialist nature, following an essentially liberal line that would not accept for publication articles likely to upset middle-class subscribers or the watchful censors, or to differ from Marx's own preference at this time for bit-by-bit reform. The change, by means of which Marx ceased to be a democratic reformer and became first a philosophical, then a revolutionary communist, occurred after the *Rheinische Zeitung* was closed down for criticism of the Prussian government in 1843.[8]

[8] It is most difficult to reach conclusions in regard to Marx's motivations as he became increasingly an active revolutionary. Much of the recent writing on Marx since the publication of the 1844 manuscripts has been so adulatory that it is nearly impossible to imagine a real man as the creator of works portrayed as the product sheer philosophic genius—and one so young. All the adulation is likely to create the impression that any individual of some intelligence and sensitivity would, in that time and place, necessarily abhor his society along with the bourgeois class and its philistinism. Clearly many artists did, and it is little noted that Marx's conception of an atomized

The papers published as *The Economic and Philosophic Manuscripts of 1844* mark a major step in the formulation of his new theory, as do the essays for the *Deutsch-Französische Jahrbücher's* only edition, i.e., "The Jewish Question" and "Introduction to the Criticism of the Hegelian Philosophy of Right."[9] The *German Ideology* contains the elements of a materialist interpretation of history, which is even more fully formulated again in 1847 in *The Poverty of Philosophy*, a book written specifically about economic affairs. Then, finally, in 1848, *The Communist Manifesto* applied the theory to the full sweep of history.

---

society, needing to be reordered so that men might establish true human relationships, asks only for what Romantic political theory—which he also abhorred—had been urging for thirty years. But few Romantic artists or political theorists linked their cause to the proletariat (in the forties in Germany more nearly a concept than a social and political reality), nor did many pursue violent revolution.

Marx's personality is a most puzzling problem. The implication of philosophic studies such as those of Avineri, Fromm, Lichtheim, and Tucker (see suggested readings) that he became a revolutionary out of humanitarianism on the one hand and sheer cerebration on the other simply does not suffice. It is a relief, in contrast, to read Marx's critics, who seek to explain his anxiety, ambition, and anger. A bitter book like Leopold Schwarzschild's *Red Prussian: The Life and Legend of Karl Marx*, trans. by Margaret Wing (New York, 1947), for all its faults, has the advantage of locating frustrations—of his poetic, academic, and journalistic hopes—that might have led him to seek outlet for his abilities in the revolutionary world. This is not to deny that in such a man as Marx, whatever his personal emotional involvement, the change would appear as an intellectual change, as if he *decided* to become a revolutionary. Leonard Krieger's essay, "The Uses of Marx for History" (*Political Science Quarterly*, vol. 75 [Sept. 1960], 355–78) is a very able analysis of the transformation. A very welcome new history tracing the early career—again far from adulatory—is Oscar G. Hammen, *The Red 48'ers: Karl Marx and Friedrich Engels* (New York, 1969).

[9] This essay includes a considerable discussion of the problems of bureaucracy in modern society—a foretaste of the important role Marx accorded it in *The Eighteenth Brumaire*. Shlomo Avineri, *The Social and Political Thought of Karl Marx* (London, 1968), pp. 48 ff., traces changes in Marx's view of bureaucracy.

Marx formulated a new philosophic position, a realist-humanism. He saw himself as ceasing to be an idealist and becoming a materialist, so that he could deal scientifically with society and shape historical conditions. He condemned the Hegelians for abstraction and "mystification." Instead of their fantasy world of philosophic consciousness, he now demanded that philosophy be practical ("Theses on Feuerbach," 1845), insisting that the truth of philosophy was to be discovered in politics and that its role was in fact political, to change the existing social reality.

At the same time Marx moved steadily away from the Hegelian conception of the importance of the philosopher and of philosophy. History he saw no longer as the history of philosophy, with a truly central role for theorists, but as the development of man in the context of his material conditions. For some time (even in 1845), he continued to see ideas as more important in social change than material conditions, but by 1848 he had concluded that most leading ideas were the ideas of the leading social group, helping to maintain its power by justifying it in the eyes of the oppressed. He had begun to formulate his conception of ideology, which was to play so large a part in all his subsequent social analysis. The role of philosophy and theorists became one of comprehending the course of historical development and aiding the downtrodden to see it. He did not conclude that his own theories (any more than the sciences) were ideological, and by the time of the 1848 revolution he was increasingly dedicating himself to the task of imparting knowledge of their truth to the proletariat. He wrote in *The Communist Manifesto*:

> Finally, in times when the class struggle nears the decisive hour, the process of dissolution going on within the ruling class, in fact within the whole range of old society, assumes such a violent, glaring character that a small section of the ruling class cuts itself adrift and joins the revolutionary class, the class that holds the future in its hands. Just as, therefore, at an earlier period, a section of the nobility went over to the

bourgeoisie, so now a portion of the bourgeoisie goes over to the proletariat, and in particular a portion of the bourgeois ideologists, who have raised themselves to the level of comprehending theoretically the historical movement as a whole.[10]

Despite his departures from the Hegelian system, Marx retained from Hegel the belief that history is a rational and intelligible process, that there is a logic of historical development, and he further accepted the belief that change is the result of contradiction, tension, or incompatibility.

His philosophic position also resembled Feuerbach's in that it centered upon evolving human needs. Marx saw man as essentially creative and productive in fulfilling those needs—defining man as a tool-making animal who realizes himself in his work. A statement in *The Poverty of Philosophy* provides virtually a pure technological interpretation of history to fit such a definition of man. "The hand-mill gives you society with the feudal lord, the steam-mill, society with the industrial capitalist."[11]

The contradiction of modern society seemed to be that it was capable of fulfilling human needs and yet failed to do so. In modern capitalist society Marx felt man had become divorced from nature, from the product of his labor, from his true self, and from his fellows; he was trapped in an unplanned network of social activities. The group most alienated was the proletariat. It constituted the one pure class, caught against its will—other classes enjoyed being entrapped. In effect, the proletariat was the negation of all other classes, and their potential conqueror. The 1844 manuscripts identified the proletariat as the bearer

10 Karl Marx, *The Communist Manifesto*, trans. by Samuel Moore (New York, 1948), p. 19. M. M. Bober considers it inappropriate to apply this statement to Marx. See *Karl Marx's Interpretation of History* (New York, 1965), p. 337.
11 Karl Marx, *The Poverty of Philosophy* (New York, 1963), p. 109. Though Marx occasionally wrote as if he were a technological determinist, most often he used more general formulations comprehending the economic structure of society as a whole.

of the future, playing a role analogous to that of a nation in the Hegelian system. The proletariat's destiny was to attain consciousness of itself as a class, and of its mission, the abolition of private property. Once accomplished, this would produce a true revolution that would abolish the proletariat and other classes as well, and permit man to be whole once again.

The years in Paris and Brussels after Marx's experience with the *Rheinische Zeitung* were years in which he extended his acquaintance with international radical circles, becoming far more of a practicing revolutionary. Paris was then, in the forties, a center of socialist thought. He met Proudhon, and as a step toward establishing later a more formal organization he sought to engage him as a contributor in an international socialist correspondence—other French socialists were too religious for Marx —but the two differed over a colleague and parted. Then Proudhon asked Marx to review his *Economic Contradictions,* with disastrous results.[12] Marx also met and got on well with the great poet Heinrich Heine—many of Marx's personal relations were wrecked by his arrogance, rancor, or vindictiveness, but this friendship was one of the exceptions that prevents easy generalization—and he met Mikhail Bakunin with whom he was later to have such bitter conflict in the International. For the first time he became involved in working-class movements and saw some real revolutionary workers and artisans (instead of mere philosophic radicals)—experiences that must have affected his growing belief that the proletariat (especially the German proletariat) would produce the revolutionary transformation of mankind.

In this period and in his subsequent stay in Brussels he came to know Friedrich Engels, the manufacturer's son who had studied working-class conditions in England. They met in 1844 and formed the alliance that was to last the rest of Marx's life. It was Engels who helped increase Marx's knowledge of the works of the English classical economists such as David Ricardo.

[12] See below, pp. 210 ff.

Besides the turn his interests took in conjunction with Engels, Marx greatly expanded in these few years his knowledge of the works of the French socialists, especially Count Henri de Saint-Simon, Charles Fourier, and, of course, Proudhon. He also undertook extensive study of the French Revolution, and even talked of writing a book on it. He thereby became acquainted with the work of such men as François Guizot and Augustin Thierry, who saw French history as the progressive rise of the bourgeoisie in contest against the aristocracy—an interpretation of history to supplement the view of class struggle available in the theories of Saint-Simon.[13]

Marx used Proudhon's publication of *Economic Contradictions* as an occasion to give his own theory still further refinement while engaging in a bitter attack—probably an unnecessarily bitter one. Marx and Proudhon differed sharply on many specific issues, but Marx's attack centered on what he felt were Proudhon's failures as an economist, philosopher, and revolutionary. Marx still defended his criticism when he wrote an obituary letter on Proudhon in 1865.[14] He seems to have found it necessary to do to Proudhon what he did to his Young Hegelian colleagues: after having admired their thought and used it, he attacked them unmercifully and insultingly. The trait is certainly one of Marx's least attractive qualities. It is not easy to explain, though it is not totally foreign to traditional academic practice to scarify those one thinks to be in error. Since Marx also thought those he attacked were misleading mankind, the vehemence of his attacks is the more understandable. We find here another clear indication that Marx still attached immense importance to ideas, since he spent so much intense en-

[13] A version of class struggle can also be found in Ricardo's economic works, of all economic writings those which Marx seems to have respected most.

[14] See below, p. 214. Marx was to return to the attack in the section on "Conservative, or Bourgeois, Socialism" in the *Manifesto* a year later, contending that such socialists as Proudhon wish for change for the benefit of the proletariat only *within* the existing bourgeois social order, are merely reformers, not revolutionaries.

ergy correcting those of others. It is clear he believed ideas could serve to shape reality if rightly and knowingly applied, despite the limits he placed on the role of consciousness in later formulations of his theory.

In his Preface to *A Contribution to a Critique of Political Economy* (1859) Marx offered a summary description of the mental evolution he went through in these years (although he telescopes the complex mental transformation). He also gives his most famous statement, and one of his clearest, of his theory of history (although the phrasing has left many puzzles for commentators to wrestle over):

. . . Some remarks as to the course of my own politico-economic studies may be in place here.

The subject of my professional studies was jurisprudence, which I pursued, however, in connection with and as secondary to the studies of philosophy and history. In 1842–43, as editor of the *Rheinische Zeitung*, I found myself embarrassed at first when I had to take part in discussions concerning so-called material interests. The proceedings of the Rhine Diet in connection with forest thefts and the extreme subdivision of landed property; the official controversy about the condition of the Mosel peasants, into which Herr von Schaper, at the time President of the Rhine Province, entered with the *Rheinische Zeitung*; finally, the debates on free trade and protection gave me the first impulse to take up the study of economic questions. At the same time a weak, quasi-philosophic echo of French socialism and communism made itself heard in the *Rheinische Zeitung* in those days when the good intentions "to go ahead" greatly outweighed knowledge of facts. I declared myself against such botching, but had to admit at once in a controversy with the *Allgemeine Augsburger Zeitung* that my previous studies did not allow me to hazard an independent judgment as to the merits of the French schools. When, therefore, the publishers of the *Rheinische Zeitung* conceived the illusion that by a less aggressive policy the paper could be saved from the death sentence pronounced upon it, I was glad to grasp that opportunity to retire to my study room from public life.

The first work undertaken for the solution of the question that troubled me was a critical revision of Hegel's *Philosophy of Law;* the Introduction to that work appeared in the *Deutsch-Französische Jahrbücher,* published in Paris in 1844. I was led by my studies to the conclusion that legal relations as well as forms of state could be neither understood by themselves nor explained by the so-called general progress of the human mind, but that they are rooted in the material conditions of life, which are summed up by Hegel after the fashion of the English and French of the eighteenth century under the name "civil society"; the anatomy of that civil society is to be sought in political economy. The study of the latter, which I had taken up in Paris, I continued at Brussels, whither I immigrated on account of an order of expulsion issued by Mr. Guizot. The general conclusion at which I arrived and which once reached, continued to serve as the leading thread in my studies may be briefly summed up as follows: In the social production which men carry on they enter into definite relations that are indispensable and independent of their will; these relations of production correspond to a definite stage of development of their material powers of production. The sum total of these relations of production constitutes the economic structure of society—the real foundation, on which rise legal and political superstructures and to which correspond definite forms of social consciousness. The mode of production in material life determines the general character of the social, political, and spiritual processes of life. It is not the consciousness of men that determines their existence, but, on the contrary, their social existence determines their consciousness. At a certain stage of their development the material forces of production in society come into conflict with the existing relations of production, or—what is but a legal expression for the same thing—with the property relations within which they had been at work before. From forms of development of the forces of production these relations turn into their fetters. Then comes the period of social revolution. With the change of the economic foundation the entire immense superstructure is more or less rapidly transformed. In considering such transformations the distinction should always be made between the material transformation of the economic conditions of production, which can be determined with the precision of natural science, and the legal, political, religious, aesthetic, or philosophic—in short, ideological—forms in which men become conscious of this conflict and fight it out. Just as our opinion of an individual is not based on what he thinks of himself, so can we not judge such a period of transformation by its own consciousness; on the contrary, this consciousness must rather be explained from the contradictions of material life, from the existing conflict between the social forces of production and the relations of production. No social order ever disappears before all the productive forces for which there is room in it have been developed, and new, higher relations of production never appear before the material conditions of their existence have matured in the womb of the old society. Therefore mankind always takes up only such problems as it can solve, since, looking at the matter more closely, we will always find that the problem itself arises only when the material conditions necessary for its solution already exist or are at least in the process of formation. In broad outlines we can designate the Asiatic, the ancient, the feudal, and the modern bourgeois methods of production as so many epochs in the progress of the economic formation of society. The bourgeois relations of production are the last antagonistic form of the social process of production—antagonistic not in the sense of individual antagonism, but of one arising from conditions surrounding the life of individuals in society; at the same time the productive forces developing in the womb of bourgeois society create the material conditions for the solution of that antagonism. This social formation constitutes, therefore, the closing chapter of the prehistoric stage of human society.[15]

Marx had been expelled from Paris in 1845 at the request of the Prussian government. Until 1848 he lived in Brussels, where he formed the Communist Correspondence Committee and maintained many of the contacts with revolutionary and worker groups he had begun in Paris. Though he never was able to establish close personal ties with workers, he gave lectures

[15] Karl Marx, *A Contribution to the Critique of Political Economy*, trans. by N. I. Stone (New York, 1904), pp. 10–13.

to them. Most important, he became involved with the revolutionary Communist League which asked Marx and Engels to produce its platform in 1847. At this juncture, Marx and Engels were very concerned to counter first the Utopian socialists and then the insurrectionist followers of Auguste Blanqui who argued for a revolutionary take-over by a small conscious minority of the working class rather than awaiting the full preparation of the proletariat. Working on the basis of a draft prepared by Engels, Marx responded to these requirements in a document that was a full-fledged economic interpretation of history, magnificently concrete portrayal of the course of development of capitalism toward its predicted inevitable collapse in the proletarian revolution, a searing polemic, one of the outstanding propaganda works of all time, and certainly the finest piece of writing Marx ever did—*The Communist Manifesto*.

Just as the revolutions of 1848 began, Marx was asked to leave Belgium and was immediately invited back to Paris by a radical member of the Provisional Government. Once there, although he believed Germany to be the true center of the revolution, he opposed the sending of an ill-prepared German legion into his homeland. He attended chiefly to German issues, working with the Communist League. After revolution had broken out in the German states in March, however, Marx and Engels became participants. Marx returned to Cologne in early April and started publishing the *Neue Rheinische Zeitung*. He poured abuse upon the moderates who were leading the German revolution, especially in the Assembly at Frankfurt am Main, where they sought to unite Germany.[16] Meanwhile, both Marx and Engels found themselves opposed by the socialists; the lead-

16 Marx was as opposed to parliaments ("parliamentary cretinism") as we will find Proudhon to have been. English factory legislation was almost the only product of such government that he approved. In his attacks on the Frankfurt Assembly and the Prussian Parliament as well, Marx kept pointing out the machinations of the forces of reaction, even while proclaiming the sure victory of the revolution.

ers of the working class had difficulty comprehending the Marxian doctrine that the workers should first support the bourgeois revolution before they could hope for their own.

Marx maintained his stance as journalist-critic despite declining funds and declining support. His radicalism regarding domestic affairs was matched on foreign issues. His article praising the June insurgents in Paris alienated his middle-class clientele. He supported the efforts of Hungary and Italy to gain freedom from Austrian domination, but his hopes for the continuation of the revolution were disappointed as the forces of the status quo steadily regained their authority. The war against reactionary Russia that he had hoped might pull together the revolutionary forces failed to occur.

After the censorship had become increasingly severe, he was forced to close down his paper for urging non-payment of taxes. He was subjected to a trial on charges of subversion at which he gave so impressive a speech in his own defense that he was acquitted and thanked by the jury. Because he had given up his Prussian citizenship, however, the government was able to ask him to leave.

Returning to Paris in July 1849, he was again asked to move on, this time to the provinces. He determined instead to go to London, which he and his family were able to reach with the aid of money raised by his revolutionary friends.[17]

He was deeply disillusioned over the failure of the German revolution, the stupidity and weakness of the German liberal bourgeoisie, and the gullibility of the masses. Although he was once again to suggest, in his "Address to the Communist League" in 1850, the need for collaboration with the petty bourgeoisie, less and less in the future did such a tactic seem to him likely to prove beneficial.[18]

[17] His wife, Jenny, had had to sell the furniture to get them out of Germany.
[18] Even here, the tactic showed a significant variation, for the workers were to disrupt the victorious petty bourgeoisie from the moment of their victory.

Marx hoped briefly for a revival of the revolutionary movement in France in the winter of 1849–50, when he thought socialist literature was taking hold—only to be disappointed.[19] Within a year however, he was arguing that since economic conditions had improved, revolution would have to wait for another crisis. The delay seemed very long. The 1857 recession and the Polish insurrection of 1863 (and momentary signs in 1868 and 1877) brought only temporary hope again. Such a negative view put Marx and Engels in conflict with many of their fellow communist revolutionary exiles.

Marx made his home in London until his death in 1883, living most of the time in dire poverty, having steady income only in the 1850s when he and Engels submitted regular articles to Charles A. Dana's New York *Tribune* and living otherwise by irregular journalism and largely on such remittances as Engels, who worked for a Manchester branch of his father's firm, was able to send him.

Besides his journalistic activities, Marx, during his years in London, engaged in controversy with other leaders of the revolutionary movement who were also living much of the time in the hectic and distorted atmosphere of exile and defeat. He tried briefly to control the local branch of the Communist League. He maintained contact and correspondence with the revolutionary movement on the Continent, especially with the developing German workers political party, and later with the International Workingmen's Association. And he dedicated his major effort to the production of the great scholarly work of his life which he left unfinished, his study of capitalist society, *Das Kapital*.

[19] E. T. Gargan, *Alexis de Tocqueville: The Critical Years, 1848–51* (Washington, 1951), pp. 278 ff. He also erroneously predicted the revision of the French Constitution to allow the re-election of Louis Napoleon; see also Karl Marx, *The Class Struggles in France*, ed. by C. P. Dutt (New York, 1935), e.g., pp. 91, 124. A week after the coup he wrote to Engels that events in Paris bewildered him, and he ventured no prediction on the outcome; see Krieger, pp. 395–96.

A large part of Marx's journalistic work in this period was on international affairs; he was a Russophobe (as were many German revolutionaries) and he underestimated the burgeoning nationalisms of the lesser nations of the era, which he tended to see as distractions from the larger task of bourgeois-capitalist economic development.[20] He also applied his considerable powers to issues of English and continental domestic politics and economics; his most memorable journalism remains, however, the articles that became *The Class Struggles in France* and *The Eighteenth Brumaire of Louis Bonaparte*.

Marx's efforts at establishing a revolutionary workers' movement attained little success in London, but his acquaintance with Ferdinand Lassalle, whom he had come to know in 1848, opened new possibilities. From the later 1850s until his death in 1864 Lassalle built the basis of the German socialist party, and he did so while leaning on Marx for counsel at long distance (Marx was still prohibited from living in Prussia). Lassalle was not a true disciple of Marx. He believed, for example, much more than did Marx in accommodation with the existing state. After Lassalle's death, his followers combated followers of Marx for leadership of the workers' movement. In 1869 a real Marxist party, the Social Democratic Workingman's Party, was formed. When, in 1875, efforts were made to unify the socialists of the newly formed German Empire by combining Lassalleans and Marxists into one party, Marx was outraged at the accommodations accorded to the Lassalleans (writing the "Critique of the Gotha Program" against them), but his protests were ineffective. The party grew rapidly, becoming the largest

[20] His opposition to the Second Empire remained evident in his disapproval of the Italian war of independence of 1859–60, and his initial anti-French position on the Franco-Prussian War. He soon became anti-Prussian over the issue of annexations. Maximilian Rubel, in *Karl Marx devant le Bonapartism* (Paris, 1960), has put together Marx's views on the Second Empire from his articles in the *Tribune* and elsewhere, and from his letters. Marx dealt extensively with the Empire's foreign policy, though he did recurrently turn to criticizing Louis Napoleon's experiments in state socialism.

socialist party in the world, and by the nineties it was also the most intransigently Marxist, as Marx's disciples increasingly achieved posts of leadership.

During his lifetime, Marx was far more successful in controlling the International Workingmen's Association, founded in 1864. It collapsed, however, by 1872, in part because of internal feuds, in part in consequence of the reaction to the Paris Commune. Marx at the start was asked to aid in the organization of the International and establish its principles. He gave its inaugural address. As the organization grew through the next few years as an amalgam of trade unionists, revolutionists, and intellectuals with national representations of varying size and varying persuasions, Marx strove to impose Marxist theory upon it and to use it to promote the ends of the proletarian revolution by demonstrations of solidarity in strikes across national lines, exchanges of information, and so on. But at the meetings of the congresses he had first to do battle with the French Proudhonists, whom he failed to defeat, and thereafter he confronted Mikhail Bakunin who sought to decentralize the International and bring it closer to his own anarchist ideal. The conflict did not imply that Marx was ceasing to believe in the need for a violent revolutionary overthrow of the bourgeois order. The opposition Marx and Bakunin developed as a deep personal antagonism between the two men, a competition for leadership as well as a fundamental disagreement over theory and tactics. Bakunin saw Marx as authoritarian and dependent upon the state; Marx saw his opponent as ignorant of the reality confronted by the working class and, through his addiction to conspiratorial tactics as a danger to the movement, the organization, and to Marx's place in them.

This conflict greatly weakened the International, and its position was further endangered by its association with the Paris Commune. The Commune was viewed internationally as a dreadful threat to all constituted authority. Marx adopted the Commune for the International (even though the ties were not very close) by writing his *Civil War in France* in praise of the Commune, claiming, in effect, the myth of the Commune for the Marxist socialist movement.[21] Suspect as the International already was, it immediately became far more so, and its opportunities for beneficial efforts were more tightly restricted. Marx and Engels decided to move its center to New York in 1872. A resolution to that effect was passed, and though it shocked much of the membership, it may have been a mere acceptance of the inevitable. Thereafter, Marx's ties with international working class organizations were maintained chiefly by correspondence, and the period of his deep involvement and leadership had passed.

Volume I of *Das Kapital* was published in 1867. In the following years Marx continued to work on the later volumes, but was unable to finish them. Engels pieced together Volumes II and III from notes after his friend's death. Marx died in 1883 after frequent visits to continental spas failed to improve his declining health.

The Eighteenth Brumaire was one of Marx's very few sustained portrayals of the class struggle that was the key part of the theory he had designed to explain the whole course of history. We have already seen that the idea of class struggle was not new, nor was its application to the Second Republic. Tocqueville, for instance, offered a similar, though less theoretically sophisticated interpretation of the June Days in his *Recollections*.

Marx himself, in a letter to Weydemeyer on March 5, 1852, said:

> And now as to myself, no credit is due to me for discovering the existence of classes in modern society or the struggle between them. Long before me bourgeois historians had described the historical development of this class struggle and bourgeois economists the economic anatomy of the classes. What I did that was new was to prove: (1) that the *existence of classes* is only bound up with *particular historical phases in the devel-*

[21] See I. M. Zeitlin, *Marxism: A Re-examination* (Princeton, 1967), p. 141.

opment of production, (2) that the class struggle necessarily leads to the *dictatorship of the proletariat,* (3) that this dictatorship itself only constitutes the transition to the *abolition of all classes* and to a *classless society.*[22]

What was especially novel here was the complexity of the class analysis, its "texture," the interplay of so many classes and subclasses, all apparently able to play significant roles in the struggle for political power.[23] Many critics—e.g., John Plamenatz and Robert Tucker—have pointed out that such a portrayal seems at least a deviation from the nearly monolithic classes of *The Communist Manifesto.* There all classes other than the proletariat and the bourgeoisie are dying out, being absorbed into the two great contestants. In *The Eighteenth Brumaire* the petty bourgeoisie, the peasants, elements of the aristocracy, etc., constitute significant factors in the political power complex that Marx treats. They may be going to die out, but until they do, they remain politically significant. Probably the most striking feature is the skill with which Marx associates each political group with an economic interest. It is also intriguing to see how little importance Marx attaches to shifts in their economic bases as he follows through the activities of the conflicting classes and subclasses.

Some of Marx's most important theoretical statements in this work concern the self-interested ideological masks adopted by these groups, particularly notable in the cases of the two monarchical parties. He points out their powers of self-deception and identifies the great importance of imitation through the whole history of the Second Republic. The history of the coup shows once again that Marx gave a greater role to mind (even though full of error) in comparison to interests, greater causal force to the superstructure in comparison to the economic sub-

[22] Karl Marx and Friedrich Engels, *Selected Correspondence, 1846–1895,* trans. by Dona Torr (New York, 1934), p. 57.
[23] Zeitlin, p. 129.

structure, than his theory as described in 1859 might have led one to expect.[24]

The most puzzling and most intriguing discussion of class in the book is his treatment of the peasantry. The matter has been a source of vital controversy in the course of the history of Marxism, because Marxism came to power in Russia where peasants made up the mass of the population. In 1851–52 Marx believed that the mass of the peasantry, apart from a few activists, were as he had described them in the *Manifesto,* backward and reactionary. In *The Class Struggles in France* he argued they were incapable of revolutionary initiative. In *The Eighteenth Brumaire* he stated they constituted no true class at all and put forward the important distinction between a class merely identifiable as such to the outside observer, and a class conscious of itself and able to act politically as a unit. The conservative peasantry lacked these latter capacities, and hence fell prey to the blandishments of Louis Napoleon. In doing this they linked their fate to that of the bourgeoisie, yet Marx also contended that their economic position created ties with the proletariat. Leonard Krieger has written that ". . . Marx wavered between his view of them as a barbarian mass whose political expression was the Napoleonic idea and his conviction that a growing section was destined for a revolutionary alliance with the proletariat."[25] It remains a question which view dominates in *The Eighteenth Brumaire.*

[24] Gargan, pp. 293–94. This is one of the bases for the recurrent assertion by sympathetic critics of Marx that he really intended to argue for a complex interplay of sub- and superstructure. Sidney Hook contends that the historical writings, such as *The Eighteenth Brumaire,* should suffice to refute those who accuse Marx of fatalism; see *From Hegel to Marx* (Ann Arbor, 1962), p. 71. Marx added notable complexities to his theory in his description of the "literary representatives" of a class, and by tracing the surprising occurrence of the *separation* of the parliamentary-political representatives of the bourgeois class from their constituency.

[25] Krieger, p. 385, footnote. Engels, traveling across France in 1848, had supplied Marx with descriptions of the French peasantry

Another major problem in the book is the question of the autonomy (or neutrality) of the state; Marx in some passages seems to adopt a view that differs from the dominant one in most of his writing, including especially the *Manifesto*. In the *Manifesto*, the state is merely an instrument of class oppression —a means by which an ascendant class exercises exploitation. Yet in this book, the historical logic Marx sees working itself out includes the perfection of the state machine. Louis Napoleon and his entourage are presented not as true representatives of the peasants (for peasant dreams rather than interests are represented), but rather as representatives of the growing state itself which in bourgeois capitalist society increasingly enhances its own power. In later journalistic writings and finally in *The Civil War in France*, Marx was to suggest even more explicitly a view of a Bonapartist state that anticipates twentieth-century despotisms. His 1852 idea of the state has been interpreted as a military administrative machine which stands over against the bourgeoisie as well as against other classes, as something more than a *mere* engine of exploitation.[26]

---

and their Bonapartism; see Wilson, p. 174. Marx and his revolutionary associates in Cologne had attempted to revolutionize the German peasants through 1848; their relatively unsuccessful experience may have affected his opinions.

E. H. Carr has argued that the failure to recognize the independent power of the peasantry is a real weakness in Marx's position (*Studies in Revolution*, New York, 1964, p. 29). It is clear, none the less, that he did recognize their central role in Louis Napoleon's rise to power, even though he did not credit them with initiative.

[26] Some of the difficulty of interpretation here can be seen in the disagreements among the following: John Plamenatz, *German Marxism and Russian Communism* (New York, 1965), pp. 145 ff., argues that an autonomous state is presented here; his *Man in Society*, vol. 2: *Bentham Through Marx* (New York, 1963), pp. 367–73 points to links between the state Marx portrays and the Fascist state. Similar views appear in James H. Meisel, *Counterrevolution: How Revolutions Die* (New York, 1966), ch. VI, and in Wilson, op. cit., p. 186. Robert H. Tucker, in *The Marxian Revolutionary Idea* (New York, 1969), pp. 71–72, disagrees. Meisel (pp. 104–5) feels that especially important is the suggested role of a class of adventurers who re-

R. N. Carew-Hunt declares that *The Eighteenth Brumaire* offers Marx's most complete exposition of his theory of revolution.[27] Yet even if the state be taken as the instrument of the bourgeoisie[28] (or one that will fall into its hands), the problem remains in the revolutionary theory: What is to be done with the state by the proletariat? The letter to Weydemeyer, quoted above, was written just as *The Eighteenth Brumaire* was completed and speaks of a dictatorship of the proletariat—as the *Manifesto* had done—yet Marx wrote to his friend Dr. Ludwig Kugelmann at the time of the Commune (April 12, 1871) as follows:

> If you look at the last chapter of my *Eighteenth Brumaire* you will find that I say that the next attempt of the French Revolution will be no longer, as before, to transfer the bureaucratic-military machine from one hand to another, but to smash it, and that is essential for every real people's revolution on the continent. And this is what our heroic Party comrades in Paris are attempting.[29]

It is by no means clear, then, what Marx's belief was in 1852 with regard to the nature of the state itself nor what he felt was the appropriate revolutionary tactic with regard to the existing state organization. It seems evident that by 1852 Marx had given up the idea of a revolutionary take-over by a Blanquist elite; such romantic politics were for the past. But it is not clear whether he thought the state a neutral instrument which might appropriately be used by victorious proletarians in establishing

---

establish the conflicting class arrangements. The interpretation most in accord with traditional Marxism sees the aggrandized state prepared to betray the peasants on behalf of the bourgeoisie. See Auguste Cornu, *Marx et la Révolution de 1848* (Paris, 1948), p. 70.

[27] R. N. Carew-Hunt, *The Theory and Practice of Communism* (Baltimore, 1963), p. 98, footnote.

[28] Marx does make clear that the bourgeoisie has an *interest* in a strong state as a source of jobs.

[29] Karl Marx and Friedrich Engels, *Selected Correspondence, 1846–1895*, p. 309. See below, p. 203, especially footnote 26.

their dictatorship (prior to the appearance of the utopian end of history with its newly fulfilled mankind) or a corrupt instrument to be done away with immediately, as he saw it at the time of the Commune. *The Eighteenth Brumaire* leaves room for question, despite the interpretation Marx gave in 1871.

Two comments may be made here. Marx's approval of decentralized administrative arrangements at the time of the Commune are naturally wrapped up with his enthusiasm for the Commune itself, despite the fact that Proudhonism and Blanquism played so large a part in it. Like other of Marx's seeming shifts or contradictions it can be comprehended in part at least if one recognizes that he was not merely a theorist, but also a revolutionary leader during times of significant change. Further, there was a tendency, not merely in Marx but also in others (including Proudhon), to equate with the state those aspects of government of which they disapproved, e.g., the military or police, and to call "administration" those functions still seen as necessary for the operation of a social order. Such terminological sleight-of-hand made talk of the disappearance of the state a good deal easier.[30]

It may fairly be stated, I think, that the concluding pages of *The Eighteenth Brumaire* are simply unclear on the questions of state and revolution. Krieger again supports this view: "In his repeated attempts to explain the rise of Louis Bonaparte, Marx not only saw him variously as the expression of the common opposition of all other classes to bourgeois political rule, as the chief of the *Lumpenproletariat*, and as the representative of the peasants, he also interpreted Bonaparte's role as the embodiment of the monstrous state-machine which had risen like a Frankenstein creation to the predominance over bourgeois society, and as a last resort of that bourgeoisie in its quest for social order against its own principles of political liberty."[31]

Marx does point unequivocally to one root contradiction in

30 Schwarzschild, pp. 354–55.
31 Krieger, p. 385.

the politics of the Second Republic, the introduction of universal suffrage, which he believed inappropriate to precommunist society and hence a source of tension, as men sought to frustrate its implications—producing in consequence the rule of Louis Napoleon.[32] One further most interesting suggestion he makes about the course of the history of the Second Republic is that it moved in a direction opposite to that of the First; after 1789, with each shift of power, a more radical group had taken over; after 1848 each change put a more conservative group in control. The implications for a sociology of revolution are unfortunate, unless we bear in mind that Marx's interpretation of the 1848 revolution in France was changing. In *The Class Struggles in France*, he had stressed that progress had been made by the revolution through 1850, class conflict had been clarified and illusions banished; now, though he still noted the same consequence, he portrayed the 1848 revolution as farce.[33] As we have noted, he had given up hope for any true social revolution in the near future in the interval between his writing of the two books. He was, then, demonstrating all the more pointedly that no real revolution had occurred.

Several commentators have compared the interpretations of the Second Republic made by the two great sociologists, Marx and Tocqueville—for example, Raymond Aron, Edward Gargan, and Leonard Krieger. Some points of similarity to note are the following: Marx resembled Tocqueville in granting a major role to tradition and to the imitation of the behavior of the revolutionaries of 1789 and of the first Napoleonic regime. Both also saw the July Monarchy as a business run for the benefit of its ruling class. Both stressed the central importance of Paris as a revolutionary center, so that the defeat of the Second Republic constituted a revolt against Paris.

Marx, like Tocqueville (and Hugo), passed moral judgement on Louis Napoleon. He did not simply restrict himself to analy-

[32] Avineri, p. 213.
[33] Krieger, p. 403.

sis—he attacked the debased character of the new regime. Stanley Edgar Hyman rightly says that Marx portrays the triumph of Louis Napoleon as both inevitable and reprehensible.[34] Marx differed here from Tocqueville and Hugo only in that he would not himself have viewed the moral dimension as central to his enterprise.

Marx differed from most of his contemporaries in his philosophic and revolutionary inclinations, but he remained very much a man of his time. He had deep faith in the possibility of discovering truth through scientific procedures. He expected to learn thereby the way in which history was tending, for he was convinced (as were many intellectuals in his era) that descriptions of the discovered tendencies of social change and historical development were analogous to scientific laws, certain enough to allow prediction. And he was of his time in believing in progress, even though his expectation that progress would come through violent conflict was less universal. For all the priority he gave to economic conditions, he believed, as was characteristic of his age, that political action—revolution—was still the way, when the time was economically ripe, to resolve existing tensions. It did not seem anomalous to him, nor to many of his contemporaries either, that he combined the roles of scientist, moralist, and practical revolutionary agitator, nor that the theory of the scientist should be loaded with intense moral animus and directed at changing the situation it purported to describe. Marx adopted the position he had portrayed in the *Manifesto* of a déclassé intellectual guide to the proletariat, assisting it toward class consciousness. The problem for him, as G. D. H. Cole puts it, was to get men to act (for philosophy must be practical), yet in his view right action does not necessarily follow from ideas[35]—as his whole theory of ideology argues. So fortified by the conviction that the whole

---

[34] Hyman, p. 110.

[35] G. D. H. Cole, *Socialist Thought: the Forerunners 1781–1850* (London, 1953), p. 237.

course of history was on his side, he sought to incorporate his ideas into practical revolutionary activity to further the ends he desired.

SUGGESTED READINGS

Shlomo Avineri, *The Social and Political Thought of Karl Marx,* London, 1968.

Isaiah Berlin, *Karl Marx,* London, 1952.

M. M. Bober, *Karl Marx's Interpretation of History,* New York, 1965.

G. D. H. Cole, *Socialist Thought: The Forerunners 1781–1850,* London, 1953.

Lloyd D. Easton and Kurt H. Guddat, eds., *Writings of the Young Marx on Philosophy and Society,* Garden City, N.Y., 1967.

Erich Fromm, *Marx's Concept of Man,* New York, 1961.

Oscar G. Hammen, *The Red '48ers: Karl Marx and Friedrich Engels,* New York, 1969.

Sidney Hook, *From Hegel to Marx,* Ann Arbor, 1962.

George Lichtheim, *Marxism: An Historical and Critical Study,* London, 1961.

Karl Löwith, *From Hegel to Nietzsche,* Garden City, N.Y., 1967.

Herbert Marcuse, *Reason and Revolution,* New York, 1954.

F. Mehring, *Karl Marx,* London, 1936.

John Plamenatz, *German Marxism and Russian Communism,* New York, 1965.

———, *Man and Society,* vol. 2: *Bentham Through Marx,* New York, 1963.

Nathan Rotenstreich, *Basic Problems of Marx's Philosophy,* Indianapolis, 1965.

Robert C. Tucker, *Philosophy and Myth in Karl Marx,* London, 1961.

Edmund Wilson, *To the Finland Station,* Garden City, N.Y., 1953.

SELECTIONS FROM MARX'S

The Eighteenth Brumaire of Louis Bonaparte

I

HEGEL REMARKS somewhere that all facts and personages of great importance in world history occur, as it were, twice. He forgot to add: the first time as tragedy, the second as farce. Caussidière for Danton, Louis Blanc for Robespierre, the *Montagne* of 1848 to 1851 for the *Montagne* of 1793 to 1795, the Nephew for the Uncle.[1] And the same caricature occurs in the circumstances attending the second edition of the eighteenth Brumaire![2]

Men make their own history, but they do not make it just as they please; they do not make it under circumstances chosen

SOURCE: Karl Marx, *The Eighteenth Brumaire of Louis Bonaparte*, vol. 1 of Karl Marx and Friedrich Engels, *Selected Works*, Foriegn Language Publishing House, (Moscow, 1951), pp. 225–41, 243–53, 255–61, 263–69, 275, 277, 282–84, 286, 288–95, 297–311.

[1] Caussidière, see above, p. 90, note 10. Louis Blanc, see above, p. 65, note 2. Marx's reference to Hegel essentially repeats a remark in Engels' letter of December 3, 1851, wherein appear in the same context the Caussidière–Danton, and Blanc–Robespierre comparisons. *Selected Correspondence*, p. 51.

[2] Napoleon's coup d'état of November 9, 1799.

by themselves, but under circumstances directly encountered, given and transmitted from the past. The tradition of all the dead generations weighs like a nightmare on the brain of the living. And just when they seem engaged in revolutionizing themselves and things, in creating something that has never yet existed, precisely in such periods of revolutionary crisis they anxiously conjure up the spirits of the past to their service and borrow from them names, battle cries and costumes in order to present the new scene of world history in this time-honoured disguise and this borrowed language. Thus Luther donned the mask of the Apostle Paul, the Revolution of 1789 to 1814 draped itself alternately as the Roman republic and the Roman empire, and the Revolution of 1848 knew nothing better to do than to parody, now 1789, now the revolutionary tradition of 1793 to 1795. . . .

Consideration of this conjuring up of the dead of world history reveals at once a salient difference. Camille Desmoulins, Danton, Robespierre, Saint-Just, Napoleon, the heroes as well as the parties and the masses of the old French Revolution, performed the task of their time in Roman costume and with Roman phrases, the task of unchaining and setting up modern *bourgeois* society. The first ones knocked the feudal basis to pieces and mowed off the feudal heads which had grown on it. The other created inside France the conditions under which alone free competition could be developed, parcelled landed property exploited and the unchained industrial productive power of the nation employed; and beyond the French borders he everywhere swept the feudal institutions away, so far as was necessary to furnish bourgeois society in France with a suitable up-to-date environment on the European Continent. The new social formation once established, the antediluvian Colossi disappeared and with them resurrected Romanity—the Brutuses, Gracchi, Publicolas, the tribunes, the senators, and Caesar himself. Bourgeois society in its sober reality had begotten its true interpreters and mouthpieces in the Says, Cousins, Royer-

Collards, Benjamin Constants and Guizots;[3] its real military leaders sat behind the office desks, and the hog-headed Louis XVIII was its political chief. Wholly absorbed in the production of wealth and in peaceful competitive struggle, it no longer comprehended that ghosts from the days of Rome had watched over its cradle. But unheroic as bourgeois society is, it nevertheless took heroism, sacrifice, terror, civil war and battles of peoples to bring it into being. And in the classically austere traditions of the Roman republic its gladiators found the ideals and the art forms, the self-deceptions that they needed in order to conceal from themselves the bourgeois limitations of the content of their struggles and to keep their enthusiasm on the high plane of the great historical tragedy. . . .

From 1848 to 1851 only the ghost of the old revolution walked about, from Marrast, the *républicain en gants jaunes*, who disguised himself as the old Bailly,[4] down to the adventurer, who hides his commonplace repulsive features under the iron death mask of Napoleon. An entire people, which had imagined that by means of a revolution it had imparted to itself an accelerated power of motion, suddenly finds itself set back into a defunct epoch. . . . The French, so long as they were engaged in revolution, could not get rid of the memory of Napoleon, as the election of December 10 proved. They hankered to return from the perils of revolution to the fleshpots of Egypt,[5] and December 2, 1851 was the answer. They have not only a caricature of the old Napoleon, they have the old Na-

[3] Jean Baptiste Say (1767–1832), French classical economist. Victor Cousin (1792–1867), philosopher of electicism, Minister of Education under Louis Philippe. Pierre Paul Royer-Collard (1763–1845), politician and political theorist of constitutional monarchy. Benjamin Constant (1767–1830), novelist and journalist of the Restoration era. François Pierre Guillaume Guizot (1787–1874), historian and politician, leading minister in the July Monarchy's last years.

[4] Armand Marrast (1801–52), see above, p. 15, note 14, "the republican in yellow gloves." Jean Sylvain Bailly (1736–93), astronomer, who was active in the first French Revolution.

[5] A reference to the first Napoleon's Egyptian campaign.

poleon himself, caricatured as he must appear in the middle of the nineteenth century.

The social revolution of the nineteenth century cannot draw its poetry from the past, but only from the future. It cannot begin with itself before it has stripped off all superstition in regard to the past. Earlier revolutions required recollections of past world history in order to drug themselves concerning their own content. In order to arrive at its own content, the revolution of the nineteenth century must let the dead bury their dead. There the phrase went beyond the content; here the content goes beyond the phrase.

The February Revolution was a surprise attack, a *taking* of the old society *unawares*, and the people proclaimed this unhoped-for *stroke* as a deed of world importance, ushering in a new epoch. On December 2 the February Revolution is conjured away by a cardsharper's trick, and what seems overthrown is no longer the monarchy but the liberal concessions that were wrung from it by centuries of struggle. Instead of *society* having conquered a new content for itself, it seems that the *state* only returned to its oldest form, to the shamelessly simple domination of the sabre and the cowl. This is the answer to the *coup de main* of February 1848, given by the *coup de tête* of December 1851. Easy come, easy go. Meanwhile the interval of time has not passed by unused. During the years 1848 to 1851 French society has made up, and that by an abbreviated because revolutionary method, for the studies and experiences which, in a regular, so to speak, textbook course of development would have had to precede the February Revolution, if it was to be more than a ruffling of the surface. Society now seems to have fallen back behind its point of departure; it has in truth first to create for itself the revolutionary point of departure, the situation, the relations, the conditions under which alone modern revolution becomes serious.

Bourgeois revolutions, like those of the eighteenth century, storm swiftly from success to success; their dramatic effects outdo each other; men and things seem set in sparkling brilliants;

ecstasy is the everyday spirit; but they are short-lived; soon they have attained their zenith, and a long crapulent depression lays hold of society before it learns soberly to assimilate the results of its storm-and-stress period. On the other hand, proletarian revolutions, like those of the nineteenth century, criticize themselves constantly, interrupt themselves continually in their own course, come back to the apparently accomplished in order to begin it afresh, deride with unmerciful thoroughness the inadequacies, weaknesses and paltrinesses of their first attempts, seem to throw down their adversary only in order that he may draw new strength from the earth and rise again, more gigantic, before them, recoil ever and anon from the indefinite prodigiousness of their own aims, until a situation has been created which makes all turning back impossible, and the conditions themselves cry out:

> *Hic Rhodus, hic salta!*
> Here is the rose, here dance!

For the rest, every fairly competent observer, even if he had not followed the course of French developments step by step, must have had a presentiment that a terrible fiasco was in store for the revolution. It was enough to hear the self-complacent howl of victory with which Messieurs the Democrats congratulated each other on the expected gracious consequences of the second Sunday in May 1852. In their minds the second Sunday in May 1852, had become a fixed idea, a dogma, like the day on which Christ should reappear and the millennium begin, in the minds of the Chiliasts. As ever, weakness had taken refuge in a belief in miracles, fancied the enemy overcome when he was only conjured away in imagination, and it lost all understanding of the present in a passive glorification of the future that was in store for it and of the deeds it had *in petto* but which it merely did not want to carry out as yet. Those heroes who seek to disprove their demonstrated incapacity by mutually offering each other their sympathy and getting together in a crowd had tied up their bundles, collected their laurel wreaths in advance and were just then engaged in discounting on the exchange market the republics *in partibus* for which they had already providently organized the government personnel with all the calm of their unassuming disposition. December 2 struck them like a thunderbolt from a clear sky, and the peoples that in periods of pusillanimous depression gladly let their inward apprehension be drowned out by the loudest bawlers will perchance have convinced themselves that the times are past when the cackle of geese could save the Capitol.

The Constitution, the National Assembly, the dynastic parties, the blue and the red republicans, the heroes of Africa, the thunder from the platform, the sheet lightning of the daily press, the entire literature, the political names and the intellectual reputations, the civil law and the penal code, the *liberté, égalité, fraternité* and the second Sunday in May 1852 —all has vanished like a phantasmagoria before the spell of a man whom even his enemies do not make out to be a magician. Universal suffrage seems to have survived only for a moment, in order that with its own hand it may make its last will and testament before the eyes of all the world and declare in the name of the people itself: All that exists deserves to perish.

It is not enough to say, as the French do, that their nation was taken unawares. A nation and a woman are not forgiven the unguarded hour in which the first adventurer that came along could violate them. The riddle is not solved by such turns of speech, but merely formulated differently. It remains to be explained how a nation of thirty-six millions can be surprised and delivered unresisting into captivity by three high-class swindlers.

Let us recapitulate in general outline the phases that the French Revolution went through from February 24, 1848, to December 1851.

Three main periods are unmistakable: *the February period;* May 4, 1848, to May 28, 1849: *the period of the constitution of the republic,* or *of the Constituent National Assembly;* May

28, 1849, to December 2, 1851: *the period of the constitutional republic* or *of the Legislative National Assembly.*

The *first period,* from February 24, or the overthrow of Louis Philippe, to May 4, 1848, the meeting of the Constituent Assembly, the *February period* proper, may be described as the *prologue* to the revolution. Its character was officially expressed in the fact that the government improvised by it itself declared that it was *provisional* and, like the government, everything that was mooted, attempted or enunciated during this period proclaimed itself to be only *provisional.* Nothing and nobody ventured to lay claim to the right of existence and of real action. All the elements that had prepared or determined the revolution, the dynastic opposition, the republican bourgeoisie, the democratic-republican petty bourgeoisie and the social-democratic workers, provisionally found their place in the February *government.*

It could not be otherwise. The February days originally intended an electoral reform, by which the circle of the politically privileged among the possessing class itself was to be widened and the exclusive domination of the aristocracy of finance overthrown. When it came to the actual conflict, however, when the people mounted the barricades, the National Guard maintained a passive attitude, the army offered no serious resistance and the monarchy ran away, the republic appeared to be a matter of course. Every party construed it in its own way. Having secured it arms in hand, the proletariat impressed its stamp upon it and proclaimed it to be a *social republic.* There was thus indicated the general content of the modern revolution, a content which was in most singular contradiction to everything that, with the material available, with the degree of education attained by the masses, under the given circumstances and relations, could be immediately realized in practice. On the other hand, the claims of all the remaining elements that had collaborated in the February Revolution were recognized by the lion's share that they obtained in the government. In no period do we, therefore, find a more confused mixture of high-flown phrases and actual uncertainty and clumsiness, of more enthusiastic striving for innovation and more deeply-rooted domination of the old routine, of more apparent harmony of the whole of society and more profound estrangement of its elements. While the Paris proletariat still revelled in the vision of the wide prospects that had opened before it and indulged in seriously-meant discussions on social problems, the old powers of society had grouped themselves, assembled, reflected and found unexpected support in the mass of the nation, the peasants and petty bourgeois, who all at once stormed on to the political stage, after the barriers of the July monarchy had fallen.

The *second period*, from May 4, 1848, to the end of May 1849, is the period of the *constitution*, the *foundation, of the bourgeois republic*. Directly after the February days not only had the dynastic opposition been surprised by the republicans and the republicans by the Socialists, but all France by Paris. The National Assembly, which had met on May 4, 1848, having emerged from the national elections, represented the nation. It was a living protest against the presumptuous pretensions of the February days and was to reduce the results of the revolution to the bourgeois scale. . . .

The *bourgeois monarchy* of Louis Philippe can be followed only by a *bourgeois republic,* that is to say, whereas a limited section of the bourgeoisie ruled in the name of the king, the whole of the bourgeoisie will now rule in the name of the people. The demands of the Paris proletariat are utopian nonsense, to which an end must be put. To this declaration of the Constituent National Assembly the Paris proletariat replied with the *June Insurrection,* the most colossal event in the history of European civil wars. The bourgeois republic triumphed. On its side stood the aristocracy of finance, the industrial bourgeoisie, the middle class, the petty bourgeois, the army, the *lumpenproletariat* organized as the Mobile Guard, the intellectual lights, the clergy and the rural population. On the side of the Paris proletariat stood none but itself. More than three thousand insurgents were butchered after the victory, and fifteen thousand were transported without trial. With this defeat the proletariat passes into the *background* of the revolutionary stage. . . .

The defeat of the June insurgents, to be sure, had now prepared, had levelled the ground on which the bourgeois republic could be founded and built up, but it had shown at the same time that in Europe the questions at issue are other than that of "republic or monarchy." It had revealed that here *bourgeois republic* signifies the unlimited despotism of one class over other classes. It had proved that in countries with an old civilization, with a developed formation of classes, with modern conditions of production and with an intellectual consciousness in which all traditional ideas have been dissolved by the work of centuries, *the republic* signifies *in general only the political form of revolution of bourgeois society* and not its *conservative form of life.* . . .

During the June days all classes and parties had united in the *party of Order* against the proletarian class as the *party of Anarchy*, of Socialism, of Communism. They had "saved" society from *"the enemies of society."* They had given out the watchwords of the old society, *"property, family, religion, order,"* to their army as passwords and had proclaimed to the counter-revolutionary crusaders: "In this sign thou shalt conquer!" From that moment, as soon as one of the numerous parties which had gathered under this sign against the June insurgents seeks to hold the revolutionary battlefield in its own class interest, it goes down before the cry: "Property, family, religion, order." Society is saved just as often as the circle of its rulers contracts, as a more exclusive interest is maintained against a wider one. Every demand of the simplest bourgeois financial reform, of the most ordinary liberalism, of the most formal republicanism, of the most shallow democracy, is simultaneously castigated as an "attempt on society" and stigmatized as "Socialism." And, finally, the high priests of "the religion of order" themselves are driven with kicks from their Pythian tripods, hauled out of their beds in the darkness of night, put in prison-vans, thrown into dungeons or sent into exile; their temple is razed to the ground, their mouths are sealed, their pens broken, their law torn to pieces in the name of religion, of property, of the family, of order. Bourgeois fanatics for order are shot down on their balconies by mobs of drunken soldiers, their domestic sanctuaries profaned, their houses bombarded for amusement—in the name of property, of the family, of religion and of order. Finally, the scum of bourgeois society forms the *holy phalanx of order* and the hero Crapulinski[6] installs himself in the Tuileries as the *"saviour of society."*

II

Let us pick up the threads of the development once more.

The history of the *Constituent National Assembly* since the June days is the *history of the domination and the liquidation of the republican faction of the bourgeoisie*, of that faction which is known by the names of tricolour republicans, pure republicans, political republicans, formalist republicans, etc.

Under the bourgeois monarchy of Louis Philippe it had formed the *official* republican *opposition* and consequently a recognized component part of the political world of the day. It had its representatives in the Chambers and a considerable sphere of influence in the press. Its Paris organ, the *National*, was considered just as respectable in its way as the *Journal des Débats*. . . . It was a coterie of republican-minded bourgeois —writers, lawyers, officers and officials that owed its influence to the personal antipathies of the country against Louis Philippe, to memories of the old republic, to the republican faith of a number of enthusiasts, above all, however, to *French nationalism*. . . .

The exclusive *rule of the bourgeois republicans* lasted only

[6] Insulting nickname for Louis Napoleon, taken from the hero of Heine's *Two Knights*.

from June 24 to December 10, 1848. It is summed up in the *drafting of a republican constitution* and in the *state of siege of Paris.*

The new *Constitution* was at bottom only the republicanized edition of the constitutional Charter of 1830. The narrow electoral qualification of the July monarchy, which excluded even a large part of the bourgeoisie from political rule, was incompatible with the existence of the bourgeois republic. In lieu of this qualification, the February Revolution had at once proclaimed direct universal suffrage. The bourgeois republicans could not undo this event. They had to content themselves with adding the limiting proviso of a six months' residence in the constituency. The old organization of the administration, of the municipal system, of the judicial system, of the army, etc., continued to exist inviolate, or, where the Constitution changed them, the change concerned the table of contents, not the contents; the name, not the subject matter.

. . . Glance through the Constitution and you will find that only the paragraphs in which the relationship of the President to the Legislative Assembly is defined are absolute, positive, non-contradictory, incapable of distortion. For here it was a question of the bourgeois republicans safeguarding themselves. §§45–70 of the Constitution are so worded that the National Assembly can remove the President constitutionally, whereas the President can remove the National Assembly only unconstitutionally, only by setting aside the Constitution itself. Here, therefore, it challenges its forcible destruction. It not only sanctifies the division of powers, like the Charter of 1830, it widens it into an intolerable contradiction. . . . On one side are seven hundred and fifty representatives of the people, elected by universal suffrage and eligible for re-election; they form an uncontrollable, indissoluble, indivisible National Assembly, a National Assembly that enjoys legislative omnipotence, decides in the last instance on war, peace and commercial treaties, alone possesses the right of amnesty and, by its permanence, perpetually holds the front of the stage. On the other side is the President, with all the attributes of royal power, with authority to appoint and dismiss his ministers independently of the National Assembly, with all the resources of the executive power in his hands, bestowing all posts and disposing thereby in France of the livelihoods of at least a million and a half people, for so many depend on the five hundred thousand officials and officers of every rank. He has the whole of the armed forces behind him. He enjoys the privilege of pardoning individual criminals, of suspending National Guards, of discharging, with the concurrence of the Council of State, general, cantonal and municipal councils elected by the citizens themselves. Initiative and direction are reserved to him in all treaties with foreign countries. While the Assembly constantly performs on the boards and is exposed to the critical light of day, he leads a hidden life in the Elysian fields, and that with Article 45 of the Constitution before his eyes and in his heart, crying to him daily: *"Frère, il faut mourir!"*[7] Your power ceases on the second Sunday of the lovely month of May in the fourth year after your election! Then your glory is at an end, the piece is not played twice and if you have debts, look to it betimes that you pay them off with the six hundred thousand francs granted you by the Constitution, unless, perchance, you should prefer to go to Clichy[8] on the second Monday of the lovely month of May!—Thus, whereas the Constitution assigns actual power to the President, it seeks to secure moral power for the National Assembly. Apart from the fact that it is impossible to create a moral power by paragraphs of law, the Constitution here abrogates itself once more by having the President elected by all Frenchmen through direct suffrage. While the votes of France are split up among the seven hundred and fifty members of the National Assembly, they are here, on the contrary, concentrated on a single individual. While each separate representative of the people represents only this or that party, this or that town, this or that bridgehead, or even only the mere necessity of electing some one of the seven hundred

[7] "Brother, you must die."
[8] Clichy was a debtors' prison in Paris.

and fifty, in which neither the cause nor the man is closely examined, *he* is the elect of the nation and the act of his election is the trump that the sovereign people plays once every four years. The elected National Assembly stands in a metaphysical relation, but the elected President in a personal relation, to the nation. The National Assembly, indeed, exhibits in its individual representatives the manifold aspects of the national spirit, but in the President this national spirit finds its incarnation. As against the Assembly, he possesses a sort of divine right; he is President by the grace of the people.

Thetis, the sea goddess, had prophesied to Achilles that he would die in the bloom of youth. The Constitution, which, like Achilles, had its weak spot, had also, like Achilles, its presentiment that it must go to an early death. It was sufficient for the constitution-making pure republicans to cast a glance from the lofty heaven of their ideal republic at the profane world to perceive how the arrogance of the royalists, the Bonapartists, the Democrats, the Communists as well as their own discredit grew daily in the same measure as they approached the completion of their great legislative work of art, without Thetis on this account having to leave the sea and communicate the secret to them. They sought to cheat destiny by a catch in the Constitution, through §111 of it, according to which every motion for a *revision of the Constitution* must be supported by at least three-quarters of the votes, cast in three successive debates between which an entire month must always lie, with the added proviso that not less than five hundred members of the National Assembly must vote. Thereby they merely made the impotent attempt still to exercise, when only a parliamentary minority, as which they already saw themselves prophetically in their mind's eye, a power which at the present moment, when they commanded a parliamentary majority and all the resources of governmental authority, was slipping daily more and more from their feeble hands.

Finally the Constitution, in a melodramatic paragraph, entrusts itself "to the vigilance and the patriotism of the whole

French people and every single Frenchman," after it had previously entrusted in another paragraph the "vigilant" and "patriotic" to the tender, most painstaking care of the High Court of Justice, the *"haute cour,"* invented by it for the purpose.

Such was the Constitution of 1848, which on December 2, 1851, was not overthrown by a head, but fell down at the touch of a mere hat; this hat, to be sure, was a three-cornered Napoleonic hat.

While the bourgeois republicans in the Assembly were busy devising, discussing and voting this Constitution, Cavaignac outside the Assembly maintained the *state of siege of Paris.* The state of siege of Paris was the midwife of the Constituent Assembly in its travail of republican creation. If the Constitution is subsequently put out of existence by bayonets, it must not be forgotten that it was likewise by bayonets, and these turned against the people, that it had to be protected in its mother's womb and by bayonets that it had to be brought into existence. The forefathers of the "respectable republicans" had sent their symbol, the tricolour, on a tour round Europe. They themselves in turn produced an invention that of itself made its way over the whole Continent, but returned to France with ever renewed love until it has now become naturalized in half her Departments—the *state of siege.* A splendid invention, periodically employed in every ensuing crisis in the course of the French Revolution. But barrack and bivouac, which were thus periodically laid on French society's head to compress its brain and render it quiet; sabre and musket, which were periodically allowed to act as judges and administrators, as guardians and censors, to play policeman and do night watchman's duty; moustache and uniform, which were periodically trumpeted forth as the highest wisdom of society and as its rector—were not barrack and bivouac, sabre and musket, moustache and uniform finally bound to hit upon the idea of rather saving society once and for all by proclaiming their own regime as the highest and freeing civil society completely from the trouble of governing itself? . . .

I have worked out elsewhere the significance of the election of December 10. I will not revert to it here. It is sufficient to remark here that it was a *reaction of the peasants*, who had had to pay the cost of the February Revolution, against the remaining classes of the nation, a *reaction of the country against the town*. It met with great approval in the army, for which the republicans of the *National Assembly* had provided neither glory nor additional pay, among the big bourgeoisie, which hailed Bonaparte as a bridge to monarchy, among the proletarians and petty bourgeois, who hailed him as a scourge for Cavaignac. I shall have an opportunity later of going more closely into the relationship of the peasants to the French Revolution.

The period from December 20, 1848, until the dissolution of the Constituent Assembly, in May 1849, comprises the history of the downfall of the bourgeois republicans. After having founded a republic for the bourgeoisie, driven the revolutionary proletariat out of the field and reduced the democratic petty bourgeoisie to silence for the time being, they are themselves thrust aside by the mass of the bourgeoisie, which justly impounds this republic as *its property*. This bourgeois mass was, however, *royalist*. One section of it, the large landowners, had ruled during the *Restoration* and was accordingly *Legitimist*. The other, the aristocrats of finance and big industrialists, had ruled during the July Monarchy and was consequently *Orleanist*. The high dignitaries of the army, the university, the church, the bar, the academy and of the press were to be found on either side, though in various proportions. Here, in the bourgeois republic, which bore neither the name *Bourbon* nor the name *Orleans*, but the name *Capital*, they had found the form of state in which they could rule *conjointly*. The June Insurrection had already united them in the "party of Order." Now it was necessary, in the first place, to remove the coterie of bourgeois republicans who still occupied the seats of the National Assembly. . . .

. . . On acceding to the presidency, Bonaparte at once formed a ministry of the party of Order, at the head of which he

155

placed Odilon Barrot, the old leader, *nota bene,* of the most liberal faction of the parliamentary bourgeoisie. M. Barrot had at last secured the ministerial portfolio, the spectre of which had haunted him since 1830, and what is more, the premiership in the ministry. . . .

III

On May 28, 1849, the Legislative National Assembly met. On December 2, 1851, it was dispersed. This period covers the span of life of the *constitutional, or parliamentary, republic.*

In the first French Revolution the rule of the *Constitutionalists* is followed by the rule of the *Girondins* and the rule of the *Girondins* by the rule of the *Jacobins.* Each of these parties relies on the more progressive party for support. As soon as it has brought the revolution far enough to be unable to follow it further, still less to go ahead of it, it is thrust aside by the bolder ally that stands behind it and sent to the guillotine. The revolution thus moves along an ascending line.

It is the reverse with the Revolution of 1848. The proletarian party appears as an appendage of the petty-bourgeois-democratic party. It is betrayed and dropped by the latter on April 16, May 15,[9] and in the June days. The democratic party, in its turn, leans on the shoulders of the bourgeois-republican party. The bourgeois-republicans no sooner believe themselves well established than they shake off the troublesome comrade and support themselves on the shoulders of the party of Order. The party of Order hunches its shoulders, lets the bourgeois-republicans tumble and throws itself on the shoulders of armed force. It fancies it is still sitting on its shoulders when, one fine morning, it perceives that the shoulders have transformed themselves into bayonets. Each party strikes from behind at that pressing further and leans from in front on that pressing back.

[9] Unsuccessful revolutionary *journées* in the spring of 1848.

No wonder that in this ridiculous posture it loses its balance and, having made the inevitable grimaces, collapses with curious capers. The revolution thus moves in a descending line. It finds itself in this state of retrogressive motion before the last February barricade has been cleared away and the first revolutionary authority constituted.

The period that we have before us comprises the most motley mixture of crying contradictions: constitutionalists who conspire openly against the Constitution; revolutionists who are confessedly constitutional; a National Assembly that wants to be omnipotent and always remains parliamentary; a *Montagne* that finds its vocation in patience and counters its present defeats by prophesying future victories; royalists who form the *patres conscripti*[10] of the republic and are forced by the situation to keep the hostile royal houses, to which they adhere, abroad, and the republic, which they hate, in France; an executive power that finds its strength in its very weakness and its respectability in the contempt that it calls forth; a republic that is nothing but the combined infamy of two monarchies, the Restoration and the July Monarchy, with an imperial label . . . the official collective genius of France brought to naught by the artful stupidity of a single individual; the collective will of the nation, as often as it speaks through universal suffrage, seeking its appropriate expression through the inveterate enemies of the interests of the masses, until at length it finds it in the self-will of a filibuster. If any section of history has been painted grey on grey, it is this. Men and events appear as inverted Schlemihls,[11] as shadows that have lost their bodies. The revolution itself paralyzes its own bearers and endows only its adversaries with passionate forcefulness. When the "red spectre," continually conjured up and exorcised by the counter-revolutionaries, finally appears, it appears not with the Phrygian cap of anarchy on its head, but in the uniform of order, in *red breeches*.

10 Senators.
11 Hero of a fairy tale by Adelbert von Chamisso (1781–1838).

We have seen that the ministry which Bonaparte installed on December 20, 1848, on his Ascension Day, was a ministry of the party of Order, of the Legitimist and Orleanist coalition. This Barrot-Falloux ministry had outlived the republican Constituent Assembly, whose term of life it had more or less violently cut short, and found itself still at the helm. Changarnier, the general of the allied royalists, continued to unite in his person the general command of the First Army Division and of the National Guard of Paris. Finally, the general elections had secured the party of Order a large majority in the National Assembly. Here the deputies and peers of Louis Philippe encountered a hallowed host of Legitimists, for whom many of the nation's ballots had become transformed into admission cards to the political stage. The Bonapartist representatives of the people were too sparse to be able to form an independent parliamentary party. They appeared merely as the *mauvaise queue* of the party of Order. Thus the party of Order was in possession of the governmental power, the army and the legislative body, in short, of the whole of the state power; it had been morally strengthened by the general elections, which made its rule appear as the will of the people, and by the simultaneous triumph of the counter-revolution on the whole continent of Europe.

Never did a party open its campaign with greater resources or under more favourable auspices.

The shipwrecked *pure republicans* found that they had melted down to a clique of about fifty men in the Legislative National Assembly, the African generals Cavaignac, Lamoricière and Bedeau at their head. The great opposition party, however, was formed by the *Montagne*. The *social-democratic* party had given itself this parliamentary baptismal name. It commanded more than two hundred of the seven hundred and fifty votes of the National Assembly and was consequently at least as powerful as any one of the three factions of the party of Order taken by itself. . . .

Before we pursue parliamentary history further, some remarks are necessary to avoid common misconceptions regarding the whole character of the epoch that lies before us. Looked at with the eyes of democrats, the period of the Legislative National Assembly is concerned with what the period of the Constituent Assembly was concerned with: the simple struggle between republicans and royalists. The movement itself, however, they sum up in the one shibboleth: *"reaction"*—night, in which all cats are grey and which permits them to reel off their night watchman's commonplaces. And, to be sure, at first sight the party of Order reveals a maze of different royalist factions, which not only intrigue against each other—each seeking to elevate its own pretender to the throne and exclude the pretender of the opposing faction—but also all unite in common hatred of, and common onslaughts on, the "republic." In opposition to this royalist conspiracy the *Montagne,* for its part, appears as the representative of the "republic." The party of Order appears to be perpetually engaged in a "reaction," directed against press, association and the like, neither more nor less than in Prussia, and which, as in Prussia, is carried out in the form of brutal police intervention by the bureaucracy, the *gendarmerie* and the law courts. The *"Montagne,"* for its part, is just as continually occupied in warding off these attacks and thus defending the "eternal rights of man" as every so-called people's party has done, more or less, for a century and a half. If one looks at the situation and the parties more closely, however, this superficial appearance, which veils the *class struggle* and the peculiar physiognomy of this period, disappears.

Legitimists and Orleanists, as we have said, formed the two great factions of the party of Order. Was that which held these factions fast to their pretenders and kept them apart from one another nothing but lily and tricolour, House of Bourbon and House of Orleans, different shades of royalism, was it at all the confession of faith of royalism? Under the Bourbons, *big landed property* had governed, with its priests and lackeys; under the Orleans, high finance, large-scale industry, large-scale trade, that is, *capital,* with its retinue of lawyers, professors and smooth-tongued orators. The Legitimate Monarchy was merely the political expression of the hereditary rule of the lords of the soil, as the July Monarchy was only the political expression of the usurped rule of the bourgeois *parvenus*. What kept the two factions apart, therefore, was not any so-called principles, it was their material conditions of existence, two different kinds of property, it was the old contrast between town and country, the rivalry between capital and landed property. That at the same time old memories, personal enmities, fears and hopes, prejudices and illusions, sympathies and antipathies, convictions, articles of faith and principles bound them to one or the other royal house, who is there that denies this? Upon the different forms of property, upon the social conditions of existence, rises an entire superstructure of distinct and peculiarly formed sentiments, illusions, modes of thought and views of life. The entire class creates and forms them out of its material foundations and out of the corresponding social relations. The single individual, who derives them through tradition and upbringing, may imagine that they form the real motives and the starting point of his activity. While Orleanists and Legitimists, while each faction sought to make itself and the other believe that it was loyalty to their two royal houses which separated them, facts later proved that it was rather their divided interests which forbade the uniting of the two royal houses. And as in private life one differentiates between what a man thinks and says of himself and what he really is and does, so in historical struggles one must distinguish still more the phrases and fancies of parties from their real organism and their real interests, their conception of themselves from their reality. Orleanists and Legitimists found themselves side by side in the republic, with equal claims. If each side wished to effect the *restoration* of its *own* royal house against the other, that merely signified that each of the *two great interests* into which the *bourgeoisie* is split—landed property and capital—sought to restore its own supremacy and the subordination of the other. We speak of two interests of the bourgeoisie, for large landed property, despite its feudal coquetry and pride of race, has been rendered thoroughly bourgeois by the develop-

ment of modern society. Thus the Tories in England long imagined that they were enthusiastic about monarchy, the church
and the beauties of the old English Constitution, until the day
of danger wrung from them the confession that they are enthusiastic only about *ground rent.*

The royalists in coalition carried on their intrigues against
one another in the press, in Ems, in Claremont, outside parliament. Behind the scenes they donned their old Orleanist and
Legitimist liveries again and once more engaged in their old
tourneys. But on the public stage, in their grand performances
of state, as a great parliamentary party, they put off their respective royal houses with mere obeisances and adjourn the restoration of the monarchy *in infinitum.* They do their real business as the *party of Order,* that is, under a *social,* not under a
political title; as representatives of the bourgeois world-order, not
as knights of errant princesses; as the bourgeois class against
other classes, not as royalists against the republicans. And as the
party of Order they exercised more unrestricted and sterner
domination over the other classes of society than ever previously
under the Restoration or under the July Monarchy, a domination which, in general, was only possible under the form of the
parliamentary republic, for only under this form could the two
great divisions of the French bourgeoisie unite, and thus put the
rule of their class instead of the regime of a privileged faction
of it on the order of the day. If, nevertheless, they, as the party
of Order, also insulted the republic and expressed their repugnance to it, this happened not merely from royalist memories.
Instinct taught them that the republic, true enough, makes their
political rule complete, but at the same time undermines its
social foundation, since they must now confront the subjugated
classes and contend against them without mediation, without
the concealment afforded by the crown, without being able to
divert the national interest by their subordinate struggles among
themselves and with the monarchy. It was a feeling of weakness that caused them to recoil from the pure conditions of their
own class rule and to yearn for the former more incomplete,

more undeveloped and precisely on that account less dangerous forms of this rule. On the other hand, every time the royalists in coalition come in conflict with the pretender that confronts them, with Bonaparte, every time they believe their parliamentary omnipotence endangered by the executive power, every time, therefore, that they must produce their political title to their rule, they come forward as *republicans* and not as *royalists*. . . .

As against the coalesced bourgeoisie, a coalition between petty bourgeois and workers had been formed, the so-called *social-democratic* party. . . . The peculiar character of the Social-Democracy is epitomized in the fact that democratic-republican institutions are demanded as a means, not of doing away with two extremes, capital and wage labour, but of weakening their antagonism and transforming it into harmony. However different the means proposed for the attainment of this end may be, however much it may be trimmed with more or less revolutionary notions, the content remains the same. This content is the transformation of society in a democratic way, but a transformation within the bounds of the petty bourgeoisie. Only one must not form the narrow-minded notion that the petty bourgeoisie, on principle, wishes to enforce an egoistic class interest. Rather, it believes that the *special* conditions of its emancipation are the *general* conditions within the frame of which alone modern society can be saved and the class struggle avoided. Just as little must one imagine that the democratic representatives are indeed all shopkeepers or enthusiastic champions of shopkeepers. According to their education and their individual position they may be as far apart as heaven from earth. What makes them representatives of the petty bourgeoisie is the fact that in their minds they do not get beyond the limits which the latter do not get beyond in life, that they are consequently driven, theoretically, to the same problems and solutions to which material interest and social position drive the latter practically. This is, in general, the relationship between the *political* and *literary representatives* of a class and the class they represent. . . .

Immediately, as soon as the National Assembly met, the party of Order provoked the *Montagne*. The bourgeoisie now felt the necessity of making an end of the democratic petty bourgeois, just as a year before it had realized the necessity of settling with the revolutionary proletariat. Only the situation of the adversary was different. The strength of the proletarian party lay in the streets, that of the petty bourgeois in the National Assembly itself. It was therefore a question of decoying them out of the National Assembly into the streets and causing them to smash their parliamentary power themselves, before time and circumstances could consolidate it. The *Montagne* rushed headlong into the trap.

The bombardment of Rome by the French troops was the bait that was thrown to it. It violated Article V of the Constitution which forbids the French republic to employ its military forces against the freedom of another people. In addition to this, Article 54 prohibited any declaration of war on the part of the executive power without the assent of the National Assembly, and by its resolution of May 8, the Constituent Assembly had disapproved of the Roman expedition. On these grounds Ledru-Rollin brought in a bill of impeachment against Bonaparte and his ministers on June 11, 1840. Exasperated by the wasp stings of Thiers, he actually let himself be carried away to the point of threatening that he would defend the Constitution by every means, even with arms in hand. The *Montagne* rose to a man and repeated this call to arms. On June 12, the National Assembly rejected the bill of impeachment, and the *Montagne* left the parliament. The events of June 13 are known: the proclamation issued by a section of the *Montagne*, declaring Bonaparte and his ministers "outside the Constitution"; the street procession of the democratic National Guards, who, unarmed as they were, dispersed on encountering the troops of Changarnier, etc., etc. A part of the *Montagne* fled abroad; another part was arraigned before the High Court at Bourges, and a parliamentary regulation subjected the remainder to the schoolmasterly surveillance of the President of the National Assembly. Paris was again declared in a state of siege and the democratic part of its National Guard dissolved. Thus the influence of the *Montagne* in parliament and the power of the petty bourgeois in Paris were broken. . . .

The bulk of the *Montagne* had left its vanguard in the lurch, having refused to subscribe to its proclamation. The press had deserted, only two journals having dared to publish the *pronunciamento*. The petty bourgeois betrayed their representatives, in that the National Guards either stayed away or, where they appeared, hindered the erection of barricades. The representatives had duped the petty bourgeois, in that the alleged allies from the army were nowhere to be seen. Finally, instead of gaining an accession of strength from it, the democratic party had infected the proletariat with its own weakness and, as is usual with the great deeds of democrats, the leaders had the satisfaction of being able to charge their "people" with desertion, and the people the satisfaction of being able to charge its leaders with humbugging it.

Seldom had an action been announced with more noise than the impending campaign of the *Montagne,* seldom had an event been trumpeted with greater certainty or longer in advance than the inevitable victory of the democracy. Most assuredly, the democrats believe in the trumpets before whose blasts the walls of Jericho fell down. And as often as they stand before the ramparts of despotism, they seek to imitate the miracle. If the *Montagne* wished to triumph in parliament, it should not have called to arms. If it called to arms in parliament, it should not have acted in parliamentary fashion in the streets. If the peaceful demonstration was meant seriously, then it was folly not to foresee that it would be given a warlike reception. If a real struggle was intended, then it was a queer idea to lay down the weapons with which it would have to be waged. But the revolutionary threats of the petty bourgeois and their democratic representatives are mere attempts to intimidate the antagonist. And when they have run into a blind alley, when they have sufficiently compromised themselves to make it necessary to give effect to their threats, then this is done in an ambiguous fashion that avoids nothing so much as the means to the end and tries to find excuses for succumbing. The blaring overture that announced the contest dies away in a pusillanimous snarl as soon as the struggle has to begin, the actors cease to take themselves *au sérieux*, and the action collapses completely, like a pricked bubble.

No party exaggerates its means more than the democratic, none deludes itself more light-mindedly over the situation. Since a section of the army had voted for it, the *Montagne* was now convinced that the army would revolt for it. And on what occasion? On an occasion which, from the standpoint of the troops, had no other meaning than that the revolutionists took the side of the Roman soldiers against the French soldiers. On the other hand, the recollections of June 1848 were still too fresh to allow of anything but a profound aversion on the part of the proletariat towards the National Guard and a thoroughgoing mistrust of the democratic chiefs on the part of the chiefs of the secret societies. To iron out these differences, it was necessary for great, common interests to be at stake. The violation of an abstract paragraph of the Constitution could not provide these interests. Had not the Constitution been repeatedly violated, according to the assurance of the democrats themselves? Had not the most popular journals branded it as counter-revolutionary botchwork? But the democrat, because he represents the petty bourgeoisie, that is, a *transition class,* in which the interests of two classes are simultaneously mutually blunted, imagines himself elevated above class antagonism generally. The democrats concede that a privileged class confronts them, but they, along with all the rest of the nation, form the *people*. What they represent is the *people's rights;* what interests them is the *people's interests*. Accordingly, when a struggle is impending, they do not need to examine the interests and positions of the different classes. They do not need to weigh their own resources too critically. They have merely to give the signal and the *people,* with all its inexhaustible resources, will fall upon the *oppres-*

sors. Now, if in the performance their interests prove to be un-interesting and their potency impotence, then either the fault lies with pernicious sophists, who split the *indivisible people* into different hostile camps, or the army was too brutalized and blinded to comprehend that the pure aims of democracy are the best thing for it itself, or the whole thing has been wrecked by a detail in its execution, or else an unforeseen accident has this time spoilt the game. In any case, the democrat comes out of the most disgraceful defeat just as immaculate as he was inno-cent when he went into it, with the newly-won conviction that he is bound to win, not that he himself and his party have to give up the old standpoint, but, on the contrary, that conditions have to ripen to suit him.

. . . The demonstration of June 13 was, above all, a demon-stration of the democratic National Guards. They had not, to be sure, borne their arms, but worn their uniforms against the army; precisely in this uniform, however, lay the talisman. The army convinced itself that this uniform was a piece of woollen cloth like any other. The spell was broken. In the June days of 1848, bourgeoisie and petty bourgeoisie had been united as the National Guard with the army against the proletariat; on June 13, 1849, the bourgeoisie let the petty-bourgeois National Guard be dispersed by the army; on December 2, 1851, the National Guard of the bourgeoisie itself had vanished, and Bonaparte merely registered this fact when he subsequently signed the decree for its disbandment. Thus the bourgeoisie had itself smashed its last weapon against the army, but it had to smash it the moment the petty bourgeoisie no longer stood behind it as a vassal, but before it as a rebel, as in general it was bound to destroy all its means of defence against absolutism with its own hand as soon as it had itself become absolute. . . .

IV

In the middle of October 1849, the National Assembly met once more. On November 1, Bonaparte surprised it with a message in which he announced the dismissal of the Barrot-Falloux ministry and the formation of a new ministry. No one has ever sacked lackeys with less ceremony than Bonaparte his ministers. The kicks that were intended for the National Assembly were given in the meantime to Barrot and Co. . . .

The Barrot-Falloux ministry was the first and last *parliamentary ministry* that Bonaparte brought into being. Its dismissal forms, accordingly, a decisive turning point. With it the party of Order lost, never to reconquer it, an indispensable post for the maintenance of the parliamentary regime, the lever of executive power. It is immediately obvious that in a country like France, where the executive power commands an army of officials numbering more than half a million individuals and therefore constantly maintains an immense mass of interests and livelihoods in the most absolute dependence; where the state enmeshes, controls, regulates, superintends and tutors civil society from its most comprehensive manifestations of life down to its most insignificant stirrings, from its most general modes of being to the private existence of individuals; where through the most extraordinary centralization this parasitic body acquires a ubiquity, an omniscience, a capacity for accelerated mobility and an elasticity which finds a counterpart only in the helpless dependence, in the loose shapelessness of the actual body politic —it is obvious that in such a country the National Assembly forfeits all real influence when it loses command of the ministerial posts, if it does not at the same time simplify the administration of the state, reduce the army of officials as far as possible and, finally, let civil society and public opinion create organs of their own, independent of the governmental power. But it is precisely with the maintenance of that extensive state machine in its numerous ramifications that the *material interests* of the French bourgeoisie are interwoven in the closest fashion. Here it finds posts for its surplus population and makes up in the form of state salaries for what it cannot pocket in the form of profit, interest, rents and honorariums. On the other hand, its *political interests* compelled it to increase daily the repressive measures and therefore the resources and the personnel of the state power, while at the same time it had to wage an uninterrupted war against public opinion and mistrustfully mutilate and cripple the independent organs of the social movement, where it did not succeed in amputating them entirely. Thus the French bourgeoisie was compelled by its class position to annihilate, on the one hand, the vital conditions of all parliamentary power, and therefore, likewise, of its own, and to render irresistible, on the other hand, the executive power hostile to it.

The new ministry was called the d'Hautpoul ministry. . . . The d'Hautpoul ministry contained only one man of parliamentary standing, the moneylender *Fould,* one of the most notorious of the high financiers. To his lot fell the ministry of finance. Look up the quotations on the Paris *bourse* and you will find that from November 1, 1849, onwards the French *fonds* rise and fall with the rise and fall of Bonapartist stocks. While Bonaparte had thus found his ally in the *bourse,* he at the same time took possession of the police by appointing Carlier[12] Police Prefect of Paris. . . .

I have not here to write the history of its legislative activity, which is summarized during this period in two laws: in the law re-establishing the *wine tax* and the *education law* abolishing unbelief. If wine drinking was made harder for the French, they were presented all the more plentifully with the water of true life. If in the law on the wine tax the bourgeoisie declared the old, hateful French tax system to be inviolable, it sought through the education law to ensure among the masses the old state of mind that put up with the tax system. One is astonished to see the Orleanists, the liberal bourgeois, these old apostles of Voltairianism and eclectic philosophy, entrust to their hereditary enemies, the Jesuits, the superintendence of the French mind. However, in regard to the pretenders to the throne, Orleanists and Legitimists could part company, they understood

[12] Achille Fould (1800–67), banker-politician who held ministerial posts under the Second Republic and the Second Empire. Pierre Carlier (1799–1858), Bonapartist and prefect of Paris police 1849–51.

that to secure their united rule necessitated the uniting of the means of repression of two epochs, that the means of subjugation of the July Monarchy had to be supplemented and strengthened by the means of subjugation of the Restoration.

The peasants, disappointed in all their hopes, crushed more than ever by the low level of grain prices on the one hand, and by the growing burden of taxes and mortgage debts on the other, began to bestir themselves in the Departments. They were answered by a drive against the schoolmasters, who were made subject to the clergy, by a drive against the *maires,* who were made subject to the prefects, and by a system of espionage, to which all were made subject. In Paris and the large towns reaction itself has the physiognomy of its epoch and challenges more than it strikes down. In the countryside it becomes dull, coarse, petty, tiresome and vexatious, in a word, the *gendarme.* One comprehends how three years of the regime of the *gendarme,* consecrated by the regime of the priest, were bound to demoralize immature masses.

Whatever amount of passion and declamation might be employed by the party of Order against the minority from the tribune of the National Assembly, its speech remained as monosyllabic as that of the Christians, whose words were to be: Yea, yea; nay, nay! As monosyllabic on the platform as in the press. Flat as a riddle whose answer is known in advance. Whether it was a question of the right of petition or the tax on wine, freedom of the press or free trade, the clubs or the municipal charter, protection of personal liberty or regulation of the state budget, the watchword constantly recurs, the theme remains always the same, the verdict is ever ready and invariably reads: *"Socialism!"* Even bourgeois liberalism is declared *socialistic,* bourgeois enlightenment socialistic, bourgeois financial reform socialistic. It was socialistic to build a railway, where a canal already existed, and it was socialistic to defend oneself with a cane when one was attacked with a rapier.

This was not merely a figure of speech, fashion or party tactics. The bourgeoisie had a true insight into the fact that all the weapons which it had forged against feudalism turned their points against itself, that all the means of education which it had produced rebelled against its own civilization, that all the gods which it had created had fallen away from it. It understood that all the so-called bourgeois liberties and organs of progress attacked and menaced its *class rule* at its social foundation and its political summit simultaneously, and had therefore become "*socialistic.*" In this menace and this attack it rightly discerned the secret of Socialism, whose import and tendency it judges more correctly than so-called Socialism knows how to judge itself; the latter can, accordingly, not comprehend why the bourgeoisie callously hardens its heart against it, whether it sentimentally bewails the sufferings of mankind, or in Christian spirit prophesies the millennium and universal brotherly love, or in humanistic style twaddles about mind, education and freedom, or in doctrinaire fashion excogitates a system for the conciliation and welfare of all classes. What the bourgeoisie did not grasp, however, was the logical conclusion that its *own parliamentary regime,* that its *political rule* in general, was now also bound to meet with the general verdict of condemnation as being *socialistic.* As long as the rule of the bourgeois class had not been organized completely, as long as it had not acquired its pure political expression, the antagonism of the other classes, likewise, could not appear in its pure form, and where it did appear could not take the dangerous turn that transforms every struggle against the state power into a struggle against capital. If in every stirring of life in society it saw "tranquillity" imperilled, how could it want to maintain at the head of society a *regime of unrest,* its own regime, the *parliamentary regime,* this regime that, according to the expression of one of its spokesmen, lives in struggle and by struggle? The parliamentary regime lives by discussion; how shall it forbid discussion? Every interest, every social institution, is here transformed into general ideas, debated as ideas; how shall any interest, any institution, sustain itself above thought and impose itself as an article of faith? The struggle of the orators on the platform evokes the struggle of the scribblers of the press; the debating club in parliament is necessarily supplemented by debating clubs in the salons and the pothouses; the representatives, who constantly appeal to public opinion, give public opinion the right to speak its real mind in petitions. The parliamentary regime leaves everything to the decision of majorities; how shall the great majorities outside parliament not want to decide? When you play the fiddle at the top of the state, what else is to be expected but that those down below dance?

Thus, by now stigmatizing as *"socialistic"* what it had previously extolled as *"liberal,"* the bourgeoisie confesses that its own interests dictate that it should be delivered from the danger of its *own rule;* that, in order to restore tranquillity in the country, its bourgeois parliament must, first of all, be given its quietus; that in order to preserve its social power intact, its political power must be broken; that the private bourgeois can continue to exploit the other classes and to enjoy undisturbed property, family, religion and order only on condition that their class be condemned along with the other classes to like political nullity; that in order to save its purse, it must forfeit the crown, and the sword that is to safeguard it must at the same time be hung over its own head as a sword of Damocles. . . .

The parliamentary majority understood the weakness of its antagonist. Its seventeen burgraves[13]—for Bonaparte had left to it the direction of and responsibility for the attack—drew up a new electoral law, the introduction of which was entrusted to M. Faucher,[14] who solicited this honour for himself. On May 8 he introduced the law by which universal suffrage was to be abolished, a residence of three years in the locality of the election to be imposed as a condition on the electors and, finally,

[13] Nickname derived from the Hugo drama of the same name, given to the leading monarchists who prepared the May 31 electoral law.

[14] Léon Faucher (1804–54), Orleanist who became a Bonapartist, Minister of the Interior during the Second Republic.

the proof of this residence made dependent in the case of workers on a certificate from their employers.

On May 31, the new electoral law went through. The *Montagne* contented itself with smuggling a protest into the pocket of the President. The electoral law was followed by a new press law, by which the revolutionary newspaper press was entirely suppressed. It had deserved its fate. The *National* and *la Presse*, two bourgeois organs, were left behind after this deluge as the most advanced outposts of the revolution.

. . . 1850 was one of the most splendid years of industrial and commercial prosperity, and the Paris proletariat was therefore fully employed. But the election law of May 31, 1850, excluded it from any participation in political power. It cut it off from the very arena of the struggle. It threw the workers back into the position of pariahs which they had occupied before the February Revolution. By letting themselves be led by the democrats in face of such an event and forgetting the revolutionary interests of their class for momentary ease and comfort, they renounced the honour of being a conquering power, surrendered to their fate, proved that the defeat of June 1848 had put them out of the fight for years and that the historical process would for the present again have to go on *over* their heads. . . .

The law of May 31, 1850, was the *coup d'état* of the bourgeoisie. All its conquests over the revolution hitherto had only a provisional character. They were endangered as soon as the existing National Assembly retired from the stage. They depended on the hazards of a new general election, and the history of elections since 1848 irrefutably proved that the bourgeoisie's moral sway over the mass of the people was lost in the same measure as its actual domination developed. On March 10,[15] universal suffrage declared itself directly against the domination of the bourgeoisie; the bourgeoisie answered by outlawing uni-

[15] By-elections of March 10, 1850, when Paris returned only Social-Democrats.

versal suffrage. The law of May 31 was, therefore, one of the necessities of the class struggle. On the other hand, the Constitution required a minimum of two million votes to make an election of the President of the republic valid. If none of the candidates for the presidency received this minimum, the National Assembly was to choose the President from among the three candidates to whom the largest number of votes would fall. At the time when the Constituent Assembly made this law, ten million electors were registered on the rolls of voters. In its view, therefore, a fifth of the people entitled to vote was sufficient to make the presidential election valid. The law of May 31 struck at least three million votes off the electoral rolls, reduced the number of people entitled to vote to seven million and, nevertheless, retained the legal minimum of two million for the presidential election. It therefore raised the legal minimum from a fifth to nearly a third of the effective votes, that is, it did everything to smuggle the election of the President out of the hands of the people and into the hands of the National Assembly. Thus through the electoral law of May 31 the party of Order seemed to have made its rule doubly secure, by surrendering the election of the National Assembly and that of the President of the republic to the stationary section of society.

V

. . . When the National Assembly met once more in November 1850, it seemed that, instead of the petty skirmishes it had hitherto had with the President, a great and ruthless struggle, a life-and-death struggle between the two powers, had become inevitable.

As in 1849 so during this year's parliamentary recess, the party of Order had broken up into its separate factions, each occupied with its own Restoration intrigues, which had obtained fresh nutriment through the death of Louis Philippe. The Legitimist king, Henry V, had even nominated a formal ministry which resided in Paris and in which members of the Permanent Commission held seats. Bonaparte, in his turn, was therefore entitled to make tours of the French Departments, and according to the disposition of the town that he favoured with his presence, now more or less covertly, now more or less overtly, to divulge his own restoration plans and canvass votes for himself. On these processions, which the great official *Moniteur* and the little private *Moniteurs* of Bonaparte naturally had to celebrate as triumphal processions, he was constantly accompanied by persons affiliated with the *Society of December 10*. This society dates from the year 1849. On the pretext of founding a benevolent society, the *lumpenproletariat* of Paris had been organized into secret sections, each section being led by Bonapartist agents, with a Bonapartist general at the head of the whole. Alongside decayed *roués* with dubious means of subsistence and of dubious origin, alongside ruined and adventurous offshoots of the bourgeoisie, were vagabonds, discharged soldiers, discharged jailbirds, escaped galley slaves, swindlers, mountebanks, *lazzaroni*, pickpockets, tricksters, gamblers, *maquereaus*,[16] brothel keepers, porters, *literati*, organ-grinders, ragpickers, knife grinders, tinkers, beggars—in short, the whole indefinite, disintegrated mass, thrown hither and thither, which the French term *la bohème*; from this kindred element Bonaparte formed the core of the Society of December 10. A "benevolent society"—in so far as, like Bonaparte, all its members felt the need of benefiting themselves at the expense of the labouring nation. This Bonaparte, who constitutes himself *chief of the lumpenproletariat*, who here alone rediscovers in mass form the interests which he personally pursues, who recognizes in this scum, offal, refuse of all classes the only class upon which he can base himself unconditionally, he is the real Bonaparte. . . . What the national *ateliers* were for the socialist workers, what the *Gardes mobiles* were for the bourgeois

16 Procurers.

174

republicans, the Society of December 10, the party fighting force characteristic of Bonaparte, was for him. . . .

The Society of December 10 was to remain the private army of Bonaparte until he succeeded in transforming the public army into a Society of December 10. Bonaparte made the first attempt at this shortly after the adjournment of the National Assembly, and precisely with the money just wrested from it. As a fatalist, he lives in the conviction that there are certain higher powers which man, and the soldier in particular, cannot withstand. Among these powers he counts, first and foremost, cigars and champagne, cold poultry and garlic sausage. Accordingly, to begin with, he treats officers and noncommissioned officers in his Élysée apartments to cigars and champagne, to cold poultry and garlic sausage. On October 3 he repeats this maneuvre with the mass of the troops at the St. Maur review, and on October 10 the same maneuvre on a still larger scale at the Satory army parade. . . .

Bonaparte, who precisely because he was a Bohemian, a princely *lumpenproletarian,* had the advantage over a rascally bourgeois in that he could conduct the struggle meanly, now saw . . . that the moment had come when he could pass from an apparent defensive to the offensive. The minor defeats meanwhile sustained by the Minister of Justice, the Minister of War, the Minister of the Navy and the Minister of Finance, through which the National Assembly signified its snarling displeasure, troubled him little. He not only prevented the ministers from resigning and thus recognizing the sovereignty of parliament over the executive power, but could now consummate what he had begun during the recess of the National Assembly: the severance of the military power from parliament, the *removal of Changarnier.*

. . . The dismissal of Changarnier and the falling of the military power into Bonaparte's hands closes the first part of the period we are considering, the period of struggle between the party of Order and the executive power. War between the two powers has now been openly declared, is openly waged, but only after the party of Order has lost both arms and soldiers. . . .

VI

The coalition with the *Montagne* and the pure republicans, to which the party of Order saw itself condemned in its unavailing efforts to maintain possession of the military power and to reconquer supreme control of the executive power, proved incontrovertibly that it had forfeited its independent *parliamentary majority*. On May 28, the mere power of the calendar, of the hour hand of the clock, gave the signal for its complete disintegration. With May 28, the last year of the life of the National Assembly began. It had now to decide for continuing the Constitution unaltered or for revising it. But revision of the Constitution, that implied not only rule of the bourgeoisie or of the petty-bourgeois democracy, democracy or proletarian anarchy, parliamentary republic or Bonaparte, it implied at the same time Orleans or Bourbon! Thus fell in the midst of parliament the apple of discord that was bound to inflame openly the conflict of interests which split the party of Order into hostile factions. The party of Order was a combination of heterogeneous social substances. The question of revision generated a political temperature at which the product again decomposed into its original constituents.

The interest of the Bonapartists in a revision was simple. For them it was above all a question of abolishing Article 45, which forbade Bonaparte's re-election and the prorogation of his authority. No less simple appeared the position of the republicans. They unconditionally rejected any revision; they saw in it a universal conspiracy against the republic. Since they commanded *more than a quarter of the votes* in the National Assembly and, according to the Constitution, three-quarters of the votes were required for a resolution for revision to be legally valid and for the convocation of a revising Assembly, they only needed to count their votes to be sure of victory. And they were sure of victory.

As against these clear positions, the party of Order found itself caught in inextricable contradictions. If it should reject revision, it would imperil the *status quo*, since it would leave Bonaparte only one way out, that of force, and since on the second Sunday in May 1852, at the decisive moment, it would be surrendering France to revolutionary anarchy, with a President who had lost his authority, with a parliament which for a long time had not possessed it and with a people that meant to reconquer it. If it voted for constitutional revision, it knew that it voted in vain and would be bound to fail constitutionally because of the veto of the republicans. If it unconstitutionally declared a simple majority vote to be binding, then it could hope to dominate the revolution only if it subordinated itself unconditionally to the sovereignty of the executive power, then it would make Bonaparte master of the Constitution, of its revision and of itself. An only partial revision which would prolong the authority of the President would pave the way for imperial usurpation. A general revision which would shorten the existence of the republic would bring the dynastic claims into unavoidable conflict, for the conditions of a Bourbon and the conditions of an Orleanist Restoration were not only different, they were mutually exclusive. . . .

A revision of the Constitution—and circumstances compelled taking it into consideration—called in question, along with the republic, the common rule of the two bourgeois factions, and revived, with the possibility of a monarchy, the rivalry of the interests which it had predominantly represented by turns, the struggle for the supremacy of one faction over the other. The diplomats of the party of Order believed they could settle the struggle by an amalgamation of the two dynasties, by a so-called *fusion* of the royalist parties and their royal houses. The real fusion of the Restoration and the July Monarchy was the parliamentary republic, in which Orleanist and Legitimist colours were obliterated and the various species of bourgeois disappeared in the bourgeois as such, in the bourgeois genus. Now, however, Orleanist was to become Legitimist and Legitimist Orleanist. Royalty, in which their antagonism was personified, was to embody their unity; the expression of their exclusive factional interests was to become the expression of their common class interest; the monarchy was to do that which only the abolition of two monarchies, the republic, could do and had done. . . .

That part of the party of Order which was eager for revision, but was divided again on the limits to revision, a section composed of the Legitimists led by Berryer and Falloux, on the one hand, and by La Rochejaquelein,[17] on the other, and of the conflict-weary Orleanists led by Molé, Broglie, Montalembert and Odilon Barrot, agreed with the Bonapartist representatives on the following indefinite and broadly framed motion: "With the object of restoring to the nation the full exercise of its sovereignty, the undersigned Representatives move that the Constitution be revised." At the same time, however, they unanimously declared through their reporter Tocqueville that the National Assembly had not the right to move the *abolition of the republic*, that this right was vested solely in the Revising Chamber. For the rest, the Constitution might be revised only in a *"legal" manner*, hence only if the constitutionally prescribed three-quarters of the number of votes were cast in favour of revision. On July 19, after six days of stormy debate, revision

---

[17] Pierre Antoine Berryer (1790–1868), Legitimist deputy during the Second Republic. Comte Alfred de Falloux (1811–86), ardent Catholic Legitimist, as Minister of Education was responsible for the famed Falloux Law extending clerical control of schools. Henri Auguste Georges Du Vergier, Marquis de La Rochejaquelein (1805–67), a leader of the Legitimist party. Count Louis Mathieu Molé (1781–1855), an Orleanist, leading minister under the July Monarchy, a leader of the Orleanists during the Second Republic. Achille Charles Léonce Victor, Duke de Broglie (1785–1870), Orleanist deputy during the Second Republic, former first minister under Louis Philippe. Charles Forbes, Comte de Montalembert, see above p. 14, note 13.

was rejected, as was to be anticipated. Four hundred and forty-six votes were cast for it, but two hundred and seventy-eight against. The extreme Orleanists, Thiers, Changarnier, etc., voted with the republicans and the *Montagne*.

Thus the majority of parliament declared against the Constitution, but this Constitution itself declared for the minority and that its vote was binding. But had not the party of Order subordinated the Constitution to the parliamentary majority on May 31, 1850, and on June 13, 1849? Up to now, was not its whole policy based on the subordination of the paragraphs of the Constitution to the decisions of the parliamentary majority? Had it not left to the democrats the superstitious belief of the Old Testament in the letter of the law, and castigated the democrats for it? At the present moment, however, revision of the Constitution meant nothing but continuation of the presidential authority, just as continuation of the Constitution meant nothing but Bonaparte's deposition. Parliament had declared for him, but the Constitution declared against parliament. He therefore acted in the sense of parliament when he tore up the Constitution, and he acted in the sense of the Constitution when he dispersed parliament. . . .

I have already indicated above that since Fould's entry into the ministry the section of the commercial bourgeoisie which had held the lion's share of power under Louis Philippe, namely, the *aristocracy of finance*, had become Bonapartist. Fould represented not only Bonaparte's interests in the *bourse*, he represented at the same time the interests of the *bourse* before Bonaparte. . . .

In its issue of November 29, 1851, *The Economist* declares in its own name: *"The President is the guardian of order, and is now recognized as such on every Stock Exchange of Europe."* The aristocracy of finance, therefore, condemned the parliamentary struggle of the party of Order with the executive power as a *disturbance of order*, and celebrated every victory of the President over its ostensible representatives as a *victory of order*. By the aristocracy of finance must here be understood not merely the great loan promoters and speculators in public funds, in regard to whom it is immediately obvious that their interests coincide with the interests of the state power. All modern finance, the whole of the banking business, is interwoven in the closest fashion with public credit. A part of their business capital is necessarily invested and put out at interest in quickly convertible public funds. Their deposits, the capital placed at their disposal and distributed by them among merchants and industrialists, is partly derived from the dividends of holders of government securities. If in every epoch the stability of the state power signified Moses and the prophets to the entire money market and to the priests of this money market, why not all the more so today, when every deluge threatens to sweep away the old states, and the old state debts with them?

The *industrial bourgeoisie,* too, in its fanaticism for order, was angered by the squabbles of the parliamentary party of Order with the executive power. . . .

With barely an exception, the bourgeois dignitaries of the Departmental towns, the municipal authorities, the judges of the Commercial Courts, etc., everywhere received Bonaparte on his tours in the most servile manner, even when, as in Dijon, he made an unrestrained attack on the National Assembly, and especially on the party of Order.

When trade was good, as it still was at the beginning of 1851, the commercial bourgeoisie raged against any parliamentary struggle, lest trade be put out of humour. When trade was bad, as it continually was from the end of February 1851, the commercial bourgeoisie accused the parliamentary struggles of being the cause of stagnation and cried out for them to stop in order that trade might start again. The revision debates came on just in this bad period. Since the question here was whether the existing form of state was to be or not to be, the bourgeoisie felt itself all the more justified in demanding from its Representatives the ending of this torturous provisional arrangement and at the same time the maintenance of the *status quo.* There was no contradiction in this. By the end of the provisional arrangement it understood precisely its continuation, the postponement to a distant future of the moment when a decision had to be reached. The *status quo* could be maintained in only two ways: prolongation of Bonaparte's authority or his constitutional retirement and the election of Cavaignac. A section of the bourgeoisie desired the latter solution and knew no better advice to give its Representatives than to keep silent and leave the burning question untouched. They were of the opinion that if their Representatives did not speak, Bonaparte would not act. They wanted an ostrich parliament that would hide its head in order to remain unseen. Another section of the bourgeoisie desired, because Bonaparte was already in the presidential chair, to leave him sitting in it, so that everything might remain in the same old rut. They were indignant because their parliament did not openly infringe the Constitution and abdicate without ceremony.

The General Councils of the Departments, those provincial representative bodies of the big bourgeoisie, which met from August 25 on during the recess of the National Assembly, declared almost unanimously for revision, and thus against parliament and in favour of Bonaparte.

Still more unequivocally than in its falling out with its *parliamentary representatives* the bourgeoisie displayed its wrath against its literary representatives, its own press. The sentences to ruinous fines and shameless terms of imprisonment, on the verdicts of bourgeois juries, for every attack of bourgeois journalists on Bonaparte's usurpationist desires, for every attempt of the press to defend the political rights of the bourgeoisie against the executive power, astonished not merely France, but all Europe.

While the *parliamentary party of Order*, by its clamour for tranquillity, as I have shown, committed itself to quiescence, while it declared the political rule of the bourgeoisie to be incompatible with the safety and existence of the bourgeoisie, by destroying with its own hands in the struggle against the other classes of society all the conditions for its own regime, the parliamentary regime, the *extra-parliamentary mass of the bourgeoisie*, on the other hand, by its servility towards the President, by its vilification of parliament, by its brutal maltreatment of its own press, invited Bonaparte to suppress and annihilate its speaking and writing section, its politicians and its *literati*, its platform and its press, in order that it might then be able to pursue its private affairs with full confidence in the protection of a strong and unrestricted government. It declared unequivocally that it longed to get rid of its own political rule in order to get rid of the troubles and dangers of ruling.

And this mass, which had already rebelled against the purely parliamentary and literary struggle for the rule of its own class and betrayed the leaders of this struggle, now dares after the event to indict the proletariat for not having risen in a bloody struggle, a life-and-death struggle on its behalf! This mass, which every moment sacrificed its general class interests, that is, its political interests, to the narrowest and most sordid private interests, and demanded a similar sacrifice from its Representatives, now moans that the proletariat has sacrificed its [that mass's] ideal political interests to its [the proletariat's] material interests. It poses as a lovely being that has been misunderstood and deserted in the decisive hour by the proletariat misled by Socialists. . . .

In the year 1851, France, to be sure, had passed through a kind of minor trade crisis. The end of February showed a decline in exports compared with 1850; in March trade suffered and factories closed down; in April the position of the industrial Departments appeared as desperate as after the February days; in May business had still not revived; as late as June 28 the holdings of the Bank of France showed, by the enormous growth of deposits and the equally great decrease in advances on bills of exchange, that production was at a standstill, and it was not until the middle of October that a progressive improvement of business again set in. The French bourgeoisie attributed this trade stagnation to purely political causes, to the struggle between parliament and the executive power, to the precariousness of a merely provisional form of state, to the terrifying prospect of the second Sunday in May 1852. I will not deny that all these circumstances had a depressing effect on some branches of industry in Paris and the Departments. But in any case this influence of the political conditions was only local and inconsiderable. Does this require further proof than the fact that the improvement of trade set in towards the middle of October, at the very moment when the political situation grew worse, the political horizon darkened and a thunderbolt from Elysium was expected at any moment? For the rest, the French bourgeois, whose "skill, knowledge, spiritual insight and intellectual resources" reach no further than his nose, could throughout the period of the Industrial Exhibition in London have found the cause of his commercial misery right under his nose. While in France factories were closed down, in England commercial bankruptcies broke out. While in April and May the industrial panic reached a climax in France, in April and May the commercial panic reached a climax in England. Like the French woollen industry, so the English woollen industry suffered, and as French silk manufacture, so did English silk manufacture. True, the English cotton mills continued working, but no longer at the same profits as in 1849 and 1850. The only difference was that the crisis in France was industrial, in England commercial; that while in France the factories stood idle, in England they extended operations, but under less favourable conditions than in preceding years; that in France it was exports, in England imports which were hardest hit. The common cause, which is naturally not to be sought within the bounds of the French political horizon, was obvious. The years 1849 and 1850 were years of the greatest material prosperity and of an overproduction that appeared as such only in 1851. At the beginning of this year it was given a further special impetus by the prospect of the Industrial Exhibition. In addition there were the following special circumstances: first, the partial failure of the cotton crop in 1850 and 1851, then the certainty of a bigger cotton crop than had been expected; first the rise, then the sudden fall, in short, the fluctuations in the price of cotton. The crop of raw silk, in France at least, had turned out to be even below the average yield. Woollen manufacture, finally, had expanded so much since 1848 that the production of wool could not keep pace with it and the price of raw wool rose out of all proportion to the price of woollen manufactures. Here, then, in the raw material of three industries for the world market, we have already threefold material for a stagnation in trade. Apart from these special circumstances, the apparent crisis of 1851 was nothing else but the halt which overproduction and overspeculation invariably make in describing the industrial cycle, before they summon all their strength in order to rush feverishly through the final phase of this cycle and arrive once more at their starting point, the *general trade crisis*. During such intervals in the history of trade commercial bankruptcies break out in England, while in France industry itself is reduced to idleness, being partly forced into retreat by the competition, just then becoming intolerable, of the English in all markets, and being partly singled out for attack as a luxury industry by every business stagnation. Thus, besides the general crises, France goes through national trade crises of her own, which are nevertheless determined and conditioned far more by the general state of the world market than by French local influences. . . .

Now picture to yourself the French bourgeois, how in the throes of this business panic his trade-sick brain is tortured, set in a whirl and stunned by rumours of *coups d'état* and the restoration of universal suffrage, by the struggle between parliament and the executive power, by the Fronde[18] war between Orleanists and Legitimists, by the communist conspiracies in the south of France, by alleged *Jacqueries* in the Departments of Nièvre and Cher, by the advertisements of the different candidates for the presidency, by the cheapjack slogans of the journals, by the threats of the republicans to uphold the Constitution and universal suffrage by force of arms, by the gospel-preaching émigré heroes *in partibus*, who announced that the world would come to an end on the second Sunday in May

[18] A reference to the seventeenth-century aristocratic opposition to the French Crown which produced civil war.

1852—think of all this and you will comprehend why in this unspeakable, uproarious confusion of fusion, revision, prorogation, constitution, conspiration, coalition, emigration, usurpation and revolution, the bourgeois madly snorts at his parliamentary republic: *"Rather an end with terror than terror without end!"*

Bonaparte understood this cry. His power of comprehension was sharpened by the growing turbulence of creditors who, with each sunset which brought settling day, the second Sunday in May 1852, nearer, saw a movement of the stars protesting their earthly bills of exchange. They had become veritable astrologers. The National Assembly had blighted Bonaparte's hopes of a constitutional prorogation of his authority; the candidature of the Prince of Joinville[19] forbade further vacillation.

If ever an event has, well in advance of its coming, cast its shadow before, it was Bonaparte's *coup d'état.* As early as January 29, 1849, barely a month after his election, he had made a proposal about it to Changarnier. In the summer of 1849 his own Prime Minister, Odilon Barrot, had covertly denounced the policy of *coups d'état;* in the winter of 1850 Thiers had openly done so. In May 1851, Persigny had sought once more to win Changarnier for the *coup;* the *Messager de l'Assemblée* had published an account of these negotiations. During every parliamentary storm, the Bonapartist journals threatened a *coup d'état,* and the nearer the crisis drew, the louder grew their tone. In the orgies that Bonaparte kept up every night with men and women of the "swell mob," as soon as the hour of midnight approached and copious potations had loosened tongues and fired imaginations, the *coup d'état* was fixed for the following morning. Swords were drawn, glasses clinked, the Representatives were thrown out of the window, the imperial mantle fell upon Bonaparte's shoulders, until the following morning banished the spook once more and astonished Paris learned, from vestals of little reticence and from indiscreet paladins, of the danger it had once again escaped. During the months of Sep-

[19] Prince of Joinville (1818–1900), son of Louis Philippe.

tember and October rumours of a *coup d'état* followed fast one after the other. Simultaneously, the shadow took on colour, like a variegated daguerreotype. Look up the September and October copies of the organs of the European daily press and you will find, word for word, intimations like the following: "Paris is full of rumours of a *coup d'état*. The capital is to be filled with troops during the night, and the next morning is to bring decrees which will dissolve the National Assembly, declare the Department of the Seine in a state of siege, restore universal suffrage and appeal to the people. Bonaparte is said to be seeking ministers for the execution of these illegal decrees." The letters that bring these tidings always end with the fateful word "*postponed*." The *coup d'état* was ever the fixed idea of Bonaparte. With this idea he had again set foot on French soil. He was so obsessed by it that he continually betrayed it and blurted it out. He was so weak that, just as continually, he gave it up again. The shadow of the *coup d'état* had become so familiar to the Parisians as a spectre that they were not willing to believe in it when it finally appeared in the flesh. What allowed the *coup d'état* to succeed was, therefore, neither the reticent reserve of the chief of the Society of December 10 nor the fact that the National Assembly was caught unawares. If it succeeded, it succeeded despite *his* indiscretion and with *its* foreknowledge, a necessary, inevitable result of antecedent developments. . . .

On the very first day of its re-opening, the National Assembly received the message from Bonaparte in which he demanded the restoration of universal suffrage and the abolition of the law of May 31, 1850. The same day his ministers introduced a decree to this effect. The National Assembly at once rejected the ministry's motion of urgency and rejected the law itself on November 13 by three hundred and fifty-five votes to three hundred and forty-eight. Thus, it tore up its mandate once more; it once more confirmed the fact that it had transformed itself from the freely elected representatives of the people into the usurpatory parliament of a class; it acknowledged once more that it had itself cut in two the muscles which connected the parliamentary head with the body of the nation.

If by its motion to restore universal suffrage the executive power appealed from the National Assembly to the people, the legislative power appealed by its Questors' Bill from the people to the army. This Questors' Bill was to establish its right of directly requisitioning troops, of forming a parliamentary army. While it thus designated the army as the arbitrator between itself and the people, between itself and Bonaparte, while it recognized the army as the decisive state power, it had to confirm, on the other hand, the fact that it had long given up its claim to dominate this power. By debating its right to requisition troops, instead of requisitioning them at once, it betrayed its doubts about its own powers. By rejecting the Questors' Bill, it made public confession of its impotence. This bill was defeated, its proponents lacking 108 votes of a majority. . . .

Cromwell, when he dissolved the Long Parliament, went alone into its midst, drew out his watch in order that it should not continue to exist a minute after the time limit fixed by him, and drove out each one of the members of parliament with hilariously humourous taunts. Napoleon, smaller than his prototype, at least betook himself on the eighteenth Brumaire to the legislative body and read out to it, though in a faltering voice, its sentence of death. The second Bonaparte, who, moreover, found himself in possession of an executive power very different from that of Cromwell or Napoleon, sought his model not in the annals of world history, but in the annals of the Society of December 10, in the annals of the criminal courts. He robs the Bank of France of twenty-five million francs, buys General Magnan with a million, the soldiers with fifteen francs apiece and liquor, comes together with his accomplices secretly like a thief in the night, has the houses of the most dangerous parliamentary leaders broken into and Cavaignac, Lamoricière, Le Flô, Changarnier, Charras, Thiers, Baze, etc., dragged from their beds, the chief squares of Paris and the parliamentary building occupied by troops, and cheapjack placards posted early in the morning on all the walls, proclaiming the dissolution of the National Assembly and the Council of State, the restoration of universal suffrage and the placing of the Seine Department in a state of siege. In like manner, he inserted a little later in the *Moniteur* a false document which asserted that influential parliamentarians had grouped themselves round him and formed a state *consulta*.

The rump parliament, assembled in the *mairie* building of the tenth *arrondissement* and consisting mainly of Legitimists and Orleanists, votes the deposition of Bonaparte amid repeated cries of "Long live the Republic," unavailingly harangues the gaping crowds before the building and is finally led off in the custody of African sharpshooters, first to the d'Orsay barracks, and later packed into prison vans and transported to the prisons of Mazas, Ham and Vincennes. Thus ended the party of Order, the Legislative Assembly and the February Revolution. Before hastening to close, let us briefly summarize its history:

I. *First Period.* From February 24 to May 4, 1848. February period. Prologue. Universal brotherhood swindle.

II. *Second Period.* Period of constituting the republic and of the Constituent National Assembly.

1. May 4 to June 25, 1848. Struggle of all classes against the proletariat. Defeat of the proletariat in the June days.

2. June 25 to December 10, 1848. Dictatorship of the pure bourgeois-republicans. Drafting of the Constitution. Proclamation of a state of siege in Paris. The bourgeois dictatorship set aside on December 10 by the election of Bonaparte as President.

3. December 20, 1848 to May 28, 1849. Struggle of the Constituent Assembly with Bonaparte and with the party of Order in alliance with him. Passing of the Constituent Assembly. Fall of the republican bourgeoisie.

III. *Third Period.* Period of the *constitutional republic* and of the *Legislative National Assembly*.

1. May 28, 1849 to June 13, 1849. Struggle of the petty bourgeoisie with the bourgeoisie and with Bonaparte. Defeat of the petty-bourgeois democracy.

2. June 13, 1849 to May 31, 1850. Parliamentary dictatorship of the party of Order. It completes its rule by abolishing universal suffrage, but loses the parliamentary ministry.

3. May 31, 1850 to December 2, 1851. Struggle between the parliamentary bourgeoisie and Bonaparte.

(a) May 31, 1850 to January 12, 1851. Parliament loses the supreme command of the army.

(b) January 12 to April 11, 1851. It is worsted in its attempts to regain the administrative power. The party of Order loses its independent parliamentary majority. Its coalition with the republicans and the *Montagne*.

(c) April 11, 1851 to October 9, 1851. Attempts at revision, fusion, prorogation. The party of Order decomposes into its separate constituents. The breach between the bourgeois parliament and press and the mass of the bourgeoisie becomes definite.

(d) October 9 to December 2, 1851. Open breach between parliament and the executive power. Parliament performs its dying act and succumbs, left in the lurch by its own class, by the army and by all the remaining classes. Passing of the parliamentary regime and of bourgeois rule. Victory of Bonaparte. Parody of restoration of empire.

VII

On the threshold of the February Revolution, the *social republic* appeared as a phrase, as a prophecy. In the June days of 1848, it was drowned in the blood of the *Paris proletariat*, but it haunts the subsequent acts of the drama like a ghost. The *democratic republic* announces its arrival. On June 13, 1849, it is dissipated together with its *petty bourgeois*, who have taken to their heels, but in its flight it blows its own trumpet with redoubled boastfulness. The *parliamentary republic*, together with the bourgeoisie, takes possession of the entire stage; it enjoys its existence to the full, but December 2, 1851, buries it to the accompaniment of the anguished cry of the royalists in coalition: "Long live the Republic!"[20]

The French bourgeoisie balked at the domination of the working proletariat; it has brought the *lumpenproletariat* to domination, with the chief of the Society of December 10 at the head. The bourgeoisie kept France in breathless fear of the future terrors of red anarchy; Bonaparte discounted this future for it when, on December 4, he had the eminent bourgeois of the Boulevard Montmartre and the Boulevard des Italiens shot down at their windows by the liquor-inspired army of order. It apotheosized the sword; the sword rules it. It destroyed the revolutionary press; its own press has been destroyed. It placed popular meetings under police supervision; its salons are under the supervision of the police. It disbanded the democratic National Guards; its own National Guard is disbanded. It imposed a state of siege; a state of siege is imposed upon it. It supplanted the juries by military commissions; its juries are supplanted by military commissions. It subjected public education to the sway of the priests; the priests subject it to their own education. It transported people without trial; it is being transported without trial. It repressed every stirring in society by means of the state power; every stirring in its society is suppressed by means of the state power. Out of enthusiasm for its purse, it rebelled against its own politicians and men of letters; its politicians and men of letters are swept aside, but its purse is being plundered now that its mouth has been gagged and its pen broken. . . .[21]

[20] The following appeared at this point in the original 1852 American editon but was omitted from subsequent editions: "The social republic and the democratic republic experienced defeat: but the parliamentary republic, the republic of the royalist bourgeoisie, has perished, just as the pure republic of the bourgeois republicans has perished." Source: Karl Marx, *The Eighteenth Brumaire of Louis Bonaparte*, trans. by Eden and Cedar Paul (London, 1926), p. 185. ED.

[21] The following passage appeared here only in the 1852 American edition: "The primary aim of the February revolution had been

Why did the Paris proletariat not rise in revolt after December 2?

The overthrow of the bourgeoisie had as yet been only decreed; the decree had not been carried out. Any serious insur-

---

the overthrow of the Orleans dynasty, and of that section of the bourgeoisie which ruled through its instrumentality. The aim was not achieved until December 2, 1851. After the coup d'état, the vast possessions of the House of Orleans, the true foundations of its influence, were confiscated. What had been expected from the February revolution, was brought about by the December revolution. The men who, since 1830, had been wearying France with their clamour, were now imprisoned, put to flight, deposed, exiled, disarmed, made a mock of. But under Louis Philippe, only a part of the commercial bourgeoisie had ruled. The other fractions of the commercial bourgeoisie had constituted a dynastic and a republican opposition, or had stood without the pale of the so-called 'legal country.' Not until the parliamentary republic came into being, were all the fractions of the commercial bourgeoisie included within the orbit of constitutional political activity. Furthermore, under Louis Philippe, the commercial bourgeoisie had excluded the landowning bourgeoisie from participation in power. Not until the parliamentary republic was established, did the two rule on equal terms, for now the July monarchy was wedded to the legitimist monarchy, and the two epochs of property dominion were fused into one. In the days of Louis Philippe, the privileged section of the bourgeoisie concealed its hegemony behind the crown. In the days of the parliamentary republic, the dominion of the bourgeoisie (now that all its elements had been united, and now that its realm had been expanded into the realm of the whole bourgeois class) was displayed without subterfuge. Thus it had been left to the revolution to create the form in which the hegemony of the bourgeois class could secure its broadest, most general, and final expression—so that it could now be overthrown without the possibility of resurrection.

In the February days, judgment had been passed upon the Orleanist bourgeoisie, the most vigorous portion of the French bourgeoisie. Not until December 1851 was that sentence carried into effect. The Orleanist bourgeoisie was now deprived of its parliament, its barristers, its commercial courts, its provincial representatives, its solicitors, its university, its rostrum and its tribunals, its press and its literature, its administrative revenues and its judicial fees, its army pay and State income, its soul and its body. Blanqui [Louis Auguste Blanqui (1805–81), see above p. 65, note 2.] had made the dis-

rection of the proletariat would at once have put fresh life into the bourgeoisie, would have reconciled it with the army and ensured a second June defeat for the workers.

On December 4 the proletariat was incited by bourgeois and *épicier* to fight. On the evening of that day several legions of the National Guard promised to appear, armed and uniformed, on the scene of battle. For the bourgeois and the *épicier* had got wind of the fact that in one of his decrees of December 2 Bonaparte abolished the secret ballot and enjoined them to record their "yes" or "no" in the official registers after their names. The resistance of December 4 intimidated Bonaparte. During the night he caused placards to be posted on all the street corners of Paris, announcing the restoration of the secret ballot. The bourgeois and the *épicier* believed that they had gained their end. Those who failed to appear next morning were the bourgeois and the *épicier*.

By a *coup de main* during the night of December 1 to 2, Bonaparte had robbed the Paris proletariat of its leaders, the barricade commanders. An army without officers, averse to fighting under the banner of the *Montagnards* because of the memories of June 1848 and 1849 and May 1850, it left to its vanguard, the secret societies, the task of saving the insurrectionary honour of Paris, which the bourgeoisie had so unresistingly surrendered to the soldiery that, later on, Bonaparte could sneeringly give as his motive for disarming the National Guard—his

solution of the bourgeois National Guard the first demand of the revolution; and the bourgeois National Guard, which in the February days had participated in the revolution in order to check its progress, vanished from the stage in the December revolution. The Pantheon itself was retransformed into an ordinary church. The eighteenth century initiators of the bourgeois regime, had declared that regime to be sacred. Now its last form had perished: its charm had been broken. When Guizot learned that the coup d'état of December 2, 1851, had been successful, he exclaimed: 'C'est le triomphe complet et définitif du socialisme.' ["This is the complete and final triumph of socialism."] Which, being interpreted, means: This is the final and complete overthrow of bourgeois dominion." (*Ibid.*, pp. 185–87)

fear that its arms would be turned against it itself by the anarchists!

. . . But if the overthrow of the parliamentary republic contains within itself the germ of the triumph of the proletarian revolution, its immediate and palpable result was *the victory of Bonaparte over parliament, of the executive power over the legislative power, of force without phrases over the force of phrases*. In parliament the nation made its general will the law, that is, it made the law of the ruling class its general will. Before the executive power it renounces all will of its own and submits to the superior command of an alien will, to authority. The executive power, in contrast to the legislative power, expresses the heteronomy of a nation, in contrast to its autonomy. France, therefore, seems to have escaped the despotism of a class only to fall back beneath the despotism of an individual, and, what is more, beneath the authority of an individual without authority. The struggle seems to be settled in such a way that all classes, equally impotent and equally mute, fall on their knees before the rifle butt.

But the revolution is thoroughgoing. It is still journeying through purgatory. It does its work methodically. By December 2, 1851, it had completed one half of its preparatory work; it is now completing the other half. First it perfected the parliamentary power, in order to be able to overthrow it. Now that it has attained this, it perfects the *executive power*, reduces it to its purest expression, isolates it, sets it up against itself as the sole target, in order to concentrate all its forces of destruction against it. And when it has done this second half of its preliminary work, Europe will leap from its seat and exultantly exclaim: Well grubbed, old mole!

This executive power with its enormous bureaucratic and military organization, with its ingenious state machinery, embracing wide strata, with a host of officials numbering half a million, besides an army of another half million, this appalling parasitic body, which enmeshes the body of French society like a net and chokes all its pores, sprang up in the days of the absolute monarchy, with the decay of the feudal system, which it helped to hasten. The seignorial privileges of the landowners and towns became transformed into so many attributes of the state power, the feudal dignitaries into paid officials and the motley pattern of conflicting medieval plenary powers into the regulated plan of a state authority whose work is divided and centralized as in a factory. The first French Revolution, with its task of breaking all separate local, territorial, urban and provincial powers in order to create the civil unity of the nation, was bound to develop what the absolute monarchy had begun: centralization, but at the same time the extent, the attributes and the agents of governmental power. Napoleon perfected this state machinery. The Legitimist monarchy and the July monarchy added nothing but a greater division of labour, growing in the same measure that the division of labour within bourgeois society created new groups of interests, and, therefore, new material for state administration. Every *common* interest was straightway severed from society, counterposed to it as a higher, *general* interest, snatched from the activity of society's members themselves and made an object of government activity, from a bridge, a schoolhouse and the communal property of a village community to the railways, the national wealth and the national university of France. Finally, in its struggle against the revolution, the parliamentary republic found itself compelled to strengthen, along with the repressive measures, the resources and centralization of governmental power. All revolutions perfected this machine instead of smashing it. The parties that contended in turn for domination regarded the possession of this huge state edifice as the principal spoils of the victor.

But under the absolute monarchy, during the first Revolution, under Napoleon, bureaucracy was only the means of preparing the class rule of the bourgeoisie. Under the Restoration, under Louis Philippe, under the parliamentary republic, it was the instrument of the ruling class, however much it strove for power of its own.

Only under the second Bonaparte does the state seem to have

made itself completely independent. As against civil society, the state machine has consolidated its position so thoroughly that the chief of the Society of December 10 suffices for its head, an adventurer blown in from abroad, raised on the shield by a drunken soldiery, which he has bought with liquor and sausages, and which he must continually ply with sausage anew. Hence the downcast despair, the feeling of most dreadful humiliation and degradation that oppresses the breast of France and makes her catch her breath. She feels dishonoured.

And yet the state power is not suspended in midair. Bonaparte represents a class, and the most numerous class of French society at that, the *small-holding [Parzellen] peasants*.

Just as the Bourbons were the dynasty of big landed property and just as the Orleans were the dynasty of money, so the Bonapartes are the dynasty of the peasants, that is, the mass of the French people. Not the Bonaparte who submitted to the bourgeois parliament, but the Bonaparte who dispersed the bourgeois parliament is the chosen of the peasantry. For three years the towns had succeeded in falsifying the meaning of the election of December 10 and in cheating the peasants out of the restoration of the empire. The election of December 10, 1848, has been consummated only by the *coup d'état* of December 2, 1851.

The small-holding peasants form a vast mass, the members of which live in similar conditions but without entering into manifold relations with one another. Their mode of production isolates them from one another instead of bringing them into mutual intercourse. The isolation is increased by France's bad means of communication and by the poverty of the peasants. Their field of production, the small holding, admits of no division of labour in its cultivation, no application of science and, therefore, no diversity of development, no variety of talent, no wealth of social relationships. Each individual peasant family is almost self-sufficient; it itself directly produces the major part of its consumption and thus acquires its means of life more through exchange with nature than in intercourse with society.

A small holding, a peasant and his family; alongside them another small holding, another peasant and another family. A few score of these make up a village, and a few score of villages make up a Department. In this way, the great mass of the French nation is formed by simple addition of homologous magnitudes, much as potatoes in a sack form a sack of potatoes. In so far as millions of families live under economic conditions of existence that separate their mode of life, their interests and their culture from those of the other classes, and put them in hostile opposition to the latter, they form a class. In so far as there is merely a local interconnection among these small-holding peasants, and the identity of their interests begets no community, no national bond and no political organization among them, they do not form a class. They are consequently incapable of enforcing their class interest in their own name, whether through a parliament or through a convention. They cannot represent themselves, they must be represented. Their representative must at the same time appear as their master, as an authority over them, as an unlimited governmental power that protects them against the other classes and sends them rain and sunshine from above. The political influence of the small-holding peasants, therefore, finds its final expression in the executive power subordinating society to itself.

Historical tradition gave rise to the belief of the French peasants in the miracle that a man named Napoleon would bring all the glory back to them. And an individual turned up who gives himself out as the man because he bears the name of Napoleon, in consequence of the *Code Napoléon,* which lays down that *la recherche de la paternité est interdite.* After a vagabondage of twenty years and after a series of grotesque adventures, the legend finds fulfilment and the man becomes Emperor of the French. The fixed idea of the Nephew was realized, because it coincided with the fixed idea of the most numerous class of the French people.

But, it may be objected, what about the peasant risings in half of France, the raids on the peasants by the army, the mass incarceration and transportation of peasants?

Since Louis XIV, France has experienced no similar persecution of the peasants "on account of demagogic practices."

But let there be no misunderstanding. The Bonaparte dynasty represents not the revolutionary, but the conservative peasant; not the peasant that strikes out beyond the condition of his social existence, the small holding, but rather the peasant who wants to consolidate this holding, not the country folk who, linked up with the towns, want to overthrow the old order through their own energies, but on the contrary those who, in stupefied seclusion within this old order, want to see themselves and their small holdings saved and favoured by the ghost of the empire. It represents not the enlightenment, but the superstition of the peasant; not his judgment, but his prejudice; not his future, but his past; not his modern Cevennes, but his modern Vendée.[22]

The three years' rigorous rule of the parliamentary republic had freed a part of the French peasants from the Napoleonic illusion and had revolutionized them, even if only superficially; but the bourgeoisie violently repressed them, as often as they set themselves in motion. Under the parliamentary republic the modern and the traditional consciousness of the French peasant contended for mastery. This progress took the form of an incessant struggle between the schoolmasters and the priests. The bourgeoisie struck down the schoolmasters. For the first time the peasants made efforts to behave independently in the face of the activity of the government. This was shown in the continual conflict between the *maires* and the prefects. The bourgeoisie deposed the *maires*. Finally, during the period of the parliamentary republic, the peasants of different localities rose against their own offspring, the army. The bourgeoisie punished them

---

[22] Cevennes, an area in southeastern France where a peasant uprising occurred in the first years of the eighteenth century. Vendée, department in the west of France where in the 1700s peasants fought against the great French Revolution.

with states of siege and punitive expeditions. And this same bourgeoisie now cries out about the stupidity of the masses, the vile multitude, that has betrayed it to Bonaparte. It has itself forcibly strengthened the empire sentiments [*Imperialismus*] of the peasant class, it conserved the conditions that form the birth-place of this peasant religion. The bourgeoisie, to be sure, is bound to fear the stupidity of the masses as long as they remain conservative, and the insight of the masses as soon as they become revolutionary.

In the risings after the *coup d'état,* a part of the French peasants protested, arms in hand, against their own vote of December 10, 1848. The school they had gone through since 1848 had sharpened their wits. But they had made themselves over to the underworld of history; history held them to their word, and the majority was still so prejudiced that in precisely the reddest Departments the peasant population voted openly for Bonaparte. In its view, the National Assembly had hindered his progress. He had now merely broken the fetters that the towns had imposed on the will of the countryside. In some parts the peasants even entertained the grotesque notion of a convention side by side with Napoleon.

After the first revolution had transformed the peasants from semi-villeins into freeholders, Napoleon confirmed and regulated the conditions on which they could exploit undisturbed the soil of France which had only just fallen to their lot and slake their youthful passion for property. But what is now causing the ruin of the French peasant is his small holding itself, the division of the land, the form of property which Napoleon consolidated in France. It is precisely the material conditions which made the feudal peasant into a small-holding peasant and Napoleon into an emperor. Two generations have sufficed to produce the inevitable result: progressive deterioration of agriculture, progressive indebtedness of the agriculturist. The "Napoleonic" form of property, which at the beginning of the nineteenth century was the condition for the liberation and enrichment of the French country folk, has developed in the course of this century into the law of their enslavement and pauperization. And precisely this law is the first of the *"idées napoléoniennes"* which the second Bonaparte has to uphold. If he still shares with the peasants the illusion that the cause of their ruin is to be sought, not in this small-holding property itself, but outside it, in the influence of secondary circumstances, his experiments will burst like soap bubbles when they come in contact with the relations of production.

The economic development of small-holding property has radically changed the relation of the peasants to the other classes of society. Under Napoleon, the fragmentation of the land in the countryside supplemented free competition and the beginning of big industry in the towns.[23] The peasant class was the ubiquitous protest against the landed aristocracy which had just been overthrown. The roots that small-holding property struck in French soil deprived feudalism of all nutriment. Its landmarks formed the natural fortifications of the bourgeoisie against any surprise attack on the part of its old overlords. But in the course of the nineteenth century the feudal lords were replaced by urban usurers; the feudal obligation that went with the land was replaced by the mortgage; aristocratic landed property was replaced by bourgeois capital. The small holding of the peasant is now only the pretext that allows the capitalist to draw profits, interest and rent from the soil, while leaving it to the tiller of the soil himself to see how he can extract his wages. The mortgage debt burdening the soil of France imposes on the French peasantry payment of an amount of interest equal to the annual interest on the entire British national debt. Small-holding property, in this enslavement by capital to which its development inevitably pushes forward, has transformed the mass of the

[23] The following sentence appeared here only in the 1852 American edition: "Even the preferential treatment of the peasantry was to the interest of the new bourgeois order. This newly formed class was the many-sided expansion of the bourgeois regime beyond the gates of the towns; was the inauguration of that regime upon a national scale." (*Ibid.*, p. 187)

French nation into troglodytes. Sixteen million peasants (including women and children) dwell in hovels, a large number of which have but one opening, others only two and the most favoured only three. And windows are to a house what the five senses are to the head. The bourgeois order, which at the beginning of the century set the state to stand guard over the newly arisen small holding and manured it with laurels, has become a vampire that sucks out its blood and marrow and throws them into the alchemistic cauldron of capital. The *Code Napoléon* is now nothing but a *codex* of distraints, forced sales and compulsory auctions. To the four million (including children, etc.) officially recognized paupers, vagabonds, criminals and prostitutes in France must be added five million who hover on the margin of existence and either have their haunts in the countryside itself or, with their rags and their children, continually desert the countryside for the towns and the towns for the countryside. The interests of the peasants, therefore, are no longer, as under Napoleon, in accord with, but in opposition to the interests of the bourgeoisie, to capital. Hence the peasants find their natural ally and leader in the *urban proletariat*, whose task is the overthrow of the bourgeois order. But *strong and unlimited government*—and this is the second "*idée napoléonienne*," which the second Napoleon has to carry out—is called upon to defend this "material" order by force. This "*ordre matériel*" also serves as the catchword in all of Bonaparte's proclamations against the rebellious peasants.

Besides the mortgage which capital imposes on it, the small holding is burdened by *taxes*. Taxes are the source of life for the bureaucracy, the army, the priests and the court, in short, for the whole apparatus of the executive power. Strong government and heavy taxes are identical. By its very nature, small-holding property forms a suitable basis for an all-powerful and innumerable bureaucracy. It creates a uniform level of relationships and persons over the whole surface of the land. Hence it also permits of uniform action from a supreme centre on all points of this uniform mass. It annihilates the aristocratic intermediate grades between the mass of the people and the state power. On all sides, therefore, it calls forth the direct interference of this state power and the interposition of its immediate organs. Finally, it produces an unemployed surplus population for which there is no place either on the land or in the towns, and which accordingly reaches out for state offices as a sort of respectable alms, and provokes the creation of state posts.[24] By the new markets which he opened at the point of the bayonet, by the plundering of the Continent, Napoleon repaid the compulsory taxes with interest. These taxes were a spur to the industry of the peasant, whereas now they rob his industry of its last resources and complete his inability to resist pauperism. And an enormous bureaucracy, well-gallooned and well-fed, is the *"idée napoléonienne"* which is most congenial of all to the second Bonaparte. How could it be otherwise, seeing that alongside the actual classes of society he is forced to create an artificial caste, for which the maintenance of his regime becomes a bread-and-butter question? Accordingly, one of his first financial operations was the raising of officials' salaries to their old level and the creation of new sinecures.

Another *"idée napoléonienne"* is the domination of the *priests* as an instrumentality of government. But while in its accord with society, in its dependence on natural forces and its submission to the authority which protected it from above, the small holding that had newly come into being was naturally religious, the small holding that is ruined by debts, at odds with society

[24] The following appeared here only in the 1852 American edition: "Under the first Napoleon, this numerous class of civil servants was directly productive. Having the coercive powers of the State at its disposal, it was able, in the form of State construction works, to do for the newly enfranchised peasantry things of a kind which the bourgeoisie could not do by the methods of private industry. State taxation was a necessary coercive measure for the maintenance of an interchange between town and country. But for this, the French smallholders, like the Norwegian smallholders and some of the Swiss smallholders, would, in peasant self-sufficiency, have broken off all connection with the towns." (*Ibid.,* p. 187)

and authority, and driven beyond its own limitations naturally becomes irreligious. Heaven was quite a pleasing accession to the narrow strip of land just won, more particularly as it makes the weather; it becomes an insult as soon as it is thrust forward as substitute for the small holding. The priest then appears as only the anointed bloodhound of the earthly police—another "*idée napoléonienne.*" On the next occasion, the expedition against Rome will take place in France itself, but in a sense opposite to that of M. de Montalembert.

Lastly, the culminating point of the "*idées napoléoniennes*" is the preponderance of the *army.* The army was the *point d'honneur* of the small-holding peasants, it was they themselves transformed into heroes, defending their new possessions against the outer world, glorifying their recently won nationality, plundering and revolutionizing the world. The uniform was their own state dress; war was their poetry; the small holding, extended and rounded off in imagination, was their fatherland, and patriotism the ideal form of the sense of property. But the enemies against whom the French peasant has now to defend his property are not the Cossacks; they are the *huissiers*[25] and the tax collectors. The small holding lies no longer in the so-called fatherland, but in the register of mortgages. The army itself is no longer the flower of the peasant youth; it is the swamp-flower of the peasant *lumpenproletariat.* It consists in large measure of *remplaçants,* of substitutes, just as the second Bonaparte is himself only a *remplaçant,* the substitute for Napoleon. It now performs its deeds of valour by hounding the peasants in masses like chamois, by doing *gendarme* duty, and if the internal contradictions of his system chase the chief of the Society of December 10 over the French border, his army, after some acts of brigandage, will reap, not laurels, but thrashings.

One sees: *all "idées napoléoniennes" are ideas of the undeveloped small holding in the freshness of its youth;* for the

[25] Bailiffs.

small holding that has outlived its day they are an absurdity. They are only the hallucinations of its death struggle, words that are transformed into phrases, spirits transformed into ghosts. But the parody of the empire [*des Imperialismus*] was necessary to free the mass of the French nation from the weight of tradition and to work out in pure form the opposition between the state power and society. With the progressive undermining of small-holding property, the state structure erected upon it collapses. The centralization of the state that modern society requires arises only on the ruins of the military-bureaucratic governmental machinery which was forged in opposition to feudalism.[26]

The condition of the French peasants provides us with the answer to the riddle of the *general elections of December 20 and 21*, which bore the second Bonaparte up Mount Sinai, not to receive laws, but to give them. . . .

As the executive authority which has made itself an independent power, Bonaparte feels it to be his mission to safeguard "bourgeois order." But the strength of this bourgeois order lies in the middle class. He looks on himself, therefore, as the representative of the middle class and issues decrees in this sense. Nevertheless, he is somebody solely due to the fact that he has broken the political power of this middle class and daily breaks it anew. Consequently, he looks on himself as the adversary of the political and literary power of the middle class. But by protecting its material power, he generates its political power anew.

[26] In the 1852 edition this paragraph ended with the following lines, which Marx omitted in the 1869 edition: "The demolition of the state machine will not endanger centralization. Bureaucracy is only the low and brutal form of a centralization that is still afflicted with its opposite, with feudalism. When he is disappointed in the Napoleonic Restoration, the French peasant will part with his belief in his small holding, the entire state edifice erected on this small holding will fall to the ground and *the proletarian revolution* will obtain *that chorus without which its solo song becomes a swan song in all peasant countries*." [This note is provided by the editor of the translation used in this volume. ED.]

The cause must accordingly be kept alive; but the effect, where it manifests itself, must be done away with. But this cannot pass off without slight confusions of cause and effect, since in their interaction both lose their distinguishing features. New decrees that obliterate the border line. As against the bourgeoisie, Bonaparte looks on himself, at the same time, as the representative of the peasants and of the people in general, who wants to make the lower classes of the people happy within the frame of bourgeois society. New decrees that cheat the "True Socialists" of their statecraft in advance. But, above all, Bonaparte looks on himself as the chief of the Society of December 10, as the representative of the *lumpenproletariat* to which he himself, his *entourage,* his government and his army belong. . . .

Bonaparte would like to appear as the patriarchal benefactor of all classes. But he cannot give to one class without taking from another. . . . He would like to steal the whole of France in order to be able to make a present of her to France or, rather, in order to be able to buy France anew with French money, for as the chief of the Society of December 10 he must needs buy what ought to belong to him. And all the state institutions, the Senate, the Council of State, the legislative body, the Legion of Honour, the soldiers' medals, the washhouses, the public works, the railways, the *état major*[27] of the National Guard to the exclusion of privates, and the confiscated estates of the House of Orleans—all become parts of the institution of purchase. Every place in the army and in the government machine becomes a means of purchase. But the most important feature of this process, whereby France is taken in order to give to her, is the percentages that find their way into the pockets of the head and the members of the Society of December 10 during the turnover. . . .

Driven by the contradictory demands of his situation and being at the same time, like a conjurer, under the necessity of keeping the public gaze fixed on himself, as Napoleon's substi-

[27] General staff.

tute, by springing constant surprises, that is to say, under the necessity of executing a *coup d'état en miniature* every day, Bonaparte throws the entire bourgeois economy into confusion, violates everything that seemed inviolable to the Revolution of 1848, makes some tolerant of revolution, others desirous of revolution, and produces actual anarchy in the name of order, while at the same time stripping its halo from the entire state machine, profanes it and makes it at once loathsome and ridiculous. The cult of the Holy Tunic of Treves he duplicates at Paris in the cult of the Napoleonic imperial mantle. But when the imperial mantle finally falls on the shoulders of Louis Bonaparte, the bronze statue of Napoleon will crash from the top of the Vendôme Column.

PIERRE-JOSEPH PROUDHON'S
APPEAL TO LOUIS NAPOLEON

It seems anomalous to us now—and it must have seemed anomalous to his fellow radicals then—that the anarchist-socialist Pierre-Joseph Proudhon (1809–65) should have appeared to offer support for the perpetrator of the coup d'état. The Republican and democratic Left was shocked when, just seven months after the coup, Proudhon published his *The Social Revolution Demonstrated by the Coup d'État* and called upon Louis Napoleon to take over the leadership of the Revolution—thereby implicitly lending the coup d'état the sanction of one of the Left's most famous voices. The argument of his book on the coup was inappropriate enough for a radical. It seemed especially out of place for Proudhon since it was a *political* appeal to Louis Napoleon, urging him to take advantage of the void left by the failures of all other political groups in the Second Republic. The anomaly involved Proudhon's avowed anarchism itself. He had frankly declared his opposition to government in 1840 and had consistently distrusted and opposed political solutions proposed by rival theorists—mostly *because* they were political solutions—and he had largely avoided personal involvement in party politics prior to 1852 (as he was to do afterwards). Now he was hoping that government itself could carry forward the progressive social change he identified with the Revolution.

The appeal to Louis Napoleon added another surprise, for the book was published just after Proudhon was released from prison, an imprisonment resulting from the bitter attacks against the Prince-President that Proudhon had printed in the journal of which he had been editor.

Proudhon was troubled by the likelihood that his book would be misconstrued. Its complexity and lack of logical structure cloud its purpose; the book moves rapidly from analysis to exhortation, touching on many diverse issues dear to Proudhon. In fact, it shares the faults of most of his writings.

He wrote in a disorderly fashion, writing much and rapidly,[1] and polemically. He was a controversialist who sought to influence the present by "the tongue, the pen, the poem, by action, and example."[2] He usually found himself engaged in critical battle over vital issues of society, politics, and philosophy. Paris in the 1840s was a center of markedly irascible revolutionary thought. The first half of the nineteenth century was one of the great ages of international debate, an era when, perhaps above all others, men truly believed that getting their ideas straight (and correcting those of others) would make a difference in fact, and Proudhon particularly believed this to be the case. He sought desperately to counteract the errors he saw proliferating around him and to express the wealth of ideas he possessed.

The Social Revolution is Proudhon's attempt to comprehend the coup d'état in revolutionary terms. Despite its lack of clarity, it does seem to have the guiding thread we have pointed to: the revolutionary role for the President. Yet Proudhon's apparent Machiavellian intent to co-opt Louis Napoleon for the Revolution remains puzzling. This intent is an oddity in his life and thought—and an oddity he himself soon rejected. It becomes

[1] His *Confessions of a Revolutionary* was completed in two months.
[2] *Second Memoir on Property,* trans. by Benjamin R. Tucker (Princeton, Mass., 1876) p. 432.

more intelligible if we see its place in the course of Proudhon's career and in the development of his ideas.

Proudhon was born in Besançon, in the department of Doubs, in 1809, son of a cooper, sometime tavernkeeper, and farmer. His mother was a peasant, who appears to have served him as a model of peasant virtue. Much of his early life he spent on a farm; he ever after retained strong provincial inclinations and a distaste for big cities. His dislike of the impact of the city, especially Paris, upon the countryside and country folk is reflected in the federalist doctrines of communal and provincial autonomy he developed and in his obvious opposition to governmental centralization. He retained a deep appreciation for rural virtues, which is unusual in a socialist but which became characteristic of nineteenth-century anarchist thought; in this he stands in marked contrast to Karl Marx. He showed a real sympathy and understanding for the farmer's intractable desire, so inhibiting to socialists and communists alike, to own his land free from debt.

Proudhon had the good fortune to obtain early schooling at the college in Besançon, but he was hampered throughout by his poverty. Upon completing his studies, he entered a printing establishment, becoming a proofreader and typesetter, and converted his work into an opportunity for further study, just as the historian Jules Michelet had done.[3] Besançon was a religious center, and much of Proudhon's early reading was in theology—so much so that we find reflections of his persisting theological concerns in almost all his works, even the most specifically social and economic. (The *First Memoir on Property* diverges into religious controversy and *The System of Economic Contradictions* begins with a discussion of the history of ideas of God.) His reading quickly ended his ties with Catholicism. He concluded that men could not become free till they,

[3] Proudhon admired Michelet's work and shared in his glorification of the Revolution as an active agency in historical change. In later life the points of view of the two diverged, especially over their doctrines of love and marriage.

like himself, had been freed from the Church. He believed both Church and State served as agencies of human subjugation, from which men were destined gradually to become emancipated. He determined to dedicate himself to aid mankind toward liberation.

After attempts to earn his living in Paris, he took the tour of France that journeymen in many trades had long taken. He learned how printing was pursued in many areas and tried briefly with a partner to set up a press. Seeking support to continue his studies in 1838, he applied to the Besançon Academy for the Suard scholarship, a three-year research scholarship at 1,500 francs per year. Despite his assertion in his application that he intended to use its emoluments for "ameliorating the physical, moral, and intellectual conditions" of his working-class brothers and fellows, he received the award. He did not retain it long. In 1839 he wrote a study on the celebration of Sunday, adumbrating many of his later views. It was his next work which branded him ever after as a radical and a revolutionary. *First Memoir on Property*—"What is Property?"—in 1840 declared in its first paragraph that property is theft. Proudhon in fact attacked only the *abuses* of property ownership, those aspects that enabled an owner to extort revenue from others and allowed for exploitation, e.g., rent, profit, interest. He continued to advocate possession per se. In the long run, such qualifications did little to alleviate the impact of his book. Even though he was concerned chiefly for property in land, his ideas remained fearsome to capitalists, and his opposition to communism as tyrannical failed to mitigate his assertion that anarchy was the future form of society. His reputation was made, and whatever his demurrers he little regretted it, even though the subtleties of his doctrine were lost. He was unequivocally the enemy of the powers established in French society in his day, and his volume on property made the enmity clear. He pursued the issues he had raised in further studies, one of which led to a court process in 1842. Although he was acquitted, it nearly kept his book from circulation.

Proudhon worked next for a shipping firm in Lyons, a position of some responsibility, which allowed him to see something of the management side of business and learn some finance, to develop a deep distaste for railways, and to come in contact with radical Mutualist workers who had been involved in uprisings in 1831–34. As was the case with Jean-Jacques Rousseau, Proudhon had the opportunity to move through and have experiences with the several ranks and classes of French society, as well as its several geographical areas. His response to his opportunity was particularly unusual for the nineteenth century, for he did not seek to climb out of his class origins. Instead, he remained a deeply involved observer, who used his experiences in his writings to further the cause of the Revolution.

In October 1847 he returned to Paris hoping to resume his studies. He had never given up his intention of continuing his intellectual pursuits. He hoped now to start a newspaper but had insufficient money and was able to obtain only hack writing jobs. He could not rely for income on the two major studies he had produced since his work on property. These had extended his powers and enhanced his reputation but had provided little income. The first, *The Creation of Order Among Men* (1843), was a major attempt at a constructive philosophy of history, for Proudhon, like many of his contemporaries including Marx, hoped to achieve a historically based science of society complete with laws of social development; the second, *The System of Economical Contradictions, or The Philosophy of Poverty* (1846), has attained considerable modern notoriety as the provocation for Marx's devastating and unfair rejoinder, *The Poverty of Philosophy*.

Proudhon and Marx had met in 1844.[4] Marx, nine years

---

[4] R. Hoffman's recent essay in *The Historian* (May 1967) effectively summarizes the relationship between the two men and concludes that despite their meeting at a time when their interests, Proudhon's in German philosophy and Marx's in French socialism, led them together, their casts of mind and the directions in which

Proudhon's junior had been impressed by Proudhon's work on property and had praised it in *The Holy Family* (1844). Marx claimed to have devoted nightlong conversations to trying unsuccessfully to teach Hegelianism to Proudhon.[5] But Marx's effort to enlist Proudhon's aid in arranging an international socialist correspondence group had failed—and brought a reply from Proudhon that pointed up significant differences between them. Though both men laid great stress upon economic conditions, Proudhon was fundamentally an idealist, where Marx was a materialist, and Proudhon opposed violent revolution while Marx supported it. Proudhon wrote:

> Let us by all means collaborate in trying to discover the laws of society, the way in which these laws work out, the best method to set about investigating them; but for God's sake, after we have demolished all the dogmatisms *a priori*, let us not of all things attempt in our turn to instil another kind of dogma into the people. Let us not fall into the contradiction of your compatriot Martin Luther, who, after overthrowing Catholic theology, addressed himself to the task of building up with all the apparatus of excommunication and anathemas, a Protestant theology. For three whole centuries Germany has been doing nothing but pull down the plasterwork of Martin Luther. Let us not, by contriving any more such restrictions, leave any more such tasks for the human race. With all my heart I welcome your idea of exposing all opinions to the light. Let us have decent and sincere polemics; let us give the world an example of learned and farsighted tolerance, let us not pose as the apostles of a new religion of logic, the religion of reason itself. Let us welcome, let us encourage all the protests; let us condemn all exclusions, all mysticisms. But never let us think of any question as closed, and even after we have

---

they were developing were such as to preclude significant influence of either man upon the other. Denis Brogan suggests (*Proudhon*, London, 1934, p. 43) that as both men were born teachers, they were likely to make poor disciples. See above, "Marx's *The Eighteenth Brumaire of Louis Bonaparte*."

[5] Karl Marx and Friedrich Engels, *Selected Correspondence, 1846–1895* trans. by Dona Torr (New York, 1934), p. 171.

exhausted our very last argument, let us begin again, if necessary, with eloquence and irony. On that condition I shall be delighted to associate with you—but otherwise, no![6]

Even though relations between the two were strained prior to the appearance of *The System of Economical Contradictions*, Proudhon asked for Marx's views on the book. The latter's *Poverty of Philosophy* produced a permanent rupture. The vaguely Hegelian implications of Proudhon's book aroused Marx's critical wrath. The accusation that Proudhon misused dialectics, while true enough as many commentators have pointed out, is of questionable relevance since Proudhon's approach, for all his use of Hegelian-sounding language, is not Hegelian. Instead, Proudhon believed in a world of conflicting antinomies, which in the social sphere should be creatively equilibrated. He spoke in this book of "syntheses," but without much clarity as to what he had in mind. In later works, he appeared to prefer equilibration to eradication, lest life and progress cease.[7] In *The System of Economic Contradictions* Proudhon demonstrated that such economic phenomena as competition, division of labor, and machinery have both beneficial and harmful effects and that these dual effects inhere in their very nature. Proudhon was developing great ability to see things and issues from at least two sides with great sensitivity. Some of the best of the book is in criticism of utopian and laissez-faire economists showing Proudhon's own polemic inclination. There are also chapters on the ideas of God and of Providence and their role in supporting the social system, which

[6] Translation from J. Hampden Jackson, *Marx, Proudhon, and European Socialism* (New York, 1962), p. 61. Proudhon's opposition to Marxian dogmatism was combined with disagreement over the appropriate treatment of a fellow socialist, Karl Grün, whom Marx had denounced.

[7] Robert C. Tucker, *The Marxian Revolutionary Idea* (New York, 1969), p. 53, contrasts Proudhon's and Marx's mature views thus: "To Proudhonian justice as equilibrium of antagonisms, Marx opposed revolution as abolition of antagonisms."

serve mainly to provide Proudhon with opportunity for considerable anti-theist comment. This combination makes the book seem disorganized and ill-digested. Despite its virtues, there was plenty of room for Marx's polemic skill.

Marx summarized his attack on Proudhon's book[8] in a letter to the German Socialist leader J. B. Schweitzer, January 24, 1865:

> There I showed, among other things, how little he has penetrated into the secret of scientific dialectics and how, on the contrary, he shares the illusions of speculative philosophy in his treatment of the *economic categories; how* instead of conceiving them as *the theoretical expression of historical relations of production, corresponding to a particular stage of development in material production,* he transforms them by his twaddle into pre-existing *eternal ideas,* and in this roundabout way arrives once more at the standpoint of bourgeois economy.

> I also show further how very deficient and sometimes even schoolboyish his knowledge is of the "political economy" which he undertook to criticize, and how he and the utopians are hunting for a so-called *"science"* by which a formula for the "solution of the social question" is to be excogitated *a priori,* instead of deriving their science from a critical knowledge of the historical movement, a movement which itself produces the *material conditions of emancipation.* But especially I show how confused, wrong and superficial Proudhon remains with regard to *exchange value,* the basis of the whole thing, and how he even tries to use the utopian interpretation of Ricardo's theory of value as the basis of a new science.[9]

[8] James Joll, *The Anarchists* (New York, 1904), p. 61, says: ". . . [Marx] was a better philosopher and a better economist than Proudhon, and much of his criticism of Proudhon's theories was justified. Yet there is also something in the remark with which Proudhon received Marx's attack: 'The true meaning of Marx's work is that he regrets that I have thought like him everywhere and that I was the first to say it.'"

[9] Marx and Engels, *Selected Correspondence, 1846–1895*, p. 172. More specifically, Marx also attacked Proudhon's treatment of the problems of money and rent. He flatly disagreed with Proudhon's op-

Although Proudhon concluded in anger that Marx was the "tapeworm of socialism," he never replied publicly. His marginal notes on *The Poverty of Philosophy* remain and are reprinted at the end of vol. 2 of *The System of Economic Contradictions* in his collected works. Marx had the last public word when he sent the letter quoted above to the German periodical *Social Democrat* in 1865 where it appeared as an obituary notice of Proudhon.[10] Marx repeated here what had become his frequent contention, that Proudhon's position was "petty bourgeois." But Proudhon was victor in the eyes of his contemporaries: in the first place, *The Poverty of Philosophy* did not sell, then Proudhonists battled Marx with considerable success through all the early years of the First International (i.e., after 1864), and despite Marxists' assertions, the tone of the Paris Commune in 1870–71 was dominantly Proudhonist (and Blanquist).

Had Proudhon intended a reply to Marx, he was soon too involved in the February Revolution of 1848 to do much about it. He had opposed its coming, for he feared the foolishness of the revolutionaries and reformers whose theories seemed unsuited to the needs of France; yet he participated despite his opposition to violent revolution when he saw hope for the solu-

---

position to strikes and trade unions. His criticism of Proudhon's inept handling of history includes the accusation that Proudhon invents genetic explanations, prefers theoretical to historical accounts, reads the present back into the past, and in a reactionary fashion expects the future to be like the present. Proudhon truly lacked Marx's historical sense. Fundamental differences between the two are that Marx favored violent revolution and hence saw Proudhon as no revolutionary, and that for Marx the class struggle was between workers and bourgeois, while for Proudhon the workers and the petty bourgeois together struggled against those above them, and finally that Marx was far more an internationalist and Proudhon a French patriot.

[10] This letter also contains the following remarks on *The Social Revolution:* "His work on the *coup d'état,* in which he flirts with Louis Bonaparte and, in fact, strives to make him palatable to the French workers . . . must be characterized as not merely bad but base . . . of a baseness which corresponds, however, to the petty-bourgeois point of view."

tion of the social problem. In the first days of the revolution he helped build barricades, he set type for a revolutionary manifesto, joined the Club of the Revolution, and received a deputation which promised him backing as editor of a journal. Amidst the great proliferation of newspapers during the first months of the Second Republic, Proudhon's *La Représentant du Peuple* became one of the leading voices of the radical Left.

At the start Proudhon supported the efforts of the Provisional Government but became increasingly its critic. He pointed to the futility of "a revolution without an Idea"—a purely political transformation. He criticized the social and economic policies that produced the ill-fated National Workshops (the doctrine of the "right to work") and argued against the state socialism of Louis Blanc. He lumped together Jacobins and socialists as simply perpetuating the regime of authority inherited from the past.

He began describing the major reform he hoped to introduce, a system of free credit, in *The Solution to the Social Problem* in the spring of 1848. He hoped that by affecting circulation of goods he could get at the sources of exploitation in society. He tried to institute the scheme through a short-lived bank of the people in 1849.

He was asked to run for the Constituent Assembly in its first election in April 1848 but lost, then was elected in the June by-election along with Victor Hugo and Louis Napoleon Bonaparte.[11] None of the newly elected members had time to become more than barely accustomed to his task (Proudhon was named to the Finance Committee) when the capital erupted in civil war. The June Days, Proudhon confessed, caught him unprepared, for he had become so busy that he had gotten out of touch with the people—as he believed all representatives must necessarily come to do. Repression of the people in the June Days demonstrated to him that he must oppose the Republic.

He was able to do little to help the workers; to have helped

[11] It will be recalled that Louis Napoleon did not accept his seat in June, but ran again in September. See above p. 2.

215

them directly in the streets would have required giving up his long-held opposition to violent revolution. After the event his paper was one of the few to speak out for their point of view. Conservatives thereupon linked him and his theories with the insurrection, and he became increasingly notorious—as is suggested by the portrayal of him in the Bagehot selection.

One of his major efforts to aid the workers after the June Days was to seek government support for a partial remission of debts. To propose it, he gave his sole major speech in the Assembly, and he was treated most unceremoniously by his disdainful and fearful colleagues. In his speech he implied a class conflict as he identified himself with the workers against the middle class; only one fellow radical voted with him against the order of the day condemning his proposal. Soon thereafter his journal was suspended.

Proudhon's antipathy toward the Republic was enhanced by the Constitution it produced. He asserted that he voted against the Constitution because it *was* a constitution. Yet he had worked for its practical amelioration; he supported efforts to have the President elected by the Assembly; like Tocqueville he feared popular election of the President. Particularly, he feared Bonaparte.[12] But he helped to split the vote of the radical Left in the presidential election by giving his support as a form of protest to Raspail, the socialist candidate, against Ledru-Rollin, the democratic Republican candidate. Both, of course, were disastrously defeated.

The end of the Republic seemed to him implicit in the presidential election of December 10. He quickly put forward the prognosis of a transformation of the Republic into another Napoleonic Empire. Now in his new journal, *Le Peuple,* he attacked the reactionary forces around the President, arguing at

[12] Proudhon warned against Louis Napoleon's election to the Assembly in June. He also was one of the first to predict the election of Louis Napoleon to the presidency; believing the mass electorate was ready to turn over France to him, he ironically urged him to consummate the shame of the French nation. See Jackson, pp. 71–72.

first in a manner anticipatory of the theme of *The Social Revolution* that Louis Napoleon himself, with his name and his tradition, was a potential revolutionary. But increasingly he attacked the President as well—describing him as a threat to the Republic, to democracy, and to socialism. He was arrested despite his membership in the Legislative Assembly after that body had stripped him of his parliamentary privilege, fined, and given a three-year sentence in March 1849. He fled to Brussels but returned to see the lady he hoped to marry, was captured, and was imprisoned in June.

For the most part, his imprisonment was mild—mild enough for him to marry and to visit his wife on parole. He could have his books and contact with the outside world.[13] He was therefore able to continue his radical journalism, aiding in the publication of *La Voix du Peuple* (later, of a new *Le Peuple*). He wrote vituperative attacks upon the President and his government and published two revolutionary books which spared neither the Republican Left nor the Party of Order. His *Confessions of a Revolutionary* is a critical history assessing the failures of the February revolution and its aftermath, combined with some autobiography. The book was finished before the end of 1849. *The General Idea of the Revolution in the Nineteenth Century* appeared in 1851, and in it he gave a rounded sketch of his theories.

Proudhon saw the Revolution as part of a process of democratization in the same apocalyptic sense Tocqueville did, but for Proudhon, quite unlike Tocqueville, the Revolution was the object of his faith.[14] The year 1848 became merely a

[13] He was twice removed from comparatively mild incarceration in Sainte-Pélagie and then the Conciergerie to the very much stricter confinement at Doullens and Bourges on occasions when the government instituted stricter measures against the radical Left, as it did after the June 13, 1849, uprising over the Roman question.

[14] Roger Soltau says that Proudhon's search for equality was to some degree inspired by Tocqueville's description of American equality; see *French Political Thought in the Nineteenth Century* (New Haven, 1931), p. 288.

part, and a generally unsuccessful part, of this process, which in its political and social aspects had begun in 1789 and would continue until men were free and equal. Proudhon's *General Idea of the Revolution* may be seen as a summary of guidelines for revolutionaries who had begun a revolution in February 1848 without a clear idea of where they were going and by 1851 had completely lost their way.

He believed the Revolution was necessarily moving toward the end of government. The experience of being governed, he sums up as follows:

> . . . To be GOVERNED is to be kept in sight, inspected, spied upon, directed, law-driven, numbered, enrolled, indoctrinated, preached at, controlled, estimated, valued, censured, commanded, by creatures who have neither the right, nor the wisdom, nor the virtue to do so . . . To be GOVERNED is to be at every operation, at every transaction, noted, registered, enrolled, taxed, stamped, measured, numbered, assessed, licensed, authorized, admonished, forbidden, reformed, corrected, punished. It is, under pretext of public utility, and in the name of the general interest, to be placed under contribution, trained, ransomed, exploited, monopolized, extorted, squeezed, mystified, robbed; then, at the slightest resistance, the first word of complaint, to be repressed, fined, despised, harassed, tracked, abused, clubbed, disarmed, choked, imprisoned, judged, condemned, shot, deported, sacrificed, outraged, dishonored. That is government; that is its justice; that is its morality. And to think that there are democrats among us who pretend that there is any good in government; Socialists who support this ignominy, in the name of Liberty, Equality and Fraternity; proletarians who proclaim their candidacy for the Presidency of the Republic.[15]

"No authority, no government, not even popular, that is the revolution." Government hitherto has been class-bound and exploitative. "Government is made for the defense of the rich

[15] Proudhon, *The General Idea of the Revolution in the Nineteenth Century,* trans. by R. B. Robinson (London, 1923), p. 294.

against the poor." "Authority, in defending rights, however established, in protecting interests, however acquired, has always been for riches against misfortune: the history of governments is the martyrology of the proletariat."[16] And Proudhon rejected the democratic creed as a solution, rejecting with it the heirs of the Jacobins. He had no faith in the ability of the multitude to choose its rulers. Plebiscites create situations in which voters are almost sure to vote wrongly. His conclusive objection was against democratic faith in government power. "The law of the majority is not my law, it is the law of force . . ."[17]

He believed the Revolution had progressed in consequence of the opposition it had generated, ideas had become clarified, the task better outlined. He hoped next to see class conflict assuaged, eventually allowing a fusion of the middle and lower classes. His opening address was, in fact, an appeal to the bourgeoisie. The ends of the Revolution—federalism, contract, and free credit—were not to be attained by political means; instead, an equilibrium of industrial forces must be achieved, retaining the benefits of competition while alleviating the degradation of man to machinery. His concluding hope was that economic forces would be so organized that the governmental system could be dissolved in the economy. On the other hand, he had earlier proposed[18] that government might begin the revolutionary process. There is a continuing inconsistency here, the same that appears in the recurring suggestion that Louis Napoleon might be a revolutionary.

George Woodcock argues that Proudhon's most general position on this question is that revolutions "from above" involve too much state power to further the cause of the Revolution satisfactorily,[19] while Denis Brogan says:

16 *Ibid.*, pp. 126, 62, 108.
17 *Ibid.*, pp. 140, 149, 205.
18 *Ibid.*, p. 187.
19 George Woodcock, *Pierre-Joseph Proudhon* (New York, 1956), p. 143. Proudhon treated this issue explicitly in his *Confessions d'un*

. . . What he wanted of a government was that it should commit suicide gracefully, giving way to the free anarchical society without trying to make the birth of the new order difficult. If the House of Orleans would put itself at the disposal of the Revolution, Proudhon would put up with the anomaly of hereditary political power. He was willing, later, to make the same bargain with the House of Bonaparte, and he saw nothing to choose between a monarchical and a democratic tyranny.[20]

It is not clear that Proudhon had fully resolved this issue even by the end of his life.

Édouard Dolléans has provided a useful chronology of Proudhon's relations with and views of the President prior to the coup in the Introduction to *The Social Revolution*.[21] It becomes evident therein that Proudhon increasingly believed in the usefulness of an alliance between the *Montagne* (the Social-Democrats) and the Bonapartists in the last months of the Republic's life and therefore had more reason for his hopes for a "revolutionary" President.

He believed the alignment had been evident in 1849 on the Roman question (see "Tocqueville's Defense of the Assembly"), in the controversy over the President's letter to Ney when he dismissed the Barrot ministry, of which Tocqueville was Foreign Minister. Proudhon had been enthusiastic over this vision of Louis Napoleon as an opponent of the Pope and the clericals. The articles Proudhon wrote as early as the winter of 1850 already urged Louis Napoleon to take over the leadership of the Revolution, for he did not expect the Republic could last and anticipated a coup d'état. He preferred an imperial con-

---

Révolutionnaire (Paris, 1929), pp. 81–82, and his remarks support Woodcock's interpretation.

[20] Brogan, p. 56.

[21] In *Oeuvres Complètes de P.-J. Proudhon*, ed. by MM. C. Bouglé & H. Moysset (Paris, 1936). Proudhon had briefly met Louis Napoleon in a famous interview arranged by the latter in September 1848, probably to seek support for the presidency.

spiracy to a monarchist one, reiterating his belief that the Napoleonic tradition carried revolutionary overtones, contending that in contrast the monarchical tradition was simply feudal. He hoped republicans and democrats would co-operate with Louis Napoleon so that the Revolution could continue. Louis Napoleon's dismissal of Changarnier was viewed as yet another service to the Revolution. It is therefore not surprising that Proudhon urged the revision of the Constitution to avoid the deadlock of May 1852.[22]

The coalition of Bonapartists and the *Montagne* seemed most clearly visible in the unsuccessful effort to repeal the suffrage law of May 31, 1850, but there was little true community of interest. After the defeat of the Quaestors' Bill, we find Proudhon again correctly anticipating a dictatorship (though not soon).

He was allowed out of prison on the morning of the coup d'état; Émile Ollivier found him reading placards and reports that he said: "So their worthies, the bourgeois, want a try at despotism! Well, it will be a good lesson for them. Despotism is the most unstable thing in the world."[23] We find a further description of his activities in Hugo's *History of a Crime*:

> These preliminary operations concluded, Lafon, taking Michel de Bourges and me aside, informed us that ex-Constituant Proudhon had remained downstairs nearly a quarter of an hour, in the hopes of seeing one of us; failing to do so, he

[22] A passage (pp. 33–37) in *The General Idea of the Revolution* shows Proudhon's awareness of the difficulty that would face the Republic in May 1852. Here he discussed the problem of revision of the Constitution, the possibility of a coup d'état, and sketched the Draconian measures that would be needed to uphold a reactionary coup against the forces of revolution. His faith was in the inevitable triumph of the Revolution, despite the machinations of royalists, the weakness of republicans, or the dangerous plans of the Bonapartists.

[23] From Octave Aubry, *The Second Empire*, trans. by Arthur Livingston (Philadelphia, 1940), p. 66. Ollivier was to become a deputy under the Empire and the leading figure in the promotion of the Liberal Empire in its last years.

had left, saying that he should await our coming on the Place de la Bastille.

Proudhon, for an offence against Louis Bonaparte, was undergoing a term of three years' imprisonment at St. Pélagie, but he was granted occasional leave of absence. By mere chance, one of these days of freedom fell on the 2d of December.

An incident worthy of special remark was that on the 2d of December Proudhon was under lawful sentence to serve his time; thus he, whom they could have legitimately detained, was allowed his liberty, while at the very moment the inviolable Representatives were illegally imprisoned. Proudhon had used his freedom to come to us.

I had seen Proudhon at the Conciergerie, where both my sons were shut up, together with my two illustrious friends, Auguste Vacquérie and Paul Meurice, and those dauntless writers, Louis Jourdan, Erdan, and Suchet. I felt sure to none of these men would liberty be granted on that day.

Xavier Durrieu whispered to me, "I have just left Proudhon down below, at the entrance of the Place close by; you will find him leaning on the parapet over the canal, where he is waiting to see you."

"I will go there," said I.

I accordingly found Proudhon at the place mentioned, buried in thought, with his elbows on the parapet. He wore the broad-brimmed hat in which I had been accustomed to see him walking up and down in the Conciergerie courtyard.

"You wish to see me?" said I, going towards him.

"Yes," he replied, shaking me by the hand.

There was no one near us. The dark and gloomy Place de la Bastille was to the left, whence nothing could be seen; but you felt the crowd by its muffled sound of breathing. Regiments were there drawn up in battle array, all ready for marching, with no signs of bivouacking; and the bayonets in the square shot forth their sparks, so perceptible at night time. Rising above this dark mass the column of July stood out in relief, straight and black.

"Listen," continued Proudhon; "I have come to give you a friendly warning. You are fostering illusions, for the people will not stir; they will be carried away by Bonaparte. And that nonsense termed the restitution of universal suffrage is only fit for simpletons. Bonaparte passes for a Socialist, and he said, 'I will be Emperor of the Rabble.' It is a piece of insolence; but impudence has a chance of success when it is supported by such as these," added Proudhon, pointing towards the sinister gleaming of the bayonets, "and Bonaparte has an object in view. His wish is to restore the populace. The Republic has made the People, but he will succeed while you will fail. He has power on his side, cannons, the peoples' errors, and the Assembly's follies. The few members of the Left to which you belong will not succeed in overcoming the *coup d'état*. You are honest, and he has the advantage over you of being a rogue. You have scruples; again has he the advantage by having none. Rely on what I say, make no further resistance, for the situation is devoid of all resources, and fighting now would be sheer madness; there is nothing left but to wait. What do you hope for?"

"Nothing."

"What do you think of doing?"

"Everything."

By the tone of my voice he knew that further persistence would be useless.

"Adieu," said he, and we parted never to meet again. He disappeared in the darkness, and I returned to Lafon's rooms.[24]

Proudhon's first reactions to the coup d'état were bitter. He condemned the coup as an insult to the nation (December 3); but he gradually returned to his work, and even offered a proposal for a colony for political prisoners which he presented in person to the Comte de Morny (December 24). Apparently Morny was more interested in his attitude toward the coup than in the proposal, but he left Proudhon with an impression that his views were of some importance to the government. Proudhon told Morny that Louis Napoleon was condemned by 7,500,000

[24] Victor Hugo, *The History of a Crime*, vol. 1, in *Hugo's Works*, Centenary Edition (Boston, 1892), pp. 149–51.

votes (in the plebiscite) to do great things for the Revolution and began to hope his advice might have some weight.

He continued to puzzle over the success of the coup d'état, attributing it to popular indifference, the fear of socialism, the discredit of the Assembly (mostly over the suffrage issue), and the failure of the *Montagne* more effectively to ally with Louis Napoleon. He continued to feel the ambivalence apparent in the remarks Hugo recalled. In February Proudhon could write that France was turned over to ruffians, robbers, and whores; yet he was one of the few Republicans who approved of the oath demanded of public officials after the coup.[25]

He began to put his views together into *The Social Revolution* at the end of March 1852.[26] He had no illusions as to the dangers his reputation ran in his writing such a book. He admitted that his conscience tortured him as he wrote. After a week he noted:

> I am giving it up. It seems to me that I am deceiving myself about the utility of this pamphlet. The more I think about it and the more I write, the more I seem to see that there is only one rational way to deal with the reigning order of things, that is with total war and by sounding the alarm against it as against a gang of robbers.[27]

[25] Perhaps some clarification is to be found in a remark he makes in his *Second Memoir on Property:* "So firm a believer am I in the philosophy of accomplished facts and the *status quo* of governmental forms, that, instead of destroying that which exists and beginning over again the past, I prefer to render everything legitimate by correcting it. It is true that the corrections which I propose, though respecting the form, tend finally to change the nature of the things corrected. . . ." This, written in 1841, sounds excessively moderate, yet it is suggestive of a technique Proudhon did not disdain. In 1851, in *The General Idea of the Revolution*, he had written: "There is, as I have said, only one way of averting the dangers of revolution. It is by making revolution legitimate." Translation from *Selected Writings of P.-J. Proudhon*, ed. by Stewart Edwards (Garden City, N.Y., 1969), p. 160.

[26] Toward the end of March, Proudhon did not believe the regime would survive for long.

[27] Quoted from *Carnets* in Alan Ritter, *The Political Thought of Pierre-Joseph Proudhon* (Princeton, 1969), pp. 186–87.

Yet he became increasingly certain that what he had to say was well worth the saying. He was impelled to write partly out of anger at the accusations against the French socialists leveled by Mazzini, blaming them for their failure as leaders of the European Revolution; Proudhon sought to rehabilitate the French revolutionary movement after the shock of December 2. He also, as his text makes clear, wanted once more to urge his favorite reform measures as those most needed for the progress of France and the Revolution. He felt his intentions were too important to abandon: to make the alliance with the republicans so desirable to the government that any monarchial restoration would be inconceivable; to make the consequences of the coup an advance toward democracy. Yet there is little doubt that the book he produced *seemed* to approve the coup and contained reasoning as tortured as that which justified its production.

After his release on June 4 Proudhon soon was ready to publish *The Social Revolution;* its sale was held up however, on July 23. Proudhon then applied directly to the President,[28]

[28] Proudhon wrote to the President on July 29. Portions of his letter follow:
Dear Mr. President:
    . . . For the five days following the *coup d'État* of December 2 and the defeat of the insurrection I felt like someone condemned to death. I had nothing to fear for myself; but the blow to the Republic left me in despair. Ah! Mr. President, you have never had, nor will you ever meet, an opponent more energetic, and at the same time, more disinterested than I. . . . I feel no more animosity against your dignity than against your person, and I am not plotting. I simply saw in you the enemy of the Republic that I had loved: you need look no farther for the cause of my opposition.
    Ever since your second rise to power I have been trying to console myself—and I would have died without this consolation—by showing myself that you were the product of inevitable circumstances, and that you, for better or for worse, were the representative of this revolution, that my friends and I had undoubtedly been thought unworthy to accomplish.
    Louis-Napoleon, I told myself, had been chosen mandatory of the revolution on pain of deposition! . . .

and on July 31 the police authorized the sale of the book. The book sold well and enhanced his hope of regaining a position of leadership in the revolutionary party. But the reviews were destructive, and he was further disappointed as it soon became

Soon afterward I wrote a book based on these thoughts: I printed this book; but the police prohibited its sale. . . .

You embody revolution of the nineteenth century, because you can be nothing else. Outside of that, December 2 would be no more than a historical accident, without any justification or significance: that is my first point. Do you realize this now, Mr. President? Do you want it to be this way? Would you dare to say it? These are risky questions, and I do not dare to resolve them: that is my second point. This is what my book amounts to: consolation for myself, hope for my coreligionists, and defiance to the counter-revolution! I gave to this book my manner, my style, my ideas, my opinions, and my fears in spite of my extreme candor, however, I did not include even the slightest attack against either the President or the government.

I did not delude myself about this book: I realized that by explaining the existence of December 2 it gave it a sort of legitimate place in the course of events; that, having thus gained historical significance, the government would gain new force; and that as soon as I had written the words: "Louis-Napoleon is the representative of the revolution," the man's popularity, so often fatal to republicans, would increase again by their seven million voices.

I said these things to myself as a man of party; as a man of the revolution, I passed over them; allow me to tell you, Mr. President, for what motive and in what hope I did this.

I realized that, as representative of the revolution, you would have to share a large part of even your smallest success with the revolution.

Therefore, in the interest of this revolution, I hoped that France, informed as to the reality of her situation, and strengthened by you against all unforeseen contingencies, would at least dare to come to terms with the question that was put to her in February: I hoped that our country, which has always dominated the intellectual movement . . . would be able without danger to continue the philosophical and social revolution of the nineteenth century, in which you yourself, Mr. President, have participated;—finally, I hoped that the spirit of democracy, stifled by exile and prisons, would find solace in my words, and that perhaps those honorable and harmless people who share my submission to the present and my hope for the future would be permitted to see their friends and homes again. . . .

I wanted the publication of my book to be an act of high morality;

clear that since he could not obtain permission to found a journal, he would have no chance to pursue his chosen career under the new regime. His efforts to enter business in Besançon also ended in failure. He was reduced to pamphlets and pot-boilers for support.

Proudhon quickly gave up the hope expressed in *The Social Revolution* that Louis Napoleon might serve as an agent of true social reform, for he found the President favored the wrong people—by the fall of 1852 he was convinced that Louis Napoleon was leaning on the feudality of industry and finance. He had hoped to counsel the government into revolutionary ways; briefly now his hopes turned to Prince Napoleon, another nephew of Napoleon I, who became heir to the throne after the establishment of the Second Empire and who had had links with the Left during the Second Republic. Proudhon corresponded with him over a project of a universal exposition, and he remained hopeful concerning him as late as the Crimean War, which he felt might require the Emperor to abdicate in the Prince's favor.[29]

The possibility of Proudhon's even living in France under

it is up to you alone, Mr. President, to make it an act of high politics. For that, my book must appear as I wrote it, with all its bitterness, its boldness, its suspicions, and its paradoxes. I condemn only those parts that may be declared criminal or offensive by the courts of justice; and I demand that the condemnation fall upon my head alone.

Four days ago, I said to myself: if there is just one man in the government of December 2 who is reasonable and sympathetic my work will pass. Must I come to you, Mr. President, to find that man?

I am, etc. . . .

Sincerely,

P. J. Proudhon

[Translated for this volume by James E. Michael and revised by the editor. From Proudhon's *La Révolution Sociale démontrée par la Coup d'État du Deux Décembre*, in *Oeuvres Complètes*, pp. 107–9.]

[29] It was to Prince Napoleon that Proudhon made his famous remark to the effect that he dreamed of a society in which he himself would be guillotined as a conservative.

the Empire ended when he published his greatest work in 1858, the multivolume study *Of Justice in the Revolution and the Church*. What began as a response to an insulting biographical sketch of Proudhon burgeoned into a major philosophical treatise on the problem of human dignity, containing a large scale attack upon the Church. Proudhon was prosecuted for the work, and to avoid imprisonment he fled to Brussels where he lived in exile with his family from 1858 to 1862.

He delayed his return to France despite an amnesty, hoping to be able to publish freely once he was back in Paris. A misunderstanding of his views on the question of nationality brought a mob outside his house in Brussels which believed he was advocating the annexation of Belgian territory to France. In consequence he hastened his departure for France. His actual view opposed the unification movement in Italy (1859–60) and French participation therein as a distraction from the Revolution. His ideal was confederation on the Swiss model, a position virtually unique and thoroughly unpopular among radicals in the mid-nineteenth century. It made him anathema to Mazzini-style democrats, in part because by adopting such views he gave the impression of supporting the Papacy, which he had always opposed.

Proudhon had completed *War and Peace* (1861)[30] and had many more works under way when he returned to France, and even though he was troubled by increasingly bad asthma attacks, he still wrote a major compendium of his social and political views, *Of the Federal Principle* (1863), and had virtually completed *Of the Political Capacity of the Working Classes* when he died in 1865.

In his last years, he filled out the political aspect of his mutualist scheme, envisioning a federalism wherein men would owe no all-absorbing loyalties, yet where, through a system of contracts reaching from the family through the commune to the

[30] Which included some glorification of martial virtues. He did believe, as our selection shows, that they are softened by civilization.

province, they might be effectively organized while yet remaining free. Alan Ritter has described this as a system of "universalized negotiation."[31] Proudhon had little faith in the parliamentary system, and he deeply distrusted universal suffrage —particularly after the coup d'état.[32] He concluded that voting made sense only in terms of vocational divisions and democracy was suitable only under a federal arrangement.

His book on the working class reflected the changing status of the labor movement and of his reputation in it. Here he sought to give advice to an increasingly organized worker group, which had just begun to enter the politics of the Empire.[33] Proudhon was concerned that the workers abstain from voting, that they avoid the political process lest they appear to lend their approval to the regime. Besides urging avoidance of politics—an attitude that came to characterize the French working class for

[31] Alan Ritter, "Proudhon and the Problem of Community," *Review of Politics*, October, 1967, p. 470.

[32] "How could universal suffrage reveal the thought, the real thought, of the people, when the people is divided by inequality of fortunes into classes subordinate one to the other and voting either through servility or through hate; when this same people, held in restraint by authority, is incapable notwithstanding its sovereignty of expressing its ideas on anything; and when the exercise of its rights is limited to choosing every three or four years, its chiefs and imposters?" (Quoted from the *Confessions* in Carr, p. 43.) Parliament is ". . . a political system invented for the express triumph of talkative mediocrity, of intriguing pendantism, of a subventioned Press, exploiting cheap advertising and blackmail, where compromises with conscience, vulgar ambitions, barren ideas, together with oratorical platitudes and rhetorical glibness are sure avenues to success: where contradiction and inconsequence, the lack of frankness and boldness, erected into prudence and moderation, are perpetually on the day's programme— such a system needs no regulation, it is enough to depict it." (Quoted from *The Political Capacity of the Working Classes*, in Soltau, pp. 277–78.)

[33] The "Manifesto of the Sixty" had urged voting by workers for working-class candidates in the elections of 1863. Proudhon had been consulted about it, and his book constituted an extended answer.

many years to come—Proudhon also revealed his continuing opposition to worker organization, unionism, and strikes.

His theories, in fact, of mutualism and federalism seem most suitable to a world without trade unions; nor is there much to indicate that Proudhon had faith in the power of the industrial plant to transform society and produce plenty. Social transformation, instead, was to come from a fundamental moral regeneration.

Proudhon's posthumous reputation was carried on in France by worker groups, which perpetuated concern for mutualist and federalist arrangements as well as avoidance of politics in the International, in the Paris Commune, and in the Syndicalist movement, whose theorist, Georges Sorel, was a profound admirer of Proudhon. Outside of France the international anarchist movement, beginning with Bakunin, especially southern European anarchism, was much influenced by Proudhon. Later in the century the work of Prince Peter Kropotkin and English Guild socialism both reveal Proudhonian influence. The Right, especially the far Right in France, has found attractive his support for peasant virtues, his intense patriotism, his abhorrence of *other* socialists, his scathing attacks on constitutions, democracy, and parliaments, as well as his anti-semitism: all these gave rightists ammunition for interpretations of Proudhon to fit their needs and quotations they could use, so an anti-fascist has seen in him a forerunner of fascism.[34]

The interpretation of Proudhon as the supporter of right-wing causes is obviously most to the point here, where once and only once he appeared to give aid to the destroyer of the Republic, to the man who committed an act of political immorality and who was the open enemy of Proudhon's supposed revolutionary allies—most of whom had just been imprisoned

[34] J. S. Schapiro, *Liberalism and the Challenge of Fascism, Social Forces in England and France, 1815–1870* (New York, 1949), ch. XIV; Alan Ritter has given a splendid resumé of the range of interpretations of Proudhon in his recent study, *The Political Thought of Pierre-Joseph Proudhon*, ch. I.

or exiled. But we need no longer hunt for forerunners of fascism—it was on the whole a very unsatisfactory historical activity that produced little but new distorted visions of figures who had not been looked at in that way before. We may simply assert that Proudhon's most invariant position was opposition to government power and that he was a radical social reformer, despite the fact that conservatives find things to please them in his writings, especially among his moral beliefs. A more significant issue is Proudhon's apparent amorality or Machiavellianism. We must, I think, at least wonder what was the range of moral choices open to him and his readers in the light of realistic alternatives; much, I think, as we should do in reading Bagehot's interpretation of the coup—another piece of writing very difficult to assess. It may very well be that Proudhon's proposal that Louis Napoleon lead the social revolution evidences a badly mistaken judgment of the man and of the situation.[35] A careful reading will help answer whether Proudhon was over-sanguine. It is well to ponder also to whom he was addressing his work. Since his audience is apparently a chastened radical Left, he seems to offer them the simple alternative: Louis Napoleon to lead the Revolution, or—nothing.

The Social Revolution treats almost all Proudhon's favorite themes, omitting only the expanded doctrines of justice, federalism, and international affairs he would later develop. It would have been unlike Proudhon to fail to take advantage of the work to portray his view of the Revolution as a whole. He reasserted the need to break the power of the Church and sketched the political and economic transformation that must occur to allow for the progressive liberation of man, the fulfillment of the anarchist ideal. He stressed the Second Republic's failure to fulfill the demands of the Revolution and included a resumé of the career of Napoleon I (which we omit) that serves to exemplify his fundamental belief in the ongoing power of

[35] Though Louis Napoleon has been subsequently interpreted as a social reformer, e.g., by Albert Gúerard.

events over their participants, in the historical necessity requiring men to carry out the idea of the Revolution (even though he insists they retain freedom of action). The application of this almost Hegelian view of the leader's mission or mandate to Louis Napoleon is, of course, central to the book's argument.

We find interesting similarities to our other selections: Proudhon and Bagehot both mistakenly expected the army to defect from Louis Napoleon, both touched on aspects of the French national character, and both *claimed* their respective works would avoid the issue of legitimacy—but in fact, the whole of Proudhon's book is an assessment of the revolutionary legitimacy of the coup d'état. Proudhon showed himself able to anatomize society into economic categories that resemble those of Marx and to link social, economic, and political factors in a similar way. He saw the political parties based on classes and their opposition supporting Louis Napoleon's power. Like Hugo, Proudhon believed the coup d'état was very close to being defeated; again like Hugo, he deflated the "red scare." Both saw the President entrapped in an inevitable current of socialism and, along with Marx, depicted Louis Napoleon shaking up everything in France. Finally, along with Hugo, Marx, and even Bagehot, Proudhon saw the coup d'état offering as one of its major lessons the destruction of illusions.

Proudhon's presentation is distinctive in its extended attempt to assess the direction in which the regime was moving after seven months in power and in its concern for foreign affairs.[36] Also particularly noteworthy is the weight he gives to the support of the old conservatives outside Paris and to the indifference of the masses in allowing the success of the coup d'état. Of special theoretical interest are his distinction between the will (or unconscious tendency) of a regime and its subjectivism (or subjectivity, i.e., the pursuit of chosen ideals) and his con-

[36] These may be compared with Bagehot's brief remarks on the possibility of a French invasion of Belgium and the unlikelihood of an invasion of England and with Hugo's criticism of the spurious "socialism" of the regime.

ception of the replacement of government by the representation of the relation of interests.

It is doubtful that Proudhon did much to clarify the "Revolutionary situation" with his book on the coup d'état. It remains a puzzling product of a puzzling writer. The reasoning is tortuous, and his concern for reform and for controversy casts the whole focus of the book upon a problematic future and distracts from the analysis of past and present. The unsystematic character of the book, of course, does allow for the insertion of some very impressive rhetorical passages.

G. D. H. Cole said of him, "Indeed, Proudhon was set on not being dogmatic or systematic. He believed in an untidy world."[37] It is also clear that his mind did grow and develop as he learned from practical disillusionment. He expressed views that changed over time.[38] For example, he urged first equality of wages, then abolition of wages, then determination of wages by production. The whole question of equality of rewards seems to be one on which Proudhon was simply equivocal. It is by no means clear, either, how much he favored austerity over comfort, or how possible he thought it might be to universalize the latter by means of the modern industrial plant. Similarly, his abhorrence of the state, intense as it is, neither prevented his calling upon government to introduce reform nor prevented his retaining remnants of it in his federal system. We have noted that he also shifted on the question of whether the Revolution could proceed from above or below—an important matter in relation to the coup d'état.

His weakness as an economist and philosopher and his shifts

[37] G. D. H. Cole, *Socialist Thought: The Forerunners, 1789–1850* (London, 1953), p. 207.

[38] Martin Buber agrees with Cole: "Proudhon's fear of 'systems' has its roots in his fundamental relationship to social reality. He observes society in all its contrasts and contradictions and will not rest until he has understood and expressed them." Buber also points to a transition from individualism in Proudhon's early books to an emphasis on the local autonomous community in his later writings. See Buber, *Paths in Utopia* (London, 1949), pp. 25, 28.

and contradictions are so notorious as to have engaged commentators and generated controversy for generations. His virtues, however, seem to speak very directly to our time, in a way they have not to intervening generations. His moral attachments formerly seemed to glow as old-style rural virtues. His personal virtues take on new coloration in the present. His rancor at those who congratulated him on his obtaining the Suard scholarship, because they saw it as a vehicle he might use to climb the social ladder rather than as a way of helping his fellows, was one expression of his refusal to leave the poverty he was born to. He hated traditional forms of deference as demeaning; he protested with real honesty and allowed himself no co-operation. He could be quarrelsome and petty; he could also show anger that is reminiscent of the biblical prophets. He truly and fully rejected the contemporary system and tried to set his fellows on the way toward a better order, feeling no other social good was worth the price of justice and liberty. In doing so he was and remains especially distinctive, in that he took this stance while opposing revolutionary violence and hoping that class amalgamation might eventuate. This last, particularly the opposition to class warfare, is the source of the Marxists' belittling allegation that he is a mere petty bourgeois. His creed argued for the small property owner, and in that sense he was, throughout his life, true to his original intention of working for the betterment of the lower classes, owners and non-owners, the unprivileged and the underprivileged. To them he was a staunch friend, as the thousands who followed his coffin to the cemetery well knew.

SUGGESTED READINGS

D. W. Brogan, *Proudhon*, London, 1934.

Stewart Edwards, ed., *Selected Writings of P.-J. Proudhon*, trans. by Elizabeth Fraser, Anchor Books, Garden City, N.Y., 1969.

J. Hampden Jackson, *Marx, Proudhon, and European Socialism*, New York, 1962.

Preston King, *The Fear of Power*, London, 1960.

Henri de Lubac, *The Un-Marxian Socialist*, London, 1948.

Karl Marx, *The Poverty of Philosophy*, New York, 1963.

Alan Ritter, *The Political Thought of Pierre-Joseph Proudhon*, Princeton, 1969.

J. Salwyn Schapiro, *Liberalism and the Challenge of Fascism: Social Forces in England and France 1815–1870*, New York, 1949.

George Woodcock, *Pierre-Joseph Proudhon*, New York, 1950.

SELECTIONS FROM PROUDHON'S

The Social Revolution Demonstrated by the Coup d'État of the Second of December

---

I
WHY I ENGAGE IN POLITICS

. . . I begin by declaring that I have nothing to say against the *coup d'État* of the Second of December, nothing against the authors, the associates, and the beneficiaries of that *coup d'État*; nothing against the vote which absolved it with 7,600,000 suffrages; nothing against the Constitution of January 15 and the forces that it organizes; nothing even against the tradition that it seems to want to bring back to life, to whose vestiges it is devoted, and that has remained in the heart of the people, as the last of its religions.

I do not at all recriminate, I do not protest, I accuse no one. I accept the *fait accompli*—just as the astronomer, fallen into a cistern, would accept his accident.

SOURCE: This selection from Proudhon is here translated for the first time. The translation was prepared by Kathryn Orbeton Greenberg and James E. Michael and revised by the editor. The text used is from Proudhon's *Oeuvres Complètes*, edited by MM. C. Bouglé and H. Moysset, Paris, 1936.

Does it follow, republicans, that, in the course of all these changes in the political scene, of which the end is perhaps not near, we are not to engage in a single conservative act; and because our convictions are found crumpled, our hopes disappointed, our faith injured, must we stagnate in this moral prostration worse than crime? Does it follow that we are to do nothing but curse the victor, awaiting the tardy hour of reparation, and thus by a stupid and guilty inertia, deserve our bad fortune?

God forbid! We have too many interests caught up in power, no matter in whose hands it falls, we are too little assured of the present and future of that power to be allowed for a single instant to annul ourselves in an abstention that claims to be virtuous, and that would only be cowardly. Therefore I will say what I think of things, even though I be accused by the energetic of having forgotten the pride of a republican because, while writing, I have once more bent under the necessity of the day; I will affirm again the republican principle in its plenitude, against every monarchy and theocracy; I shall foretell its triumph while the dynasties are preparing their return; I shall oppose to the politics of men the necessity of things: I shall try, as best I can, and without forgetting the conditions that the present power imposes upon me, to light the darkness of our situation with an idea, to give the country an awareness of its condition, to lift it back up in its own esteem and in the eyes of foreigners; to take precautions, in this time of sudden catastrophes, against a possibly revolutionary substitution; finally, to restore to ideas a perspective, to interests a direction, to courage a new strength, to the condemned understanding and calm. . . .

After this, let power, which I shall perhaps have served in revealing it to itself and to others, take advantage of my information; I do not hold power in awe as my religion. If the occasion presents itself, I will be happy for its progress. I, who in history recognize only governments in fact, and in theory repudiate them all, who wanted no government at all for my contemporaries, I ask nothing better than to see the one I am paying for make some changes and proceed according to my principles.

And who does not already see how much the government of the Second of December, which imagines itself to be so strong and wise, needs its most mistreated adversaries to show it the way? . . .

It is an unhappy condition of human societies, which especially the democrats should reflect upon, that a people cannot, in any circumstance, separate itself from its governors, and that unless it crushes them in revolt, which it cannot always do, it is condemned ceaselessly to set them up again even when it most detests them!

But what am I saying? That which we are tempted to take as fatal and regrettable support, what is it other than the eternal absorption of power in liberty? And in this intimate solidarity of citizen and State, in this close and indissoluble bond between our interests and the government, can we fail to recognize at this point the symptom of an impending revolution?

Is it not, indeed, the triumph of the idea of revolution, based on the very nature of things, that the ability to practice politics is from now on so linked with the exercise of every professional ability that political technique, otherwise called reason of the State, depends on a million sovereigns, and becomes an impossibility; that whoever involves himself with one branch of the general production or consumption participates in that way in the management of power and has a deliberative and fatally disturbing voice in the State; that therefore the government is no more able to be detached from the activity of producers, manufacturers, merchants, craftsmen, laborers, writers, artists, than the latter are in their work to make abstraction from the policies of government, and industrial initiative continually transforms itself into political initiative, and inevitably converts authority into *an-archy*?

It used to be thought that in order to repress the terror of democracy it was necessary, by an extreme concentration of power, to take away the sovereignty of the nation, to isolate the masses from politics, and to prohibit all writers not responsible to the ministry from dealing with political matters. The suspension of the right to engage in politics, everywhere and at all times, the restoration of authority—such was the *mot d'ordre* of the counterrevolution. Indeed, what government would be possible, they said, with the constitutional right to question the government? What religion could survive with free enquiry? What could come out of tumultuous assemblies formed of such disparate elements? The Second of December simply applied this powerful theory to the best of its means, apparently unaware that in every society the sovereign only legislates and the prince only executes from the abundance of opinion, and imagining that the best way to make the brain think is to practice ligature of the nerves and stopping up of the senses! . . .

So no more of these vain matters of delicacy and false scruples, please! Politics, surpassed, subordinated by the economy, but obstinately holding on to a separate, superior, impossible position—that is the secret of our situation and the thing that forces me, in spite of all the delicacy of the subject, to perform at this moment a political act. . . . For three years, an imbecile reaction has preached the restoration of authority, the absorption of individual liberties into the State. The present power is only the first term of this counterrevolutionary succession—I was going to say, its first dupe. Others will bring to trial the author of the *coup d'État*, recount the *Mysteries of the Second of December*,[1] give the *unrelenting orders*, name the multitude of suspects, give the names of the victims. As for me, to whom exile does not accord such freedoms (and I thank the prison which protected me with its walls), I respond to other duties. I will not permit the mystical and holographic testament of December 3 to be opened, nor a surreptitious restoration to be prepared abroad, nor worse yet a second try at constitutional corruption to be organized in the shadows, without expressing my reservations beforehand. Responsible, whether I like it or not, as a citizen, writer, and head of a family, for the acts of a power I was not in favor of; convinced, moreover, that in the

[1] Title of an anti-Bonapartist book on the coup by M. H. Magen which appeared in 1852.

event of the Second of December there is still something other than a conspiracy; having no guarantee, far from it, that either a democracy, a true democracy, will in time return, nor that another palace revolution will cause us to enjoy a regime more complete in its liberty; not trusting any prominent man, either princely or popular, with the care of the general interest and public liberties: once more I take up the course of my publications. While conforming to the laws, I make use of what initiative remains to me; I present to my fellow citizens, and through them to the President of the Republic, my reflections on the causes that have brought about the most recent events and the results that, according to me, they must produce; and without shame I beseech Louis-Napoleon to look at the situation as soon as possible, for truly, for himself and for us, I dare say that it is urgent!

For him, first of all. They say that like the Emperor he has faith in his star. If such is his superstition, far from laughing at him I congratulate him. Indeed no glass is needed to see this star, nor a table of logarithms to calculate its course. It is seen with the naked eye, and everyone can say where it is going.

On February 24, 1848, a revolution overturned the constitutional monarchy and replaced it with a democracy; on the Second of December, 1851, another revolution substitutes for this democracy a ten-year presidency; in six months perhaps a third revolution will drive out the presidency and re-establish a legitimate monarchy on its ruins. What is the secret of this continuing change? The same propositions, reproduced in other terms, will reveal it to us.

What Louis-Philippe could not understand produced the downfall of Louis-Philippe and brought on the Republic; what the republicans did not dare affirm produced the downfall of the republicans and decided the success of Louis-Napoleon; what Louis-Napoleon is unable to furnish will in turn bring his downfall, and it will be likewise for as many of his successors as present themselves, supposing that the country consents to pay indefinitely the cost of such unfaithfulness.

Thus, since 1848, and I could go much farther back, a *spell* has been cast on the political leaders of France: this *spell* is the problem of the proletariat, of the substitution of economics for politics, of interests for authority, in a word, the social idea. That is why the mission of Louis-Napoleon is no different from that of Louis-Philippe and the republicans, and those to come will not have one that is any different. In politics, one is not a man's heir, one is the carrier of an idea. He who best carries it into effect is the legitimate heir.

Of what importance is it then that the social idea no longer raises irritating disputes in the press, that it has ceased passionately to interest the crowd, that the capitalist thinks himself delivered from the nightmare, that the commissioners of Louis-Napoleon congratulate him in their reports for having brought the monster down . . . if the power that was to crush it expresses, by the fact of its institution and its needs, in spite of the official protests and proscriptions, only socialism, the absorption of the political order into the economy; if Louis-Napoleon, in his most important decrees, shows the irresistible tendency that is pushing him toward social revolution?

No, socialism is not defeated because it has not yet been demonstrated; because as yet it has only encountered insults and bayonets; because there is not one interest that is expressing it; because the government of the Second of December, after proscribing it, had to set itself up as its interpreter; because the Second of December borrows its popularity, inspires itself with its solutions, seems held back only by the desire to reconcile the existing interests with those which it would like to create; because, in a word, according to some reports to which one may give some credence, Louis-Napoleon may be *the worst*, or if you wish, the first, *of the Socialists*, the last of the men of government! Is it Louis-Napoleon, then, who will bring about social revolution? Is it the grandson of Charles X, the grandson of Louis-Philippe, or anyone else you would like? . . . because in truth we can no longer say in the evening who we will be governed by in the morning. Again, of what importance is the name of the person? The same star rules them all. . . .

II
THE SITUATION OF FRANCE ON FEBRUARY 24, 1848

There are some people who, referring to the *Fall of the Roman Empire,* say to you quite seriously of the Second of December: The French nation is corrupt, degenerate, and cowardly. She has forsaken her providential mission and given up her glory. We can expect no more from her; let another take her place and wear her crown.

Many Frenchmen, quick to condemn themselves, repeat these foolish things.

Others, affecting a Hippocratic air, blame socialism. Socialism, they assure us, is what has killed democracy. The people, by themselves, were pure, virtuous, devoted, and full of good sense. But the spirit of the people was made materialistic by the preachers of socialism, and their heart was distracted from the public interest and diverted from action. It is because of the influence of these destructive ideas that the people were misled as to the significance of the *coup d'État,* and that they applauded when the Assembly was violated and when the generals were arrested. They had been taught to suspect their own representatives: they did not respond when the representatives called upon them and, in the treacherous scheme of the Second of December, they saw only the re-establishment of their right to universal suffrage.

Citizen Mazzini, the archangel of democracy, made himself the spokesman of this opinion.

Here are some other variants on the same event:

It was the Left that assured the success of the *coup d'État* when, on November 17, it voted against the Quaestors' motion.

It was the press of the Élysée that frightened the bourgeoisie with its stories and kept it indignant.

It was the attitude of the army, fierce and corruptible, that discouraged patriotism among the citizens.

This did it, that did it!

Little causes are always used to explain big events! Other countries have also taken note of these miserable defeats, and cannot understand how thirty-six million men, in the space of one day, could be hoaxed and muzzled; they all jeer at us and proclaim that our country is fallen. People who do not know us, or who do not realize what kind of a revolution we are undergoing, or who having heard a little bit about the revolution and, like our conservatives, believe it to be absurd, heap sarcasms on our chosen race, and give us up to opprobrium. The Englishman has trouble containing his delight and blushes at our experience, while devouring our territory in anticipation; the American with the insolence of the emancipated, spits on our name; one after another, the metaphysical German, the feudal Hungarian, and the bigoted Italian all pillory us. While the Holy Father makes us kiss his toes, the prophet Mazzini presents us the sponge dipped in gall and pronounces our *Consummatum est!* What a triumph for the envy throughout Europe! And what a lesson for posterity! France of 1848, daughter of 1792 and of 1830! France, the emancipator, commits an adultery one moment and gives birth to socialism. Immediately she betrays the nationalities and assassinates the republics; she kneels down before the cadaver of the papacy, kisses the ghost of tyranny, and dies!

Oh! would that I had only to answer to ignorant pedants! If it were once again a simple matter of lashing out at those mystagogues—sycophants of revolutions which they failed to foresee and which pass them by—But I have a more serious duty to perform. I must justify my nation in the eyes of history, by removing the weight of this disgrace, with which her rivals hope to crush her. One miserable day of sorrow for France is a hundred thousand times greater than the passion of the Son of God

—If it is possible, then, let us all forget our grievances; let us reason deliberately and review the causes and effects. Let history, showing us in our errors the causes of our defeats, teach us finally how to correct them. In the fire of adversity, let parties and sects disappear; let intolerance be quelled, and liberty alone be valued. . . .

IV
UNIVERSAL PREJUDICE AGAINST REVOLUTION ON FEBRUARY 24. WITHDRAWAL OF THE REPUBLICANS

In search from cause to cause through the history of society, I seem to see that what has deceived nations for four centuries and still shackles the human mind, what produced all the evils of the first revolution and caused the movement of 1848 to miscarry, is the generally held prejudice concerning the nature and effects of *progress*. Things happen in society in a certain way; we conceive of them in another, into which we struggle to put them. As a result there is constant contradiction between the practical reason of society and our theoretical reason; that is the source of all the noises and disturbances of revolution. . . .

We draw our conception of *progress* from the sciences and industry. There we observe that discovery is added unceasingly to discovery, machine to machine, theory to theory; that a hypothesis admitted at first as true and later demonstrated false is immediately, necessarily, replaced by another. The result is that there is never any void or empty place in knowledge, rather, accumulation and continuous development.

We apply this idea of progress to society; I mean to say to the great organisms that up to now have served as its forms. Thus we want every political constitution to be an improvement on the previous one; every religion to present a doctrine richer, more complete, more harmonious than that which it replaces;

and all the more, we want every organization of the economy to realize an idea more vast, more comprehensive, more complete than that of the preceding system. We would not think that while society is advancing on one point it might be regressing on another. And the first question that we ask the innovators who talk of reforming society, abolishing this and that institution, is: *What do you put in its place?*

The men who involve themselves with government, the minds biased with religious ideas, those impassioned with metaphysical constructions and utopias for society, and, in their turn, the common people, are incapable of imagining that reason, consciousness, and even more, society, do not have an ontology, an essential constitution—the increasingly explicit affirmation of which is the perpetual *profession of faith* of humanity. One system destroyed, they search for another; they need the sense of their minds' being within universals and categories, their liberty within prohibitions and licenses. A surprising thing—most revolutionaries, like the conservatives they are in combat with, dream only of building prisons for themselves. . . .

Nothing is more false than this concept of social progress.

The first task of any society is to make a set of rules for itself, essentially subjective, a work of speculative minds, accepted by the vulgar without discussion, which from time to time is honored by the cleverness of some just prince; but having no foundation in the life of the species, it sooner or later degenerates into oppression. A labor of opposition to power begins immediately and does not stop. Liberty, taken as the principle of criticism, tends to occupy all the space; while the political man is making efforts to reform the State and seeks perfection for the system, the philosopher perceives that what claims to be a system is nothingness; that the true authority is liberty; that instead of a *constitution of created powers,* what society is looking for is the equilibrium of its natural forces.

This is the way, furthermore, with all things that proceed from pure reason. At first these constructions seem necessary, endowed with positiveness of the highest degree, and the problem seems to be to grasp them in their absolute state. But soon analysis, taking up these pure products of understanding, demonstrates their emptiness and allows to stand in their place only the faculty which caused them all to be rejected, that of criticism. . . .

. . . There are not two types of government, there is only one: it is the government of hereditary monarchy, more or less hierarchical, concentrated and balanced, following on one hand the law of property and on the other the division of labor. That which is called aristocracy here, democracy or republic there, is only monarchy without a monarch—just as the Church of Augsburg, the Church of Geneva, the Anglican Church, etc., are papacies without popes, just as the philosophy of Monsieur Cousin[2] is an absolutism without an absolute. Now, once the royal form of government is cut into by democratic control, whether the dynasty is conserved as in England or abolished as in the United States, is of little importance; it is necessary that, progressing step by step downward, this form perish completely, without the emptiness that it leaves ever being filled. In the matter of government, after royalty there is nothing.

Certainly, the passage cannot be accomplished in a day; the human mind does not pass in one bound from *something* to NOTHING; and the reasoning of the public is still so weak! But what is important is to know where we are going and what principle leads us. . . . In a democracy there is no place, in the last analysis, for either constitution or government. Politics, about which so many volumes have been written, and which is the specialty of so many brilliant minds, is reduced to a simple contract of mutual guarantee, of citizen to citizen, commune to commune, province to province, people to people, variable in its provisions according to the subject matter, and revocable *ad libitum*, endlessly. . . .

Thus progress in the oldest institutions of humanity—philosophy, religion, and the State—is a continual process of negation,

2 See above, p. 143, note 3.

not without compensation, but without possible reconstruction. . . .

In the economic order there is no agricultural-commercial-industrial system; there will never be one, no more than there is for free thought any philosophic system; for the conscience, a theology; for liberty, a government. It is wasted time, ignorance, folly to look for it; it is counterrevolution. Economic perfection lies in the absolute independence of the worker, just as political perfection lies in the absolute independence of the citizen. This high perfection, impossible to realize in its ideal form, is approached progressively by society in a continuous movement of emancipation. To reduce indefinitely the burdens on production, the deductions from salaries, the restraints imposed on circulation and consumption; to reduce the weariness of work, the difficulties of manual labor, the hindrances to credit and to commercial opportunity, the slowness of apprenticeship, the convulsions of competition, the inequities in education, the accidents of nature, etc., by means of a contract of guarantee and mutual aid—there you have, in the economic order, the whole Revolution, there you have progress. . . .

. . . No more dogmatic religions, governmental constitutions, industrial organizations; no more utopias, either on earth or in heaven. Like reason, conscience, liberty, and work can bear neither authority nor protocol. . . .

Neither conscience, nor reason, nor liberty, nor labor, pure forces, primary and creative faculties, can, without perishing, be mechanized, become constituent or integral parts of any subject or object whatever—they are by nature without a system and one of a kind. Within themselves is their reason for being, in their works is where they must find their reason for acting. In this consists the human person, a sacred entity that appears in its plenitude and radiates with all its glory at the instant when it casts off all sentiment of fear, all preconception, all subordination, all participation, and can say with Descartes, *Cogito, ergo sum;* I think, I am sovereign, and, exalted to ecstasy, I am God.

If the men of the Provisional Government had been convinced of the truth of these ideas, how easy the Revolution would have been for them! With what calm and security they would have received the clamor that started to rise against democracy and which, left without response and giving rise only to embarrassed, sheepish protestations, was so soon to engulf it: "What! always negate! always destroy! always ruins! always nothingness! That is what one calls progress and liberty!" . . .

The men of the Provisional Government made the *Republic* a symbol of MORALITY. They were pious, modest, full of honor and scruples, prompt with self-sacrifice, slaves of legality, incorruptible guardians of democratic decency, above all sincere. They carried high republican heroism. Of all the things they could have done toward Revolution, their religion dared allow itself only one, and it found out that this one thing, demanded by principle, was, from the point of view of the cause, too advanced, and sovereignly impolitic: universal suffrage!

Now the Revolution having been signaled and not effected . . . what could come of the situation? . . .

The essence of all revolution is to displace the mass of interests, to crumple a few, to create a much greater number of them. For that reason, any revolution has as natural adversaries the interests that it endangers, just as it has as partisans those which it fosters. . . .

. . . A coalition formed against democracy, made up of all who wrongly or with reason had been afraid: property owners, manufacturers, business men, the Bank, the clergy, the peasants, bodies authorized by the Constitution, military staffs, that is, two thirds of the country. On May 15,[3] on June 24, revolutionary democracy tries to regain command: It is opposed with its own law, universal suffrage—it is crushed. So the duel is moved to the ground of the new Constitution. But, alas, that Constitution, no matter how it might turn out, was the sign of the retreat of the democrats.

[3] May 15, 1848, when a demonstration on behalf of Poland led to an invasion of the Constituent Assembly.

As for me (I do not conceal it), I worked with all my strength for political disorganization, not out of revolutionary impatience, not for love of vain celebrity, not for ambition, envy, or hate, but with the expectation of an inevitable reaction, and in any case with my certitude that in the form of government in which it persisted in maintaining itself, democracy could not do anything for the good. As for the masses, as impoverished as was their intelligence, as feeble as I knew their virtue to be, I feared them less in full anarchy than with a ballot. With the people, as with children, crimes and offenses stem more from mobility of impressions than from perversity of heart; and I found it easier for a republican elite to accomplish the education of the people in political chaos than to have it exercise its sovereignty, with some chance of success, the electoral way.

New developments made useless that desperate tactic for which I have long braved public censure; and I joined wholeheartedly the honest men of all parties, who, understanding that *democracy* is *demopedy* (education of the people), accepting this education as their task and placing LIBERTY above everything, desire sincerely, along with the glory of their land, the well-being of the workers, the independence of nations, and the progress of the human spirit.

V
THE SECOND OF DECEMBER

The situation set, the events are to take their course.

While the wealthy class swears hate for the Republic, and the Republican party, fallen into constitutionalism, withdraws, Louis Bonaparte, carried by five and a half million votes, becomes the organ of the Revolution. So goes the logic of things—the competition of parties, the crisscross of intrigue, the excitement of personalities do not permit us to understand it.

No matter who was elected December 10, being the product,

in effect, of a revolutionary situation, he was forced to become the organ of revolution, under penalty of a prompt fall from power. The coalition of reactionaries, in supporting Louis Bonaparte, acts as if in making sure of the man it could exorcise the thing; as for democracy, in persisting after the election in an opposition too well justified, also too often forgot that its cause could not depend on the good pleasure of the man whom the Revolution had just given itself as leader—a contradiction on both sides which was to bring on a host of others. . . .

Louis Bonaparte, independent of the popular feeling that had raised him to power, was therefore, after December 10, the representative of the Revolution; judging from his alliance with the chiefs of the old parties and the opposition of the Republicans, he was, on the contrary, the head of the counterrevolution. This reversal of roles, which put everything in a false situation, almost cost the new President dearly. He would have been irreparably ruined if from the end of 1849 he had not disavowed, in a fairly direct and formal manner, the politics of the majority; if, above all, that majority had not contrived for him, in the law of May 31, 1850, a lifeline.

Let us pass by the years 1849, 1850, 1851, and then arrive at the Second of December.

The appearance of democracy in public affairs had in reality produced only one result, which was to make universal suffrage popular, at least for a while, in representing it to the people as the infallible instrument in social revolution. Now the law of May 31 had reduced by a third and falsified universal suffrage by the system of exclusions; democracy, in turn, was making the maintaining of this law a *casus belli* for 1852. The occasion was a decisive one for Louis Bonaparte. His re-election depended on his popularity, and his popularity on the conduct he was going to follow concerning the re-establishment of universal suffrage. The whole question for him was to know whether, in supporting the law that his ministers had voted for, he would make himself the Monck[4] of a new restoration, or whether in joining the Republicans he would become a second time the visible leader of the Revolution. With the royalist majority, Louis Bonaparte would descend from the presidential chair, like Cincinnatus, Monck, Washington, all of them, not taking even a retirement pension. Joined with the democrats, that is to say, with the democratic principle, he was at the head of a superior force and without a possible competitor. The Constitution was dismissing him, that is true; but the people would call him back! Louis Bonaparte, of his own initiative, proposed therefore the abrogation of the law of May 31, thus placing the cause of universal suffrage under his protection: All his popularity came back to him at that instant; he became *ipso facto* and in spite of everything master of the situation.

And he gained from this action two immense advantages: the first was to have vote with him, for him, whatever repugnance it felt about it, the whole Left, and in that way he appeared in the eyes of the people as the head of the Revolution because he was in agreement with the revolutionaries; the second was to give the majority the unhappy alternative of either being entirely subordinated and discredited if it followed the President or of itself giving the signal for civil war if it persisted. To him the handsome role, to it the odious character. This latter choice was the worst, because while the majority would be expressing its support for maintaining the law, sacrificing to a point of honor all the hopes for its cause, the President would be refusing to lend a helping hand to its decrees. In this conflict between the monarchy and democracy Louis Bonaparte appeared simultaneously to the people as the defender of its rights and to the bourgeoisie as the protector of its interests.

It was however that way of action the majority chose. History will brand these decrepit minds, these impure consciences, who

---

[4] General George Monck, (1608–70), lieutenant general under Cromwell; in 1660 he supported the Stuarts, dissolved Parliament, and caused the election of a new parliament which restored the Stuart monarchy.

preferred the risking of liberties to a reconciliation with the Left, and who, in such a clear situation, capable with a word of annulling the good fortune of Bonaparte, worked with all their powers, with all their cunning, for the triumph of the man they hated.

From November 4 to November 30 the action proceeds with a military quickness. The Élysée proposes, in its message, the repeal of the law of May 31: the *Montagne* gives its support. The Élysée abstains from voting on the municipal law:[5] the *Montagne* does likewise. The Élysée, seizing upon the system of abstention, recommends to the electors that they not attend the Paris electoral meeting. Democracy, obligated by precedents, also abstains. The Élysée finally rejects the proposition of the Quaestors: the *Montagne* votes with it. The *Montagne* and the Élysée are one body, the fusion appears complete.

This last vote of the Montagnards has been criticized—unjustly, in my opinion. Already they were dominated, absorbed: an about-face to the side of the majority would have only made the situation more complicated, more dangerous, without removing any of the advantages for the President. . . .

As for me, I share completely the opinion expressed by Michel de Bourges[6] and Victor Hugo. They could not, as they have said, strengthen the law of May 31, the counterrevolution; they could not, without abandoning the politics of principles for those of personalities, at this point set their conduct in opposition to their words. The rejection of the repeal of the law of May 31 and the proposal of the Quaestors were two solidary acts, which good sense prevented splitting up. For as much as one returned within the bounds of the Constitution with the proposal of the Élysée, equally, one departed from it with the proposal of the Quaestors, true equivocation. To vote today for universal suffrage was to obligate oneself to vote tomorrow against erecting a dictatorship in opposition to the presidency: the whole misfortune

[5] A reduction in residence requirements for voting in local elections.
[6] Michel de Bourges (1797–1853), was a leading parliamentary spokesman for the Social Democrats.

of the *Montagne* at this occasion, was not to embrace resolutely the situation that was made for it, not to accept, just as it was, its alliance of the moment with the Élysée and follow its consequences through to the end. . . .

If the thought of February 24 was without comparison more grandiose, more elevated, than the fatality of the Second of December, it is far from holding as profound a lesson. That a government collapses beneath the distaste of the public; that a democracy shows itself at the beginning to be peace-loving, conciliatory, pure of violence, lies, and corruption; that it carries its considerateness to minutiae, the respect for people, opinions, and interests to the point of sacrifice of itself—all this, the product of an already advanced civilization, material for poetry and eloquence . . . has nothing momentous for the spirit, nothing for philosophy.

But that a man in the state of dilapidation that Louis-Napoleon was in before the Second of December, a President on his way out, having since his election done nothing that asserted his person, absorbed or overshadowed as he was by his ministers, thwarted, contradicted, abandoned by those who were faithful to him, watched by all the parties, having nothing to recommend him but an uncle who died in the islands, thirty-two years back! That this man, I say, alone and against everyone, with known means and the help of two or three men in his trust, quite unknown until then, attempts a *coup d'État* and succeeds: that is what, better than any other event, shows the force of situations and the logic of history. That, Republicans, is what we must profoundly reflect upon, and what must put us on guard hereafter against all subjective and arbitrary politics.

Let it be repeated indefinitely that the Second of December was a trap, the act of a highway robber, a situation in which the army showed itself to be fierce, the people cowardly, power villainous—all that only confuses the enigma. To be sure, it was necessary to be a little the man of Strasbourg and Boulogne[7]

---

[7] A reference to Louis Napoleon's youthful attempts at invading France in 1836 and 1840.

to accomplish the Second of December; but in assigning to the event all the characteristics that one does, this still remains to be explained: how he who failed so miserably at Boulogne and Strasbourg, in circumstances which, according to our insurrectionary customs, could only gain him a certain esteem, succeeds in Paris in odious conditions; how, in the nick of time, the soldier, so sympathetic to the worker, under the pretext of discipline, acted pitilessly; why the people were cowardly, more cowardly than the government overturned by them in 1848; why, one morning, they were seized with hate for liberty, scorn for the Constitution, and adoration for force!

It is certain that no matter what one has said of the courage of the army on the Second of December, that courage was singularly excited by the complete defection, or rather by the formal approval, of the people. It is certain that for a moment, on the third and the fourth, a handful of insurgents would have sufficed to render doubtful the *coup d'État*, and that if at that time the people, filling up the streets, had mesmerized the soldiers, fate would have turned against Louis Bonaparte.

The masses (it is necessary to acknowledge it, because it is more honorable than keeping quiet), from top to bottom, were accessories, here by their failure to act, there by their applause, elsewhere by real co-operation with the *coup d'État* of the Second of December. I saw it, and a thousand others, as little suspect of Bonapartism, also saw it: It is not the armed force, it is the people, indifferent, or rather sympathetic, that decided the movement in favor of Bonaparte.

The battle was won before it was fought. For three years the Revolution, misjudged, insulted, put in peril, was calling for a leader, by that I mean to say, no longer a writer or an orator—it had more of them than it needed—but a man in a position to defend it. Bonaparte had only to answer with these three words: "I am here!" He said them, and since in politics intentions are nothing, actions everything, since for a month Bonaparte's actions had been revolutionary, the Revolution took him at his

word. It gave him victory, and only later did it have to reckon
with him. . . .

In 1848 the centralization[8] created by the Republic, the Empire, and the Constitutional Monarchy was tending to dissolve,
when suddenly once again democracy found herself the mistress
of things. Then, as if the analogy of situations was to bring back
perpetually the same antinomies, the influence given back to
the people again had the result not of fulfilling the wish of the
middle classes for decentralization, but of awakening the thought
of a dictatorship. The days of March 17, April 16, May 15[9]
had no other purpose; finally, in the June Days, the dictatorship was set up in the person of General Cavaignac, the man
who was least eager for it, against those who wanted it the most.
The example, covered by the pretext of public welfare, was not
lost: In 1849 a new try at dictatorship and again against democracy. From that moment, democracy prepared its revenge for
1852 and no longer cherished any other idea.

On the Second of December the masses were exhausted, incapable of deliberation or initiative; the bourgeoisie was anxious,
wishing to lean on a leader who would obligingly guard its interests; all parties were prepared for the great measure, from
which decisive results were expected. On the side of the Republicans, that which distinguished the *men of action* from the
sleeping ones, was that the first wanted to proceed with an energetic dictatorship, while the second were maintaining all the

[8] In an earlier chapter, Proudhon had described this centralized
authority as of 1848: "An organized *clergy*, including approximately
50,000 priests and other individuals of both sexes distributed among
the religious institutions, having at its disposal 300 million francs
worth of properties not including the churches . . . etc. . . . An
army of 400,000 men. . . . A *central* administration which had control of the police, the public schools, the public works, the taxes, the
customs, and the public lands, employing over 500,000 officials . . .
controlling everything and everybody. . . . A strongly hierarchical
magistracy extending, in its turn, its inevitable arbitration over social
relations and private interests. . . ."

[9] Days of revolutionary unrest in the first months of the Second
Republic life. See note 3, above.

same that one should remain within the bounds of Constitution.

Let us add that the monarchist ideas brought forth daily with insulting openness especially helped the progress of opinion in favor of a dictator. The principle of authority admitted by the royalists as necessary, by democracy as transitory, the thinking at that time was the same: there was disagreement only on the wording. On both sides, personal power, the authority of a single man, appeared as the logical organ and indispensable means of solution. Also, at the end of 1851 it was no longer a question of reform, of various ameliorations. Above all, it was a question of fighting. All parties were arming themselves, manufacturing powder, capturing the favor of the military men. For some, the future dictator was Changarnier, for others, Ledru-Rollin, or no matter who. The situation, which everyone was responsible for, but which no one could reckon with, demanded that it be Bonaparte. . . .

Bonaparte dissolves the Assembly by force: there is the *man of action*, the *dictator!*

Bonaparte calls on the people: there is *universal suffrage!*

Bonaparte refers himself to the ideas of 1789: there is the REVOLUTION!

The people are logical, not in the manner of philosophers who make distinctions and arguments; they are logical like the ball that comes out of the cannon, like the little hammer in a clock. . . . How could they have been opposed to the enterprise of Louis Bonaparte? They would have been obliged . . . to accept universal suffrage with one hand and push away with the other the Constitution of the year VIII; applaud in their hearts the discomfiture of the reactionary majority and support with their votes the principle of national representation: subtle operations which the masses are incapable of.

That is not all. Formerly the President had made himself known with some socialist writings: his conservative friends had practically begged the country's pardon for him. The people, which judges men after itself, knows that they can be traitorous and sell themselves, but they do not change. It said (the words are historic) *Barbès*[10] *asked for a million from the rich for us: Bonaparte will give it to us!* Largesse! as in the time of kings. That is the socialism of the people.

Soon they learn that Generals Changarnier, the terror of the working class population of the *faubourgs*, Cavaignac, so odious since the June Days, Bedeau, Lamoricière, and Colonel Charras, were taken from their homes and locked up at Mazas, to be sent on from there to Ham. The people takes joy in the satisfaction given to its hates; it recalls the words of Changarnier to the representatives—"*Deliberate in peace*"—and laughs.

A meeting of representatives, having at its head Messieurs Berryer, O. Barrot, Creton, Vitet, etc., is formed in the Tenth Arondissement. It is removed by troops and conducted between two rows of soldiers to the Quai d'Orsay. The citizens, at the passage of this fallen power, remove their hats; the people, cruel like children, without generosity insult their disaster: *They asked for it!* In vain they invoke the Constitution.—"The Constitution!" says the people. "You have first and knowingly violated it. It's a scrap in a basket."

But the *Montagne!* Its most popular members, Greppo, Nadaud, Miot, are also arrested. . . . The people, ungrateful, unfaithful in friendship, summons as a response to this news only ignoble raillery on the loss of the twenty-five francs. The Montagnards had lost popularity—do you know why? Because they were indemnified. The people, which accepts without a raising of an eyebrow a civil list of twelve million—fine, it says, if it promotes business—regards the indemnity of its representatives as theft from its purse. Twenty-five francs per day! democrats! Democracy is greed.

There was nothing, including the boldness of a surprise attack, that would not amuse the people. It seemed delightful to have the men who that evening had talked of putting Bonaparte in Vincennes and doing away with the Republic seized

10 Armand Barbès, see above, p. 65, note 2.

in their beds. "Bravo! good hit!" said the working class. No victory of the Emperor impressed them more.

This act of the Second of December remained nonetheless essentially an offense against the Constitution and the Assembly, consequently against the Republic itself. The appeal to the people could not cover it up: Calling on the people by one man cannot prevail over the written rights of the people. For the appeal to the people to be taken into consideration would have necessitated, first of all, putting things back *in statu quo*. From the legal point of view, Bonaparte was therefore guilty, liable under Article 68 of the Constitution. It was very true that this Constitution had been violated many times by those who now talked of defending it. But after all it was the law, the monument of the Revolution and of liberty. Far from having to tear up the pact, democracy had its only support in it.

The people did not want to hear anything. The people is always in favor of whoever calls it, and by the mere fact that Bonaparte submitted himself to its decision, he was sure of being acquitted.

The future will tell, in view of the acts of Louis-Napoleon, whether the *coup d'État* of the Second of December was, I will not say legitimate, there is no legitimacy against the law, but, from the point of view of public utility, excusable. My only duty is to investigate the elements, the signification, the inevitability; it is, in doing justice to those who armed themselves to combat the *coup,* to save the national honor.

The *Montagne* did its duty nobly. It marked with its blood a just cause, but a hopeless one. The blood, that of several thousand citizens, and the proscription *en masse* of the democratic party cleansed the country and regenerated the Revolution. . . . The welfare of the country, I wish to believe, and the politics of Louis-Napoleon, politics of progress no doubt, required that he obtain at any price a prorogation and extension of authority. The Republicans could not, without cowardice and perjury, permit this usurpation. They sacrificed themselves: my respects to them! Let their principles be rejected, their theories condemned, their persons proscribed, well done! Let the sycophants of the tribune, the press, and the pulpit receive the reward for their calumnies: it is their right. Posterity will render a pious justice to the vanquished, France will say their names with pride. . . .

Let the foreigner, better informed on the state of our country, the question posed in February, the degree of intelligence of the masses, the play of situations, the progress of the parties, condemn us at present if he dare! The French nation which has already accomplished such great things has not attained its majority. Lively prejudices, a superficial education given by civilized corruption rather than by civilization; romanesque legends in the guise of historical instruction; fashions rather than customs; vanity rather than dignity; a proverbial foolishness that already served the fortune of Caesar as much as the courage of his legions; a levity that betrays its childishness; the taste for parades and for public demonstrations taking the place of public spirit; admiration for force and the cult of daring replacing the respect for justice: this is a thumbnail sketch of the French people. Of all civilized people, it is still the youngest; what will this child do when grown? We have always followed our masters, and, our school-day quarrels dividing us into a multitude of bands, we have always succumbed in our protestations against authority when we have not had for an ally a fraction of the authority itself.

On the Second of December after a campaign of thirty months by the Legislative Assembly against the institutions it was charged with defending, the executive power, master of the army, supported by the clergy, the bourgeoisie, and a considerable part of middle class which feared the eventualities of 1852, tried a *coup d'État*. Like Charles X on July 15, 1830, the government divided the national representation and the higher classes, leaving the people. But while Charles X, in violating the charter, attacked the Revolution, Bonaparte claimed friendship with the Revolution and did not tear up the compact; he said so, at least, to manage the royalist parties: from that moment, the masses, if they were not fully for him, became neutral. The workers of the Saint-Antoine district distinctly refused to march. . . . The bourgeois, parvenus, ragpickers, shot by drunken soldiers in their homes, nonetheless applauded the repression of the *brigands*. . . . The peasants in several places descended on the towns with their wives and sacks. . . . But scarcely did the news spread that at Paris the *reds* were overthrown than the peasants retired and pronounced for Bonaparte. . . .

You are surprised after that by the 7,600,000 votes given Louis-Napoleon on December 20? Oh; Louis-Napoleon is really the elect of the people. The people, you say were not free! The people were deceived! The people were afraid! Vain pretexts. Are men afraid? Are they deceived in similar cases? Do they lack liberty? It is we Republicans who repeated on the faith of our most doubtful traditions: *The voice of the people is the voice of God*. Well! The voice of God has named Louis-Napoleon. As the expression of popular will he is the most legitimate of sovereigns. And to whom do you want the people to give their votes? We have had dealings with this people of 1789, 1792, 1793; they have always known nothing but the imperial legend. . . . The people know only two things, the good God and the Emperor, as formerly they knew the good God and Charlemagne. If the people's morals have incontestably softened since 1789, its reason has remained on the same level. . . .

We will finally learn that the Republic cannot have the same principle as royalty, and that to take universal suffrage as the basis for public law is to affirm implicitly the perpetuation of monarchy! We are refuted by our own principle; we have been defeated, because . . . we have not wished to recognize that monarchy is the direct and almost infallible product of popular spontaneity; because, after having abolished government by *the grace of God*, we have pretended, by the aid of another fiction, to form a government by *the grace of the people*; be-

cause, instead of the educators of the masses, we have become
their slaves. . . .

Pardon these bitter reflections of a writer who so many times
has played the role of Cassandra! I do not put democracy on
trial, no more than I nullify the vote that renewed the mandate
of Louis-Napoleon. But it is time that this school of false revolutionaries disappeared; speculating more on agitation than on
understanding, on surprise attacks more than on ideas, they
think themselves all the more vigorous and logical, flattering
themselves that they represent the latest strata of the common
people. And so do you believe that it is to please this barbarity,
this wretchedness, and not to combat it and heal it that we are
Republicans, socialists, and democrats? Courtiers of the multitude, secret agents of monarchies, which liberty sweeps away
and universal suffrage reinstates, it is you who block the
Revolution.

Who then elected the Constituent Assembly, full of legitimists, dynastics, nobles, generals, and prelates? Universal
suffrage.

Who produced December 10, 1848? Universal suffrage.

Who produced the Legislative Assembly? Universal suffrage.

Who gave full powers on December 20? Universal suffrage.

Who chose the legislature of 1852? Universal suffrage.

Couldn't one also say that it was universal suffrage that began the reaction . . . that remained deaf to the appeal of June
13; that watched the passing of the law of May 31, which
simply folded its arms on December 2!

And I repeat, when I thus accuse universal suffrage, I in
no way mean to attack the established Constitution and the
present principle of power. I myself have defended universal
suffrage, as a constitutional right and law of the State; and
because it exists, I do not at all ask that it be suppressed, but
that it be instructed, that it be organized, and that it live. But
the philosopher and the Republican must be permitted to state,
for the understanding of history and the experience of the future, that, for a people whose education, with its materialist

and heliocentric form, has been as neglected as ours, universal suffrage, far from being the organ of progress, is the stumbling block to liberty.

Poor inconsequential democrats! We have made violent speeches against the tyrants; we have preached respect for nationalities, the free exercise of the sovereignty of peoples; we wanted to take up arms to support, toward and against all, these beautiful, incontestable doctrines. And with what right, if universal suffrage was our rule, were we to suppose that the Russian nation was the least bit troubled by the Tsar; that the Polish, Hungarian, Lombard, or Tuscan peasants would sigh for deliverance; that the lazzaroni would be full of hate for King Bomba,[11] and the Trasteverans full of horror from Monsignor Antonelli; that the Spaniards and Portuguese would blush about their queens Dona Maria and Isabella, when our own people, in spite of the appeal of the representatives, in spite of the duty written into the Constitution, in spite of the blood spilled and the pitiless proscription, because of fear, stupidity, constraint, or love, I let you choose, gives 7,600,000 votes to the man whom the democratic party most detested, whom it prided itself in having worn down, ruined, demolished, with three years of criticism, excitation, and insults; when it makes this man a dictator, an emperor! . . .

VI
LOUIS-NAPOLEON

. . . I want to tell Louis-Napoleon's future. I make only one reservation about my predictions: it is that he remains thoroughly the master, at his risk and peril, to make me lie, and to outwit irrevocable destiny. The decree is inflexible but the man has the liberty to disobey and lose his soul! . . .

[11] King Ferdinand II of the Two Sicilies (1810–59); so nicknamed because of his bombardment of towns that angered him.

Louis-Napoleon . . . has his mandate, all the more imperative because he pronounced it upon himself in full strength. Does he know it? In the speech at the opening of the Legislative Body, he let it be understood that if the parties were not well behaved he could make himself Emperor, otherwise he would content himself with the title of President. What was that? Prince, you do not know exactly what you represent, the Empire or the Republic! . . .

To draw up the horoscope of a man, two conditions are necessary: to know his historical and functional meaning and to ascertain his inclinations. The destiny of the man will be what results from these two factors.

A man, in all the circumstances of his life, is no more than the expression of an idea. According to it he is made strong or is destroyed, depending on whether he procures its manifestation or proceeds counter to its influence. Especially the man of power, by reason of the general interests that he represents, can have no will, no individuality, except the idea itself. He ceases to belong to himself, he loses his free will, he is a serf of destiny. If he presumed, with personal views, to depart from the line that his idea has traced for him, or if by error he deviated from it, he would no longer be the man of power, but a usurper, a tyrant . . .

So, first of all, in terms of his historical meaning, what is Louis-Napoleon? Such is the first question we must answer.

I have already said it: Louis-Napoleon is, just as his uncle was, a revolutionary dictator, but with this difference—the First Consul came to close the first phase of the Revolution, whereas the President opens the second. . . .

Let us pass over the Estates General of Louis XVI, in which, after one hundred seventy-five years of despotism, the nation took up again its traditional Constitution, to reform it and develop it; let us pass over the Constituent Assembly, the Legislative Assembly, the Convention, and the Directory, which after all did nothing but relink this chain of time the kings had broken. But the Emperor, who called back the nobles and the priests and did not bother, however, to give back their wealth; who reopened the churches, while sanctioning the civil constitution of the clergy and the secularization of religion—that is revolution. And the Charter of 1814, which gave birth to those of 1830 and 1848—that is the revolutionary covenant.

He who was elected for the first time President of the Republic in virtue of this covenant; who, taking advantage of the same covenant, even though he tore up its last article and with pretexts of monarchist conspiracies has just had himself re-elected head of this same Republic for ten years—how could that man dare, I say, denying his principle, his right, if I may say so, his own legitimacy, support the counterrevolution!

Now not only does Louis-Napoleon carry within him, on the forehead and on the shoulder, the revolutionary stigma; he is the agent of a new period, he expresses a superior form of the Revolution. Because history is neither stationary nor does it repeat itself, no more than the life of plants and the movement of the universe. What, then, is this form whose turn seems to have arrived, and what must Louis-Napoleon represent or risk meaning nothing?

Is it that honest and moderate Republic, wisely progressive, reasonably democratic, which prevailed after February 24? But Louis-Napoleon has overturned it; he pursues its defenders everywhere. . . .

Constitutional and bourgeois monarchy?—Retire in that case, I will say to Louis-Napoleon; it is not for you to dispense this civil list, it is the Comte de Paris's work.[12] Because you have not violated the contract only to put things back *in statu quo*; get on with you then. The bourgeoisie understands how to conduct its affairs; as for power, it wants it for itself; it recognizes in the chief of state only the authority that it has measured out to him. Its maxim is well-known: *The King reigns and does not govern.* . . . The bourgeoisie is sullen with you, sep-

[12] The Orleanist pretender.

arating itself from you more and more; it would be absurd for you to be its representative.

So-called legitimate monarchy?—Then the place belongs to the Comte de Chambord![13] You are not the KING, you are the *Usurper*. Henry V makes it quite understood when he engages his faithful servants and subjects to lend you their support in all that you do against the Revolution and at the same time enjoins them to refuse you the oath.

Empire? It is said that the government appears to think that way. Perhaps it would yield to the idea!—But, I will admonish you, take care. You confuse your family tradition with your political mandate, your certificate of baptism with your IDEA. A tradition, however popular it may be, when it has reference only to the dynasty and is not based on the tendencies of an epoch, far from being a vital force, is a danger. One can use it to escalate power: it is useless for exercising power. That is why in history tradition appears constantly defeated: faith of our fathers, royalism of our fathers, ways, customs, prejudices, virtues, and vices of our fathers, you are finished forever! And you, sublime Emperor, remain also on your column: you would lose your stature if you decided to come down from it. . . .

And then, with what is an empire made and sustained? With an army, it is said. Now, with all due respect to the soldier, the modern mind loathes this influence. Napoleon, who was Emperor only because of the army, who had so many legions maneuver with so much success, experienced the fact himself. *"They want no more of it!"* he said at the end of his career. The truth is that, indeed, with the best will in the world, we could stand no more. Now the causes of the weakening of the warrior spirit, which in the most warlike nation and the most favorable circumstances got the best of the Emperor, have redoubled in intensity; and without sharing the illusions of the

13 The Bourbon pretender; Legitimists proclaimed him to be Henry V.

Congress of Peace,[14] one can doubt that Napoleon himself, had he lived in our time, would have been other than a Lamoricière[15] or a Changarnier. France, as much as, and perhaps more than, the rest of Europe, with its myriads of separate industries, its parceled out property, its needy population, living from one day to the next, looking for work, not able for a single moment, even for the defense of public liberties, to be distracted from its labors, France has become rebellious against the military profession. The bourgeoisie, the middle class, even the people are less and less sympathetic to the uniform: now only the priest fraternizes with the soldier. The country counts the expense and waits for an opportunity to call these children back to their homes, armed for defending order and maintaining the country's dignity. He who could prove the uselessness of this soldierly protection would have defeated Empire, so much do the inclinations of this country leave little chance for this hypothesis of government!

Empire, constitutional and legitimate monarchy, republic of moderation and virtue: none of these furnish the Second of December with a reason for existence nor explains the role of Louis-Napoleon. Therefore one must conclude (just as it resulted for us from the situation of France on February 24) from the empty spaces left by the first Revolution, from questions brought up by socialism, the eviction of the democrats, the proclamation of the Second of December, the approval by the people of the promises contained in that proclamation, that the Second of December is the signal for movement forward on the revolutionary road, and that Louis-Napoleon is its general. Does he want that? Does he know it? Can he bear the burden? That is what the outcome will teach us. As for the present, for us it is a question, I repeat, not of the inclinations or the capacity of the subject, but of its meaning. Now the

[14] An international peace congress had met in Paris in 1849; Hugo was its president.
[15] Christophe-Léon-Louis Juchault de Lamoricière (1806–65), general, Minister of War under Cavaignac, opponent of Louis Napoleon.

meaning of the Second of December, history demonstrates, is *democratic and social Revolution*. . . .

Could the Church, called on by the State, furnish the irrevocable mother idea, the *aliquid inconcussum* which all powers pursue and whose mobile image, similar to those nocturnal fires that make the traveler lose his way, draws them one after the other to the depths of the abyss?

I say no. . . .

. . . The year 1825 was the great era of missions, followed, in 1826, by the jubilee. Well, what this excitation of consciences produced! Several *débauchés*, without ideas and without shame, some decrepit Jacobins, for whom nothing had happened since Robespierre, taken in by the words of our young missionaries: those are the shining conversions which enriched the celebrations of faith at this time. Moreover, the same phenomena that had manifested themselves in 1801 in the bourgeoisie reappeared in 1825 in the people. It was the people's time to say its last farewell to its religion and its forefathers. I was witness, in my bigoted city, to this intemperate, intermittent devotion, I was able to observe all its symptoms. I saw men, women, youths, girls, cross themselves, be confessed, and spread at the foot of altars the superabundance of their tenderness. Because they were full of love they thought themselves faithful. But it was only a fire of straw, serving to warm their sensuality, as was shown in the intrigues of pretty singers with worldly vicars. The missionaries, using pious seduction, had had the idea of composing their hymns to the tunes of the Revolution. A strange way to make one forget it! In 1829 the revolutionary spirit blew from all directions; *libertinism* had reclaimed its rights; the people and the middle class, shaken by the mission, had gotten to know each other: it became evident in the elections of 1830, in which the clergy exhausted its influence and which decided the catastrophe of July. Religion collapsed with the throne. The cross-bearers of the missionaries, who had become national guardsmen, began everywhere to destroy the monument of their piety to the tune of the "Marseillaise": so trustworthy is the conversion of a revolutionary race!

What more? Progress is the belief of the century. Humanity runs ahead at an unbridled pace and you want me to believe in the resurrection of Christianity! Would Christ have to endure two Passions for the salvation of mankind? . . .

. . . Louis-Napoleon cannot separate himself from the society he is head of: therefore Louis-Napoleon represents, from the point of view of Catholicism, revolutionary impiety, impiety that is not only part of one era, but also dates back six centuries. What is this impiety? The leveling of classes, the emancipation of the proletariat, freedom of work, freedom of thought; in a word, the end of all authority. Louis-Napoleon, the chief of socialism, is for the Church an antichrist!

Now in politics, just as in economics, *one lives only from what one is and what one creates:* this aphorism is more certain than all of Machiavelli's. Let Louis-Napoleon therefore take his fatal title boldly; let him raise in the place of the cross the emblem of the Freemasons—the level, the square, and the plumb; it is the sign of the modern Constantine to whom victory is promised, *in hoc signo vinces!* Let the Second of December, abandoning the false position made for it by party tactics, produce, develop, and organize without delay the principle that is to make it live—anti-theocracy, anti-capitalism, antifeudalism; let it wrest from the Church, from inferior life, the baptised children of God and the Church, who lack knowledge, work, and bread, and make the proletariat the grand army of universal suffrage into men. That is its mandate, that is its power.

To make citizens from serfs of the soil and the machine; to change stupefied believers into wise men; with the most beautiful of races, to produce a whole people; then with this transformed generation, to revolutionize Europe and the world—

either I am as alienated from civilization as from the Christian god, or I am correct in saying there is enough here to satisfy the ambition of ten Bonapartes.

VII
SEVEN MONTHS OF GOVERNMENT

I have said what the Second of December was according to the *necessity of things*: it remains to be known what it claims to be through its *will*.

I call "will" in a government not intention, which is understood only in terms of persons and can always be presumed to be good, but the tendency, impersonal and collective, that its acts reveal. Actually, however despotic a government may seem, its acts are always determined by the opinions and interests that group themselves around it, that hold it in dependence upon them (far more than it holds them in dependence), and to which opposition, if it tried to defy them, would infallibly lead to its downfall. In the last analysis, sovereignty of a single man does not exist anywhere.

But if will in a ruling power is impersonal, it still does not exist without motives; it rests on considerations, true or false, which, adopted by the government and introduced into history, become there in turn, by the train of consequences, a second necessity. Thence it follows that for all governments in which the will is not identical and adequate to the reason for being, there are two types of necessitating causes. The first are objective, the result of the historical given; the second are subjective and have as bases the more or less interested considerations which govern it.

As an impartial historian, free from all party resentment, I have stated, for the benefit of the Second of December, the historical, objective, and fatal reason for its existence. In the same way, without malignity or indiscretion, remaining always within pure philosophy, I am going to descend into the heart of this power to find the secret of its decisions, a secret that the power itself, I would almost dare assert, does not know. Polemics and satire are forbidden to me; I feel no regret about that. I wish that my readers, too, would admit that it was no loss for me.

So what is the tendency of the new power, since that alone, after the sequence of facts, is important to history and politics? What is the secret, spontaneous reasoning that, perhaps unknown to it, guides the Élysée? While its historical meaning assigns its goal as Revolution, where, with a common effort, do its attractions and influences push it? Where is it actually going?

Toward EMPIRE! That is the uniform response. And satisfied with one solution that only touches the surface of things, opinion comes to a standstill, awaiting with more anxiety than sympathy this imperial manifestation.

It is useless to deny that empire can be seen in the mood of the house, in the style and etiquette of the Élysée. It appears in the restoration of emblems, the imitation of prescribed forms, the commemoration of ideas, the imitation of means, the more or less disguised ambition for title. But all this points to a memory rather than a principle, a passing fancy rather than spontaneity. We seek the idea and are shown the symbol. If the Empire were proclaimed tomorrow I would still ask why and in virtue of what does the Empire exist, all the more since reestablishing the name does not mean repeating the thing. Let Louis-Napoleon have himself crowned one Second of December, by the hands of the Pope, in the church of Notre Dame: he will no more be Emperor than Charlemagne, acclaimed in 800 by the Roman people, was Caesar. Between Napoleon, Emperor, and Louis-Napoleon, President of the Republic, too many things have happened for the latter to become the continuation, pure and simple, of the former. Just as the first and second Roman Empires had nothing in common, the first and second French Empires would have nothing in common, nothing, I say, except perhaps for despotism. Now it is precisely concerning this despotism, its origin and reason, in the conditions of the epoch, that we would demand to be informed.

The impulses that the Second of December obeys, that make up what I call its reason or private will, in contrast to its historical reason, all have their origin in the way it understands its commission.

For the Second of December, just as for the vulgar, the man chosen by the people is not, like the Roman dictator, the organ of the necessity of the moment, enclosed in a circle of historical, economic, strategic, etc., conditions that delineate its mandate. The man chosen by the people, in the thinking of the Élysée, is free of all circumstantial considerations; he acts in the absolute independence of his inspiration. He does not receive the law of things from the outside, he produces it from the depths of his wisdom. Instead of seeking, as we have done, with indefatigable analysis, the necessity of each day, in order to convert it into law and procure its accomplishment, he creates an ideal for himself, which each of his acts are then directed toward realizing, and which he applies with authority to the nation. It is in that way that the Catholic Church, by virtue of the mission it assigns itself from on high, tends unceasingly to reshape society according to the Church's pattern, taking no account of the givens of economics, philosophy, and history. Such is humanity according to the faith, it says; nothing more or less. The Second of December pursues exactly the same conduct. It moves in a sphere of ideas of its own; it governs according to a certain spontaneity of reason that causes it to accept or reject the instruction of facts, depending on whether it judges them to be conforming or contrary to its own design. . . .

That is what I call *subjectivism* in power, in opposition to OBJECTIVE law, which reveals the generation of facts and the necessity of things. Subjectivism is common to all the parties, to the democrats as well as the dynastics; its action is more intense in our country than in any other. From this subjectivism comes the mania for strong governments and the clamor in favor of an authority which is less likely to be reached the more it is sought in such a way.

The first fruit of subjective politics, in effect, is to raise as much resistance as it has ideas and interests, consequently to isolate power, to give it a constant need for restrictions, defenses, censures, interdictions; finally, to rush it through hatred and discontent on the roads of despotism, which are convenience, violence, and contradiction. . . .

I. OPINION OF THE SECOND OF DECEMBER AS TO ITS OWN MEANING

. . . Louis-Napoleon, according to the manner in which he interprets the commission given him by the people, does not clearly accept the Revolution except with reservations and within the bounds of his own thinking. Instead of subordinating himself to it, he tends, with an exaggerated opinion of his power, to subordinate it to himself; finally, having all the parties against him and not being able, not knowing, or not daring either to declare himself for one of them or create a new one that would be his, he finds it necessary to divide his enemies, and, to maintain himself, he invokes one after the other the Revolution and counterrevolution. In a certain world this would pass for prudence, cleverness; but it is what I call utopia, lack of understanding of the mandate, betrayal of destiny, unfaithfulness to his star. The Chief of State in the place of reason of the State, the man substituting himself for the nature of things: there is no longer in the government either unity of view, or sincerity, or strength. He thinks that he is sure and he is groping, that he is intelligent and he doesn't know what he is doing or where he is going. He calls himself Bonaparte or Napoleon and he cannot say what his nature and his title are. . . .

2. ACTS OF THE SECOND OF DECEMBER
CONCERNING THE CLERGY

On December 7 . . . a decree of the President of the Republic gave the Pantheon back to the Church. It was natural—from the point of view of subjectivity!

Since 1848 the clergy, while following its own designs, had rendered only good services to Louis-Napoleon, whose origin, tradition, and reason for being it however repudiated. The election of December 10 had been for the clergy the occasion for a campaign against the infidels; the expedition against Rome, carried out for the clergy's benefit, had found it no less ardent; and in the *coup d'État,* which crushed socialism, it saw a manifestation of Providence. With this system of providential interpretation, the Church serves whom it wants as much as suits it; it never gets entangled in its panegyrics and anathemas: it sings for all the powers who co-operate with its designs, swears by all the principles, affirming today the sovereignty of the people, *Vox Populi,* tomorrow divine right, *Vox Dei.* It alone has the privilege of giving its word without engaging its conscience, like giving to whomever it sees fit *the host without confession.* Its subjectivity raises it above all law. The President of the Republic, who has only a simple faith, did not consider the clergy's intentions: he showed that he was grateful. After the Pantheon, he relinquished the colleges to the clergy, declared the cardinals members of the Senate with full rights, reinstated the chaplains in the regiments, abolished (to the satisfaction of the Jesuits) the chairs of philosophy and the École Normale, the hotbed of ideologists, assigned to the old curates a retirement pension from the Orléans, wealth, etc. Could he do less for his loyal allies? . . . So let us be fair, and although philosophy is presently forbidden, let us consider things philosophically.

Undoubtedly Louis-Napoleon, in giving the clergy such a brilliant show of gratitude, wanted simply to preserve for himself, over against hostile parties, an ally that enters into and goes through them all. Moreover, he was flattering the religious fervor so suddenly awakened after February. People do not want the inventor of a religion. Yet, "A religion is needed for the people!" clamored reaction. So Louis-Napoleon finds Catholicism under his hand; he takes hold of Catholicism. If it is not transcendent genius, it is at least facile practicality; and as for me I praise Louis-Napoleon unreservedly for not having dogmatized on the subject of faith.

But in binding himself to the clergy, Louis-Napoleon performed a purely personal political act, and, as cunning as it may be, it does not compromise in the least the true principle, which is revolution. Since Charles X, the priests' party no longer existed; the decrees of the President brought it back to life. Louis-Napoleon himself understood that; and as his intention in making the clergy an instrument of power for himself apparently was not to accord it more than the Emperor had, he imposed in advance a limit to the encroachments of the Church, in the regulation of studies which rids the teaching of the sciences of literary requirements and reserves for the State the right of superior inspection over the ecclesiastical schools. . . .

. . . It is not in the character of the Church to stand for limits to its apostolate; it does not accept sharing; it wants everything—ask *L'Univers*.[16] The right of inspection, among other things, offends it deeply. By that right, in effect, it is made a dependency of the State; the divine authority that it prides itself in, revelation, the Scriptures, the councils, all this is negated. Hardly lifted up by the secular arm, the Church aspires to dominate it; the antagonism of the two powers, spiritual and temporal, starts up again: one can foresee what will come of it.

Let us suppose for the present regime a certain duration. One of two things will happen: either it will move back toward democracy and return to the revolutionary movement, for which

[16] A leading conservative Catholic journal edited by Louis Vieullot.

the first act will be to eradicate Catholicism from the institutions of the country; or it will persist in its plan of initiative, and in this case, having only the Church, with the army, to oppose the hostile activity of parties, it will be led to sacrifice to its ally, concession by concession, all the remaining liberties maintained by the Constitution.

Then once more the cry of Voltaire against the Church will resound: *Écrasez l'infame!* Then, too, the clergy will answer the free-thinkers with reprisals of intolerance; the considerations of simple conformity that the law requires in favor of religion will be changed into an obligation to practice publicly, and any profession of unbelief, manifest or tacit, will be prosecuted as an outrage to religion and a scandal to morals. . . . By virtue of the principle that the child belongs to the Church before belonging to the family, the Church will insinuate itself into the household, seat itself at the domestic fireside, take by surprise the secret of the unbelieving father, whom it will then denounce as a betrayer of his God, his country, and his children, and hand over to the secular arm. These days of triumph for the Church are not so far away perhaps. Does it not have possession of public instruction, with which it proposes to remake the next generation? Was there not a question of making the sanctification of Sunday obligatory? And who would assure me that in the great raids that followed the Second of December, the crime of lack of piety was not, for many citizens, the first cause of transportation and banishment?

And now! Let the government and the Church receive my profession of faith.

I stand on the *principles* of 1789, guaranteed by the Constitution of January 15. Since the war for Rome, for myself and my people I have broken with the Church, and I loudly proclaim my free will. Let the priest lavish his services on those unfortunate beings, still close to the brutes, depraved by their excess of animal nature, who, in order to act justly need an infernal sanction: I praise this charity, which as yet no institution has been able to replace; and if, in assisting the weakness of my brothers, the priest respects my conscience, I thank him in the name of humanity. But as for me, I believe that I have no need for these mystical formulas; I reject them as harmful to my dignity and my morals. The day I would be forced by law to recognize the Catholic, Apostolic, and Roman religion as the religion of the State, to appear in church and at the confessional, to send my children to baptism and to the communion table, that day would have struck my last hour. Defenders of the family, I would show you what a father of a family is! I fear nothing for my person: neither prison nor the galleys would force from me an act of worship. But I forbid the priest to touch my children; otherwise, I would kill the priest.

3. ACTS OF THE SECOND OF DECEMBER TOWARD THE REPUBLICANS

I understand what one calls, through an assimilation of man's convenience into the order of things, reason of State. I know that politics is no more charity than it is ethics, and I admit that a leader of a party who undertakes to give peace to his country and reform its institutions by suddenly seizing power, next insures himself of the inaction of his adversaries by arresting their persons. *Who desires the end wants the means*: once outside of legality, this principle knows no limits. And that is why I am opposed to dictatorship and any type of *coup d'État*.

But even while I myself grant these immoral grounds for power, I still maintain that there are for the dictator some considerations that regulate the exercise of his power and dominate his subjectivity. The arbitrary, in a word, is not the truth, even in the service of the arbitrary: how could one make it, for a single day, a principle of government?

Louis-Napoleon had proposed to do away with the parties: one could judge what a difference he saw among them and with what unequal measure he treated the dynastics and the republicans. Let us first establish the facts.

From 1848 Louis-Napoleon, because of the co-operation of

the conservative parties and the opposition of the varieties of republicanism, which supported against him for the presidency Messieurs Cavaignac, Ledru-Rollin, and Raspail, found himself in reality the ally, the leader, of the reaction. This obviously false position, which I for one admit was the hope of the republicans until the Second of December, was not to last longer than the electoral period. Other opinions directed the Élysée: since as a token of agreement he had adopted the politics of the reactionaries, he sought his ministers from them. June 13, the elections of March and April 1850, the law of May 31, etc., tightening more each day the bonds that linked the President to the counterrevolution, deepened the abyss that separated him from the Republic.

In 1851 began the scission that was to set him free from the majority and end in the *coup d'État*. With Louis-Napoleon thus coming into the truth of his role, it was logically expected that while he would be subject to attack by the majority, he would be supported by the republican Left. But the evolution that was just completed in the Assembly was far from winning over the country. While the majority and minority were becoming more and more hostile to Bonaparte, the conservative masses, as unhappy with the majority as the republican party was with the *Montagne,* frightened above all of 1852, continued to group themselves around the President. These are the dispositions in which the *coup d'État* found the country. On the Second of December, when the republicans rose up to defend the Constitution, the conservatives rose up against the republicans. The *coup d'État* was thus turned, like the election of 1848, to the benefit of those it threatened; having begun by calling for Revolution, it finished with a St. Bartholomew[17] of revolutionaries.

Because we were in a dictatorship, it was the dictator's duty, while taking precautions against men, to declare himself on things. Why did he not say, now that nothing could bother

[17] The massacre of Protestants begun in Paris in 1572 on St. Bartholomew's Day (August 24).

him, and in a way that he would be understood: *I am the Revolution, both democracy and socialism!* Barely escaped from the trap of the Quaestors, how did he allow himself for a second time to be drawn by the fatal sway of reaction? Certainly one would not report to Louis-Napoleon those funereal tables of names drawn up by the military commissions and which survived the state of siege. Does he know one out of a thousand of the individuals proscribed? Does he know the names of all the citizens, craftsmen, laborers, wine-growers, manufacturers, men of law, scholars, landowners, whom the Decembrist terror struck down? No. He simply allowed it to happen. Why? What is the meaning of this quadrille in which the Revolution is invoked as principle and means, and the revolutionary personnel proscribed? In which the dynastic principle is denied and the partisans of the dynasties chosen for advisors and auxiliaries?

God forbid that I come to sow new seeds of hate in my country! But how will we manage to re-establish harmony, without which we will never have liberty, if we do not learn to know the fatal mechanics that make us take up arms against each other and move us to exterminate ourselves? It is those terrified of 1852 who suddenly became terrorists in 1851; it is Bourbon, Orléans, who, while Napoleon was throwing them out the windows in Paris, were lending a helping hand in the departments to the soldiers. They are the men of the old monarchies, who, from before December 10, 1848, filling up the administrations, law courts, and military staffs, landowners, capitalists, and grand entrepreneurs, alarmed by the threats of several madmen, trembling for their fortunes and their lives, directed the arrests, the investigations, the executions, and decided, in the transport of their egoism, the victory of the *coup d'État* against their own leaders.

Now what is the situation?

Louis-Napoleon flatters himself that he has destroyed the dynastic parties in taking their place and ruining their princes; these parties, on the other hand, believe it a success to have obtained the Élysée, and as part of the spoils, the proscription of the democrats. Who has won, who has lost, in this campaign of counterrevolution? It is easy to take the count.

Now that the Republic appears crushed, the population purified, and the country placed under such strong authority that the old monarchies can already represent themselves in perspective with a liberal veneer, the partisans of the dynasties are separating themselves from Louis-Napoleon. . . . *Liberty—Property*, that is the motto of the royalists, no longer against democracy, but against Louis-Napoleon. As for the *coup d'État*, although they accept its fruits, they declare themselves innocent of it. . . .

4. ACTS OF THE SECOND OF DECEMBER RELATED TO ECONOMIC REFORM

To dissolve the bourgeoisie and the proletariat into the middle class[18]—the class which lives off its income and the class which lives off its wages into the class which, properly speaking, has neither income nor salary, but which invents, undertakes, improves, produces, exchanges, which alone determines the economy of society and truly represents the country—such is . . . the true question of February.

Here, as in several other instances, I like to recognize that the Second of December did not fail in intention. It is indeed in the acts related to the blending of classes that Louis-Napoleon showed best to what point he understood his mandate. But here again purely subjective considerations turned the Second of December away from its true goal and neutralized its good intentions. At the time when the President of the Republic should have been recruiting adherents by the thousands each day, his

18 In an earlier passage, Proudhon had written of the middle class as being "composed of entrepreneurs, landowners, shopkeepers, manufacturers, farmers, scholars, artists, etc. They are like the proletariat and unlike the bourgeoisie in that they live more from their own earnings than from their capital, privileges, or properties. . . . They are self-employed . . . whereas the proletarian is hired and works for wages."

groundwork passed almost unnoticed by the middle class and the people and stirred up suspicion and discontent in the bourgeoisie. Others will praise this policy of so-called equilibrium and imperceptible progress, which disaffects the influential classes and leaves the masses indifferent: I complain about it in the name of public welfare and the Revolution.

Nothing is easier, when one wants it, than to accomplish, without the smallest shock, the social revolution. Waiting for it is paralyzing France and Europe.

First of all one understands that for *the most numerous and most impoverished class*—the Revolution consisting in guarantee of work, improvement of well-being, development of knowledge and moral sense—no opposition to revolutionary measures can arise from that sector. The proletariat, having everything to receive, will never obstruct a revolution that has as an end giving it everything.

As for the middle class, it must be considered as being at the same time an acting party, a giving party, and a taking party: all in all, its account with the Revolution, if I may reason in such a way, comes out in its favor, through an increase in business, profits, power, popularity, and security. This class is the monitor of the people in the mutual instruction of Revolution and the mainspring of progress: the government must simply bring the middle class to heel by setting it an example, and then let it act freely. From this sector also there would be no resistance to fear, no difficulty.

All the problems come from the bourgeoisie, whose existence must be transformed and which must be led, by the conviction that it is necessary for the care of its interests, to change voluntarily the use of its capital, if it does not want to run the risk of consuming it in unproductive activity and as a result arrive promptly at total ruin.

How was this conversion of the bourgeoisie undertaken . . . ? Only justice was needed: invective and spineless dealings occurred.

Since according to the newspapers of the Élysée, which

haven't yet finished exploiting this miserable theme, the *coup d'État* had been directed exclusively against the *reds, socialists, communalists, brigands,* and *peasants;* since the beneficiaries of the Second of December are therefore the capitalists, stockholders, landowners, the privileged, monopolists, sinecurists, in a word, everything that is BOURGEOIS, the consequence was, it seems, that they were given that illusion as long as possible. Government policy, at least that of the court, prescribed treating this rancorous class with caution, making it more and more an accomplice, involving it at first by means of its vanities, prejudices, and fears, then by the authority of these first measures, bringing it into the new reforms. . . .

. . . The desire was to push back the new feudality, but without destroying it, and only while it could challenge central power; to serve the people, but without raising it above its station. For me, at least, that is the result of the acts of the Second of December. . . .

. . . Not to extend ourselves too much, we will mention, of those which concern the bourgeoisie, the decrees of January 22 concerning the Orléans family, the institution of the *crédit foncier,* the reduction of the rate of discount, the conversion of rent completed ulteriorly by the reduction of interest on Treasury bonds;—of those which concern the proletariat, a certain development of public works, notably in Paris, the creation of mutual aid funds, the memoranda of Ministers of the Interior and of the police in favor of the working classes. . . .

Such is nearly the whole of the measures taken by the Second of December in regard to the two extreme classes, and in the end, will I speak of a revolutionary transformation? A bit, but chiefly of a general subordination. . . .

What I object to in the decrees concerning discount, income, and credit based on land is their incoherence, the lack of co-ordination that one senses in them, and that betrays again the totally subjective preoccupations in the Second of December.

Since the government had the intention—assuredly quite admirable—of reducing discount, converting income, and organizing land-based credit, the first thing that it had to do, before stopping the number of reductions, was to look for the relationships between different values, so as to act then in order to obtain a desired result. For example, did one wish to make capital, which was flowing into the Exchange, flow back towards commerce and industry? It was necessary to press more on unearned income in such a way as to offer to capitalists the lure of a greater income on limited partnerships than on debts. The contrary took place: I have the right to ask why.

The organizations of land-based credit have been authorized, the bases of their constitution established. But it is one thing to authorize credit, another thing to give credit. The decree of February 28 has opened the floodgate, no doubt, but the canal is dry. Why was it not seen that in order to direct capital to the societies of land-based credit, it was necessary to force it out of the Exchange; better than that, to decree the reduction of the interest on all mortgage debts and at the same time extend the time of all the returns from two to five years? . . .

Power in France will never make anything solid, the budget will not cover its deficits, Louis-Napoleon in particular will not triumph over the bourgeois opposition and will not bring true relief to the people nor a real guarantee to the middle class; the nation, finally, will not succeed in overcoming foreign competition and reduce its tariffs—until central power, by its laws on interest, will have forced capital to demand from investments the returns offered it by the public debt and mortgages. Louis-Napoleon has the authority: let him use it, accepting in turn the authority of necessity, and he will have nothing to fear from the judgments of history nor from conspiracies. When the reason of State is simply the reason of things, the State, no matter what its Constitution, is as sovereign as it is free, and the citizens are also.

Is it in a tyrannical spirit that the Élysée has completely disregarded these principles of true political policy? No, in a spirit of comradeship. . . .

All in all, the financial reforms of the Second of December, conceived from purely personal considerations, corporative conveniences, arbitrary transactions, have not at all produced what one had hoped for. . . .

5. ACTS OF THE SECOND OF DECEMBER CONCERNING
POLITICAL INSTITUTIONS:
THE PRESS, THE OATH

The object of Louis-Napoleon's mandate is to procure either revolution or counterrevolution: I do not think that anyone disputes this pair of choices. In both cases his power, obtained and organized in view of this mandate, is dictatorial: the control, such as it is, of the council of state or the legislative body could not weaken this second proposition.

I call dictatorship the power conferred by the people on a single man for the execution, not of the personal projects of that man, but of what necessity commands in the name of public welfare. Thus dictatorial power, unlimited in means, is particularly special in reference to its object: everything that is outside of this object is removed for that reason from the authority of the dictator, whose powers cease as soon as he has fulfilled his mission.

I have already said how much I am repelled by dictatorship, so familiar to the Romans, and the abuse of which will in the end engender Caesarian autocracy. I consider it a theocratic and barbarous institution, in every case a menace to liberty; I abhor it even more when the delegation of power it supposes is indefinite in its object and unlimited in its duration. To me, dictatorship is only tyranny: I do not discuss it, I hate it, and if the occasion presents itself, I assassinate it.

I admit that Louis-Napoleon, in taking dictatorship, did not want tyranny. He set the conditions and placed the limits to his power by means of a Constitution. It was as if he had said to the country: "France has a Revolution to accomplish, a Revolution which in this divided state of minds cannot come out correctly from an Assembly, and which requires, perhaps for a whole generation, the command of a single man. I assume the burden of this Revolution with the consent of the people, and here are what my prerogatives will be."

In fact and in right, the Constitution of January 15 is no more than this agreement.

Just as I understand reason of State, which however I would like to keep muzzled, I also understand dictatorship, which I like not at all in spite of the examples that history furnishes. And because universal suffrage in 1851 wanted it that way, I have actually no objection to the Constitution of January 15: my observations are purely formal.

I wonder why the Constitution of January 15, having as its function the organization of dictatorial power, essentially transitory, makes decrees as if this power were definitive; its object being exclusively revolutionary, why does it assume a general comprehensiveness; why does it not define anything regarding either reforms to bring about, institutions to introduce, foreign relations, boundaries, colonies, commerce, or the combination of means that the accomplishment of the mandate requires? . . . The Constitution of January 15, except for several unimportant restrictions, organizes a quasi-hereditary dictatorship, because the President of the Republic has the right to designate, secretly, his successor: for what end this dictatorship? One does not know. . . . How many years, centuries, will this dictatorship last? The Constitution of January 15 gives no further information.

I have given too much proof of my indifference to constitutions to attribute to the act of January 15 more importance than it deserves or to make it a text for attacks against the government of the Second of December. I know as well as anyone else that a government does not live from the Constitution that defines it, no more than a manufacturer lives from his patents: a government lives from its acts, just as a manufacturer lives from his products. The value of the acts makes the value of the government. Nevertheless, I have the right to find out whether or not there is agreement between established power and the idea that it serves, because it is that agreement, observed in greater or lesser degrees, that shows the understanding that power has of its reason for being. I am told that the Constitution of January 15 is copied from that of the year VIII! But with the leave of the author, I answer that the year VIII is no more relevant here than the year 40: the question is social revolution or counter-revolution. . . .

Now what did the Second of December want? To serve the Revolution, and to this end to organize, under popular control, a dictatorial power? The Constitution of January 15 does not say a word about it: it only lets one see, beneath appearances borrowed from representative theory, the exorbitance of the presidential prerogative, without giving the least reason for this exorbitance. To found a regular state, the expression of the middle class, having as its purpose the development of all the resources of the country and the peaceful education of the people? . . . In that case a reform of the Constitution of January 15 is indispensable. To live its normal life, cultivate the soil, exploit the mines, exchange products, France does not need to be held in readiness for war, led to a drum beat, in the silence of the rostrum and the press, as if it were a matter of a departure for Madrid, Wagram, or Moscow.[19] The powers of the President are out of proportion to his duties; it is not the idea which rules, it is the man. . . . Why, contrary to the principles of 1789 and by a thoroughly feudal reversal of ideas, has the chief of state arrogated to himself the initiative power while the representatives have only the veto? . . . Why cannot the representatives of the people interpellate the government, demanding what it has done with their money and their children? Why cannot these representatives, deliberating without publicity as well as without witnesses, give an account to the people of the manner in which they have fulfilled their mandate? . . . And as the public mind is only formed according to what is expressed, not what is implied, sooner or later this machine, poorly constructed for the job it must do, will betray the mechanic: he will be thrown off. . . .

[19] References to campaigns of the first Napoleon.

What shall I say of the oath? One more inconsequential thing. The partisans of legitimacy, on the advice of the Comte de Chambord, refuse to give it: they have good reason, and their refusal demonstrates their loyalty. According to royalist ideas, the oath is an act of vassalage that links, with a unilateral and personal bond, him who gives the oath to him who receives it. But I confess that I would not be able to accept this political delicacy in a republican, and the reasons of Messieurs Cavaignac and Carnot[20] have not convinced me. The oath for a republican is simply a recognition of the sovereignty of the people in the person of the head of state, consequently a reciprocal contract that puts both parties in equal obligation. The royalist swears on the Gospel, the republican on the Revolution: a very different matter. It is in the latter way that Garnier-Pagès,[21] Lamartine, and Ledru-Rollin swore an oath to Louis-Philippe. Would Louis-Napoleon intend it otherwise? What is certain is that he would not dare to say so. It is my opinion, therefore, that the republican representatives, having participated in the elections under the regime of the Second of December should have also participated in the work of the legislative body and conditioned their oath by their opposition. There would be neither perjury nor mental reservation in that: it would be coming into accord with oneself and affirming the Republic. But subjectivity blinds us all: in our judgments we see only men; in our adversaries, only men; in the events that weigh upon us, only men and always men. . . .

One cannot refuse Louis-Napoleon the merit, decisive in the time of revolutions, of having dared; of having in several weeks touched everything, shaken everything, put everything in question—property, rent, interest, irremovability, official privileges, bourgeoisie, dynasty, constitutionalism, Church, army, schools, administration, justice, etc. What socialism attacked only by

[20] Hyppolyte Carnot (1801–88), of a famous Republican family, Minister of Education in the provisional government.
[21] Louis-Antoine Garnier-Pagès (1803–78), Republican, member of the provisional government, became mayor of Paris and Minister of Finance.

opinion, the Second of December—in spite of the chaos of its ideas, the confusion of its personnel, the contradictions of its decrees, the programs launched, retracted, denied—proved by its acts how fragile was the structure, how poor the principles, and how superficial the stability. The old institutions, sacred traditions, alleged monuments of national genius, were made to dance like Chinese shadow puppets; thanks to him, it is no longer possible to believe in necessity, in the duration of any of the things that have been the object of parliamentary discussions for years, and the defense of which, poorly understood, has cost the Republic so much blood and tears. Let democracy, defeated in December, return when it wishes: it will find the minds prepared, the road open, the plow in the furrow, the bell on the neck of the animal; as in 1848, it can still join to the merit of radicalism that of moderation and generosity.

With all this, it is impossible to conceal from oneself:

That in the acts of the Second of December the reason of the man, instead of being hidden beneath the reason of things, essentially stands apart from it, and sometimes obeys it, sometimes subordinates it to itself;

That this subjective tendency has its source in the manner in which the Second of December, like the multitude that it represents, the legitimists who refuse to swear, even a fraction of republicans, understands delegation of power;

That the end this tendency is leading to, the meaning that it is giving itself, is none other, in the last analysis, than itself, authority for authority, art for art, the pleasure of commanding thirty-six million men, to make their ideas, their interests, their passions, excited one after the other, serve fantasies, almost like the kings of Egypt who would consume twenty years of rule and all the forces of the nation to erect a tomb and believe themselves immortal.

Thus the Second of December, born in the history of the mistakes of men and the necessities of time, having tried some useful reforms, abandons itself, like its forebears, to the arbitrariness of its conceptions and falls back, without suspecting it perhaps, without knowing how or why, from social reality into personal emptiness.

History shows, however, that societies function and governments endure only insofar as there is unity, perfect accord of interests and views, between the prince and the nation. . . .

IX
DON'T LIE TO THE REVOLUTION

. . . I could show the Revolution time after time invoked and rejected, as under the Consulship and the Empire, finally abandoning the Second of December and Louis-Napoleon, betrayed like his uncle by his personality, and show once more the example of the revenge of Destiny. . . .

I prefer, for the instruction of my country, the edification of its leaders, present and to come, and as a measure of insurance against factions which, equally lacking in intelligence and good will, already mentally devour the succession of the Second of December, to demonstrate one last time, and with a new argument, the inviolability of revolutions.

I shall say to the Élysée, No, you cannot continue calmly in this unhappy parody of the imperial era. And if, as certain philosophers would be led to believe, you are a new incarnation of your uncle, you have not come back in order to fall into your former mistaken ways, but to do penance for them. You owe us the expiation of 1814 and 1815, which means the ten years of imperial servitude; the expiation of the legitimacy which you have restored; and the expiation of quasi-legitimacy, which you have made possible. Put yourself, therefore, at one with your time and your country, because you cannot make it alone, no more than the Italy of Mazzini, *Italia fara da se!*[22] Your star does not want it, the people do not want it; the groaning, un-

[22] Mazzini's slogan claiming Italy's ability to free itself without aid.

purified spirit of Napoleon does not want it; and I, your benevolent astrologer who only wishes, like so many others, to be done with all this, I do not want it either.

To begin with, what should be your point of departure? I have told you—Revolution.

Revolution, both democratic and social, understand, is from now on for France, for Europe, a mandatory condition, almost an accomplished fact—how shall I say it?—the only refuge which remains for the old world against imminent dissolution.

As long as a sick man has gangrene, he gives rise to vermin. Similarly, as long as society is left to a haphazard economy, it is inevitable that there will be *exploiters* and *exploited,* a parasitism and a pauperism, that will gnaw away at it like teeth in upper and lower jaws. As long as society provides itself with a concentric and *forceful* power to sustain this parasitism and cover up its ravages, there will be parties that dispute this power, power that enables the victor to drink from the skull of the loser, that enables one to make and unmake revolutions. Finally, as long as there are antagonistic parties and classes hostile to one another, power will be unstable and the existence of the nation precarious.

Such is the family history of society, abandoned to speculators, usurers, charlatans, the police, and the factions! The vices of this economic regime produce inequality of fortunes and in consequence class distinction; then, to defend itself, class distinction calls for political centralization; political centralization gives rise to parties, with which power is necessarily unstable and peace impossible. Only radical economic reform can pull us out of this circle: it is rejected. It is the conservatives who hold society in a revolutionary state.

France, the country of logic, seems to have given herself the mission of bringing about, point by point, this *a priori* thesis of poverty, oppression, and civil war.

There exists in France and as long as the revolution is not brought about in the economy there will exist: (1) A *bourgeoisie* which claims to maintain into perpetuity the old ties of work and capital, even though work is no longer spurned as servitude, but claimed as a right, and the circulation of goods being able to take care of itself practically without discount, the privilege of the capitalist no longer has a reason for existence; (2) a *middle class*, in whose bosom the spirit of liberty lives and moves, that holds the reason of the future, and, suppressed in high and low places by the insolence of the capitalist and the envy of the proletariat, forms nonetheless the heart and mind of the nation; (3) a *proletariat*, with all its vigor, intoxicated by socialist sermonizing, and that shows itself with good reason to be intransigent on issues of work and well-being.

Each of these classes vies for power, the first in order to keep down the Revolution which endangers its interests, the second to hold it in control, the third to take off on it at full speed. The division of classes then changes to a division into the following parties: (1) The party of *legitimacy*, the representative of Salic law and feudal tradition, solely capable, according to itself, of stopping the Revolution; (2) the party of *constitutional monarchy*, more bourgeois than noble, which . . . reminds the country of the benefits and glories of 1830; (3) the party of the *moderate republic*, very circumspect in the matter of economic reforms; nevertheless, it does not want royalty, nor nobility, nor a presidency; (4) the party of the *red republic*, still more administratively than economically oriented, which has taken as its program the Constitution of 1793; (5) the *Bonapartist* party, which tends to satisfy or deceive the appetite of the proletariat with war; (6) finally the *priests'* party, which, fully informed on the way that this century is going, no longer sees a way out for society, nor salvation for itself, other than in the re-establishment of the spiritual and temporal omnipotence of the Pope. I do not count the socialists as a party, although they are more republican and radical than the reds, because in none of their schools are they men of power—rather men of SCIENCE and solutions.

Three classes and *six* parties, in all, NINE great antagonistic divisions: that is France under the regime of a Malthusian economy and political centralization. That is the outcome of the *unity* of which we are so proud, which is envied by foreigners, and to which we should give as an emblem the head of Medusa and her serpents!

Now I challenge all power that will not be revolutionary—the power of Henry V as well as that of the Second of December, the theocracy and the bourgeoisie alike—to stop this division of parties and classes; and for the same reason I defy all power at this point to stand up against it. For a while you can support yourself with the antagonism of parties, like the lamp of the Pantheon on the buttresses of the dome, but this equilibrium, which was the only stability Louis-Philippe had, is precarious. Just at the moment, on the first occasion, that the parties cease to counterbalance each other, the classes to menace each other, power falls. The suppression of liberties, the torment of the press, the state of siege, the prisons of the State, institutionalized ostracism—all these instruments of the old tyranny will be able to do nothing. A government with nothing but force and millions of votes in its favor will be obliged, like Robespierre, to *purge* society incessantly, until it is *purged* itself.

The Emperor believed that he was stopping the corrosion done by parties by means of war: a detestable recourse, which shows less the despotism of the man than the extremes to which he saw himself reduced and his profound ignorance of revolutionary matters. Very well, war had the last word with the Emperor. And then, what war would Louis-Napoleon make? For what reason? Against whom? With what? I ask these questions without pressing the matter: I would not want to say anything that had a shadow of challenge or irony. So let us pass over political policy based on war. And since the Second of December is almost forbidden to give the people this imperial poetry, except in the case of taking the side of the Revolution, in act and aspiration—since it is condemned to make vile prose, economic and social, let us tell it that ideas are combatted only with ideas, that consequently there is only one way to eliminate parties, which is to form one that engulfs them all. I have explained elsewhere how in the given circumstances this absorptive party has to be composed of the middle class and the proletariat: I refer the reader to my former indications on the subject.

To deny, in the current economy of society, the necessity of parties: impossible.

To govern with them, without them, or against them: impossible.

To impose silence upon them by means of the police or to sidetrack them with war or extraordinary ventures: impossible.

It remains for one of them, no matter which, to become the instrument for absorbing them all: that is what is possible.

Then let the Second of December—and what I say to this government I say to all those to come—let the Second of December openly embrace its reason for being; let it affirm the Social Revolution without restriction or equivocation; let it declare the purport of its mandate with full voice to France and abroad; let it call to its side a true representation of the middle class and proletariat to take the place of a body of men who do not speak; let it prove the sincerity of its political position with acts that are explicitly liberal; let it purge itself of all clerical, monarchical, and Malthusian influence; let it transfer the forty-two million thrown to the priests, to the corps of teachers and doctors, the former impoverished, the latter subjected to shameful wages; let it drive out of society this band of connivers with neither faith nor law, Bohemians, spies for the most part, who plunder us; let it abandon to the pillory of opinion those damnably genteel literary men whose corrupt, pestilential breath fills the sail of any tyranny; let it loose to the free judgment of the most royal democracy all those turncoats, court dramatists, pamphleteers for the police, dealers in anonymous consultations, spies from prisons and cabarets, who after eating the dry bread of socialism lick the greasy plates of the Élysée. . . .

Do not try to outsmart the Revolution; do not try to turn it to your personal ends, setting it in opposition to your competitors and at the same time cutting out of its scarf[23] a cloak for an Emperor or a King. Neither you nor any of those who aspire to replace you can bring forth one valid idea, bring to fruition the smallest undertaking, outside of the given of the Revolution. The Revolution has foreseen everything, conceived of everything; it has set forth the plan of work to be done. Seek and when with an upright mind and docile heart you have found it, give yourself together with your country only to the accomplishment of the Revolution. . . .

"Among the many religions that contradict each other," said Rousseau, "only one is the good one, if there be one." Likewise, of the many political policies that the fantasies of parties and the presumption of men of State bring forth, only one can be true—it is the one which through constant, harmonious conformity with the nature of things acquires such a quality of impersonality and reality that each of its acts seems to be a decree of nature itself. This policy can be formulated at the Academy, in the workshop, in the public square, in consultations of experts, wherever men gather to deal with each other, just as well as in an assembly of representatives and a council of state. Elevated to the degree of authenticity where it draws completely from things and nothing from man, politics is the pure expression of general reason, the immanent law of society, its internal order, in a word, its *economy*. . . .

It is a principle in this political philosophy, which is both rational and real, that without work there is no wealth and that any fortune that does not come from work is for that reason suspect; that the value of labor is always rising and the cost of things diminishing; that consequently a minimum salary and a maximum number of hours of work cannot be assigned; that if the hectoliter of wheat is worth twenty francs, no decree from the Prince can have it sold at fifteen or twenty-five, and that any artificial raising or lowering of prices by the authority

[23] A reference to the scarf of the parliamentary deputy.

of the state is robbery; that under the regime of interest the proportional tax, equitable in itself, becomes a graduated tax to the disadvantage of the poor, without anything in the world being able to prevent it; that another corollary of interest is customs protection, so that any attempt to abolish the latter without touching the former is a contradiction; that any tax that affects items of luxury, instead of being borne by the consumer, will surely be borne by the worker, because buying is optional and the price freely fixed, and the producer of objects of luxury always needs more to sell than the consumer to buy.

How many stupidities of governments and their arbitrary policies would have been prevented! How many vexatious measures, miscalculations, deficits, how much suffering prevented! How many deadly trends stopped at their source if for sixty years these propositions, with their corollaries, had had the rank of demonstrated truths and articles of law in the general consciousness! With a dozen propositions of this type and a free press, I would like to stop short the government of the Second of December in all its escapades. What? Could it be that Louis-Napoleon reigns only because of the imbecility of the French people?

On the subjects of man in society, work, salaries, revenue, property, lending, exchange, taxation, public services, religion, justice, war, there exists a mass of similar truths, of which just a simple abstract, accompanied with examples, would rid governments of all other political philosophies and soon would rid society of the governments themselves. That is our true constitution: a constitution in command of all difficulties, leaving nothing to the wisdom of princes, which finds dictators and tribunes a joke. Its theorems, linked to one another as in a mathematical proposition, lead the mind from the known to the unknown in the ways of society, furnish solutions for all circumstances; and anything that is against this constitution, wherever it comes from, is nothing, being without its support, and can be considered tyranny. The power that will teach the citizens this constitution—and this education is beginning to be possible—will have done more for humanity than all the Emperors and Popes: afterwards the revolutions of the species will be like those of the planet, nothing will trouble them and no one will any longer feel them.

In the early enthusiasm of the *coup d'État*, rectifying the long negligence of our assemblies, the Second of December felt itself able to decree, in rapid succession, railroad concessions, allocations of public works, extensions of privilege, reductions of discount, attachments of real estate, seizures of estates, conversions of stock, continuations of taxes, etc., etc.—a mass of things that, if society had been taught its true constitution, would have been done a long time ago, and done better, or would never be done. The vulgar crowd, which entrusts everything to the will of the leader . . . admired the fecundity of decrees and parasitically applauded this strong and active power! But soon the fever of reforms calmed: more than once the Second of December had to retract resolutions under pressure, withdraw projects which the council of state already strongly favored, and one can foresee that if the government doesn't learn to read better the book of eternal politics, it will soon appear to be just as powerless, just as incapable, just as overly bold and crazy as it forebears, not excepting the Emperor himself. . . .

I do not want my observations to degenerate into attacks, and it is for that reason that I express them in juridical style, limiting myself to showing, with the aid of several comparisons, and in the most concise forms, how much the exercise of authority, so much clamored for these days by lawyers without learning, publicists without philosophy, statesmen equally lacking in practice and principles, has become incompatible with the most elementary notions of economics and law. No matter from what side one looks at it, the Second of December—and when I say the Second of December, do I need to keep repeating that I mean any dictatorial or dynastic form of government? —the government, I say, is caught between *an-archy* and *expediency*, obliged to choose between the natural tendencies of society and the arbitrariness of man! And that arbitrariness is perpetual violation of law, negation of science, revolt against necessity; it is war on the mind and on work! Impossible.

I will not finish, having touched upon the domestic impossibilities, without saying something about those on the outside.

If there is one thing that the Second of December ought to have at heart, it is unquestionably to rectify the disasters of 1814 and 1815, to restore the influence of our nation in the European concert, to bring it back up to the rank of a first-rate power, supporting if need be this legitimate claim with arms.

Is the Second of December capable of this in the ambiguous situation it has put itself in, between the Revolution and counterrevolution?

There have been rumors circulated, and they still have believers, about plans for descent into England, invasion of Belgium, incorporation of Savoy, etc. These rumors have been denied seriatim: indeed, those are things that one does not believe without having seen them, and when one has seen them one still does not believe them. . . .

Up to now Louis-Napoleon has only served the Holy Alliance in striking down democracy and Revolution; far from being able to protest against the treaties of 1815, in fact he adheres to them. It would be childish for him to expect from his allies, as recompense, the border of the Rhine. The only recompense that Louis-Napoleon could obtain from the Holy Alliance is that it tolerate him, support him, protect him, as guardian and subduer of the Revolution, until circumstances, made favorable by him, permit the allies to give us back for a third time our legitimate princes. . . .

Now let Louis-Napoleon, using his prerogative, call for war. . . . But let him also know that in a demand thus made, public opinion would not follow him: it would see in his policy only a conqueror's fantasy, a national or domestic point of honor without moral character, and by abandoning him it would paralyze his efforts. So true is it that there is something legal in the treaties of 1815 that cannot be unbound except by a superior legality.

The Revolution in the nineteenth century is this legality.

Let us recall what was said earlier: since Louis-Napoleon, like the Emperor, has as his principal enemy capitalist feudality, represented outside the country by England, the real way to combat England is not to attack Egypt, Australia, or India, no more than it is to cross the Channel: it is to strike the enemy first at home, in its relations with work and capital.

From the time before the Revolution of 1789, England had begun the conquest of the globe: how? By armed force? No, it leaves that method to the French. By the accumulation of its invested capital, the power of its industry, the extension of its commerce. It did not lack success: there is no country today where it does not reap profits. We ourselves pay tribute to its workers, engineers, and capitalists, and already through the acquisitions of property being made by English subjects, Great Britain is preparing to re-establish its preponderance on our territory. *Free trade*, to which its bourgeois invite the people of the world, is crushing all competition, is the last blow that it is preparing to deal to the liberty of nations. . . .

It is therefore necessary that to a war of capital we respond before everything else, within the country and outside, with a system of credit which nullifies the superiority that England draws from its capitalized masses: then we will be able to speak to the Holy Alliance. Already, with its financial decrees, the Second of December has set the goal: let it follow through to the end, let it not wait for more imperious necessities to constrain it. Whether it is thinking of trade or preparing for war, let it begin by making itself economically strong. Let it dare to accomplish in six months what its newspapers show in a perspective of fifty years; by the combined reduction of rents and interest to the simple expenses of the task, let it totally change the relations of work and capital; let it cut—if I may express it this way—the ties to the bourgeois feudality, and then let it declare in turn to England, not the *continental system*, the madness of Napoleon I, but *free trade;* lastly, let it abolish the customs duties. . . .

Outside the country, Belgium, Savoy, a part of Switzerland and of Piedmont will gravitate, with all the force of their industrial interests, toward France, a free market of thirty-six million consumers, consuming, according to what has just been said, like forty-five million! . . .

After these neighboring countries . . . in Italy, Rome, the center of uprising, projects the national flame to the north and the south of the peninsula. Say to Italy, President of the humanitarian republic, that you want her to live by means of herself and for herself, and she will live. In a word, you will have resuscitated that nationality, slaughtered by you within the walls of Rome after having been betrayed on the battlefield of Novara! . . .

With France revolutionized, foreign policy is easy to follow. The European center of gravity is displaced, the new Carthage yields to the new Rome, and if it is necessary to fight, the war is holy, the victory sure. But where, then, would Louis-Napoleon, deserting the idea of Revolution, find a pretext for making in the name of France the least demonstration on the continent? Benevolent and gratuitous jailer of democracy, confederate and dupe of the counterrevolution, he does not even have the right to utter a wish. He has received the compliments of the Tsar: how could he make demands in behalf of Poland? On the side of the Jesuits and with the soldiers of Austria and Naples, he conducted the campaign of Rome: having returned things to the *status quo,* what remained for him to say in favor of the Italians? Thanks to his powerful diversion, reaction is the mistress everywhere in Europe, on the Po, on the Rhine, on the Danube: what principle would the family of the Emperor represent, in the eyes of the Neapolitans, Romans, Lombards, Dutch, Westphalians? Does the Bonaparte family think that people seek it for its nobility? And do Messieurs Louis, Jerome, Napoleon, Pierre, Charles, Anthony, Lucien Bonaparte and Murat think they are the clay that forms those sovereigns by the grace of God, the legitimate princes, the absolute kings? And what of the valets? . . .

X
ANARCHY OR CAESARISM—CONCLUSION

If there is any one fact that attests to the reality and the force of the Revolution, it is, without a doubt, the Second of December. Let France understand it and all of Europe be told it: the days in December 1851 are, after those of February and June 1848, like the third eruption of a volcano.

We should realize that this shake-up, more than any other, has made a decisive step for the Revolution.

Throughout her history, from the Romans and the Franks through Charlemagne and the Capetians, France has been continually moving toward 1789; after 1789 comes 1848.

In 1848, as in 1789, everything IN THE EVENTS call for a Revolution. But the difference between 1789 and 1848 is that in 1848 there is nothing, or hardly anything, *in the ideas* which points toward it. The time is ripe, but public opinion is behind. All the events that were to follow rise from this discord between events and ideas.

First, socialist preaching.

Since the Revolution was coming about by force of necessity, and since public opinion was suspicious of it because it was unacquainted with it, the first task was to introduce the socialist revolution in the country. While the Provisional Government, the Executive Commission, and General Cavaignac were busy keeping order, socialism was organizing its propaganda, with all the energy that the circumstances gave it. It has been said that socialism *frightened* people; it is still accused today of having gone too far, compromised the Republic and brought about its ruin! Yes, socialism frightened people, and it is proud of it!

People die of fear, just as they die of any illness, and the old society shall not recover from it. Socialism frightened people! Were we supposed to keep quiet just because nobody else did anything, could do anything? Were we supposed to mute our drums and give up the idea along with the action? Socialism frightened people! Powerful spirits, to have been frightened by socialism without having trembled before universal suffrage!

Since socialism is terrifying at first sight (all new ideas are frightening at their first appearance), it could not have avoided arousing a violent reaction. Since, however, it was already established by history and institutions, it had to happen, on the one side, that socialism would grow under a general reaction; in the second place, that it would expose the inconsistency of all its adversaries, from the men of the *Montagne* to the dynasts, and by that revelation of their inconsistency, socialism would dash them down, one after the other, from the power they had been using against it.

All the facts point to the progress of socialism and to the successive and inevitable overthrow of its adversaries.

Why is it that between February and December 1848 all kinds of republicans were progressively ousted? It is because these people remain outside of socialism, which is the Revolution, and because outside of the Social Revolution the Republic has no meaning: it seems like a middle ground, a *doctrine,* an arbitrariness.

But why do republicans who worshipped 1793[24] remain outside of the movement in 1848? It is because they realize from the outset that the Social Revolution is the negation of all political and economic hierarchy; because this *emptiness* shocks their preconceptions about organization and their governmental habits; and because their minds, stopping at the outward appearances of things, and failing to discover the distinct bond of the new social order under the bareness of the form, draw back from this new sight as if from an abyss. . . .

[24] A reference to Robespierrist radical Jacobins.

On December 10, Louis Bonaparte won the election over General Cavaignac who, nonetheless, had *deserved well of his country*: whose good citizenship, disinterestedness, and modesty will be revealed by impartial history. Why was this election so unjust? Because General Cavaignac, by a quirk of fate, had, in the name of law and order, fought against the Social Revolution; because subsequently he presented himself, in the name of the Revolution, as an avowed republican and an adversary of the dynastic parties; and finally because against this rigidity at once constitutional and republican, the name of Bonaparte presented itself to the masses as a hope of a quicker Revolution and to the partisans of the altar and the throne who pushed them as the hope of a counterrevolution. Revolution, counterrevolution, the *yes* and the *no*: what difference does it make? It is always the same passion that excites and the same idea that provides the direction.

Against whom was the war for Rome later waged? Against Mazzini? Surely not! The people who started the war for Rome were just as democratic as Mazzini. Like Mazzini and like Rossi they carried flags that said: *Separation of Church and State! Free and secular government!* The Revolution of Rome was fought against the Social Revolution.

Against whom was the law of May 31 passed?—Against the Revolution.

How did the man who had been elected by five and a half million votes succeed, in 1849 and 1850, in becoming unpopular? He did it by allying himself with the reactionaries. How did he then recover his popularity? He did it by confirming universal suffrage, which is supposed to be the voice of the Revolution. . . .

Here we are at the elections of 1852: on the Left we have the proposition for recall of the Élysée; on the Right, the obstinacy of the law of May 31; and behind us, insurrection. The situation could not be more revolutionary: what will come of it?

At this point we can no longer judge events from a legal

or moral point of view concerning the correct use of power, respect for the Constitution, or the religion of the oath. History will judge the morality of the acts; what we must do now is to ascertain the inevitable part. Constitution, oath, and laws all have failed in the midst of the ardent competition: one man's bad conscience absolves that of another, and when royalty is declared in the tribunes, why should not the Empire rise from the public square? When constitutional faith has been trampled by the majority, the only recourse is to violent and *immoral* action, ambitions and parties, the blind instrument of destiny.

Such were the antagonistic forces in November 1851: the Revolution is represented by the republican Left, and incidentally by the Élysée, which joins the Revolution in order to recall the law of May 31; the voice of the counterrevolution is the majority, and incidentally also the Élysée, which joins it for everything else, against the Republican party.

The Élysée is an ambiguous element, without any importance by itself; at this moment it is being fought by two sides, each of which is equally anxious to eliminate it. In effect, the question is whether France will turn to the Revolution or to the counterrevolution. Who is M. Bonaparte, that he feels he can say, "Neither one nor the other; France will be mine"?

What does the country think at the sight of this arena where her destinies are going to play themselves out? The country hates to move backwards, but it fears revolutionaries. It is no longer merely socialism that frightens her: she also fears a reaction from the *Montagne* and the reprisals of democracy! This state of mind, which impartially rejects, on the one hand, *the principle of reaction* and, on the other, *the men of the Revolution,* is what assures the success of the Élysée. The very same circumstances that could have crushed it between two armies are the cause of its triumph over both of them: it confirms the Revolution, and it protects the conservatives! The solution is bilateral and contradictory, but logical nonetheless given the state of public opinion and almost inevitable under the circumstances.

302

The significance of the Second of December and the idea that it represents are therefore, quite authentically, REVOLUTION. The rest is the business of *individuals*—in other words, party intrigues, arrangements of cliques, private acts of vengeance, autocratic demonstrations, measures taken for the public good and in the interest of reason of state. That is the freedom that is left for the convenience of the government by the law of revolutions.

But this ambiguity cannot last: every principle must produce its consequences, and all power must unfold its idea. We now must ask: what is Louis-Napoleon going to do? . . .

In 1849, the negation of authority, followed by the disappearance of all governmental organisms, was still an obscure idea; after the Second of December not even the slightest cloud remains. The Second of December made, in present-day France, the contradictions between the government and the economy and between the State and the society stand out sharply; things we could only guess at by the rules of logic four years ago, facts, the infallible interpreters, have made palpable to us: the paradox has become a truth.

Let us summarize these facts and prove, by analyzing them, the truth of this triple proposition, which represents the entire movement of the past sixty-four years:

Personal or despotic government is impossible;

Representative government is impossible;

Government is impossible.

The principles upon which French society has rested since 1789, in fact, on which every free society can be said to rest, principles anterior and superior to the very notion of government, are:

1. *Free property,* which was called "quiritarian" by the Romans and "alodial" by the barbarian invaders. This is absolute property, or at least inasmuch as it is possible for men to have anything absolute; it is property that is answerable directly and exclusively to the proprietor, who administers it, rents it, sells

it, gives it, or pawns it at his own convenience, without being accountable to anyone.

Property will undoubtedly have to be transformed by the economic revolution, but not insofar as it is free: on the contrary, its freedom and its safeguards will increase indefinitely. . . .

2. *Free work,* with all its derivatives such as free speech, free commerce, free credit, free science, free thought and religion: in other words, the absolute right, *a priori,* without restriction or control, of every citizen to work, manufacture, cultivate, extract, produce, transport, exchange, sell, buy, lend, borrow, compound, invent, learn, think, discuss, popularize, believe or disbelieve, etc., as far as his means will permit him, subject only to the condition of meeting his commitments and of not preventing anyone else from exercising the same right.

Work must also be revolutionized, like property; but only with respect to its safeguards, not its initiative. To take corporate organization as a guarantee of work would be to go back to the Middle Ages and eradicate slavery by feudalism.

3. *The natural, egalitarian, and free distinction* between the specialties of industry, of commerce, of science, etc., according to the principle of the division of labor, outside of any class consciousness.

These are the *principles of 1789,* the object of the famous *Declaration of the Rights of Man and of the Citizen,* recognized by the last Constitution; since then they have been the basis of our society.

M. de Bonald[25] has said that government should be the expression of society; one wonders what could be the government of a society established on such principles.

It could not be a territorial feudal system, because property is free; nor an industrial, commercial, or financial feudal sys-

[25] Louis-Gabriel Ambroise, Vicomte de Bonald (1754–1840), conservative French politician and political theorist of the revolutionary and restoration era.

tem, since there is, or is likely to be, free work, free commerce, and free credit; nor a caste system, since, according to their economic principle, professional businesses are free; nor a theocracy, since there is also free conscience. Will it be an absolute monarchy? No, because the powers of the man and of the citizen—work, trade, property, etc.—when converted into *rights,* are free; and when these rights can be freely exercised there is no longer motive or object for any kind of authority, and the sovereign, formerly the visible, personal incarnation of the divine right, becomes an abstraction, a myth—that is to say, the people.

If, then, in a society thus constituted, a government comes into being, this government must be the result of a delegation, convention, or federation—in a word, of the free and spontaneous consent of all the individuals who make up the people, each one of them stipulating his interests and subscribing to the guarantee of interests. With the result that the government —if there is a government—instead of BEING AUTHORITY as before, will *represent the relation* between all the interests engendered by free property, free work, free commerce, free credit, and free science and will consequently have of itself only a representative value, like paper money, whose value depends upon the value of the écus it represents. . . .

Thus the democratic and representative nature of the government proceeds from the essentially free nature of the interests whose relations it denotes: given these interests, a return to any kind of authority becomes nonsensical. . . .

Do I have to repeat what everybody knows? The philosophy of 1789, and of all the Constitutions which have emerged from it, was to organize the movement in such a way that it would be the representation of the free interests on which society rests; and this is still the claim of the Second of December. The Second of December, like all the powers that have preceded it since 1789, flatters itself with representing *par excellence* the relation of those interests that are recognized *a priori* and by nature as being free. Neither it nor any of its predeces-

sors otherwise aspiring to authority, has ever suspected wha
it means for a government, to be a *representation*, the repre
sentation of a *relation*, the relation between *interests*, and o
interests which are *free!!!* . . .

The most positive result, the only positive result of all the gov
ernments that have passed over France since 1789, is to have
brought to light this truth, which is as simple as a definitior
and as clear as an axiom: *Government is the relation betweer
liberties and interests.*

And given this first proposition, the consequences are quicl
to follow: from now on, the difference between politics anc
economics is lost; in order for relations to exist between in
terests, the interests themselves must be present, responsive
stipulating, responsible, and effective; the intellect of society
is exactly the same thing as its living emblem; and in the las
analysis, when everybody is the government, government is no
more. Thus, the negation of government arises from its own
definition: whoever speaks of representative government speaks
of the relation of interests; whoever speaks of the relation of
interests speaks of the absence of government.

And, in fact, the history of the last sixty years proves that
interests are no more free nor in harmony under representative
government than under despotic government. In order to maintain themselves in the conditions of their declaration, which
are also those of their existence, these interests must deal directly
among themselves, following the LAW of their solidarity, and
without any intermediary. That failing, property once again
becomes fief, work becomes slavery, and commerce becomes
toll; corporations are formed again and philosophy is in the
hands of the Church; science . . . says only those things that
happen to be pleasing to the established theology and to the
Pope: there are no longer any liberties nor any interests! . . .

What do I have to say to you, race of sheep, to prove to you
that a relation or an idea cannot be represented, as you would
like to think? Liberty, for the strongest reason, cannot be repre-

sented either: to represent it is to destroy it. On the day when our fathers created the *Declaration of the Rights of Man* before God and men and established in principle the free exercise of the faculties of the man and the citizen, authority was denied in the heavens and on the earth, and government, even by delegation, was made impossible.

If you like, you can return to the feudal customs, to theocratic faith, or to the piety of Caesar; go back ten, twenty, or forty centuries, but stop talking about represented liberties: because liberties and interests, in their collectivity and their relations, cannot be represented, and the representative of a nation, like the representative of a family, of an estate, or of an industry, can only be its chief and its master. Representation of interests is reconstitution of authority!

So you have the choice: anarchy or Caesarism. . . . Stop trying to evade the issue, there is no middle course. During the last sixty years all the middle courses have been exhausted and experience has shown you that they, like Dante's purgatory, are only a transitional phase, where souls in an agony of mind and conscience, are prepared for a superior existence.

Anarchy or Caesarism, I tell you: you cannot avoid that. You did not want a Republic that was honest, moderate, conservative, progressive, parliamentary, and free; you are caught between the *Emperor* and the *Social Republic!* Decide now which of these you prefer: for, in fact, if Louis-Napoleon falls, he, like his uncle, will fall only by and for revolution; and regardless of what happens, the proletarian will get less tired than you. Is it not for him that the Revolution will be made, and in awaiting the Revolution is he not the friend of Caesar?

But Caesarism! Has the joyous counsellor of the Élysée fully reflected? Caesarism became possible for the Romans when, to assure sustenance, the conquest of the world was added to the victory of the plebs over the patricians. Then Caesar was able to reward his veterans with lands captured abroad, pay his praetorians with the tributes of foreign countries, and feed his people with foreign produce. . . . This is what Caesarism consisted of: the pillage of nations, organized for the use of the lazy, savage, and hideous Roman people and for the Emperor's security. . . .

Today we are talking about quite another thing. We have lost all our conquests, both those of the Emperor and those of the Republic. From abroad we are not getting so much as a centime to give charity to the last of the Decembrists, and Algeria costs us 100 million, year in, year out. In order to triumph over the capitalistic, landed bourgeoisie, to contain the industrious, liberal middle class, and to rule the people, it is no longer a question of feeding the people with the spoils of conquered countries. The question is of their living on what they produce; in a word, of making them work. How would Caesar go about it? There is the question. However he would do it—be it by consulting Saint-Simon, Fourier, Owen, Cabet, Louis-Napoleon, etc.—we are in the middle of socialism, and the last word in socialism is, with *non-interest, non-government.*

An indiscreet and perhaps spiteful person will now ask me this question: Do you believe that the Second of December will accept the revolutionary role in which you have enclosed him . . . ? Do you trust his liberal inclinations? And on the basis of the necessity for Louis-Napoleon's mandate, which you have shown so well, will you rally to his government, as the best, or as the least objectionable, transition? That is what they want to know, and that is where they are waiting for you!

I will answer this somewhat ticklish question with another one:

After my ideas have been so unsuccessful for the last four years, do I have the right to suppose that the head of the new government will adopt them and make them his own? Have they, in the eyes of the public, taken on the impersonality, the reality, and the universality which would impose them on the state? And if these relatively new ideas are still scarcely the ideas of one man, how could I hope that the Second of December, who is also a man, would prefer them to his own ideas!

I am writing so that others will reflect in turn and, if necessary, contradict me. I am writing so that the truth will be known, elaborated by public opinion, and the Revolution, with, without, or even against government, be fulfilled. As for men, I believe freely in their good intentions, but I believe even more in their bad judgment. . . . I believe therefore, for the misfortune of us all, that the revolutionary idea, badly defined in the public mind and badly served by its vulgarizers, still leaves all political options open to the government; I believe that the government is surrounded by impossibilities that it does not see, by inconsistencies of which it is unaware, and by traps that are hidden by universal ignorance. I believe that any government can last if it wants to, by affirming its historical meaning and by putting itself in control of the interests that it is called on to serve; but I also believe that men do not change very much, and that if Louis XVI wanted to stop the Revolution as soon as he had started it, and if the Emperor, Charles X, and Louis-Philippe preferred oblivion to the Revolution, then it is unlikely that their successors will immediately and spontaneously make themselves its promoters.

It is for that reason that I remain outside of the government, which I feel more disposed to pity than to fight; devoted only to my country, I rally myself body and soul to that elite body of workers at the head of the proletariat and of the middle class, who favor work and progress, liberty and thought, and who accept as their goal and their motto the *education of the people*. They understand that authority means nothing, that popular spontaneity is unreliable, that liberty which does not act is lost, and that interests which need an intermediary for their relations are interests sacrificed.

O my country, O France, country of the bards of the eternal Revolution! Country of liberty, for in spite of your servitude there is no place on earth—neither in Europe nor in America—where the spirit, which is all of man, is as free as it is here! Country that I love with the accumulated love that the growing son feels for his mother and that the father feels growing for his children! Will I see you suffer much longer, not only for yourself but for the whole world, which pays you with its envy and its insults? You are innocent, yet you suffer because you do not know yourself. At every moment it seems to me that you are going through your last ordeal! Wake up, Mother: your princes, your barons, and your counts can do nothing for your health, and your prelates cannot comfort you with their benedictions. If you like, you can remember those who have done well, and you can pray at their graves from time to time: but do not try to find their successors. They are finished! Begin your new life, oh first of the immortals; show yourself in all your beauty, Venus Urania; spread your fragrance, flower of humanity!

And humanity will be rejuvenated, and its unity will be created by you: because the unity of mankind is the unity of my country, just as the spirit of mankind is nothing more than the spirit of my country.

VICTOR HUGO'S INDICTMENT
OF LOUIS NAPOLEON'S CRIME

At the time of the coup d'état, Victor Hugo (1802–85) was one of the most famous men in France. He was a major playwright, novelist, and above all poet, probably France's greatest poet of the nineteenth century, the leader of the rebellious Romantic youth of the thirties, member of the Academy, peer of France, and member of the Assembly through most of the life of the Second Republic. An outspoken supporter of humanitarian causes, opponent of the death penalty and slavery, proponent of social welfare schemes, of international federation and world peace, a leading spokesman for freedom of speech and press and education, in 1851 he ranked as a leading figure among Republicans. After the coup, in exile, and from the Empire's fall when he returned to France until his death, he was to become a living legend, an object of real idolatry.

He had not always been a Republican. His mixed political heritage helps account for some of the early shifts in his political views. He was the son of an officer who had had a checkered career in the Napoleonic armies, rising at last to the rank of general and right-hand man to Joseph Bonaparte in Spain. His mother was a monarchist, a Voltairian skeptic, who during the long separation from her husband, which lasted most of her children's youth, helped an anti-Napoleonic conspirator who was caught and shot. Mme. Hugo naturally welcomed the re-establishment of the Bourbon monarchy after the fall of Napoleon.

Victor Hugo began to make his mark as a poet while still in his teens, receiving honorable mention for work submitted to the French Academy and prizes from the Joux Floraux of Toulouse. In his early poetry he showed respect for throne and altar in accord with the dominant sentiments of the Restoration. His royalism, which lasted into the regime of Charles X, seems closely tied to his affection and respect for his strong-willed mother. Hugo maintained his Catholic religiosity for a brief time, though subsequently anti-clericalism became one of his more stable attitudes.[1] Even prior to the accession of Charles X in 1824, his loyalty and ability were rewarded by a royal pension which allowed him to marry. He had badly needed the money, for following his mother's death in 1821 he had experienced very real poverty, which gave him a basis for the sympathy with the lot of the poor that was to mark so much of his later work. His growing success was further demonstrated by his being made a knight of the Legion of Honor, along with his friend and fellow poet Alphonse de Lamartine in 1825.

By 1830, however, he showed increasing disaffection for the regime, a growing Bonapartist inclination (especially in his *Ode à la Colonne*, 1827), and a vehement patriotism to go with it. Such sentiments seem to have developed in conjunction with closer ties with his father between 1822 and the latter's death in 1828; but the imaginative appeal of Napoleonic glory to a poet such as Hugo must have played a central role as well. Hugo was now demonstrating some social-reformist inclinations, publishing *The Last Day of a Condemned Man* in 1829, his first effort in what became a lifelong humanitarian battle against the death penalty.

[1] For instance, André Maurois says of Hugo's novel, written in 1831, "*Notre-Dame de Paris* is not a Catholic, or even a Christian, book." *Olympio* (New York, 1956), p. 147.

But his major reforming efforts in this period were in the arts. He had achieved a position of leadership in the growing Romantic movement, which set him increasingly at odds with the established authorities. He was seeking fame as a dramatist only to find himself in opposition to both government censorship and the entrenched attitudes of the traditionalist classical critics. He began to identify the new rebellious movement in the arts with political liberalism.[2] At first he had believed poetry should be royalist and Christian; by 1830 he could say, in his preface to *Hernani*, "Liberty in art, liberty in society, that is the two-fold goal toward which all consistent and logical minds should strive in unison."

His personal experiences were such as to push him into opposition. In 1829 the production of his play *Marion de Lorme* was prohibited; he was harassed by government criticism in preparing *Hernani* in 1830. The actual production of *Hernani* was to become one of the most famous episodes in the history of the arts in the nineteenth century. Hugo gathered a claque of outlandishly dressed young artists and art lovers to support the opening of his play in the winter of 1830—a play that outraged the established classical canons of dramatic taste. The radical artists cheered wildly to overcome the conservative opposition of the well-dressed bourgeois audience and the critics. Hugo and Romanticism won the melodramatic episode just before the Revolution of July 1830 ushered in a more liberal regime—a regime dominated by the bourgeoisie.

Hugo was not very persistently rebellious. He had not been an active political rebel under the Restoration monarchy, recipient as he was of a government pension. Under its successor he had difficulties only at the start, some further censorship problems when *Le Roi S'Amuse* was closed in 1832. This was the

[2] An early expression of his views appeared in his famous preface to the play *Cromwell* (1827), a kind of Romantic manifesto. He wrote: "The train of the eighteenth century is still dragging in the nineteenth; but we, we young men who have seen Bonaparte, are not the ones who will carry it."

time when Hugo seems briefly to have hoped for a Napoleonic restoration, for he corresponded with Joseph Bonaparte, but the death in 1832 of the Duc de Reichstadt, the heir apparent, ended the matter. In general, however, Hugo's attitude toward the new July Monarchy was approving.[3]

Hugo had a driving ambition to attain the same sort of leadership in politics he had already attained in the arts. During the eighteen-year life of the July Monarchy, this ambition took shape in pursuit of two goals: to enter the French Academy and to become a peer. He lacked the necessary property to attain the peerage without membership in the Academy, hence that membership came first. After three unsuccessful attempts, he was elected in 1841, partly in consequence of having become a protégé of the Duc and Duchesse d'Orléans, heir to the throne and his wife. The peerage came in 1845, allowing Hugo his first true forum for practical politics.

He had made earlier tentative political gestures of a literary sort. In 1834 his essay on Mirabeau contained a conclusion addressed to the needs of the present, and his story "Claude Gueux" offered education and Christian hope as the prime solutions to the sufferings of the poor.[4] In his initial address at the Academy, he surprised his audience in that august literary setting with political remarks of liberal and Bonapartist flavor. In 1842

[3] In his *Journal of a Revolutionary of 1830* Hugo wrote: "What we need after July 1830 is a republic in fact, but a monarchy in name"; and again: "The kings have today, the peoples have tomorrow." If these remarks accurately depict his views at the time, he remained after his Bonapartist fling a monarchist anticipating a republic in the long run, but accepting the existing regime without major reservations, and with increasing approval as he attained increasing success.

[4] Later, despite his acquaintance with socialist writings, Hugo came to depend for this purpose primarily upon beneficent capitalism to supplement education. Much of *Les Misérables*, which expresses this position, was composed during the period before 1848. In *Napoleon the Little* we find him again basing his version of socialism on education.

his travel letters published as *The Rhine* ventured into foreign
policy at a time of considerable tension between France and the
German states, especially Prussia.[5] In the Chamber of Peers
itself, his most interesting speech was in support of the petition
to allow the return of the Bonaparte family to France.[6]

As Hugo pursued his political ambitions his literary output
was reduced. Though his poetry continued, his dramatic production declined in the forties, and after his first truly great
novel, *Notre-Dame de Paris*, appeared in 1831, his next was
not to be published until 1862 when he was in exile. His attention remained centered upon his political career. Sir Frank Marzials sums up his political development to this point:

> A republican in theory, a monarchist in practice, a liberal
> in his acceptance of the sonorous watchwords of liberalism, a
> conservative in his conviction that great immediate changes
> would be an unmixed evil, a poet in his sympathy for the
> poor and downtrodden, a practical man in his appreciation of
> the fact that any bettering of the condition of the masses
> must be the work of time and patience—such was Victor

[5] In a long concluding essay, Hugo contended that France must
reacquire the left bank of the Rhine—insisting it was traditionally
more French than German—and in compensation, Prussia should receive the kingdom of Hanover and an outlet to the sea. The sentiments were nobly expressed and glowingly patriotic (and patronizing
to the Germans). The whole was at the time blatantly impractical,
anticipating as it did an improbable alliance of France and Germany
that could only be fashioned against the will of England and Russia.
Hugo still wrote and spoke in the same vein in the era of the Franco-
Prussian War, declaring in 1870 that France should have the Rhine
(letter of 2 August to M. d'Alton Shée)—this despite his expectations
of an eventual united states of Europe and world peace. See *Letters
of Victor Hugo*, ed. by Paul Meurice (Boston, 1896), vol. 2, p. 229.

[6] His other addresses concerned the state of the French sea coast,
the continued sufferings of the Poles, and an enthusiastic endorsement
of Pius IX in his reformist phase when the Pope gave hope to supporters of Italian unity—rather surprising praise coming from the anticlerical Hugo, though Hugo recurrently revealed a Bonapartist tendency to favor reforms instituted by strong leaders.

Hugo when the Revolution of February 1848 broke suddenly upon the constitutional monarchy in France.[7]

The Revolution of 1848 abolished the peerage, and Hugo's ambitions had to take new directions. At the Revolution's outbreak, Hugo bravely and unsuccessfully tried to promote the regency of the Duchesse d'Orléans in the streets among the excited Parisian crowds. Had he been successful he might have had reason to hope for a ministerial position. Yet, though he preferred the maintenance of a monarchy, he could not oppose entirely the coming of a Republic that instituted universal suffrage and abolished the death penalty. Hugo wrote immediately to congratulate Lamartine—already a leading member of the Provisional Government—upon the latter decision. He discussed a ministerial appointment with Lamartine, but was merely appointed honorary mayor of his arrondissement.

He failed when he tried for election to the Constituent Assembly in April. He ran again in June and, like Proudhon, was elected just in time to take his seat before the outbreak of the June Days.

Hugo's political course after 1848 showed a gradual leftward tendency, so that at the end of his life, in his seventies under the Third Republic, he was a thoroughly radical democrat. By 1852 he was far more liberal and democratic than in 1848. But the transition was slow and halting. In his first election to the Assembly he was associated with the conservative group centered in the rue de Poitiers. He spoke early in June in favor of the gradual dissolution of the National Workshops, and his efforts were on the side of law and order during the June Days. As did Tocqueville, Hugo had the task of visiting the barricades, haranguing the insurgents and the troops and informing them of the decisions of the Assembly—actions Hugo appears to have performed with exemplary bravery.

Hugo's position on the Right remained manifest in his sup-

[7] Sir Frank Marzials, *Life and Writings of Victor Hugo* (London, 1888), p. 133.

port for legislation introduced under Cavaignac's dictatorship after June, for example, the state of siege and the restrictions of assembly, but he began to oppose limitations on the press,[8] partially perhaps because he was involved in midsummer in the founding of the journal *L'Événement,* which became an organ for his opinions. *L'Événement* first showed approval of Louis Napoleon by supporting his election to the Assembly in September, then it strongly supported his presidential candidacy in October, stressing the social welfare implications of Bonapartism. Here all Hugo's early Bonapartist associations revived. Along with much of the Right and the lower classes, Hugo was swept up in support of a man who posed a major threat to the Republic.

It was already a Republic of which Hugo was not overfond. *L'Événement* had supported the effort to get a right-to-work proposal into the preamble to the new Constitution, and Hugo had voted for the motion to elect the President by popular vote. But when it came to the whole Constitution, he rejected it on two grounds: it did not provide for an upper house, and rather than by plebiscite, it was to come into effect by Assembly vote—a procedure he considered undemocratic. (Ironically both of these complaints were to be resolved by the Napoleonic Constitution of 1852, a Constitution Hugo excoriated in *Napoleon the Little.*[9])

Hugo was a supporter of the President, even a guest at the Élysée Palace, during the early months of Louis Napoleon's regime. His break with the party of Order and with the President did not come until after the disbanding of the Constituent

---

[8] Naturally Hugo joined the opposition to Proudhon's July proposal for a reduction of debts.

[9] Pierre Lacretelle has pointed out a series of such paradoxes that emerge in Hugo's behavior at the time of the coup d'état. Besides that just mentioned, Hugo castigated Louis Napoleon for violating an oath against which Hugo had voted; similarly he urged the workers into the streets in insurrection, the sort of action he had condemned in the June Days. See *Vie Politique de Victor Hugo* (Paris, 1928), p. 173.

and the election to the Legislative Assembly in 1849. In the interval, the one issue that seems most clearly to have separated Hugo from his conservative colleagues was once again dissemination of information and freedom of the press—he opposed unsuccessfully some of their efforts to restrict the Left's journals. Otherwise his record suggests little of the democratic republicanism that was to make him a leading figure on the Left in the next two years. His hopes are suggested by a program that appeared in *L'Événement* after the presidential election, calling for international organization and disarmament, the opening of the Suez and Panama canals, the westernization of China, domestic progress especially in industrialization and in improving the lot of the poor, and the furtherance of artistic and intellectual pursuits.[10]

The break with the Right seems to have come over the issues of social reform and the Roman expedition.[11] Hugo broke sharply with his colleagues on the Right who failed to support the Melun proposal in July for an investigation into the condition of the poor. Hugo's humanitarianism was outraged by what he saw as the cynical adoption of a laissez-faire policy on the part of the Party of Order. The Roman issue widened the rift with both the Party of Order and the President. Hugo had voted for the credits that allowed the original force to go to Rome out of disapproval of the Mazzinian republic, but he disapproved of papal oppression far more. When the consequences of the Pope's reinstatement became clear in October and the President was complaining in his letter to Ney, Hugo joined in the debate in which Tocqueville found himself defending both government policy and the Pope's *motu proprio*. Hugo denied that the letter to Ney and the Pope's pronouncement could be brought into accord, only then to discover that the

[10] Maurois, p. 270.

[11] See Elliott M. Grant, *Victor Hugo During the Second Republic*, Smith College Studies in Modern Languages, vol. 17, no. 1 (October 1935), pp. 28–31, 44–48.

President intended to take no further action. By opposing the papacy he had thought he was supporting the President and opposing the Right, while in fact the President was accommodating to the Right and leaving Hugo thoroughly disillusioned.

In 1849 he briefly had hopes for a moderate party of "blues," which the President might lead and which could grow up between the extremes of Right and Left. But through 1850 he found himself more and more consistently in alliance with the Left. Two outstanding moments in that transition were his opposition to the passage of the Falloux law, increasing clerical control of education, and his memorable speech against the May 31, 1850, bill restricting the suffrage, in which Hugo argued that possession of the suffrage took the rifle out of the revolutionaries' hands.

While there may be some truth to the suggestion that Hugo's failure to obtain a ministerial post under Louis Napoleon's presidency made him readier to join the opposition, such major issues as these also led to the breach. It should be added that the imprisonment of Hugo's sons for press violations exacerbated the situation.

Hugo participated in all the political activity that preceded the coup, voting for repeal of the law of May 31 and against the Quaestors' Bill and even being named vice president of the Committee of Surveillance of the democratic Left of the Assembly. His July 17 speech opposing revision of the Constitution (in which Hugo described the President as "Napoleon the Little") made perfectly clear that he saw the dangers threatening the Republic from monarchists and imperialists and most strongly from the President. Yet in *The History of a Crime* Hugo writes that the coup d'état was thought unlikely on its very eve. And he admitted twenty-five years later that its coming surprised him.[12] Although he recognized the imperial ambitions, he may have come to believe, like many of the Left,

[12] Françoise Herbault, preface to Hugo's *Napoleon le Petite* (Paris, 1964), p. 17.

that Louis Napoleon would act only after the 1852 elections—
a possibility John Plamenatz has pointed out.[13]

Hugo's behavior during the days following the coup suggests
real daring, but it is hard to be certain of the details. The full-
est account is his own, in *The History of a Crime*, and it has
been subjected to considerable criticism as to its accuracy. Certainly his portrayal of the villainy of the supporters of the President, and the heroism of the republicans seems more than a
touch melodramatic.[14] It is certain, however, that Hugo was a
leader in forming the Comité de Résistance and that for three
days he participated in the attempts of republican deputies, still
not arrested, to arouse some sort of opposition to the coup; that
he moved about Paris encouraging workers to begin a serious
émeute; and that he engaged in a great deal of proclamation
writing (the presidential forces had the printing shops under
control, but secret presses became available), declaring the President a traitor, etc. He risked arrest—an attempt was made to
arrest him at his home on December 3—and perhaps death,
since orders were out to shoot those who posted appeals and proclamations inviting an uprising. As we have noted, however,

[13] John Plamenatz, *The Revolutionary Movement in France,
1815–71* (London, 1952), p. 97. Since Hugo also seems to have
taken himself seriously as a potential candidate for the presidency
in 1852, it seems fair to accuse him of some naïveté in the winter
of 1851. Yet even Tocqueville said just after the coup that he thought
the coup had originally been planned for March 1852; *Memoir, Letters, and Remains,* ed. by Gustave de Beaumont (Boston, 1862) vol.
2, p. 191.

[14] Victor Schoelcher, another republican deputy, published his
own bitter summary and condemnation of the coup d'état in the
summer of 1851, one which resembled Hugo's *History of a Crime.*
Hyppolyte Magen also published a republican interpretation at about
the same time. Both confirm Hugo's central role on the committee, and
Schoelcher locates Hugo at several barricades, but for the details of
his activities, Hugo's own grandiloquent description remains the chief
source. Schoelcher, *Histoire des Crimes de Deux Décembre* (Paris,
1852); M. H. Magen, *Mystères du 2 Décembre* (Paris, 1852). Of
course, Hugo was a dramatist, and his politics, like his plays, were
often melodramatic.

June 1848 had taken the heart for street fighting out of the Parisian republican lower classes, and they were unlikely to be aroused by deputies most of whom (including Hugo) had opposed them in June 1848. The death of one of the deputies at a barricade, the "massacre" of civilians on December 4, and the crushing of minor resistance in working-class districts were enough to convince the leaders of the republican resistance that their presence was likely to produce fruitless bloodshed and death; a more suitable move was flight and exile. Aided by his mistress, Juliette Drouet, Hugo escaped to Brussels a week after the massacre, disguised as a worker and carrying a forged passport.

There is a real difficulty in interpreting Hugo's actions after the coup and his flight into exile. Elliott Grant, one of the most sympathetic American Hugo scholars, speaks of Hugo's "suffering the indignity of not being arrested."[15] Hugo was not arrested on the night of the coup as one of the most dangerous deputies; he was not with those taken at the Tenth Arrondissement with Tocqueville; the possibility remains that efforts to catch him were *not* intense.[16] He may not have been considered a sufficiently important republican leader to warrant being sentenced to Lambessa in Algeria or to Cayenne, or alternatively there might have been too great danger of embarrassment to the government had he been taken. It appears his flight across the border was very easy, as if exile were the solution preferred by the President for the less dangerous republicans and perhaps especially for a famous poet. Hugo's funds were not confiscated, though he disdained to use them. The possibility remains, that Hugo felt belittled and that the tone of *Napoleon the Little* was

[15] Grant, p. 66.
[16] In this connection, consider the interesting remark attributed to Morny when he ordered the seventy-eight pre-dawn arrests: "There is no longer any need for people to suffer hardship in prison, and intelligent arrests may prevent civil war. To arrest a man in such circumstances is to do him a great service." See René Arnaud, *The Second Republic and Louis Napoleon* (London, 1930), p. 55.

affected thereby—a possibility welcomed by Hugo-haters and rejected by Hugo-laters who accept Hugo's own version of the coup.[17]

Once in Brussels, Hugo began gathering data from fellow fugitives for his indictment of the coup, *The History of a Crime*, a book he was unable to publish because of the Belgians' fear of a too powerful neighbor; it was not published until 1877, some years after the fall of the Second Empire. The *History* he had believed would "be a signal victory of intelligence over brute force—inkstand against cannon." (Letter to his wife, February 25, 1852).[18] Undeterred, he decided to write a shorter attack upon the new regime, and in the course of one month, between June 12 and July 14, 1852 (it appeared in August), he produced *Napoleon the Little*.

The title employed the epithet Hugo had made famous in his speech on constitutional revision. The notorious phrase appeared after a series of damning contrasts between the glory of the uncle and the pettiness of the nephew. Then Hugo had exclaimed: "What! because we have had a Napoleon the Great must we now have a Napoleon the Little?" Unlike the longer narrative *The History of a Crime, Napoleon the Little* is a condensed attack on the author of the event. Again Hugo had trouble finding a publisher; eventually a London house agreed to bring it out with Hugo sharing the expense.

The book appeared after Hugo was on his way from Brussels to the island of Jersey, concerned lest he become unwelcome in Belgium after its publication. Eventually his entire ménage was established off the French coast, first in Jersey, then in Guernsey, where he remained throughout the life of the Empire.

---

[17] Philip Guedalla, *The Second Empire* (London, 1922), pp. 213, 220, presents a forceful deflation of Hugo's self-glorification, but does little to solve the difficulties. Pierre Lacretelle gives the most extended negative treatment; Sir Frank Marzials takes the same view. More favorable views are offered by André Maurois and Elliott M. Grant. And see also Camille Pelletan, *Victor Hugo, Homme Politique* (Paris, 1907).

[18] Meurice, p. 91.

There he produced another attack upon Louis Napoleon, *Les Châtiments,* a volume of bitter and ironic verse, often in the tone of an Old Testament prophet. This was the second half of his indictment; *Napoleon the Little,* being in prose, constituted only half the work. He wrote to Alphonse Esquiros (March 5, 1853): "The wretch is roasted on one side only; I turn him over on the gridiron." In *Les Châtiments* Hugo asserted he would not return to France so long as Louis Napoleon remained in power.[19]

At the start he did not expect a long exile. Like Tocqueville, he thought the Russian war in the Crimea would topple the regime (see letter to Mme. Girardin, January 4, 1855).[20] But he gradually adjusted to the expectation of a longer wait and to playing the role of symbolic exile. As early as January 6, 1852, he wrote to André van Hasselt: "It is not I who am banished, dear sir, but liberty; it is not I who am exiled, but France. France is outcast from Truth, from justice, from greatness, is in exile and a stranger to herself."[21] He remained in splendid exile, disdaining the amnesty the Emperor declared in 1859, and thereby served as a symbol for opposition to the regime and as a center of support for a variety of liberal causes. He formed close ties with Garibaldi and the campaign for Italian unity; he attacked slavery and condemned the execution of John Brown; and above all he made clear his sympathy for the lower classes, especially in his most famous novel, *Les Misérables* (1862). He said in the preface:

> So long as, by the effect of laws and of customs, social degradation shall continue in the midst of civilization, making artificial hells, and subjecting to the complications of chance

[19] "Yes, whilst he's there, or struggle some or fall, O France, dear France, for whom I weep in vain, Tomb of my sires, nest of my loves—my all! I ne'er shall see thee with these eyes again"; Victor Hugo, *Poems,* vol. 3, in *Hugo's Works,* Centenary Edition (Boston, 1892), p. 318. Meurice, p. 118.

[20] Meurice, p. 127.

[21] *Ibid.,* p. 68.

the divine destiny of man; so long as the three problems of the age—the debasement of man by the proletariat, the ruin of woman by the force of hunger, the destruction of children in the darkness—shall not be solved; so long as anywhere social syncope shall be possible: In other words, and from a still broader point of view, so long as ignorance and misery shall remain on earth, books like this cannot fail to be useful.

Besides *Les Misérables* and other novels, his production of poetry during the years of exile was immense. He was able to publish in France after 1856, and his reputation became such that he was an object of adoration to young artists. He also attempted the role of seer, prophet of a new faith, and devoted much of his verse to religious and philosophic subjects.

When the Second Empire fell in 1870, Hugo returned to Paris to be greeted by an overwhelming reception. Soon after his return, the Prussian siege of Paris began. The Parisians with whom Hugo shared the hardships, especially the food shortages, looked to him for spiritual leadership, with great affection and respect. After the armistice he was immediately elected to the new National Assembly, which had to accept the peace terms. He wished the Left to resign as soon as it had accepted the humiliation of giving up Alsace and Lorraine, but few agreed. He himself resigned when the Assembly refused to seat Garibaldi.

He had very mixed feelings about the Commune and went to Brussels again; but there he made a dramatic gesture, to his own harm. He offered asylum to fleeing Communards. His house was attacked by disapproving Belgians, as Proudhon's had been for other reasons. He moved on to Luxembourg, returned briefly to a pacified Paris and suffered an electoral defeat in the new conservative mood of the country. In 1872 he went back to Guernsey, finally in 1873 returning to Paris where he spent his last years.

He became a senator of the Third Republic in 1876 and worked for the amnesty of the Communards. In 1877 *The*

History of a Crime was published as a warning against another presidential coup d'état, which Hugo considered imminent at the time. He remained a great popular symbol. At his death in 1885 Paris witnessed one of the most dramatic funerals it had ever known; one imagines Hugo would have predicted just such a funeral's occurring. The body lay in state beneath the Arc de Triomphe. Then, in the pauper's hearse he had asked for, followed by millions of mourners and French and foreign dignitaries, with all the panoply of a state funeral, his coffin was borne to the Pantheon where he was buried.

Hugo believed that knowledge precedes action, just as education must precede the vote. The politician, journalist, poet, and seer, (Hugo in all his roles) each provides the ideas that will move men. The special character of such leadership is expressed in Hugo's early essay on Mirabeau:

> . . . By the magic of words and by a sort of mysterious alchemy, he converted into thoughts, into systems, into precise plans of improvement and reform, the vague instincts of the multitudes; he nourished the spirit of his time with all the ideas which his great intelligence absorbed and distributed among the crowd . . . He held sway over the Assembly only through the people. What Mirabeau said, the crowds repeated with applause; and under the command of their applause, against its will, the Legislative Assembly wrote as he, Mirabeau, dictated.[22]

Hugo's glorification of the French tribune in *Napoleon the Little* (so contrary to Bagehot's criticisms of such oratory) suggests the same view. The emphasis in Hugo's own parliamentary speeches as well as in his political writings was on ideals and objectives rather than on the "precise plans" he mentions in the above quotation. His special function in politics was to convert political ends into objects of moral attachment.

Hugo showed considerable consistency in the fundamental

22 As translated in Matthew Josephson, *Victor Hugo* (Garden City, N.Y., 1942), p. 234.

objectives of his political activity, the ultimate ends he pursued. An 1830 statement describes his republican ideal:

> The republic, in the view of some persons, is the warfare of those who possess neither a halfpenny, nor an idea, nor a single virtue, against whomsoever possesses any of these three things. The republic as I understand it—that republic *which is not yet ripe, but which will embrace the whole of Europe a century hence*—is society entirely self-governed; self-protected through the national guard; self-judged through the jury; self-administered through the municipality; self-directed through the suffrage. In that republic the four members of the monarchy—the army, the magistracy, the administrative organization, the peerage—are only four inconvenient excrescences which will gradually wither and soon die.[23]

The passages in *Napoleon the Little* that describe the four chief deterrents to the establishment of the democratic ideal—the standing army, centralized administration, office-holding clergy, and the irremovable magistracy—reflect the same temper and the same hopes. In June 1862 he wrote to Lamartine that he aspired toward a

> society without kings, humanity without frontiers, religion without sacred books. Yes, I combat the priest who sells lies and the judge who administers injustice, to universalize property (which is the reverse of abolishing it) by getting rid of parisitism, i.e., to achieve the following object, every man an owner of property and no man master, that is my idea of true social and political economy.[24]

He had assurance such hopes would eventually be realized, as the references in *Napoleon the Little* to the impossibility of blocking the Revolution reveal. But they were very distant aspirations, and it is doubtful that Hugo wanted them soon. He was a member of an elite, a man so accustomed to adulation from childhood that he accepted adoration as his due, a man

[23] Marzials, pp. 132–33; italics added.
[24] Meurice, p. 168.

motivated by intense ambition, first to succeed in the arts, then to attain a high place in politics. His ideals closely resemble those that Proudhon sought to share in as equal with other men. Hugo did not see himself as an equal. The poet was to lead, the politician was to lead, the seer was to save. Too much, I think, can be made of Hugo's humanitarianism, particularly if we contrast it with Proudhon's. Hugo was always patronizing; comprehending the problems of the poor from outside, he sentimentalized and moralized about them. This, to be sure, was more than many of his contemporaries did, but Hugo's distance remains evident.[25]

Hugo played the leading role he sketched in the Mirabeau essay when, in *Napoleon the Little,* he sought to serve as conscience for us, his readers. Questions of practical action to be taken have no place beside the central issue of moral judgment of the usurper, whom he felt was a murderer as well. Elsewhere Hugo sometimes seems moved by petty rancor; here his hatred is epic. Albert Guérard says of him in *Napoleon III,* "In his resistance to the *coup d'État* he may have been pragmatically mistaken, but he was morally right. He struck superb attitudes of defiance; but however theatrical they were none the less inspired by his conscience."[26] However we may judge Hugo's conscience, there is no doubt about the superb self-confidence with which he sat in judgment on the perpetrators of the coup.

Besides the judgment on Louis Napoleon, Hugo includes some interesting commentary. He points out the importance to the middle classes of business peace, as did Bagehot, but, along with Proudhon, he sharply denounces Louis Napoleon and his supporters for employing a spurious "red menace" to justify

[25] See, for example, his remarks on June 1848 in *Les Misérables,* vol. 4, bk. I, ch. I; see also Roger Ikor's essay "Le Romancier populaire," in Jacques Lacretelle, *et al, Victor Hugo* (Paris, 1967), especially p. 146. It is also worthy of comment that Marx never got very close to workingmen either. See above, pp. 122, 126.

[26] Albert Guérard, *Napoleon III* (Cambridge, Mass., 1943), p. xx. It is important to recognize that for many the crime of Louis Napoleon was as much the "massacre" as the coup d'état.

their crime, thereby taking major exception to Bagehot's interpretation. There also is a useful sketch of the President's bases of support in the Church, the army, and the bureaucracy; and a denial to match Proudhon's of any real social policy on the part of the new regime. This last appears in a context resembling Proudhon's portrayal of Louis Napoleon as nonetheless entrapped in a necessarily victorious "socialist" tide. Like Marx, Hugo drew hope from the conclusion that the coup served a progressive function by destroying illusions, contending that February 1848 ended the terror of the Republic, and the coup ended the prestige of the Empire. Particularly interesting, when compared to Proudhon's and Marx's treatments, both of which assert that the coup d'état expresses the development of an inherent historical logic, is Hugo's belief that the coup reveals the working-out of the logic of "order," showing it as mere naked force.

It is, I believe, fairly evident that Hugo was not as profound a political thinker as the other theorists included in this volume. He had some visions of the future that were not far from the mark—e.g., a continental Europe which would edge out England and Russia and bring France and Germany closer together. But he had little understanding of the mechanisms by which such changes might occur. His political thought was primarily visual, moral, and dramatic, but he lacked other categories to comprehend and deal with the issues he confronted. His statements of his ideals are too often utopian. He concentrated on ends rather than means, seldom employing operational terms and leaving the work of concrete, pragmatic, detailed planning and criticism aside. He had, in fact, something of the weakness of many nineteenth-century liberals, believing that ideals can work out by their sheer intrinsic beauty or by men's merely believing in them.

Hugo kept asking his colleagues just after the coup (he tells us in The History of a Crime) to put on the scarves that designated them as representatives and march through the streets of Paris, to arouse the Parisians to protest the violation of the Constitution. Saner heads blocked his urge for the dramatic gesture. He ended by writing *Napoleon the Little,* a magnificent and doubtless more successful dramatic gesture. Men in his century knew the book, it meant much to them, whereas Marx's articles, for instance, were scarcely heard of. Hugo's fame suggests the way many nineteenth-century people thought about politics, as his limitations as a politician suggest something of the political reality. His books, his life, and his fame demonstrate that there was no total "change in the public spirit of Europe" after 1851, that in fact Romantic politics continued.

SUGGESTED READINGS

Marie Duclaux, *Victor Hugo,* New York, 1921.

Raymond Escholier, *Victor Hugo,* trans. by Lewis Galantière, New York, 1930.

William F. Giese, *Victor Hugo: The Man and the Poet,* New York, 1920.

Elliott M. Grant, *The Career of Victor Hugo,* Cambridge, Mass., 1945.

——, *Victor Hugo During the Second Republic,* Smith College Studies in Modern Languages, vol. 17, no. 1 (October 1935).

Matthew Josephson, *Victor Hugo,* Garden City, N.Y., 1942.

Frank T. Marzials, *Life and Writings of Victor Hugo,* London, 1888.

André Maurois, *Olympio,* New York, 1956.

SELECTIONS FROM HUGO'S

Napoleon the Little

BOOK I
THE MAN

I
THE 20TH OF DECEMBER, 1848

ON Wednesday the 20th of December, 1848, the Constituent
Assembly was in session, surrounded by an imposing array of
troops. It had met to hear the report of the Commission charged
with the verification of the ballots read by Representative Wal-
deck Rousseau. The full significance of this report is summarized
in the following sentence:—

SOURCE: *Napoleon the Little*, from *Hugo's Works*, Centenary Edition (Boston, 1892), with minor changes by the editor. Pp. 165–74,
177–78, 180–83, 189–94, 196, 202, 220–22, 226–33, 235–36, 238–
40, 242–43, 245–48, 251, 255–57, 261–65, 271–72, 283–84, 289–98,
309–14, 316–17, 329, 333–35, 341–43, 354–55, 362–65, 369, 393–
401, 406–7, 410–11, 416–19, 421–23, 425–26, 428–44.

By this admirable execution of the fundamental law the nation places the sanction of its inviolable power on the Constitution, which it thereby renders sacred and inviolable.

Amid the profound silence of the crowded Chamber, almost at its full complement of nine hundred members, the President of the Constituent National Assembly rose and said—

"In the name of the French People!

"Whereas Citizen Charles Louis Napoleon Bonaparte, born in Paris, possesses all the qualifications of eligibility required by the forty-fourth article of the Constitution—

"Whereas in the election, open throughout the whole extent of the Republic, he has received the absolute majority of votes—

"The National Assembly, by virtue of the forty-seventh and forty-eighth articles of the Constitution, proclaims him President of the Republic from this day until the second Sunday of May, 1852."

There were signs of emotion among the people who thronged the benches and tribunes; the President of the Constituent Assembly added:—

"According to the terms of the decree, I invite the President of the Republic to ascend the tribune and take the oath."

The Representatives who were blocking up the lobby on the right returned to their seats and left the passage free. It was about four o'clock in the evening, night was coming on, the immense hall of the Assembly was half plunged in shadow; chandeliers hung from the ceiling, and the ushers had just placed the lamps on the tribune. At a sign from the President, the door on the right opened.

Then a man still young, dressed in black, with the badge and broad ribbon of the Legion of Honour on his breast, entered the hall and quickly took his place in the tribune.

All eyes were turned upon this man—a pallid face whose spare angular lines were brought out with distinctness by the lamp-reflectors, a nose coarse and long, a lock of hair curled

331

over a straight forehead, eyes small and dull, a timid and troubled demeanour, a likeness to the Emperor nowhere; it was Citizen Charles Louis Napoleon Bonaparte.

During the confused murmur that succeeded his entrance, he stood motionless for some moments, with his right hand in his buttoned coat, on the tribune which bore on its front the dates: 22, 23, 24 *fevrier,* and above, these three words: *Liberté, Égalité, Fraternité.* . . .

At length there was stillness. The President of the Assembly rapped the table with his gavel, the last murmurs died away, and the President of the Assembly rose and said:—

"I am about to read the formula of the oath."

The moment seemed to bring with it a sense of religious awe. The Assembly was no longer the Assembly, it was a temple. The immense import of this oath derived additional significance from one fact—it was the only oath taken throughout the whole extent of the Republic. February had rightly abolished the political oath, and, with equal right, the Constitution had preserved no oath but that of the President. This oath had the twofold impress of necessity and grandeur. The executive power, which is a subordinate power, swore obedience to the legislative power, which is a superior power; nay, it meant even more than this. Inverting the monarchic fiction, in which the people swore allegiance to the man invested with power, it was the man invested with power who swore allegiance to the people. The President, as a functionary and a servant, took the oath of fidelity to the sovereign people. Bending before the national majesty made manifest in the omnipotent Assembly, he received the Constitution from the Assembly, and swore to obey it. The Representatives were inviolable, and he was not. He was, we repeat, a citizen responsible to his fellow-citizens, and the only man in the nation controlled by such a bond. And hence there was in this exceptional and supreme oath a solemnity that took entire possession of the heart. He who writes these lines was in his place in the Assembly on the day when this oath was taken. He is one of those who, in presence of the civilized world called to witness the act, received that oath in the name of the people; he is one of those who still hold it in their hands. It is worded thus:—

"In presence of God and before the French People, represented by the National Assembly, I swear to remain faithful to the democratic Republic, one and indivisible, and to fulfil all the duties imposed on me by the Constitution."

The President of the Assembly, standing up, read this majestic formula.

Then, while the entire Assembly listened in impressive silence, Citizen Charles Louis Napoleon Bonaparte raised his right hand and said in a loud and firm voice—

"I swear!" . . .

The Constitution to which Louis Napoleon Bonaparte swore obedience on the 20th of December, 1848, "in the face of God and of men" contained the following articles among others:—

ARTICLE 36. The Representatives of the People are inviolable.

ARTICLE 37. They cannot be arrested on a criminal charge, except taken in the very act, nor can they be prosecuted until the Assembly has permitted the prosecution.

ARTICLE 68. Every measure by which the President of the Republic dissolves the National Assembly, prorogues it, or places an obstacle in the way of the exercise of the powers delegated to it by the people, is a crime of high treason.

The President, by the very fact, forfeits his office; all citizens are bound to refuse him obedience, the executive power passes in full right to the National Assembly. The Judges of the High Court shall meet immediately, under penalty of forfeiture; they shall convoke juries in the place by them designated for the trial of the President and his accomplices; they shall themselves name the persons charged with the functions of the public ministry.

Less than three years after that memorable day, on the 2d

333

of December, 1851, might be read at daybreak the subjoined proclamation posted on every street-corner of Paris:—

IN THE NAME OF THE FRENCH PEOPLE.

THE PRESIDENT OF THE REPUBLIC

DECREES:

ARTICLE 1. The National Assembly is dissolved.

ARTICLE 2. Universal suffrage is restored. The law of the 31st of May is repealed.

ARTICLE 3. The French people is convoked in its electoral districts.

ARTICLE 4. The state of siege is decreed throughout the first military division.

ARTICLE 5. The Council of State is dissolved.

ARTICLE 6. The Minister of the Interior is charged with the execution of the present decree.

Given at the Palace of the Élysée, the 2d of December, 1851.

LOUIS NAPOLEON BONAPARTE.

At the same time Paris was informed that fifteen of the Representatives of the People—the inviolable Representatives—had been arrested during the night, at their own homes, by order of Louis Napoleon Bonaparte.

II

MANDATE OF THE REPRESENTATIVES

The Representatives of the People who on behalf of the people received in trust the oath of the 20th of December, 1848, above all, the Representatives of the People who, twice invested with the confidence of the nation, saw that oath sworn to as constituents and violated as legislators, had two duties imposed upon them by their mandate. The first was to rise on the very day when that oath was violated, to stake their lives, careless of the number of the enemy or of his strength, to cover with their bodies the sovereignty of the people, and to lay hold of every arm for the overthrow of the usurper, from the law in the code to the paving-stones of the street. The second duty was, after accepting the struggle with all its vicissitudes, to accept proscription with all its miseries; to remain eternally erect before the traitor, with his oath in their hands; to forget their inward sufferings, their private sorrows, their families dispersed and mutilated, the ruin of their fortunes, the wounds of their affections and their bleeding hearts; to forget themselves, and henceforth feel but one wound—the wound of France; to cry aloud for justice; to scorn the thought of submission or resignation; to be implacable; to seize the odious crowned perjurer, if not by the hand of the law, at least with the pincers of truth, and redden in the fires of history the letters of his oath and brand them on his face!

He who writes these lines is one of those whom no danger deterred from the fulfilment, on the 2d of December, of the first of these duties; by publishing this book he discharges the second.

III

DEMAND IN DUE FORM OF LAW

. . . The present situation, which seems calm to the unthinking, is violent. On this point there must be no misunderstanding. When public morality suffers eclipse, the social order is pervaded by an appalling shadow. All guarantees disappear, all supports fall to the ground. . . .

Surely this is a grave state of things. To allow one's self to fall asleep in such a situation is an added ignominy. . . .

IV

THERE WILL BE AN AWAKENING

But it will not be so; there will be an awakening. The single aim of this book is to do away with this sleep. France must not adhere to this Government even with the acquiescence of lethargy. At certain times, in certain places, beneath certain shades, to sleep is to die.

Moreover, at the present moment—it is a strange thing to say, but yet the truth—France knows nothing of what took place on the 2d of December and on the ensuing days, and this is her excuse. But thanks to several noble and courageous publications, the facts are becoming known. It is the object of this work to shed light on some of them, and with God's help, depict them all in their true colours. It is important that mankind should know what Monsieur Bonaparte is. . . . In the eyes of France, in the eyes of Europe, the 2d of December still wears a mask. This book is a hand issuing from the darkness, and tearing off that mask.

Yes, we shall expose this triumph of order; we shall paint this vigorous Government—this Government so firm, secure, and strong; this Government which has in its favour a crowd of poor young creatures, better supplied with ambition than with shoes, showy coxcombs and sorry paupers at the same time. . . .

We are in Russia. The Neva is frozen. Houses are erected on it; heavy chariots roll along its surface. It is no longer water; it is rock. Men go and come across this marble floor that was once a river. In an instant a city is built on it; streets are laid out and shops are opened, and men buy and sell, and eat and drink, and light their fires above this water. All are free to do as they like. Pray, do not be afraid; do whatever it seems good to you to do. Laugh and dance, for this is more firm than the solid earth. Yes, really, it sounds like granite under one's feet. Hurrah for winter! hurrah for the ice! it will last to eternity.

And then, look at the sky; is it day or is it night? A pale and sickly streak of light shimmers along the snow; it seems as if the sun were dying.

No, thou art not dying Liberty! Some day, at the very moment when thou art least looked for, at the very hour when thou art most forgotten, thou shalt rise! O dazzling spectacle! We shall see thy starry face mount upward on a sudden from the earth and shine in thy glorious splendour above the horizon. Over all this snow and ice, over this hard white plain, this water turned to stone, over all this hideous winter, thou wilt launch thy golden arrows, thy gleaming, burning rays, light, warmth, and life! and then, hark! do you hear that dull and rumbling sound? Do you hear that deep, tremendous report? It is the breaking up of the ice! It is the Neva that is sinking down! It is the river resuming her course! It is the living waters, joyous and terrible, upheaving the dead and ghastly ice and dashing it to pieces. It was granite, you said; see, it splits like glass! It is the breaking up of the ice; it is truth returning once more; it is progress renewing her work; it is humanity resuming her march and driving, tearing, hurling along in her course, striking, crushing, and drowning in her waves, as 't were no more than the wretched furniture of some poor hovel, not only the freshly constructed empire of Louis Bonaparte, but all the erections and all the works of ancient and eternal despotism! Look at all this as it passes away. It is disappearing forever. You shall never behold it again. That book, half submerged, is the hoary code of iniquity! That frame which is being fast ingulfed is the throne! That other frame which is vanishing from sight is the scaffold!

And for this immense ingulfment, for this supreme victory of life over death, what was needed? A glance of thine, O sun! One of thy rays, O Liberty!

VI

A PORTRAIT

. . . There is now in Europe, deep sunk in every mind, even beyond the limits of France, a feeling of profound stupefaction, a feeling of something like a personal indignity; for the interests of Europe, whether she wills or not, are incorporated with those of France, and whatever degrades the one humiliates the other.

Before the 2d of December, it was a common saying among the leaders of the Right with regard to Louis Bonaparte: "He is an idiot." They were mistaken. Certainly that brain of his is muddy, has gaps here and there; but thoughts logically connected and interlinked may, to some extent, be discerned in places. It is a book from which certain pages have been torn out. Louis Bonaparte is a man of one fixed idea, but a fixed idea is not idiocy. He knows what he wants, and marches to his aim. Over justice, over law, over reason, honour, and humanity, if you will, he still marches to his aim.

He is not an idiot. He is a man of other times than ours. He seems absurd and mad because he has no counterpart. Transport him to Spain in the sixteenth century, and Philip II will recognize him; to England, and Henry VIII will smile on him; to Italy, and Cæsar Borgia will throw his arms about his neck. . . .

His partisans—he has some—are ready to draw a parallel between his uncle the first Bonaparte and him. They say: "One made the 18th of Brumaire, the other has made the 2d of December; one was eager for power, so is the other." The first Bonaparte wished to restore the Empire of the West, to make Europe his vassal, to dominate the continent by his power and dazzle it by his greatness, to sit on a chair of state and give footstools to kings, to make history say, "Nimrod, Cyrus, Alexander, Hannibal, Cæsar, Charlemagne, Napoleon," to be a master of the world. And he was. For this he made the 18th of Brumaire. The second Bonaparte wishes to have horses and mistresses, to be called Monseigneur, and to live well. For this he has made the 2d of December. Eager for power both. Yes, the comparison is just. Let us add that, like the first, he too would be emperor. But what renders the comparison a little more tranquillizing is the circumstance that there is perhaps some difference between conquering the empire and filching it. . . .

The great talent of Monsieur Louis Bonaparte is silence. . . . Yet this silence is sometimes broken by Louis Bonaparte. Then he does not speak, he lies. This man lies as other men breathe. He announces that his intentions are honest; beware! he affirms; distrust! he takes an oath; tremble! Machiavelli has begotten children. Louis Bonaparte is one of them.

To blazon forth a flagitious villainy at which the world exclaims, to disavow it with indignation in the name of all that is good and holy, to declare himself an honest man, and then at the very moment every one is reassured and laughing at the possibility of the villainy in question, to execute it—this is his method. He has carried it into effect for the *coup d'état,* for the decrees of proscription, for the spoliation of the princes of Orleans; he will carry it into effect for the invasion of Switzerland and of Belgium and for all that remains. It is his method; think of it as you please. It serves him, he likes it, it is his own concern. He will have to reckon with history. . . .

Monsieur Louis Bonaparte has succeeded. From this forth he has on his side money, the Bank, the Bourse, the stockmarket, the counting-house, and all those who pass so easily from one shore to the other when they have only to stride over shame. . . .

VII
THE PANEGYRICS CONTINUE

. . . When the man is measured and found so little, and his success is measured and found so enormous, it is impossible for the mind not to experience some surprise. We ask ourselves: How has he done it? We analyze the adventure and the adventurer, and, laying aside the advantage he derives from his name, and certain facts which aided him in scaling the ramparts, we can discover nothing at the bottom of the man and of his actions but these—craft and money. . . .

Money, and with money debauchery, such was his manner of operating in his three enterprises, at Strasburg, at Boulogne,[1] at Paris. . . .

There has been, then, in France—we must endeavour to succeed in speaking calmly of these things—in France, in the land of the sword, the land of the chevaliers . . . there has been a day when one man, aided by five or six political sharpers, experts in ambuscades and jobbers in *coups d'état*, there has been a day when a man, leaning back in his gilded cabinet with his feet on the fender and a cigar between his lips, has drawn up a tariff of military honour, has weighed it in his scales as if it were merchandise, as if it were a thing purchasable and salable, has estimated this general at a million, that soldier at a louis, and has said of the French conscience, "It is worth so much."

And this man is the nephew of the Emperor. For that matter, this nephew is not too proud; he knows how to accommodate himself to the requirements of his adventures, and assumes with ease the character which destiny allots him. Set him down in London, and, if he have an interest in pleasing the English Government, he will not shrink from the task; and

[1] See p. 253, note 7.

with that hand which would seize the sceptre of Charlemagne, he will grasp the policeman's club. . . .[2]

BOOK II
THE GOVERNMENT

VII
THE ADHERENTS

. . . One class of men has been unanimous in rallying to the new order—the fools. . . .

We know these worthy dupes well. Their leaders were skilful manipulators, and succeeded in inspiring them with terror— the surest way of conducting them into whatever path was desirable. These same leaders, having discovered that the old scarecrows, *jacobin, sans-culotte,* were decidedly out of date, furbished up anew the word *demagogue.* Accustomed as they were to all sorts of intrigues, they made good use of "the Mountain;" they flourished this terrible and magnificent memory with great skill. With some few letters of the alphabet, arranged in syllables and properly accented—"demagogism," "montagnards," "anarchists," "communists," "reds"—they threw an awful glare in front of the eyes of idiots. They had found a way of perverting the brains of their simple colleagues, and inlaying them as it were with a kind of dictionary, in which every one of the expressions in use among the orators and writers of democracy is found at once with its appropriate translation. "Humanity" read "ferocity"; "universal happiness" read "chaos"; "republic" read "terrorism"; "socialism" read "pillage"; "frater-

[2] Louis Napoleon had served as a special constable in London during the Chartist disturbances in 1848.

nity" read "massacre"; "gospel" read "death to the rich." So when an orator of the Left said, for example, "We wish for the suppression of war and the abolition of the penalty of death," a crowd of unhappy creatures among the Right heard distinctly these words: "We wish to ravage everything with fire and sword," and shook their fists furiously at the speaker. After discourses dealing solely with liberty, universal peace, happiness by the agency of labour, concord, and progress, Representatives belonging to the category mentioned at the head of this paragraph would rise up quite pale; they were not quite certain that they were not already guillotined, and went in search of their hats to make sure they had still their heads. These poor scared creatures did not haggle about their adhesion to the 2d of December. It was for them especially that the saying was invented, "Louis Napoleon has saved society."

And then there were all those eternal prefects, and those eternal mayors; and those eternal *capitouls,* and those eternal aldermen, and those eternal adorers of the rising sun or the lighted lamp, who the day after a success besiege the conqueror, the victor, the master—his Majesty Napoleon the Great, his Majesty Louis XVIII, his Majesty Alexander I, his Majesty Charles X, his Majesty Louis Philippe, Citizen Lamartine, Citizen Cavaignac, Monseigneur the Prince President—kneeling, smiling, joyous, bearing the keys of their cities on dishes, and the keys of their consciences on their faces. But the fools are of ancient date; the fools have always made part of all institutions, and are almost an institution in themselves. And as to the prefects and the *capitouls,* as to these adorers of every tomorrow, insolent in their good fortune and their vapidness, they too have been seen in all times. Let us do this justice to the *régime* of December—it has not only partisans of the kind alluded to, it has adherents and creatures that belong to itself only; it has produced notabilities of quite a novel species. Nations never know how rich they are in the product of rascaldom. It is only from such commotions and disarrangements as this that they are enabled to form any idea on the subject.

Then people stand amazed at the sight of what springs from the dust; it becomes a glorious object of their contemplation. . . . Every adventurer dons an official costume, rests his head on a pillow stuffed with bank-notes, takes a sheet of white paper and writes thereon, "End of my adventures."

"You know So-and-so, don't you?"

"Yes."

"He is in the galleys?"

"No, he is a minister."

VIII
MENS AGITAT MOLEM[3]

. . . Now, will Monsieur Bonaparte be emperor or will he not? . . .

Make up your mind to it, he is emperor *in petto;* one of these fine days he will be emperor in broad daylight. To do so only requires the trifling formality of having his oath consecrated, crowned, and ratified in Notre Dame. Then everything will be glorious; look out for a spectacle of imperial splendour. . . .

IX
OMNIPOTENCE

Passing over for a moment this man's 2d of December, passing over his origin, let us see what is his political capacity. Do you wish to judge him during the eight months he has reigned? Place his power on one side and his deeds on the other. What can he do? Everything. What has he done? Nothing. With such authority as his, a man of genius would in eight months have changed the face of France, perhaps of Europe. He would

[3] "Mind moves matter."

not have, most assuredly, effaced the crime of his origin, but he might have covered it up. By the successful promotion of the material well-being of the people he might possibly succeed in hiding his moral abasement. Given a dictator of genuine sagacity, and, we must confess, the thing was not even difficult. A certain number of social problems, elaborately prepared during these last years by several robust intellects, seemed ripe for actual and relative solution; and such solution would redound to the great advantage and contentment of the nation. Louis Bonaparte does not seem to have even suspected this. He has not approached or caught a glimpse of a single one of these problems. He has not been able to discover in the Élysée an old remnant of his socialistic meditations in Ham.[4] To his first crime he has added several new ones, and in this he has been consistent. These crimes excepted, he has effected nothing. Limitless power and no initiative. He has seized France by the throat and knows not what to do with her. In truth, one is tempted to pity this eunuch struggling in the arms of omnipotence.

Surely, this dictator exerts himself—we must do him this justice; he is not quiet for a moment. He feels solitude and darkness around him, and he is appalled. Those who are afraid sing during the night; he fidgets. He turns everything topsy-turvy, meddles with everything, runs wild after every scheme. Not being able to create, he decrees; it would seem as if he were seeking to dupe his own incapacity. It is perpetual motion; but alas! the wheel turns in a vacuum. Conversion of government stock? What profit has resulted from it up to the present hour? A saving of eighteen millions. Granted; the fund-holders lose these eighteen millions which the President and Senate pocket. The gain for France, nothing. But there is the *crédit foncier*? No capital is coming into it. Railways? They are decreed; then the decrees are repealed. It is the same with all these things as it is with the workingmen's towns—Louis

[4] The town where Louis Napoleon was imprisoned after his attempted invasion of France in 1840.

Bonaparte subscribes, but does not pay. As to the budget, that budget controlled by the blind in the Council of State and voted by the dumb in the Legislative Body, an abyss yawns beneath it. The only real and effective economy possible would bear upon the army. Two hundred thousand soldiers left in their homes would mean two hundred millions saved. Attempt, then, to meddle with the army! It is true the soldier, who would become a freeman, might applaud; but what about the officer? And at bottom it is not the soldier, it is the officer, who requires to be petted. Besides, Paris and Lyons have to be watched, and all the other cities as well; and then, when we are emperor, we must have a little war now and then in Europe. You see the gulf!

If from financial questions we pass to political institutions, oh, then we find something to dazzle the neo-Bonapartists; then we find creations! And, good God! what creations! A constitution after the Ravrio[5] style, adorned with carvings of palm-leaves and swans' necks, brought with old arm-chairs in the furniture wagons to the Élysée; the *sénat-conservateur*, new-gilt and trimmed; the Council of State of 1806 smartened and tricked-out with some furbished trappings; the old Legislative Body refitted, repaired, and repainted, with a Lainé[6] the less and a Morny the more! with a bureau of public opinion for the liberty of the press, and for individual liberty the ministry of police.

All these "institutions"—we have passed them in review—are simply the old drawing-room furniture of the Empire. Beat and dust them, take off the cobwebs, daub them with splotches of French blood, and you have the establishment of 1852. This *bric-à-brac* governs France. These are your creations! But where is common-sense, where is reason, where is truth? There is not a single sound feature in contemporary opinion that is not

[5] Antoine-André Ravrio (1759–1814), maker of carvings and author of vaudevilles.

[6] Vicomte Joseph Louis Joaquim Lainé (1767–1835), politican of the restoration era.

wounded, not a real conquest of the century that is not hurled to the earth and dashed to pieces. All sorts of extravagance are now possible. Since the 2d of December we see a mediocre man broken loose, riding at full gallop through the absurd.

These men, the malefactor and his accomplices, have immense power,—power unrivalled, unlimited, absolute, and sufficient, we repeat, to change the face of Europe. This power they use to minister to their pleasures. To amuse and enrich themselves—such is their "socialism." They have stopped the budget on the highway; the coffers are opened; they stuff their wallets and have money for the taking. All salaries have been doubled or tripled. . . .

Monsieur Bonaparte has three hundred blood horses, the fruits and vegetables of the national châteaux, and parks and gardens once belonging to kings. . . . The Élysée will soon have its hundred and forty-nine kitchens, like the castle of Schoenbrunn; drinking, eating, laughing, and banqueting are the order of the day—a banquet at the residence of every minister . . . a wallowing in all sorts of profusion and intoxication.

And the man of the people, the poor day-labourer, without work, shoeless, and in rags, to whom summer brings no bread and winter no wood, whose aged mother is expiring on a rotten heap of straw, whose young daughter is forced to prostitute herself at the corner of the street in order to live, whose little children shiver with hunger, fever, and cold in the kennels of the Faubourg Saint Marceau, in the garrets of Rouen, in the cellars of Lille—do they think of him. What becomes of him? What do they do for him? Die, dog! . . .

X

THE TWO PROFILES OF MONSIEUR BONAPARTE

. . . The Jesuit and the corporal sum up this entire *régime*. Every political expedient of Monsieur Bonaparte is made up of two hypocrisies—a swashbuckler hypocrisy directed towards the soldiers, and a catholic hypocrisy directed towards the clergy. . . .

To enjoy life to the utmost; to devour the budget; to believe nothing, and turn everything to account; to compromise at the same time two sacred things, military honour and religious faith; to stain the altar with blood, and the flag with the holy-water sprinkler; to render the soldier ridiculous and the priest just a little savage; to mingle the Church and the Nation, the Catholic conscience and the patriotic conscience, in the gigantic political swindle which he calls his power—such is the method of Bonaparte the Little. . . .

The present government—a hand bathed in blood steeping a finger in the holy-water font!

XI

CAPITULATION

But people say to us: "Are you not going a little too far? Are you not unjust? Allow him something. Has he not to some extent carried socialistic measures into effect?" And then we are told of the *crédit foncier,* the railways, abatement of rents, etc.

We have already estimated these measures at their full value; but even admitting that there was something of "socialism" in all this, you would be very simple to attribute any credit for it to Monsieur Bonaparte. It is not he that marches on the path of socialism; it is the time.

A man is swimming against a rapid current; he struggles with unheard-of efforts, he buffets the waves with hand and forehead, with shoulder and knee. You say he will ascend. You look a moment after; he has descended. He is much lower in the river than he was when he started. Without knowing and without suspecting, at every effort he makes he is losing ground. He imagines he is going up, and he is going down always. He believes he is advancing, and he is receding. You are quite right as to *crédit foncier;* you are quite right as to abatement of rent.

Monsieur Bonaparte has issued several of those decrees which you are good enough to qualify as socialistic, and he will issue more of them yet. M. Changarnier would have done so, if he, instead of Monsieur Bonaparte, had triumphed. Henry V would do so if he returned to-morrow. The Emperor of Austria is doing so in Galicia, and the Emperor Nicholas in Lithuania. And now, finally, what does all this prove? That this current, whose name is Revolution, is stronger than this swimmer, whose name is Despotism.

But what is this socialism of Monsieur Bonaparte? Real socialism? I deny it. Hatred of the *bourgeoisie,* granted; socialism, no. The Ministry of Agriculture and of Commerce had, if any, a socialistic feature; he abolishes it. What does he give in compensation? The Ministry of Police. Another socialistic ministry is the Ministry of Public Instruction. It is in danger. One of these mornings it will be suppressed. The starting-point of socialism is education, is gratuitous and primary instruction, is light. To take the children and make men of them, to take the men and make citizens of them—intelligent, honest, useful, and happy citizens—is the essential thing. First intellectual progress, moral progress first; material progress afterward. The first two, from their very nature, lead inevitably to the last. Well, what is Monsieur Bonaparte doing? He is persecuting and stifling education on all sides. There is a pariah in this France of ours of to-day; it is the schoolmaster. . . .

Well, to-day, thanks to the predominance of the priest party, as it is not desirable that the schoolmaster should work for this future, as it is desirable that this future be made up of darkness and brutality and not of intelligence and light, would you know in what fashion this great and humble magistrate, the schoolmaster, is made to execute his functions? The schoolmaster serves Mass, rings the bell at vespers, arranges the chairs, sings at the music-desk, renews the flowers before the Sacred Heart, polishes the altar candlesticks, dusts the tabernacle, folds the copes and chasubles, keeps the linen of the sacristy in order, puts oil in the lamps, beats the cushions of the confessionals, sweeps the church and sometimes the presbytery; what time is left him, he may, on condition he pronounce not these words of the Evil One—Country, Republic, Liberty—employ in teaching the little children to spell A B C; that is, if he feels so inclined. . . .

What he [Louis Napoleon] attacks, what he pursues, what they all pursue in his company, what they all rage about, what they all would crush, burn, suppress, destroy, annihilate, is it that poor obscure man who is called the primary instructor, is it that sheet of paper called a journal, is it that bundle of leaves called a book, is it that engine of wood and iron called a press? No, it is thou, Thought; it is thou, Human Reason; it is thou, Nineteenth Century; it is thou, Providence; it is thou, God! . . .

" 'T is easy talking," some incorrigible worthies of the ex-party of order exclaim. "Lash yourself into a fury of indignation, mock, flout, stigmatize; it is little we care. Stability forever! Whatever you may say, we have, on the whole, a solid government."

Solid! well, we have already called attention to this solidity. Solid! yes, I admire this solidity.

If it snowed journals in France for even two days, on the morning of the third not a man would know the spot over which Monsieur Louis Bonaparte passed. . . .

Let us give a summary of this government. Who is in the Élysée and Tuileries? Crime. Who sits in the Luxembourg? Baseness. Who sits in the Palais Bourbon? Imbecility. Who sits in the Palais d'Orsay? Corruption. Who sits in the Palace of Justice? Prevarication. And who is in the prisons, in the forts, in the cells, in the dungeons, in the hulks, at Lambessa, at Cayenne, in exile? Law, honour, intelligence, liberty, Right. . . .

BOOK III
THE CRIME

. . . Whence has this government issued? See there! It is still running, it is still smoking. It is blood.

The dead are far away; the dead are dead. Ah, have we reached a point where men already no longer think of this? It is frightful to think so; it is frightful to say so.

Because men eat and drink; because coach-building is prosperous; because you, navvy, find work in the Bois de Boulogne; because you, mason, get your forty sous a day in the Louvre; because you, banker, have made a profit out of the metallurgic industries in Vienne or the shares of Hope and Company; because titles of nobility are restored; because people can call each other Monsieur le Comte or Madame la Duchesse; because processions march on Corpus Christi; because amusement and laughter are the order of the day; because the walls of Paris are placarded with announcements of celebrations and theatres—because of all this must the dead bodies that lie underneath be forgotten? . . .

. . . Thanks to the reservations of the official historiographers of the 2d of December, it is not sufficiently known how near the *coup d'état* was to its fall, and none know fully by what means it was saved. Let us place this special fact before the eyes of the reader.

I

DAY OF THE 4TH OF DECEMBER.
THE COUP D'ÉTAT AT BAY

The resistance had assumed unexpected proportions. The combat had become threatening; it was no longer a combat, it was a battle, and was waged in all directions. In the Élysée and in the ministerial palaces men were growing pale. They had asked for barricades; they had them.

The entire centre of Paris was becoming covered with re-doubts got up at a moment's notice. . . .

The impulse had indeed been given, and the outburst of anger and hatred had become universal. The *coup d'état* seemed lost; one shock more, and Louis Bonaparte was ruined. Let the day end as it had begun, and all was over. The *coup d'état* was in despair. The hour for some supreme resolution had come. What was it going to do? It had to strike hard; it had to strike a blow that would be unforeseen—a blow that would be horrible. It was reduced to this situation—to perish, or to save itself by an atrocious deed.

Louis Bonaparte had not left the Élysée. He stayed in a cabinet on the ground-floor, adjoining that splendid gilded salon, where, in 1815, he, then a child, was present at the second abdication of Napoleon. He was there, alone; orders had been given to allow no one to come near him. From time to time the door half opened, and the grey head of General Roguet, his *aide-de-camp*, appeared. No one except General Roguet had permission to open this door and enter. The news brought by the General had become more and more alarming, and frequently ended with the words "It does not get on," or, "It is getting on badly." When he finished, Louis Napoleon, leaning on a table, seated, with his feet on the fender, before a big fire, turned his head half round on the back of his arm-chair, and without apparent emotion, invariably replied in his coldest and most phlegmatic tones: "Let my orders be executed!" The last time General Roguet entered with his usual bad news, it was near one o'clock. (He has himself since related these details as reflecting honour on the impassiveness of his master.) He informed the Prince that the barricades in the central streets were holding out successfully, and others were multiplying; that on the boulevards cries of "Down with the dictator!"—he did not dare to say of "Down with Soulouque!"[7]—and hisses were heard in every direction as the troops marched by; that in front of the Galerie Jouffroy an adjutant-major had been pursued by the crowd, and at the corner of the Café Cardinal a staff captain was torn from his horse.

Louis Bonaparte half rose from his arm-chair, and fixing his eyes on the General, said calmly: "Well! let Saint Arnaud be told to execute my orders."

"What are those orders?"

"You shall see." . . .

III

A little after one o'clock, a quarter of an hour after the last order given by Louis Bonaparte to General Roguet, the boulevards throughout their entire length from the Madeleine were suddenly covered with infantry and cavalry. The Carrelet division, almost at its full complement, composed of the five brigades of Cotte, Bourgon, Canrobert, Dulac, and Reybell, and presenting an effective force of 16,410 men, had taken position and formed in echelons from the Rue de la Paix to the Faubourg Poissonnière. Each brigade had its battery with it. On the Boulevard Poissonnière alone eleven pieces of ordnance were counted. Two of these were placed back to back, and pointed, one at the entrance of the Rue Montmartre, the other at that of

[7] Faustin Soulouque (c. 1782–1867) was the black President of Haiti who in 1849 proclaimed himself Emperor; his name was used as a derisive nickname for Louis Napoleon.

the Faubourg Montmartre, for no reason that any one could see, as neither showed signs of any barricade. The people whom curiosity brought to the sidewalks and windows were astounded at this jumble of gun-carriages, sabres, and bayonets.

"The troops were laughing and chatting," says one witness; another witness says, "Most of them, with the butt-ends of their muskets resting on the ground, were supporting themselves on the barrels, and seemed to be in a half-staggering condition from fatigue or from something else." One of those old officers who have made it their study to sound the very depths of the soldier's soul, General L——, said, while passing the Café Frascati: "They are drunk." . . .

About two o'clock, howitzers were levelled at the extremity of the Poissonnière boulevard, a hundred and fifty paces from the little demi-lune barricade of the Bonne Nouvelle station. . . .

At half-past two—we must follow step by step and minute by minute the details of this hideous drama—firing began in front of the barricade, languidly, and, as it seemed, at random. The military leaders appeared to have their minds fixed on something else besides a combat. We shall know what they were thinking of.

The first shot, badly aimed, passed above all the barricades. The projectile killed a young lad in the Château d'Eau who was drawing water from the fountain. The shops were shut, and nearly all the windows as well. One casement, however, remained open in the upper story of a house at the corner of the Rue du Sentier.

Influenced by curiosity, more and more people came flocking into the boulevard, thronging on the sidewalk on the south especially. It was a crowd, and nothing more—men, women, children, and greybeards, on whom the barricade, which was hardly attacked or defended, produced all the effect of a sham battle.

This barricade remained a spectacle until it became a pretext.

IV

For about a quarter of an hour there was some poor firing on the part of the soldiers, replied to in a way, by the barricade, but not one wounded on either side, when suddenly as if by an electric impulse an extraordinary and terrible movement was made, first by the infantry, then by the cavalry. In a moment the soldiery wheeled completely round.

The historiographers of the *coup d'état* have related that a shot fired at the soldiers came from an open window at the corner of the Rue du Sentier. Others have said from the top of the house at the corner of the Rue Notre-Dame-de-Recouvrance and the Rue Poissonnière. Others again say it was a pistol-shot fired from the roof of the high house at the corner of the Rue Mazagran. The shot is disputed; but what there can be no dispute about is, that for firing this problematic pistol-shot, which may, after all, have been nothing else than the noise made by a door shut to with violence, a dentist living in the neighbourhood was executed. After all, did any one hear either gun-shot or pistol-shot fired from one of the houses on the boulevard? Is the story true? Is it false? It is denied by a crowd of witnesses. If the shot was fired, another question remains to be cleared up. Was it a cause, or was it a signal?

Be this as it may, on a sudden, as we have just said, cavalry, infantry, and artillery faced about and confronted the multitude massed on the sidewalks, and without warning, without any one being able to guess why, without motive, without a summons to disperse, (*sans sommation*) . . . from the Gymnase to the Chinese Baths—that is to say, along the whole length of the richest, the most animated and joyous boulevard in Paris, a butchery was begun.

The soldiery commenced to shoot down the people with their muskets close to the people's breasts. Who shall describe the horrors that ensued!—the cries, the arms raised to heaven, the surprise, the terror, the crowd flying in all directions, a hail of balls raining down on the pavements and rising again to the roofs, the dead bodies scattered in a moment along the causeway, young men falling with the cigar still between their lips, women in velvet robes dropping stone dead, two booksellers slaughtered on the threshold of their shops without knowing in what they had offended, shots fired through the openings in cellars and killing it mattered not whom, the Bazaar riddled with shells and bullets, the Hôtel Sallandrouze bombarded, the Maison d'Or raked with grape-shot, Tortoni carried by assault, hundreds of corpses on the boulevard, the Rue Richelieu a stream of blood!

And here the historian must again be allowed to interrupt his narrative for a while.

In presence of these deeds without a name, I who write these lines proclaim myself the recording officer who registers the crime; I bring the cause before the court. All my function is in this. I cite Louis Bonaparte; I cite Saint Arnaud, Maupas, Morny, Magnan, Carrelet, Canrobert, Reybell, his accomplices; I cite the others whose names will be found elsewhere; I cite the executioners and the murderers, the witnesses and the victims, the red-hot cannon and smoking sabres; the drunkenness of the soldiery, the agony of families, the dying and the dead, the horror, the blood and the tears, before the bar of the civilized world. . . .

VI

. . . From this forth it is certain, it is proved beyond doubt and beyond question, it is as clear as the noonday sun, that on the Thursday of the 4th of December, 1851, the inoffensive inhabitants of Paris, the inhabitants who took no part in the combat, were mowed down by grape-shot *sans sommation,* and massacred for the simple purpose of intimidation. . . .

The execution lasted until nightfall. For more than an hour

the boulevard was the scene of something like an orgy of musketry and artillery. During cannonading and platoon firing, the soldiers interchanged shots at random, and at certain moments killed one another. The battery of the 6th regiment of artillery, which formed a part of the Canrobert brigade, was dismounted; the horses, rearing amid the bullets, smashed the gun-carriages in front, and the wheels and shafts of others; and of the whole battery there was but one piece left fit for action. An entire squadron of the 1st Lancers was obliged to take refuge in an outhouse on the Rue Saint-Fiacre. The next day, the lance pennants were found to be pierced with seventy holes made by bullets. Fury had seized on the soldiery. At the corner of the Rue Rougemont, a general, in the midst of the smoke, was seen attempting to restrain them by violent gesticulations; an assistant surgeon-major of the 27th narrowly escaped death at the hands of the soldiers whom he was trying to hold back. A sergeant said to an officer who seized his arm: "Lieutenant, you are a traitor." The soldiers no longer knew what they were doing; they seemed maddened by the crime they were forced to commit. There comes a time when the very abomination of the wickedness you are doing compels you to do it with redoubled energy. Blood is a sort of horrible wine; massacre intoxicates. . . .

IX

Let us get rid at once of these frightful details.

On the morrow of the 5th, in the cemetery of Montmartre, a horrible thing was seen.

A vast space, vacant until that day, was "utilized" for the provisional interment of some of the massacred. They were buried with their heads above the ground, in order that their families might recognize them; most had their feet also exposed, with a little earth on their breasts. The curious came there in crowds, pushing, jostling one another, and wandered amid the graves; sometimes the ground would sink when trodden on—it was really the stomach of a corpse. On turning round and looking, you saw boots and sabots or women's dress shoes rising from the earth; opposite was the head which on account of your pressure on the body had made a movement. . . .

It is evident then, and we urge this point earnestly, that at first the *coup d'état* made not the slightest pretence at concealment of its crime. It did so because it saw its profit in doing so. It was later on that it became bashful. But on the first day it made, on the contrary, a parade of its iniquity. Atrocity was not enough; it needed cynicism. To massacre was but the means; to terrify was the aim.

X

Was this aim reached? Yes.

From the 4th of December the public effervescence subsided immediately. A dull stupor froze the blood of Paris. The indignation that raised its voice in presence of the *coup d'état* was suddenly dumb in presence of the butchery. Nothing resembling this had ever occurred in history before. Men felt they were dealing with some monstrous individuality heretofore unknown. . . .

BOOK IV
THE OTHER CRIMES

I
SINISTER QUESTIONS

. . . On the first day Louis Bonaparte made a public display of his massacre. We have said why. It was useful to him to do so. Having gained by this course of action all the advantage he desired, he then concealed it. Orders were given to the Elysian gazettes to be silent, to Magnan to omit, to the historiographers to ignore. The dead were buried after midnight, without torches, without funeral procession, without chant, without priest, by stealth. Families were forbidden to weep too loudly. . . .

. . . He has sought to enshroud his ambuscade in thicker darkness, and he has in part succeeded. Whatever be the efforts of history, the 2d of December will for a long time still, perhaps, be plunged in a species of awful twilight. This crime is composed of audacity and of shadow. On one side it parades cynically in the broad daylight; on the other, it steals away and vanishes in the fog; a malignant and hideous shape, a front of brass, hiding under its mantle monstrosities that are unknown.

What we get a glimpse of is enough for our purpose. On one particular side of the 2d of December all is darkness, but we see graves dimly in that darkness.

Under that greatest of crimes we have a confused perception of a crowd of others. . . .

Yes, we repeat, in what is styled "the act of the 2d of December" you find crime throughout the whole depth; perjury on the surface, assassination at the bottom; partial murders, wholesale slaughters, volleys of grape-shot in broad daylight, nocturnal fusillades—from every part of the *coup d'état* arises a vapour of blood.

Look into the common graves of the cemeteries, search under the pavements of the streets, under the slopes of the Champs de Mars, under the trees of the public gardens, search the bed of the Seine. There are few revelations. It is easily understood why. Bonaparte has had the monstrous art of binding to himself a multitude of unhappy men in the official class by a frightful universal complicity, the nature of which words are powerless to reveal. The stamped papers of the magistrates, the inkstands of the recording-clerks, the cartridge-boxes of the soldiers, the prayers of the priests, are his accomplices. He has flung his crime around him as if it were a net, and in it he has caught prefects, mayors, judges, officers, and soldiers. This complicity gravitates from the general to the corporal, and soars again from the corporal to the president. The police-agent feels as much compromised as the minister. The gendarme, the muzzle of whose pistol has touched the ear of some unfortunate, and whose uniform has been daubed with brains, knows that he is as guilty as the colonel. Atrocious men on high have given orders which have been executed by ferocious men below. Ferocity keeps the secret of atrocity. Hence this hideous silence. . . .

Is this, then, all? Is this, then, ended? Does God allow and accept such entombments as these? Do not believe it. Some day, under the feet of Bonaparte, that trench shall open suddenly, and we shall see rise up one after another between the marble flagging of the Élysée or of the Tuileries every corpse with its wound—the young man shot through the heart, the old man shaking his white head pierced by a ball, the sabred mother holding her slaughtered babe in her arms—all standing livid and terrible, and fixing on their assassin their blood-shot eyes. . . .

On the evening of the 4th of December Louis Bonaparte would have been torn from the Élysée, and the law would have triumphed, if he had been one of those men who hesitate before a massacre. Happily for him, he was not troubled by any such squeamish delicacy. What do a few dead bodies, more or less, matter? Forward! kill! kill at random, sabre, fusillade, cannonade, crush, mangle, strike terror into this hateful city of Paris! The *coup d'état* was tottering to its fall; this grand murder restored it. The felony of Louis Bonaparte all but ruined him; his ferocity saved him. . . .

II

CONTINUATION OF THE CRIMES

. . . Let us continue.

To what we have just related, add all the other crimes to which we shall have more than one opportunity of reverting, and which, if God spares us our life, we shall relate in detail. Add the incarcerations *en masse* accompanied by every circumstance of ferocity, the prisons overflowing, the sequestration of the goods of the proscribed in ten departments, notably in the Nièvre, in the Allier, and in the Lower Alps; add the confiscation of the property of the Orleans family, a morsel of it being thrown to the clergy . . . ; add the Mixed Commissions, and the so-called Commission of Clemency; the councils of war in conspiracy with the examining magistrates and multiplying abominations, exiles hurried off in batches, three thousand two hundred banished or deported from one department alone, the Herault; add that frightful proscription, worthy of comparison with the most tragic desolations of history, which, for a mere leaning, for an opinion, for an honest dissent from this government, for a word becoming a freeman spoken even before the 2d of December, takes, seizes, apprehends and drags the labourer from his field, the artisan from his trade, the proprietor from his house, the doctor from his patients, the notary from his study, the councillor-general from the people of his department, the judge from his tribunal, the husband from his wife, the brother from his brother, the father from his children. No one escapes. . . .

Add Africa, add Guiana . . . hovels, each containing a hundred and fifty human beings, under the sun of the tropics, promiscuously living amid filth and vermin, and where all these innocent creatures, all these patriots, all these honest people are dying, far from those dear to them, in fever, in misery, wringing their hands in horror and despair. . . .

III
WHAT 1852 WOULD HAVE BEEN

But supposing this 2d of December had not occurred, "necessary" as it was, according to the accomplices and their dupes subsequently, what would have taken place in France? Great heavens! this simply.

Let us go some steps backward and recall briefly the situation as it was before the *coup d'état*. The party of the past, under the name of order, resisted the Republic—in other words, resisted the future. Oppose it or not, consent to it or not, leaving all illusion aside, the Republic is the future, far or near—the inevitable future of nations.

How shall this Republic be established? It can be established in two ways—by strife or by progress. The democrats would have it by progress; their adversaries, the men of the past, would seem to wish to have it by strife.

As we have just recalled, the men of the past resist. They resist obstinately; they strike the tree with their axes, and fancy they can arrest the course of the ascending sap. They are lavish of their strength, their childishness, and their rage.

Let no bitter word be flung at our old adversaries, fallen the same day as ourselves, and many fallen with honour, let us confine ourselves to the statement that the majority of the Legislative Assembly of France from the first days of its installation, from the month of May, 1849, had entered on this strife.

This policy of resistance is a fatal policy. This wrestling of man with God is necessarily vain; but null as to result, it is fruitful in catastrophes. What ought to be shall be, what ought to flow must flow, what ought to fall must fall, what ought to be born must be born, what ought to grow must grow; but place an obstacle in the way of these natural laws, trouble arises, disorder begins. And the sad thing is that this disorder has been called order.

Tie up a vein, you become sick; dam a river, you have an inundation; bar the future, you have revolutions. Preserve with obstinate determination in your midst, as if it were alive, the part which is dead, and you produce a sort of moral cholera. Corruption spreads around; it is in the air—you breathe it. Entire classes of society, functionaries, for example, fall into rottenness. Keep the dead bodies in your houses, and a plague will burst forth.

From a kind of fatality this policy blinds those who practise it. Those men calling themselves statesmen cannot understand that they, with their own hands, with great toil and with the sweat of their brows, have themselves produced those terrible events which they lament, and that those catastrophes which overwhelm them have been constructed by them. What would be said of the peasant who made a weir from one bank to the other of a river in front of his cabin, and who, when the river, having become a torrent, casts down his dike, overflows its banks, and carries away his roof, should say, "Wicked river!" The statesmen of the past, those grand constructors of dikes across currents, spend their time in crying, "Wicked people!" Take away Polignac[8] and the ordinances of July—that is to say, the dike— and Charles X would have died in the Tuileries. Reform the electoral law in 1847[9]—that is to say again, take away the dike —and Louis Philippe would have died on the throne.

Do I mean to say that the Republic would not have come? No. The Republic, we repeat, is the future. It would have come, but step by step, progress by progress, conquest by conquest—as a river that flows, and not as a deluge that devastates; it would have come at its hour, when everything had been made ready to receive it; it would have come, not certainly with more vitality, for now it is indestructible, but with more tranquillity, without a possible reaction, without princes waylaying it, without a *coup d'état* behind it.

The policy of resistance to the movement of humanity excels —let us insist on this point—in creating artificial cataclysms. Thus it succeeded in making of the year 1852 a formidable

[8] Auguste Jules Armand, Prince de Polignac (1780–1847), a leading minister under Charles X, 1829–30; his reactionary policies helped bring on the July revolution.

[9] Proposals for electoral reform helped trigger the disturbances leading to the February 1848 revolution.

eventuality, and this always by the same method—by means of a dike. A train is going to pass over yonder railway in an hour: throw a beam across the rails; when the train reaches that point it will be crushed to pieces; you will have Fampoux.[10] Take away the beam before the arrival of the train: the travellers are carried through without even suspecting that there was any danger there. This beam is the law of the 31st of May. The leaders of the majority of the Assembly had flung it across 1852, crying, "It is there! society will be crushed!" The Left said to them: "Take away the beam! take away the beam! let universal suffrage pass over freely!" This is the whole history of the law of the 31st of May. There are things which a child might understand, and which the "statesmen" do not understand.

Now to answer the question we proposed a moment ago: "But for the 2d of December, what would have taken place in 1852?" Suppress the law of the 31st of May; take from the people its dike; take from Bonaparte his lever, his arm, his pretext; let universal suffrage alone; take the beam from the rails—do you know what would have happened in 1852?

Nothing. Some elections. A few calm Sundays on which the people would have come to vote; yesterday toilers, to-day electors, to-morrow toilers, always sovereign.

But the retort comes: "Yes, elections! You speak of them at your ease. But what about the 'Red Chamber' that would spring out of these elections?" Was it not proclaimed that the Constituant of 1848 would be a "Red Chamber"? Red Chambers, red ogres—all these predictions have their value. Those who parade these fantastic apparitions before the scared inhabitants of the rural districts know perfectly what they are doing, and laugh behind the horrible rag they wave. Under the long scarlet robe of the phantom to which the name "1852" has been given, it is easy to recognize the heavy boots of the *coup d'état*.

10 The site of a major railway accident in 1846.

IV
THE JACQUERIE

However, after the 2d of December—the crime being finished and done with—it became necessary that public opinion should be put on the wrong scent. The *coup d'état* at once set about crying, "Stop the Jacquerie!" like the assassin who cried, "Stop thief!"

Let us add that a *Jacquerie* had been promised, and Monsieur Bonaparte could not, without some inconvenience, fail in all his promises at the same time. What was the "red spectre" if not the *Jacquerie*? Some reality must be given to this spectre. It was absolutely necessary. You cannot abruptly break out into a roar of laughter in presence of the whole people and say, "There was nothing the matter! I have the whole time been making you afraid of yourselves."

There has, then, been a *Jacquerie*. The promises of the proclamation have been kept. The set around Louis Bonaparte gave their imaginations full scope; . . . Implications and inventions became the order of the day. As the press was done away with, the thing became very simple: to lie is easy when you have previously torn out the tongue of the person lied to. The cry was: "Look out, *bourgeois*! Had it not been for us, you would have been ruined. We mowed you down with grape-shot, but it was for your good." . . .

There was in the departments what there was in Paris—a legal resistance; the resistance prescribed for citizens by Article 110 of the Constitution, and by that which is above the Constitution, by natural right. There has been legitimate defence (this time the word is in its proper place) against the "saviours"; there has been the struggle of men armed by the law and by the right against the infamous insurrection of power. The Republic, surprised by an ambuscade, and the *coup d'état* have collared each other. That is the whole. Twenty-seven departments arose. . . .

It was this resistance, at once legal, constitutional, and virtuous—this resistance in which all the heroism was on the side of the citizens, and all the atrocity on the side of power—it was this resistance which the *coup d'état* has called the *Jacquerie.* But let us repeat, a little of the "red spectre" was useful. This *Jacquerie* had two ends; it served in two ways the policy of the Élysée; it offered a double advantage. On one side it forced an affirmative vote on the question of the plebiscite; to force a vote under the sabre and in face of the spectre; to suppress the intelligent, to frighten the credulous; terror for one, fear for the other, as we shall explain later on—all the success and all the secret of the vote of the 20th of December lie in this. The other end was to give a pretext for proscriptions. 1852 did not, then, contain in itself any real danger. The law of the 31st of May, killed morally, was dead before the 2d of December. A new Assembly, a new President, the Constitution purely and simply put in practice, and some elections—nothing more. Take away Monsieur Bonaparte, and you had 1852. But it was necessary for Monsieur Bonaparte to go; that was the difficulty, and from that came the catastrophe. . . .

BOOK V
PARLIAMENTARISM

III
THE TRIBUNE

. . . The French tribune! A book were needed to tell all that word contains. The French tribune!—it has been for sixty years the open mouth of the human mind—of the human mind saying all, blending and combining all, fructifying all; the good and the evil, the true and the false, the just and the unjust, the high and the low, the horrible and the beautiful, dream and reality; passion, reason, love, hatred, matter, the ideal. But its sublime and eternal task is that it makes night in order to draw day from it, chaos to draw life from it, the Revolution to draw the Republic from it. . . .

IV

THE ORATORS

. . . Let us insist on this: Beginning with Mirabeau, there has been in the world, in the fellowship of humanity, in civilization, a culminating point, a central spot, a hearth, a summit. This summit was the French tribune—that admirable starting-point of the nations marching on, that dazzling pinnacle in peaceful times, that beacon in the obscurity of catastrophes. From the extremities of the intelligent universe the people fixed their eyes on that height whence the human mind radiated. When some sudden cloud enveloped them they heard from there a great voice, which spoke to them in the shadow . . . a voice that suddenly, like that of chanticleer announcing the dawn, like the cry of the eagle calling to the sun, rang out like a clarion of war or a trumpet of doom; and at that sound all those heroic dead nations—Poland, Hungary, Italy—stood erect, terrible, shaking their winding-sheets and seeking swords in their sepulchres! And so, at this voice of France, the glorious sky of the future half opened; the old blinded and frightened despotisms bowed down their heads in the darkness beneath, and mankind saw Liberty appear—Liberty, the archangel of nations; her feet on the cloud, her brow among the stars, her great wings open in the azure! . . .

V

THE POWER OF SPEECH

. . . Such was this grand tribune from whose height a man spoke to the world. From this tribune, ever in ceaseless vibra-

tion, issued perpetually sonorous surges, immense oscillations of
sentiments and ideas which ran from billow to billow and from
people to people, to the very limits of the earth, stirring up those
thinking waves called souls. Often no one knew why such a
law, such an edifice, such an institution was staggering yonder,
farther than our frontiers, farther than our seas—the Papacy
beyond the Alps, the throne of the Czar at the extremity of
Europe, slavery in America, the penalty of death everywhere.
It was because the tribune of France had trembled. At certain
hours a shiver of this tribune is an earthquake. The tribune of
France spoke! all that thinks here below became meditative;
the words spoken sank into the darkness, travelled through space,
at random, it mattered not where. "It is only wind, it is only
noise," said those barren minds whose lifeblood is irony—and the
next day, or three months later, or a year later, something fell or
something arose on the surface of the globe. What had caused
this? This "noise" that had vanished, this "wind" that had
passed. This "wind" this "noise" was the Word—a sacred force.
From the Word of God were all beings created; from the word
of man shall spring the fellowship of the nations. . . .

VII

WHAT THE TRIBUNE DID

Two great problems are suspended over the world: war must
disappear, and conquest must continue. These two necessities
of growing civilization would seem to exclude each other. How
satisfy the one without losing the other? What could solve the
two problems at once? What was resolving them? The tribune.
The tribune is peace, and the tribune is conquest. As for conquest by the sword, who wants it? No one. The nations are the
fatherlands of their inhabitants. Conquest by idea, who wants
it? Every one. The nations are humanity.

Now, two brilliant tribunes were dominating nations—the English tribune, by doing its own work; the French tribune, by creating ideas. The French tribune had elaborated since '89 all the principles that form the political Absolute; and it had begun since 1848 to formulate all the principles that form the social Absolute. Once a principle was drawn from limbo and born into life, it threw that principle into the world armed at all points, and said, "Go!" . . . and to those who asked, "Who art thou?" it answered: "I am Truth!" and to those who asked, "Whence comest thou?" it answered, "I come from France!" Then he who questioned it stretched forth his hand, and it was better than a province—it was an intelligence annexed. Henceforth between Paris—the metropolis—and this man isolated in his solitude, and this city lost in the depth of woods or steppes, and this people bent under the yoke a current of thought and of love was established. . . . Slowly and gradually the French nation, in the cause of universal progress, was assimilating other nations. Thanks to that admirable French language, composed by Providence with a marvellous balancing of consonants enough to be pronounced by the peoples of the north, and vowels enough to be pronounced by the peoples of the south— thanks to that language, which is a power of civilization and humanity, step by step, by the force of its own radiance, that lofty central tribune of Paris was conquering the nations and making them France. . . .

This is what the tribune was; this is what it was doing for France. . . .

And this is what Monsieur Bonaparte has suppressed! . . .

BOOK VI
The Absolution

First Form
THE SEVEN MILLION, FIVE HUNDRED THOUSAND VOTES

I
THE ABSOLUTION

They say to us: "Are you not dreaming! All these facts which you call crimes are henceforth 'facts accomplished,' and consequently respectable. All this is accepted, all this is adopted, all this is legitimated, all this is covered, all this is absolved."

"Accepted, adopted, legitimated, covered, absolved!—by what?"

"By a vote."

"What vote?"

"The seven million, five hundred thousand votes."

"Oh, indeed! Yes, there has been a *plebiscite,* and vote, and seven million, five hundred thousand yes's. Let us speak of them."

II
THE DILIGENCE

A brigand stops a diligence at the corner of a wood. He is at the head of a determined band. The travellers are more numerous, but they are separated, disunited, penned in compartments, half asleep, surprised in the middle of the night, seized unexpectedly and without arms. The brigand orders them to de-

369

scend, to utter no cry, to suffer no word to escape their lips, and to lie flat on the ground. Some resist; he blows out their brains. Others obey, and lie on the road dumb, motionless, terrified, jumbled together with the dead, and like the dead themselves. The brigand, while his accomplices have their feet on the backs of the passengers and their pistols at their heads, rummages their pockets, breaks open their trunks and takes all he finds worth his while. The pockets emptied, the trunks pillaged, the *coup d'état* over, he says:—

"Now, in order to make things right with the law, I have written on a paper that you acknowledge that all I have taken belongs to me, and that you surrender it fully and freely. I conclude that this is your opinion. A pen will be placed in your hand, and without saying a word, without making a gesture, without quitting the attitude in which you are [the belly on the ground and the face in the mud], you shall stretch out your right hands and sign this paper. You see the muzzle of my pistol: still you are free."

The travellers stretch out their hands and sign. When this is over the brigand raises his head and says:

"I have seven million, five hundred thousand votes." . . .

IV

WHO REALLY VOTED FOR MONSIEUR BONAPARTE

We declare, then, purely and simply, that on the 20th of December, 1851, eighteen days after the 2d, M. Bonaparte has rummaged with his hand in the conscience of every individual, and from every individual has stolen his vote. . . .

Let us however be understood. Do we mean to imply that no one really voted for Monsieur Bonaparte; that no one voluntarily said *yes*; that no one freely and knowingly accepted this man? Not at all. Monsieur Bonaparte had for him the vulgar rabble of functionaries, the twelve hundred thousand parasites on the budget and their connections and underlings—the corrupt, the compromised, the crafty—and in their train the fools, a not inconsiderable mass. He had for him the cardinals, the bishops, the canons, the curés, the vicars, the archdeacons, the deacons, the sub-deacons, the prebendaries, the vestrymen, the sacristans, the beadles, and the "religious" men so-called. Yes, we have no difficulty in acknowledging that Monsieur Bonaparte had for him all those bishops who cross themselves after the fashion of Veuillot and Montalembert, and all those religious men (a precious race, somewhat antique, but very much increased and recruited since the terror of the property-owners in 1848) who pray in these terms: "O my God! send up my Lyons railway shares! Sweet Lord Jesus, let me gain twenty-five per cent on my Rothschild-Naples certificates! Holy Apostles, sell my wines! Blessed martyrs, double my rents! Holy Mary, Mother of God, Virgin immaculate, Star of the Sea, deign to cast a favourable eye on my little business at the corner of Rue Tirechappe and Rue Quincampoix! Tower of Ivory, grant that the shop opposite me turn out ill!"

All these have really and incontestably voted for Monsieur Bonaparte: first category, the functionary; second category, the fool; third category, the religious Voltairian-proprietor-manufacturer.

Let us say at once that in the human intellect—and the bourgeois intellect in particular—there are some singular enigmas. We know this, and have no desire to conceal it, that from the shopkeeper to the banker, from the petty trader to the stockbroker, a good number of men engaged in commerce and manufactures in France—that is to say, a good number of those men who know the meaning of a well-placed confidence, of a deposit faithfully guarded, of a key put into safe hands—have voted, after the 2d of December, for Monsieur Bonaparte. If you had happened to meet one of these men of trade, you might very likely have exchanged with him some such dialogue as the following:—

"Have you voted for Louis Bonaparte to be President of the Republic?"

"Yes."

"Would you take him for your cashier?"

"No, certainly not!" . . .

VII

AN EXPLANATION TO MONSIEUR BONAPARTE

Let us try to probe somewhat these strange things. Learn this fact then, Monsieur Bonaparte: that which separates man from the brute is the notion of good and evil. . . . That is the abyss. The animal is a complete being. The greatness of man consists in this, that he is incomplete; that he feels himself, in a multitude of directions, beyond the finite; that he perceives something beyond himself and on this side of himself. This something beyond man and on this side of man is the mystery; it is (to employ those weak human expressions that never express more than one aspect of a thing) the moral world. In this moral world man is steeped as much as in the material world; nay, more. He lives in what he feels more than in what he sees. Creation may beleaguer him, want may assail him, enjoyment may tempt him, the beast that is in him may torment him; his perpetual aspirations towards another world hurl him irresistibly beyond creation, beyond want, beyond enjoyment, beyond the beast. Always, everywhere, at every moment, he has a glimpse of the superior world; and with this vision he fills his soul, and by it he rules his actions. He does not feel himself perfected in the life here below. He bears in himself, so to speak, a mysterious exemplar of the world anterior and ulterior—of the perfect world, with which, unceasingly and in spite of himself, he is comparing this imperfect world, himself, his infirmities, his appetites, his passions, and his actions. When he recognizes that he is approaching that ideal model, he is joyous; when he recognizes that he is removing from it, he is sad. He understands thoroughly that there is nothing useless, and that nothing in this world can be destroyed. Justice and injustice, good and evil, good works and bad deeds, fall into the gulf but are not lost, depart into the infinite to the trouble or the benefit of those who accomplish them. After death they are found again, and the total reckoning is determined. To be lost, to fade away, to be annihilated is no more possible for the moral atom than it is for the material atom. Hence that great and twofold sentiment in man of his liberty and of his responsibility. He can be good or he can be wicked. That is an account he will have to settle. He can be guilty; and that—it is a striking fact, and one upon which I insist—is his greatness. Such is not the case with the brute. For it there is nothing but instinct—to drink when thirsty; to eat when hungry; to procreate in due season; to sleep when the sun sets, to wake when it rises; to do the contrary if it be a beast of night. The animal has but a sort of obscure individuality, which no moral glimmer enlightens. All its law, I repeat, is instinct. Instinct is a species of rail along which irresistible nature drags the brute. No liberty, no responsibility; consequently no other life. The brute does neither good nor evil; it does not know them. The tiger is innocent.

Now, if perchance you were innocent like the tiger? At certain times we are tempted to believe that, not having any inward monitor more than he, you have no more responsibility. In truth, there are hours when I pity you. Who knows? You are perhaps only a blind, unhappy force. Monsieur Louis Bonaparte, the notion of good and evil you have not. You are perhaps the only man in all humanity who has not this notion. This shuts you off from the human race. Yes, you are formidable. It is what constitutes your genius, we are told. I agree that in any case it is what at the present moment constitutes your power.

But do you know what is born of that kind of power?

The fact? Yes. The right? No. Crime tries to deceive history as to its true name; it comes and says, "I am success." Thou art crime! You are crowned and masked. Off with your mask! Off with your crown! Ah, you have your labour for your pains, for your appeals to the people, your plebiscites, your ballots, your additions, your executive commissions proclaiming the sum total, your streamers with these figures on gilt paper—7,500,000! You will get nothing from this scenic display. As to certain things the universal sentiment cannot be put on a wrong scent. The human race, taken in the mass, is an honest man. Even in your environment you are judged. There is not a person in your household, gold-laced or embroidered, not a groom of your stables or a groom of your senate, who does not say quite low what I say aloud. What I proclaim they whisper—that is all the difference. You are omnipotent; they bow before you—nothing more. They salute you, their cheeks flushing with shame. They feel that they are vile, but they know that you are infamous.

And now, as you are ready to give chase to all those you call "the revolted of December," since it is on them that you let slip your dogs; since you have instituted a Maupas and created a Ministry of Police especially for this—I denounce to you that rebel, that revolter, that insurgent, *the conscience of each individual!* You give money, but it is the *hand* that receives it, not the conscience. The conscience! While you are about it, inscribe it on your list of exile. It is a stubborn opponent, that— obstinate, tenacious, and inflexible—an opponent that causes trouble everywhere. Hunt me that out of France: you will be tranquil then. Would you know how it treats you, even among your friends? Would you know in what terms a worthy chevalier of Saint Louis, eighty years old, a great adversary of "the demagogues," and a partisan of yours, defended himself for voting for you? "He is a wretch," he said; "but *he is a necessary wretch.*" No! there are no necessary wretches. No! crime is never useful. No! crime is never good. Society saved by treason, blasphemy!—leave such sayings as that to the archbishops. Nothing good has evil for its basis. God does not impose on humanity the necessity of wretches. There is nothing necessary in this

world but justice and truth. If this old man looked less on life
and more on the tomb, he would have seen this. These words
are surprising in the mouth of an old man; for a light from God
enlightens those who are approaching the grave, and shows them
the truth. Never do righteousness and crime meet. The day they
could be united, the words of human speech would change their
meaning, all certitude would vanish, and darkness would over-
spread society. When by some chance (this has occasionally
been seen in history) it happens, for a moment, that crime has
the force of law, something trembles in the very foundations of
humanity. . . .

IX

WHERE MONSIEUR BONAPARTE HAS BEEN MISTAKEN

Thus then, whatever be your figures, controverted or not,
extorted or not, true or false, it little matters. Those who live
with their eyes fixed on justice will say, and keep on saying,
that crime is crime, that perjury is perjury, that treason is treason, that murder is murder, that blood is blood, that dirt is dirt,
that a rascal is a rascal. . . . They say this, and they will repeat
it in spite of your figures, because seven million five hundred
thousand votes weigh nothing against the conscience of the
honest man; because ten millions, a hundred millions, the unanimity even of the human race voting *en masse* would not
count before this atom, this particle, of God—the soul of the
just man; because universal suffrage, which has entire sovereignty over political questions, has no jurisdiction over moral
questions. . . .

BOOK VII
THE ABSOLUTION

Second Form
THE OATH

VI
SWEARING ON ALL SIDES

. . . There has been swearing here, swearing there, swearing on all sides—at Paris, in the provinces, at sunrise, at sunset, in the north and in the south. During one entire month France has been a scene of arms stretched out and hands uplifted; with the final chorus, "Let us swear!" etc. The ministers have sworn before the President, the prefects before the ministers, the herd before the prefects. What does Monsieur Bonaparte do with these oaths? Does he make a collection of them? Where does he put them? It has been noticed that the oath is seldom refused except by unpaid functionaries—councillors-general, for example. The oath has in reality been taken to the budget. On the 29th of March a certain senator was heard to protest in a loud voice that his name had been passed over, which must have happened through some sort of fortuitous decency. . . .

And yet an oath is a holy thing. The man who takes an oath is no longer a man; he is an altar on which God descends. . . .

O oath! admirable confidence of justice in itself! sublime permission to make a solemn averment granted by God to man! It is ended; it exists no longer. One more glory of the soul faded away into space!

BOOK VIII
PROGRESS CONTAINED IN THE COUP D'ÉTAT

I
THE QUANTITY OF GOOD CONTAINED IN THE EVIL

Among us democrats many sincere spirits have been stricken with stupor by the events of the 2d of December. Some have been disconcerted, others discouraged, many dismayed; some of those whom I have seen have cried out, "Finis Poloniæ!" As to myself, I—since at certain moments it becomes necessary to say I, and to speak in presence of history as a witness—I have seen this event without anxiety, and I proclaim the fact. I say more —there are moments when the 2d of December finds me a satisfied observer.

When I succeed in abstracting myself from the present; when it is in my power to turn away my eyes for a moment from all these crimes, from all the blood spilt, from all the victims, from all the proscribed, from the death-rattle on the convict-ship, from the frightful prisons of Lambessa and Cayenne where death is quick, from that exile where death is slow, from that vote, that oath, from that enormous blot of shame staining France and widening every day; when, forgetting for some minutes these painful thoughts—thoughts that habitually possess my soul—I succeed in shutting myself up in the austere coldness of the statesman, and considering no longer the fact but the consequences of the fact;—then, among many results doubtless disastrous, I see real, considerable, nay immense progress; and at that moment, while I am always one of those whom the 2d of December rouses to indignation, I am no longer one of those whom it grieves. With my eyes fixed on certain

377

aspects of the future, I arrive at this conclusion: the proceeding is infamous, but the fact is good.

Efforts have been made to account for the unaccountable victory of the 2d of December in a hundred fashions. A balance has been taken between the different sorts of resistance possible, and they have been set off one against the other. The people have been afraid of the *bourgeoisie*, the *bourgeoisie* has been afraid of the people; the Faubourgs have hesitated before the restoration of the majority—fearing, wrongly for that matter, that their victory would bring back to power that Right which was so profoundly unpopular; the shopkeepers have recoiled before the Red Republic, the people did not understand, the middle classes shuffled. Some have said, "What kind of persons are we likely to send to the Legislative Palace?" Others have said, "What kind of people are we likely to see in the Hôtel de Ville?" In fine, the harsh repression of 1848, the insurrection crushed by cannon, the casemates, the banishments, the transportations—it was a living and terrible memory; and then, If the rappel could have been beaten! if a single legion had turned out! if M. Sibour had been M. Affre,[11] and had thrown himself in front of the balls of the pretorians! if the High Court had not let itself be dispersed by a corporal! if the judges had done as the Representatives, and the red robes as well as the scarves had been seen on the barricades! if a single arrest had failed! if a regiment had hesitated! if the massacre on the boulevard had not occurred, or had fared ill for Monsieur Bonaparte! etc. All this is true; and nevertheless that has been which ought to have been. Let us repeat that beneath this monstrous victory and in its shadow a vast and certain progress has been accomplished. The 2d of December succeeded because—I say again—from more than one point of view it was perhaps good that it should succeed. All explanations are just and all explanations are vain.

[11] Marie Dominique Auguste Sibour (1792–1857), Archbishop of Paris at the time of the coup d'état; he gave it his approval. Denis Auguste Affre (1793–1848), Archbishop of Paris, killed during the June Days.

The invisible hand is concerned in all this; Providence has made the event. It was in fact necessary that *order* should reach its logical conclusion. It was well that it should be known, and known forever, that in the mouth of the men of the past this word "order" means false swearing, perjury, robbery of the public funds, civil war, councils of war, confiscation, sequestration, deportation, transportation, proscription, fusillades, police, censorship, dishonour of the army, negation of the people, the abasement of France, the senate mute, the tribune prostrate, the press crushed, the political guillotine, the butchery of liberty, the strangling of right, the violation of the laws, the sovereignty of the sabre, massacre, treason, and ambuscade. The spectacle before our eyes is a useful spectacle. The things seen in France since the 2d of December are the orgies of *order*.

Yes, Providence is concerned with this event. Think again of this; that for fifty years the Republic and the Empire filled all imaginations—the one with its reflection of terror, the other with its reflection of glory. In the Republic men saw only 1793 —that is to say, the formidable necessity of revolutions, as fiery furnaces; in the Empire they saw only Austerlitz. Hence, a prejudice against the Republic and a prestige in favour of the Empire. Now, what is the future of France? Is it the Empire? No! it is the Republic.

It was necessary to change this situation—to destroy the prestige of what cannot be revived, and destroy the prejudice against what must be. Providence has done it; it has destroyed two mirages. February came, and took from the Republic its terror; Louis Bonaparte came, and took from the Empire its prestige. Henceforth, 1848 (fraternity) is superimposed on 1793 (terror); Napoleon the Little is superimposed on Napoleon the Great. Two great things—of which the one frightened, the other dazzled—retire from the field: '93 is seen no longer except through its justification, and Napoleon is seen no longer except through his caricature; the senseless dread of the guillotine is dissipated, the vain popularity of the Empire has vanished. Thanks to 1848, the Republic no longer alarms; thanks to Louis

Bonaparte, the Empire no longer fascinates. The future has become possible. These are the secrets of God.

Moreover, the word "Republic" is not enough; it is the *thing* republic that is wanted. Well, we shall have the thing with the word. Let us develop this point.

II
THE FOUR INSTITUTIONS OPPOSED TO THE FUTURE

While waiting for the marvellous but ultimate simplifications which the union of Europe and the democratic federation of the continent must one day bring to pass, what will be in France the form of the social edifice which the thinker sees dimly at present, whose vague and luminous lineaments he traces through the darkness of dictatorships? This form will be as follows:—

The commune sovereign, administered by an elected mayor; universal suffrage everywhere, subordinate to the national unity only in what touches general interests: so much for the administration. Syndicates and trades-councils regulating the private differences of associations and industries; the jury, magistrate of the fact, instructing the judge, himself the magistrate of the law; the judge elected: so much for the judiciary. The priest excluded from everything except the Church; living with his eye fixed on his book and on heaven; a stranger to the budget, ignored by the State, known only by his followers; having no longer authority, but having liberty: so much for religion. War confined to the defence of the territory; the nation a national guard divided into three bands, and able to rise like one man: so much for power. The law everywhere, the right everywhere, the vote everywhere; the sabre nowhere.

Now, to this future, to this magnificent realization of the democratic ideal, what were the obstacles? There were four obstacles, and they were these:—

A permanent army.

A centralized administration.

A paid clergy.
An irremovable magistracy.

III

SLOWNESS OF NORMAL PROGRESS

What these obstacles are, what they were even under the Republic of February, even under the Constitution of 1848; the evil they produced, the good they prevented, the past which they perpetuated, the excellent social order which they delayed —these the political writer saw imperfectly, the philosopher knew, the nation was ignorant of. These four institutions— enormous, ancient, and solid, buttressed one upon the other, intermingled from their base to their summit, growing like a forest of huge old trees, their roots under our feet and their branches over our heads—were stifling and crushing all the scattered germs of new France. Where there should have been life, movement, association, local liberty, communal spontaneity, there was administrative despotism; where there should have been the intelligent vigilance, armed if needful, of the patriot and the citizen, there was the passive obedience of the soldier; where the living Christian faith might have gushed forth, there was the Catholic priest; where there should have been justice, there was the judge. And the future was there under the feet of the suffering generations, which could not emerge from earth and were waiting.

Was this known among the people? Was it suspected? Was it surmised? No, far from it. In the eyes of the greatest number, and of the middle classes in particular, these four obstacles were four supports. The magistracy, the army, the administration, and the clergy were the four virtues of order, the four social forces, the four holy pillars of the ancient French formation. Attack that if you dare! I do not hesitate to say that in the state of blindness to which the best minds were a prey, with the methodical march of normal progress, with our assemblies (which no one will suspect me of disparaging, but which when they are at once honest and timid, as often happens, are willing to be governed by their average; that is to say, by mediocrity), with the commissions of initiative, the delays and repeated ballotings—if, in this state the 2d of December had not come with its astounding demonstration, if Providence had not interfered, France would have been condemned indefinitely to endure an irremovable magistracy, a centralized administration, a permanent army, and a paid clergy.

Certainly it is not I who will seek to contest, much less to depreciate, the power of the press and the power of the tribune, these two great combined forces of civilization. But see, nevertheless, what efforts of every kind and in every sense and under every form have been required for the tribune and the newspaper, for books and eloquence, to succeed even in shaking the universal prejudice in favour of these four fatal institutions. What gigantic struggles would be needed, then, to overthrow them; to brandish the evidence before all eyes; to overcome the resistance of the interested, the passionate, and the ignorant; to enlighten thoroughly public opinion, the public conscience, the official powers; to make this fourfold reform penetrate first into ideas and then into the laws! Reckon up the discourses, the writings, the articles in the journals; the projects of law, the counter-projects; the amendments, the amendments on amendments; the reports, the counter-reports; the facts, incidents, polemics, discussions, affirmations, denials, the storms; the steps forward, the steps backward; the days, weeks, months, years; the quarter of a century, the half century! . . .

V
WHAT PROVIDENCE HAS DONE

But Providence acts differently. It puts the thing under your eyes, illuminated on all sides, and says, "See!"

One fine morning a man arrives; and what a man!—the first comer, the last comer, without a past, without a future, without genius, without glory, without prestige. Is he an adventurer? Is he a prince? This man has quite frankly filled his hands with money, bank-notes, railway shares, places, decorations, sinecures; this man bows to his functionaries and says, "Functionaries be traitors!" The functionaries become traitors. All—without exception? Yes, all. He addresses the generals and says, "Generals, massacre!" The generals massacre. He turns towards the irremovable judges and says: "Magistrates, I break the Constitution; I perjure myself; I dissolve the sovereign Assembly, I arrest the inviolable Representatives; I pillage the public treasury, I sequestrate; I confiscate; I banish whoever displeases me, or as my fancy dictates; I shoot down without notice, I fusillade without a trial; I commit all that men have agreed to call crime, I violate all that men have agreed to call right: behold the laws, they are under my feet!"

"We shall pretend not to see," say the magistrates.

"You are insolent!" replies the providential man. "To turn away your eyes is to insult me. I intend you to assist me. Judges, to-day you shall congratulate me—me, who am force and crime —and to-morrow you shall try those who resisted me, those who stand for honour, right, and law, and you shall condemn them."

The irremovable judges kiss his boot, and set about examining into the *affair of the troubles*. Into the bargain, they take an oath to him.

Next he perceives the clergy in a corner, endowed, gilded, crossed, coped, and mitred, and says to them: "Ah, you are there, archbishop! Come here; you shall bless all this for me." And the archbishop intones his *magnificat*. . . .

CONCLUSION

First Part
PETTINESS OF THE MASTER, SHABBINESS OF THE SITUATION
I

Be tranquil! history has him in its grip. Still, if to be laid hold of by history flatters the vanity of Monsieur Bonaparte; if he chance to have (and really it looks like it) any mental illusion as to his value as a political scoundrel—let him discard it. He must not imagine that because he has piled horror on horror he will ever be able to hoist himself up to the level of the great bandits of history. We have done wrong, perhaps, in some pages of this work to draw a parallel between him and these men. No; although he has committed great crimes, he himself remains paltry. He will never be anything but the nocturnal strangler of liberty; he will never be anything but the man who intoxicated soldiers—not with glory, as did the first Napoleon, but with wine; he will never be anything but the pygmy tyrant of a great people. The stature of the individual is entirely incompatible with greatness, even in infamy. As a dictator he is a buffoon; as emperor, he will be grotesque. That will finish him. It will be his destiny to make the human race shrug its shoulders. Will his punishment be the less harsh on account of this? No; disdain in no way lessens resentment. He will be hideous, and he will continue ridiculous—nothing more. History while laughing at him smites him. Even the indignation of those most indignant cannot get him out of this position. Great thinkers take a delight in chastising great despots, and sometimes enlarge them a little to render them worthy of their wrath; but what can the historian do with such a personage as this? The historian can only lead him to posterity by the ear. . . .

III

If there were not before long an abrupt, imposing, and striking termination; if the present situation of the French nation were prolonged and extended—the great injury, the terrific injury, would be the moral injury.

The boulevards of Paris, the streets of Paris, the fields and towns of twenty departments in France, have been strewn on the 2d of December with citizens killed and dying; fathers and mothers have been butchered on the threshold of their homes, children sabred, the hair of women matted with blood and their bosoms torn by grape-shot; suppliants have been massacred in their houses, others shot in heaps in their cellars, others dispatched by bayonets under their beds, others laid low on their own hearths; the marks of bloody hands are still imprinted here on a wall, there on a door, there on an alcove. After the victory of Louis Bonaparte, Paris tramped for three days through a reddish mud—a cap filled with human brains has been seen hanging from a tree on the Boulevard des Italiens. I who write these lines have seen among other victims on the night of the 4th, near the Mauconseil barricade, an old man with white hair extended on the pavement, his breast perforated by a musket-shot and his collar-bone broken; the gutter of the street that flowed under him carried away his blood. I have seen, have touched with my hands, have aided in undressing, a poor child of seven years killed, I was told, in the Rue Tiquetonne; he was pale, his head moved backward and forward on his shoulders while we were taking off his clothes; his eyes, half-shut, were fixed, and on leaning over near his mouth it seemed as if you could hear him feebly murmur from his half-open lips the word "mother!"

Well! there is something more poignant than that murdered child, more lamentable than that old man dabbled with blood, more horrible than that rag stained with human brains, more frightful than those pavements red with carnage, more irreparable than those men and women, those fathers and mothers, butchered and assassinated: it is the vanished honour of a great people! Certainly, those pyramids of dead bodies seen in the cemeteries after the wagons which came from the Champ de Mars had discharged their burdens, those immense open trenches filled hastily in the morning before the twilight brightened into day, brought terror to the hearts of the witnesses; but it is more frightful still to think that at the present moment the peoples of the earth are in doubt, and that for them France, that great splendour of morality, has disappeared! More heart-rending than the heads cloven by the sabre, than the breasts riddled with bullets; more disastrous than violated houses, than murder filling the streets, than blood spilt in the gutters—is the thought that now among all nations it is said: "That nation of nations, that people of the 14th of July, that people of the 10th of August, that people of 1830, that people of 1848, that race of giants which crushed bastiles, that race of men whose visage shone with light; that fatherland of mankind, which produced heroes and thinkers who made all revolutions and gave birth to all births; that France whose name meant liberty, that soul of the world which radiated over Europe, that light—well! some one has walked over it, and has extinguished it. France is no more; it is ended. Look! darkness everywhere! The world is groping on all fours!" . . .

Alas! Louis Bonaparte has done more than kill persons; he has made souls shrink, he has made smaller the heart of the citizen. It is necessary to belong to the race of the indomitable and the invincible, to persevere in the rugged path of renunciation and of duty. Some horrible gangrene of material prosperity is menacing public honesty with destruction and rottenness. Oh, what happiness, after all, to be banished, to be fallen, to be ruined! Is it not so, brave workmen? Is it not so, honest peasants, hunted out of France, without an asylum and without shoes? What happiness to eat black bread, to sleep on a mattress on the ground, to be out at elbows, but to be beyond this, and able to meet those who say, "You are a Frenchman!" with the answer, "I am proscribed!"

And what a miserable spectacle is the delight of self-interest and of cupidity as they gorge themselves at the trough of the 2d of December! "Let us live! Let us do business—job in zinc shares and railway shares. Let us get money: it is ignoble, but, faith! it is excellent. A scruple lost is a louis gained; so let us sell our souls at this rate!" And so men run, jostle one another, dance attendance, and drain all shame to the dregs. If a railway concession in France or lands in Africa cannot be obtained, a place is asked for. A crowd of fearless and devoted beings besiege the Élysée and throng around the man. Junot,[12] near the first Napoleon, braved the splashes from the howitzer-shell in the sand; those near the second brave the splashes of mud. What care they if they share his ignominy, provided they share his fortune. There is a struggle as to who shall be first in this cynical traffic in one's self; and among these people there are young men, with pure and limpid eyes and all the appearances of ingenuous youth, and there are old men who have only one fear—namely, that the place solicited may not reach them in time, and they may die before succeeding in dishonouring themselves. One would surrender himself for a prefecture, another for a receivership, another for a consulship; this one wants a tobacconist's shop, that one an embassy. All want money—some more, some less; for it is of the salary they are thinking, not of the office. Each has his hand outstretched; all offer themselves for sale. One of these days an assayer of consciences will be appointed, just as there is an assayer of coin. . . .

Let us get ahead with this painful question, and examine it in all its aspects.

The mere spectacle of such good fortune as that of Monsieur Bonaparte placed on the summit of the State would suffice to demoralize a people. There always is, and that through the fault of social institutions, which ought, above all, to enlighten

12 Andoche Junot (1771–1813), Napoleonic general.

and civilize—there always is among a population as numerous as that of France a class which is ignorant, which suffers, which covets, which struggles, placed between the bestial instinct that urges to take and the moral law that invites to labour. In the painful and distressed condition in which it still exists, this class to keep upright and honest needs all the pure and holy light which is found in the Gospel; it needs that the spirit of Jesus on the one hand, and the spirit of the French Revolution on the other, should address it in the same manly language, and show forth unceasingly, as the only beacon worthy of the eyes of man, the lofty and mysterious laws of human destiny—abnegation, devotion, self-sacrifice, labour which conducts to material happiness, probity which conducts to interior happiness. Even with this perpetual teaching, at once human and divine, this class, so worthy of sympathy and fraternity, often succumbs; suffering and temptation are stronger than virtue. Now, do you understand the infamous counsels which the success of Monsieur Bonaparte gives to this class? A poor man in rags, without resources, without labour, is there in the shadow, at the corner of the street, seated upon a post; he is meditating and at the same time resisting a bad action; now he wavers and now he is strong; he is hungry, and he would like to steal; to steal, he must have a false key, he must climb a wall; then, the false key made, and the wall climbed, he reaches the money-box; if any one awakens, if he is hindered, he will have to kill; his hair stands on end, his eyes grow wild; his conscience, the voice of God, revolts, and cries to him: "Stop! it is wrong! these are crimes!" At that moment the head of the State passes by; the man sees Monsieur Bonaparte in the uniform of a general, with the red ribbon, and lackeys in gold-laced liveries, riding at full gallop towards his palace in a carriage drawn by four horses. The wretch, halting in presence of his crime, drinks in greedily this splendid vision; and the serenity of Monsieur Bonaparte, and his gold epaulets and the red ribbon and the livery and the palace and the carriage with four horses say to him, "Succeed!" He hangs on to this apparition; he follows it; he runs to the

Élysée. A splendidly arrayed crowd is following in the wake of their prince; all kinds of carriages pass through this gate, and he gets a glimpse of men happy and joyous. Yonder is an ambassador; the ambassador looks at him and says, "Succeed!" Yonder is a judge; the judge looks at him and says, "Succeed!" Yonder is a bishop; the bishop looks at him and says, "Succeed!" So for him henceforth the whole moral law consists in getting clear of the police. To rob, pillage, stab, assassinate, is bad only when you are stupid enough to allow yourself to be taken. Every man who meditates a crime has a constitution to violate, an oath to infringe, an obstacle to destroy. In a word, take your measures well; be clever—succeed. The only guilty actions are those that miscarry. . . .

Succeed! that is everything. Ah, this is a thing to be dreaded. On the day when the human conscience becomes abashed, on the day when success makes right, all is over. The last flickering ray of morality ascends again to heaven; darkness is in the soul of man. All that is left you is to devour one another—ferocious beasts!

To moral degradation is joined political degradation. Monsieur Bonaparte treats France as a conquered country. He effaces republican inscriptions; he cuts down the trees of liberty and makes fagots of them. There was in the Place Bourgogne a statue of the Republic—he uses a pickaxe on it . . .

Go on! continue! heap insult upon insult! disfigure this France prostrate on the pavement! render her unrecognizable! crush the face of the people with repeated blows of your heel! Oh, grant me, find out for me, invent, discover for me any way, short of the dagger (which I will not have: a Brutus for this man! shame! shame! he does not deserve even Louvel[13]—find me any means whatever of casting down this man and delivering my country; of casting down this man—this man of craft, this man of falsehood, this man of success, this man of woe! Any means, the first at hand—pen, sword, paving-stone, riot, by the

---

[13] Louis-Pierre Louvel (1783–1820), saddler who killed the Duc de Berry, third heir presumptive to the throne, in 1820.

people or by the soldier—yes, whatever it be, provided it be loyal and open, I lay hold of it, we all lay hold of it, we the proscribed, if it can restore liberty; deliver the Republic, raise our country out of shame, and send back into the dust, into his past oblivion, into the slums from which he emerged, this imperial ruffian, this pickpocket prince, this vagabond of kings, this traitor, this circus-rider, this radiant ruler, unshaken, satisfied, crowned by his happy crime; who comes and goes, and walks peacefully through shuddering Paris, and who has everything in his favour—the Bourse, the shop, the magistracy, all influences, all guarantees, all invocations, from the *Nom de Dieu* of the soldier to the *Te Deum* of the priest! Truly, when one keeps his eyes fixed too long on certain aspects of this spectacle there are times when a kind of giddiness seizes the firmest minds. . . .

SECOND PART
MOURNING AND FAITH
I

Providence, by the mere fact of universal life, leads on to maturity men, things, events. In order that an old world fade away, it is sufficient for civilization, ascending majestically towards her solstice, to illuminate ancient institutions, ancient prejudices, ancient laws, and ancient manners. Her radiance burns up the past and devours it. Civilization enlightens (this is the visible fact), and at the same time consumes (this is the mysterious fact). Under its influence, that which should decline declines, and that which should grow old grows old, slowly and without shock; wrinkles come to things condemned, be they castes, or codes, or institutions, or religions.

This travail of decrepitude is in some sort its own work— fertilizing decrepitude under which germinates the new life. Destruction goes on gradually; deep crevices which we do not see branch out in the shadow and reduce to dust the interior of that venerable formation which still seems massive from the outside; and then suddenly, some fine day, that antique pile of worm-eaten facts which compose decaying societies becomes unsightly; the edifice cracks, splits, and leans forward. After this nothing can hold together. Let one of those giants peculiar to revolutions arise; let this giant raise his hand, and all is over. There has been such an hour in history, when a blow of Danton's elbow would make Europe crumble. 1848 was one of those hours. Old Europe, feudal, monarchic, and papal, staggered. But a Danton was lacking. The fall did not take place.

It has been often said, in the threadbare phraseology employed in such cases, that 1848 had opened a gulf. No. The corpse of the past was stretched over Europe; it is still so now. 1848 opened a ditch, and was proceeding to throw that corpse into it; it is that ditch that was taken for a gulf. In 1848, all who clung to the past, all who lived on the corpse, saw that ditch close by them. Not only were the kings on their thrones, the cardinals under their birettas, and the captains on their warhorses thrown into agitation; but whoever had any interest whatever in this thing that was about to disappear; whoever cultivated a social fiction for his profit, and leased or rented an abuse; whoever was the guardian of a falsehood, the door-keeper of a prejudice, or the farmer of a superstition; whoever utilized the people for his own ends and ground it down with usury, with taxes, and with lies; whoever sold with false weights—from those who alter a balance to those who falsify a Bible, from the bad trader to the bad priest, from those who manipulate figures to those who coin miracles—all, from the Jewish banker, who is somewhat of a catholic, to the bishop, who is somewhat of a Jew—all the men of the past leaned their heads towards one another and trembled. That yawning ditch into which all their fictions, their treasury, were so near falling—fictions that weighed over man for so many centuries—they resolved to fill up. They resolved to wall it in, to pile stones and rocks on it, and on the heap to erect a gibbet, and to hang on that bloody and gloomy gibbet the great criminal—Truth! They resolved to have done once for all with the spirit of enfranchisement and emancipation, and to tread down and crush forever the ascending forces of humanity.

The undertaking was a serious one. What it was we have already indicated, more than once, in this book and elsewhere. To undo the labours of twenty generations; to take the nineteenth century by the throat and slay in it three centuries—the sixteenth, the seventeenth, and the eighteenth (that is to say, Luther, Descartes, and Voltaire—religious inquiry, philosophical inquiry, universal inquiry); to crush throughout Europe that immense vegetation of free thought—a great oak here, a blade of grass there; to marry the knout and the holy-water sprinkler; to put more of Spain in the South and more of Russia in the North; to resuscitate all that could be resuscitated of the Inquisition, and stifle all that could be stifled of intelligence; to stupefy youth—in other words, to brutalize the future; to force the world to be present at the *auto-da-fé* of ideas; to overturn the tribunes, to suppress the journal, the public poster, books, utterances of every sort—a cry, a murmur, a whisper; to create silence; to hunt down thought in the printer's case, in the composing-stick, in the leaden letter, in the stereotype plate, in the lithograph, in the theatre, in the mouth of the actor, in the copy-book of the school-master, in the pack of the pamphlet-hawker; to preach to man material interest as his faith, his law, his aim, and his God; to say to the people, "Eat, and think no longer"; to displace the brain of man and put it in his stomach; to extinguish individual initiative, local life, national aspirations, all the profound instincts that urge man towards rectitude; to annihilate that *ego* of nations which is called fatherland; to destroy nationality among divided and dismembered populations, constitutions in constitutional states, the Republic in France, liberty everywhere, and everywhere to stamp out human effort: in a word, to close up that abyss which is named "progress"—such was the vast, enormous plan, extending over Europe, which no person conceived singly, for not one of those men of the old world had the genius to do so, but which all followed. . . .

Parties live on words. These men, these ringleaders, who were terrified and united by 1848 had, as we have said before, found their words—"religion," "family," "property." Certain obscure phrases of what is called "socialism" they turned to account with that vulgar adroitness which suffices to impress timidity. It was necessary "to save religion, property, the family, the flag!" they said; and the rabble rout of scared interests flocked to their side. They coalesced, faced around, formed a square. They crowded together; and this crowd was composed of diverse elements. The proprietor entered it because his income had diminished; the peasant, because he had to pay the forty-five centimes;[14] such a one who did not believe in God believed it necessary to save religion because he was compelled to sell his horses. The force which this crowd contained was released and made available. With it repression became the order of the day everywhere, and by means of everything—by law, by arbitrary power, by assemblies, by tribunes, by the jury, by the magistracy, by the police; in Lombardy by the sabre, in Naples by the dungeon, in Hungary by the gibbet. To muzzle intellects, to fetter minds again (slaves escaped for a moment), to prevent the disappearance of the past, to prevent the birth of the future, to perpetuate the power of kings, and of all powerful, privileged, and fortunate personages—everything became good, everything became just, everything became legitimate. For the necessities of the struggle a moral ambuscade against liberty was contrived and spread over the world—put in action by Ferdinand at Palermo, Antonelli at Rome, Schwarzenberg[15]

14 Reference to a tax imposed by the Provisional Government soon after its assumption of power; its incidence was chiefly on the peasantry.

15 King Ferdinand II of the Two Sicilies (1810–59); Giacomo Cardinal Antonelli (1806–76), Chief Minister to the Pope; and Prince Felix von Schwarzenberg (1800–52), Prime Minister of the newly strengthened Habsburg Empire.

at Milan and Pesth, and later on, by the men of December at Paris, those wolves of the human race.

There was among the peoples one people which was a sort of eldest brother in the family of the oppressed, which was like a prophet in the tribune of mankind. This people took the initiative in all the movements of humanity. It said, "Come!" and all followed. As a complement to the fraternity of men which is in the Gospel, this nation taught the fraternity of nations. It spoke by the voice of its writers, of its poets, of its philosophers, and its orators as by a single mouth; and its words went to the extremities of the world, to settle like tongues of fire on the brows of all nations. It presided at the Divine Supper of human intelligence; it multiplied the bread of life to those who wandered in the desert. One day a storm encompassed it; it walked over the abyss and said to the frightened peoples, "Why fear ye?" The waves of the revolutions it raised grew calm under its feet, and far from engulfing, glorified it. Nations sick, suffering, and feeble pressed around it. This one limped; the chain of the Inquisition, riveted on her limbs for three hundred years, had lamed her: it said, "Walk!" and she walked. This other was blind; the old Roman papism had filled her eyes with fog and with night: it said to her, "See!" and she opened her eyes and saw. It said: "Throw away your crutches; that is to say, your prejudices. Throw away your bandages; that is to say, your superstitions. Stand up erect, raise your heads, look at the heavens, contemplate God! The future is yours, O peoples! You have a leper—ignorance; you have a plague—fanaticism; there is not one of you that does not bear one of those frightful maladies which is termed a despot. March on, forward! break the bonds of evil! I am your deliverer, your physician!" Through all the earth there was a grateful shout from the peoples which these words were restoring to health and strength. On one day it approached dead Poland; it lifted its finger and cried, "Arise!" and dead Poland arose.

This people the men of the past, whose fall it prophesied, dreaded and hated. By craft, and tortuous patience and audacity, they seized and succeeded in garoting it at last. For more than three years the world has witnessed a gigantic execution, a frightful spectacle. For more than three years the men of the past, the scribes and pharisees, the publicans and the high-priests, are crucifying, in presence of the human race, the Christ of the peoples—the French people. Some have furnished the cross, others the nails, others the hammer. Falloux has placed on her brow the crown of thorns; Montalembert has pressed the sponge of gall and vinegar on her lips; Louis Bonaparte is the wretched soldier who has pierced her side and forced from her the last cry, "Eli! Eli! Lama Sabacthani!"

And now it is all over. The French people is dead. The great tomb is opened to receive it for three days.

II

Let us have faith. Let us not be cast down. To despair is to desert.

Let us look to the future. The future! We know not what storms separate us from the port, but the far-off and radiant port is before our eyes. The future, we repeat, is the Republic for all; let us add—the future is peace with all.

Let us not adopt the vulgar caprice of calumniating and dishonouring the age in which we live. . . .

. . . Let us proclaim it aloud, proclaim it in downfall and defeat. This century is the grandest of centuries! And do you know why? Because it is the mildest. This century, the immediate issue of the French Revolution and its first-born, is freeing the slave in America, raising the pariah in Asia, extinguishing the suttee in India, and tramping out the last embers of the stake in Europe. It is civilizing Turkey; getting the spirit of the Gospel even into the Koran; elevating woman; subordinating the right of the stronger to the right of him who has more justice on his side; suppressing pirates; diminishing penalties; improving the sanitation of prisons; throwing the branding-iron into the sewer; condemning the penalty of death; taking away the ball from the legs of criminals; abolishing torture; discrediting and stigmatizing the sword . . . and tearing from tyrants their claws. This age proclaims the sovereignty of the citizen and the inviolability of life; it crowns the people and consecrates the man. In art it has genius of all kinds—writers, orators, poets, historians, publicists, philosophers, painters, sculptors, and musicians; majesty, grace, power, strength, splendour, depth, colour, form, and style. It steeps itself at once in the real and the ideal, and bears in its hands the two thunderbolts—the true and the beautiful. In science it accomplishes all miracles; it makes a saltpetre out of cotton, a horse out of steam, a workman out of Volta's battery, a messenger out of the electric fluid, a painter out of the sun. It opens on two infinities two windows, the telescope and the microscope—the one on the infinitely great, the other on the infinitely little; and it finds in the abyss of the insects as well as in the abyss of the stars a proof that God is! It suppresses duration, it suppresses distance, it suppresses suffering; it writes a letter from London to Paris, and receives a reply in ten minutes; it cuts off a thigh from a man, and the man sings and smiles. There is one more progress to be realized, and it is drawing near to it—a progress that is nothing in comparison with the other miracles which it has already performed: it has but to find the means of guiding in a mass of air a lighter bubble of air. It has already the bubble of air—it holds it imprisoned; it has but to find the impulsive force, to make the vacuum before the air-balloon, to burn the air before it as the flare does before itself: it has only to resolve in any fashion whatever this problem, and it will resolve it—and do you know what will happen then? That very instant frontiers vanish, barriers are effaced; the entire Chinese wall around thought, around commerce, around industry, around nationalities, around progress, falls down. In despite of censorships, in despite of indexes, it rains books and journals on all sides; Voltaire, Diderot, Rousseau, fall in hail-showers on Rome, Naples, Vienna, St.

Petersburg; the human word is manna, and the serf picks it up in the furrows; fanaticisms die, oppression is impossible. . . . No more hatreds, no more self-interests devouring one another, no more wars; a new life made up of harmony and light prevails and tranquillizes the world; the fraternity of nations traverses space and communicates in the eternal azure; men meet one another in the heavens!

While watching for this last progress, observe the point to which this century has conducted civilization already. Once there was a world in which men walked with slow steps, with bent back and with bowed head; . . . in which a town like Dijon was separated from a town like Paris by the necessity of making a will, by robbers at all the corners of the woods and a ride of ten days in a coach; in which a book was a kind of infamy and filth, which the executioner burned on the steps of the Palace of Justice; in which superstition and ferocity gave each other the hand; in which the Pope said to the Emperor, "Jungamus dexteras, gladium gladio copulemus";[16] in which crosses were met at every step from which hung amulets, and gibbets from which hung men; in which there were heretics, Jews, and lepers; in which houses had loop-holes and battlements; in which the streets were closed by a chain, the rivers by a chain . . . the cities by walls, kingdoms by prohibitions and penalties; in which except for authority and force, always in the closest union, all was divided, severed, kept apart, alienated, set at variance, hating and hated, scattered and dead—men dust, power a block of iron. To-day there is a world in which all is living, united, interlinked, and incorporated—a world in which reign thought, commerce, and industry; in which political ideas, becoming more and more fixed, are tending towards an amalgamation with science—a world in which the last scaffolds and the last cannon are hastening to cut off the last heads and vomit forth the last shells—a world in which distance has disappeared; in which Constantinople is nearer to Paris than Lyons was a

16 "Give us your hand and join swords with ours."

hundred years ago; in which America and Europe throb with the same heart-beat—a world of universal dissemination and of universal love, whose brain is France, whose arteries are railways, and whose fibres are electric wires. Do you not see that to expound such a situation is to explain everything, to demonstrate everything, and to resolve everything? Do you not feel that the old world had of necessity an old soul—tyranny; and that on the new world a young soul is about to descend necessarily, irresistibly, divinely—liberty? . . .

Let us have faith! Self-mockery is the beginning of baseness. Let us affirm the truth. It is by such affirmation we become good; it is by such affirmation we become great. Yes, the enfranchisement of intelligence, and the consequent enfranchisement of peoples, was the sublime task the nineteenth century was accomplishing in co-operation with France; for the double providential travail of the time and of the men, of maturity and of action, was blended in the common work, and the great nation was the beacon of the great epoch.

O my country! it is now, when we behold thee bleeding, lifeless, with drooping head and closed eyes, and open mouth that no longer speaks; with the marks of the whip on thy shoulders, and the imprint of the nails of the boots of thy executioners on thy entire body, naked and soiled, and like unto the dead; the object of hatred and, alas! object of derision—it is now, O my country! that the heart of the proscribed overflows with love and respect for thee! Thou liest motionless. The men of despotism and of oppression laugh, and delight in the haughty delusion that thou art to be feared no more. Fleeting will be their joy. The nations who are in darkness forget the past and see only the present and despise thee. Pardon them; they know not what they do. Despise thee! Great God! despise France? And who are they? What language do they speak? What books have they in their hands? What names do they know by heart? What posters are pasted on the walls of their theatres! What form have their arts, their laws, their manners, their garments, their pleasures, their fashions? What is the great date for them as for us? '89! If they take France out of their soul, what is left them? O peoples! though Greece were fallen, and fallen forever, would she be despised? Is Italy despised? Can France be despised? Gaze on those paps! she is your nurse. Gaze on that womb! she is your mother. If she sleeps, if she is in a lethargy, silence and hats off! If she is dead, on your knees!

The exiles are scattered; the winds of destiny disperse men as a handful of ashes. Some are in Belgium, in Piedmont, in Switzerland, where they have no liberty; others are in London, where they have no shelter. . . . There is no one who does not stand aside respectfully as they pass by; there is no one who does not contemplate with deep emotion, as one of the grandest spectacles afforded to mankind, all these serene consciences, all these broken hearts. They suffer and are silent; in them the citizen has immolated the man; they look adversity calmly in the face; they do not cry out even under the pitiless scourge of misfortune, "Civis Romanus sum!" But at evening, the season of meditation, when all in the foreign town is arrayed in sadness (for that which seems cold in the daytime becomes funereal in the twilight)—at night, when sleep comes not, souls the most stoical become the prey of sorrow and dejection. Where are the little children! Who will give them bread; who will give them their father's kiss? Where is the wife; where is the mother; where is the brother; where are they all? And those songs, heard in the evening in the mother-tongue—where are they? Where is the wood, the tree, the pathway, the caves full of nests, the belfry encircled by tombs? Where is the street, where the suburb, the lamp lit before the door, the friends, the workshop, the accustomed toil! And the furniture sold at public auction,[17] the sale invading the sanctuary of home. . . .

The proscribed are silent; or if they complain, it is among themselves. They know one another, and are doubly brothers,

[17] Hugo's wife handled the auctioning of his household effects before joining him on Jersey.

having the same country, and being victims of the same proscription; and so they retail their miseries, brother to brother. He who has money shares it with those who have none; he who has firmness gives a portion to those who lack. Recollections are interchanged, aspirations, hopes. With out-stretched arms they turn in the darkness to that which they have left behind. Oh, how happy yonder are those who no longer think of us! Each suffers, and at moments each becomes incensed. On all memories are engraved the names of all the executioners. Each has something which he curses—Mazas, the prison-ship, the casemate, the informer who betrayed him, the spy who lay in wait for him, the gendarme who arrested him, Lambessa where there is a friend, Cayenne where there is a brother. But there is one thing which they all bless; it is France! Ah, a complaint, a word against thee, France! No, no! never has the fatherland a stronger hold on the heart than in exile. They will do their whole duty with tranquil soul and steadfast perseverance. No longer to behold thee is their sorrow; never to forget thee, their joy. But oh, the sadness of it all! And after eight months it is still in vain we tell ourselves that things are as they are. That yonder is the spire of Saint-Michel and not the Pantheon, that Sainte-Gudule is before our eyes and not Notre Dame; we cannot believe it! But it is true; it cannot be denied, and must be acknowledged, though we were to expire from humiliation and despair, that what is yonder, stretched prostrate on the earth, is the nineteenth century, is France!

What! it is this Bonaparte who has consummated this disaster? What! it is in the centre of the greatest people of the world, in the middle of the greatest century of history, that this man has arisen and triumphed? To make France his prey, great God! What the lion would not have dared, the ape has done! what the eagle would have feared to seize in his talons, the parrot has clutched in its claws! what Louis XI would have failed in, what Richelieu would have hurled himself against in vain, what Napoleon would have been unequal to—in one single day, between the dark and the dawn, the absurd has become possible;

axioms have become chimeras, and everything that was a lie has
become a living fact! What! the most signal co-operation of men,
the most magnificent movement of ideas, the most tremendous
concatenation of events, that which a Titan could not have
restrained, that which a Hercules could not have turned aside,
the river of humanity in its onward flow, with France surging
ahead, civilization, progress, intelligence, revolution, liberty—
all has been brought on one fine morning to a stand, has been
absolutely and at a moment's notice, stopped by this mummer,
this dwarf, this stunted Tiberius, this abortion, this nothing! God
was marching onward; Louis Bonaparte, with plume on head,
threw himself across the path and said to God, "Thou shalt go
no farther!" And God has stopped.

And do you imagine that this is so! And do you fancy that
this plebiscite exists; that this Constitution of some day or other
in January exists; that this Council of State and Legislative Body
exist? Do you imagine that there is a lackey called Rouher, a
valet called Troplong, a eunuch called Baroche,[18] and a sultan,
a pacha, a master, named Louis Bonaparte? You do not see,
then, that all this is a chimera! you do not see, then, that the
2d of December is only a monstrous illusion, a pause, a halt, a
sort of stage curtain behind which God, that wonderful mecha-
nist, is preparing and building up the last act—the supreme and
triumphal act of the French Revolution! You are gazing stupidly
at the curtain, at the things painted on that coarse canvas—the
nose of this one, the epaulets of that one, the big sabre of that
other; at those peddlers of cologne-water in their gold lace whom
you term generals, those baboons whom you style magistrates,
those simple creatures whom you dub senators; and you take this
medley of caricatures and spectres for realities! And you do not

18 Eugène Rouher (1814–84), Minister of Justice 1849–52, Bona-
partist, held several posts under the Second Empire. Raymond-
Théodore Troplong (1795–1869), magistrate and legal theorist, a
Bonapartist appointed to high legal posts after the coup d'état. Pierre-
Jules Baroche (1802–70), deputy and cabinet member and promi-
nent Bonapartist.

hear, in the shadow beyond, that muffled sound! you do not hear some one moving backward and forward! you do not see that the breathing of that which is behind makes the canvas tremble!

CONCLUSION:

THE MEANINGS OF THE COUP D'ÉTAT

INTELLECTUALS faced with Louis Napoleon's coup d'état had to comprehend it within some scheme of meaning designed to make sense out of great public events. In one way their task was easier than it might be today—they had such schemes available, e.g., theories of progress, providential plans anticipating the triumph of liberty, or democracy, or socialism, or communism through the course of human history. The Christian habit of viewing historical events as part of God's plan, and the course of history as directional, helped greatly; the Romantic movement, plus Hegelian philosophy in the early nineteenth century, provided formal philosophies of history that subsumed all historical events under great unfolding plans. Both Tocqueville and Proudhon saw the coming of democracy as providential. Similarly Hugo felt the triumph of a democratic republic was predestined. Marx never lost faith in the victory of the proletariat. Bagehot was least clearly a believer in progress in 1852; he was later to produce, however, in *Physics and Politics,* a classic philosophy of historical progress through conflict, a liberal Darwinism.

Their assurance about where the course of history was going allowed the five writers included here to speak with assurance about the meaning of the coup d'état. (Today our pretensions might be less.) Only Bagehot, because he has so little to say about the larger issue of how the coup fit into some overarching scheme, seems to remain at a pragmatic level. Yet even Bagehot believed that lessons should be drawn from the post-1848 experience. These lessons were largely practical, permitting him to attack his readers' illusions about the easy transfer of institutions; but we may wonder whether for him there does not still lurk the expectation that historical events possess value, that the lessons come from happenings as much as from the interpreter (as in Hugo's case a chapter title, "The Quantity of Good Contained in the Evil," clearly suggests).

Tocqueville shared with Marx, Hugo, and Proudhon a deep disillusionment over the results of the 1848 Revolution and the coup d'état. Not surprisingly all four found one of the events' major lessons the dispelling of old illusions. Bagehot's conclusion resembles theirs even though he was less committed. Tocqueville, deeply depressed, concluded that universal suffrage could work only when conservatives learned that the police state constituted self-imprisonment.[1] Marx had seen the whole early course of the Second Republic (in *The Class Struggles in France*) as a clarification of class relationships and the illusions that accompanied them. Now he agreed with Proudhon that socialists were learning they could not count on parliamentary government and hoped that the failure of 1848 had discredited some mistaken socialist theories,[2] and that the conservative peasants would now lose their Bonapartist illusions. Proudhon also believed the contradiction between government and economy had been made more evident by the coup d'état. Hugo found some consolation in the fact that the image of the Empire had been besmirched and the fear of the Republic lessened.

All felt the need to discover in the aftermath of the coup some positive result; however much they disapproved the Sec-

[1] E. T. Gargan, *Alexis de Tocqueville: The Critical Years, 1848–1851* (Washington, 1951), p. 231.
[2] *Ibid.*, pp. 231, 268.

ond Republic, a military coup and a potential Empire were unlikely to be improvements. Tocqueville could not find any hopeful meaning. The events fitted too perfectly his long-held fears of democratic despotism. Marx, Proudhon, and Hugo made real efforts to be sanguine. Marx, despite his new conviction that a successful revolution was a long way off, was still seeking to contribute to its development, and his hopes recurrently revived. Proudhon's book was an attempt to make sure the coup was a step in the march of the Revolution, a warning against Caesarism. Hugo saw himself engaged in the battle that would lead to the fall of the evil regime and the victory of the Republic.

The need for positive conclusions perhaps helps to explain the surprisingly poor job of prophecy the five authors do. All were aware of the sources of strength of Louis Napoleon's regime, yet only Bagehot thought it had much hope of surviving. He suggested that it suited the French and might last a considerable time (however long that might be), but would fail at last before the progress of liberalism—which, in the form of the liberalized Empire of the late 1860s, is just what it did.[3] None of the other authors came close to so effective a prediction. Marx, for all his magnificent engine of social analysis and prediction, moralized and hoped and misjudged, even though his analysis of the current situation is outstanding. Proudhon, when he stopped trying to paint a future or to cajole the regime into establishing his version of anarchy, could scarcely believe the regime's broad power base and minimized its impulse to empire although he fully recognized them both. Hugo condemned and excoriated and vented his fury—and admitted the seven million plebiscite votes. Then he denied that anything so immoral could last. Tocqueville's predictions were scattered and various. All of them except Bagehot seem to have suffered to some degree from self-delusion, from hoping against hope. It does not greatly im-

[3] But Bagehot shared with Proudhon the wrong prediction that the army would be disloyal. I also think it more reasonable to suppose that Proudhon's belief that the regime could not persist as a despotism is an anticipation of revolution rather than of liberalization.

prove the cases of Marx and Hugo that their predictions were *eventually* fulfilled. They had expected a short reign for Louis Napoleon; eighteen years is not a short reign.

Bagehot's comparative success in prediction may stem in part from his lack of involvement; more important, I think, is his relativism, revealed in his comparative study of national character. His emphasis upon the differences he remarked in French political behavior when contrasted to English traits suggests a kind of early social anthropology. It may be that prediction is more readily attained through the feel or intuition of a culture than it is through the more structured sort of analysis Marx engaged in. Marx was certainly a relativist as well, but he anticipated variant expressions of a necessary course of capitalist development, and for him the causal hierarchy was settled. For generations Marx's critics have pointed out his continuous failures as a prophet; he kept expecting the Revolution that did not come, he expected increased misery of the working class, etc. But although his theory failed as a machine for prediction, it was a great success as an engine of analysis.

John McManners has written:

> Contemporary history, so far as it is possible, can best be written by fanatics—or at least by men with powerful motives for operating some trenchant system of selectivity, by men with a formula, provided it is big enough. Marx had invented such a formula which, in its pristine freshness, must have seemed a veritable incantation bringing lucid explanation out of the most chaotic happenings.[4]

There can be no doubt that Marx's tracing of the forces in conflict in the Republic, his explanation of the success of the coup d'état, is far more cogent and satisfying than the explanations offered by Tocqueville, Bagehot, Proudhon, and Hugo. Marx's own assessment of Proudhon and Hugo in the well-known 1869

[4] John McManners, *European History, 1789–1914; Men, Machines, and Freedom* (New York, 1969), p. 332.

preface to *The Eighteenth Brumaire,* however, is less than fair.
Marx writes:

> Of the writings dealing with the same subject approximately
> *at the same time* as mine, only two deserve notice: Victor
> Hugo's *Napoleon the Little* and Proudhon's *Coup d'État.*
>
> Victor Hugo confines himself to bitter and witty invective
> against the responsible publisher of the *coup d'état.* The event
> itself appears in his work like a bolt from the blue. He sees in
> it only the violent act of a single individual. He does not no-
> tice that he makes this individual great instead of little by
> ascribing to him a personal power of initiative such as would
> be without parallel in world history. Proudhon, for his part,
> seeks to represent the *coup d'état* as the result of an antecedent
> historical development. Unnoticeably, however, his historical
> construction of the *coup d'état* turns into a historical *apologia*
> for its hero. Thus he falls into the error of our so-called *ob-*
> *jective* historians. I, on the contrary, demonstrate how the *class*
> *struggle* in France created circumstances and relationships that
> made it possible for a grotesque mediocrity to play a hero's
> part.[5]

Hugo *does* recognize the bases of Louis Napoleon's power,
and he associates him with the general European reaction. He
also gives him a role in the providential development of the
Republic of the future, i.e., he fits him into the sweep of history as the conclusive demonstration that the instruments of
"order" oppose the democratic ideal. Yet all this is admittedly
incidental to just that attack of which Marx accuses him.

In Proudhon's case, the long-range historical explanation is
probably less effective (perhaps because it is largely an expression of Proudhon's faith) than Proudhon's description of the

[5] *Karl Marx and Friedrich Engles, Selected Works,* (Moscow,
1951) vol. 1, pp. 221–22. Édouard Dolléans notes that Marx wrote
his articles in freedom in London, while Proudhon wrote his book
"en pleine bataille," as *"une instrument de combat."* E. Dolléans,
introduction to *La Révolution Sociale Demontrée par la Coup d'État*
(Paris, 1936), p. 105.

condition of France during the Second Republic. Here the catalogue of forces resembles Marx's description of competing classes and parties, but is less well-connected to the coup d'état. Marx obviously ignores Proudhon's appeal to the President or interprets it in his own way; it remains difficult to find in *The Social Revolution* an apology for Louis Napoleon.

Marx's concluding sentence points up another important aspect of these selections—the issue of the ability and power of the President. All, to one degree or another, belittle him. Marx may be correct that Hugo credits him with power (in reverse, so to speak)—but Hugo gives man a larger causal role in history than does Marx or Proudhon. His explicit view of Louis Napoleon is certainly negative. So is that of Marx, who says the coup succeeded despite Louis Napoleon's indiscretions. Tocqueville is more ambivalent; Proudhon remains hopeful, though his historical theory does not appear to leave the President much scope for action. Bagehot is the most realistic as to the skills of the President.

As for the other elements in the pre-coup situation: setting aside Tocqueville for the moment, there seems general agreement that the bureaucracy, Church, and army were mainstays of Louis Napoleon's power. Similarly, it seems to have taken little insight to see the President's tie to the peasantry—clearly they voted for him—but only Marx deals with the matter at length. The intriguing thing to discover in each selection is what the author can make of these connections. Of special note is Marx's new emphasis, in 1852, on the strength of the bourgeois order, buttressed by the peasantry.[6] Such a recognition certainly reduced his expectation of successful revolution in the near future.

Two concluding points might be made. We have said that Hugo is representative of the continuation of Romantic politics after 1848. He is of the same breed as Mazzini and other exiled revolutionaries who remained idealistic and hopeful in the

[6] Gargan, pp. 72, 89.

period when it has been said that a new realism came into politics. Some of that new realism may be visible in Bagehot's "Letters." Marx's *The Eighteenth Brumaire*, portraying the Second Republic as farce, is an expression of bitter disillusionment.[7] Proudhon's effort at Machiavellianism, transparent as it is, also suggests a moral code under strain. We may have here, then, a selection of readings that represent the shift that was occurring in the aftermath of 1848, when with the defeat of internal revolution the generous hopes of the springtime of the peoples were replaced by the calculations of diplomacy.

A second comment is brought to mind by remarks of Wilhelm Liebknecht's, comparing Marx's book to Hugo's:

> Here a comparison suggests itself to me. Napoleon's coup d'état, treated by Marx in his *Eighteenth Brumaire*, was also made the subject of a famous publication by Victor Hugo, the greatest French romancer and phrase-juggler. What a contrast between the two publications and the two men! There the monstre-phrase and the phrase-monstre, here the facts, methodically arranged—the coolly meditating man of science and the politician, wrathful, but never losing his serene judgment through his wrath.
>
> There fleeting, resplendent spray. Eruptions of pathetic rhetoric, grotesque caricatures—here every word a well-aimed dart, every sentence a weighty charge loaded with facts, the naked truth, overwhelming in its nakedness—no indignation, only demonstration, fixing of that which is. Victor Hugo's *Napoleon le Petit*—Napoleon the Little—had ten rapidly following editions and is to-day forgotten. And Marx's *Eighteenth Brumaire* will be read admiringly after thousands of years. Victor Hugo's *Napoleon the Little* was a lampoon—Marx's *Eighteenth Brumaire* is a historic work that will be to the economic historian of the future—and the future will not know

[7] Jacques Barzun, in *Darwin, Marx, and Wagner*, (Boston, 1941), has viewed Marx as representative of a new harshness in European thought. In the period just before 1848 Marx and Engels consciously gave up much of their earlier Hegelian language because it resembled too closely that of the humanitarian True Socialists.

any other but economic history—just as indispensable as to us
the history of the Peloponnesian War by Thucydides.[8]

If, setting aside the Tocqueville letter to the *Times* and comparing the other works, we ask why Hugo's *Napoleon the Little,*
or for that matter Proudhon's *Social Revolution,* are relatively
forgotten and Marx's *Eighteenth Brumaire* remembered, we can
accept some of Liebknecht's answer, which is to say that Hugo's
rhetoric is dated.[9] But then so is some of Marx's, while other
parts of it have simply become current jargon. And Marx is
perhaps less the cool scientist than Liebknecht paints him to be.
More important, perhaps, a good many of both Hugo's and
Proudhon's enthusiasms as well as their hatreds are dated. The
two selections best known in their own day are least known
now, which may suggest they were what was most needed
then, that they constitute very clear expressions of mid-
nineteenth-century thought. Marx's and Bagehot's works were
then little known. Both seem to speak to us much more readily
today, Bagehot because he had distance on the events, Marx
because he had a sociology that allowed him the semblance of
distance. Marx had a further advantage. He did not let himself
get trapped by his theory; he wrote history of a much less rigidly
structured sort than might have been expected. The consequence is a book with the peculiar timelessness of good history.

All of these documents in varying degrees possess relevance
to other times and places. They to not simply reveal their authors' minds and reflect their times; they offer more. They exemplify varieties of commentary on political behavior—forms of
analysis and judgment showing how remarkably intelligent men
may react to a significant historical happening.

[8] Wilhelm Liebknecht, *Biographical Memoirs,* trans. by Ernest
Unterman (Chicago, 1908), pp. 88–89. And see above, p. 114, note
2.

[9] The image of France as the crucified Christ of nations—also to
be found in Proudhon—may serve as a pertinent example.

INDEX

French Revolution (*cont'd*)
ment to, 258; spirit, 388; successors, 395
Fromm, Erich, 119 n, 140
Fronde, 184 *and* n

Gargan, Edward, 27, 138
Garibaldi, Giuseppe, 7, 323, 324
Garnier-Pagès, Louis, 286 *and* n
Germany, 122, 127, 129, 130–31, 214, 243, 328; France, 315 *and* n; Marx, 116–17; philosophy, 210 n; revolution, 127, 128; revolutionaries, 130, Marx and, 134 n–35 n. *See* Luther
Girardin, Émile de, 70 *and* n, 97–98, 99–100; Mme., 323
Government, 108–9, 349, 361, 365–68; Bagehot, 58–59, 66; Hugo, 341–49; national self-government: French aptitude for, 83–88, 103 ff., 108; Proudhon, 206, 218–20, 229 *and* n, 231, 234, 237 ff., 246, 269–88, 303 ff., 306, 309; "will," 269 ff. *See under* country *and* Politics
Grant, Elliott, 321, 322 n
Granville, Lord, 101
Greece (Ancient): national character, 80
Greppo, M., 257
Grün, Karl, 212 n
Guedalla, Philip, 322 n
Guérard, Albert, 16, 327
Guernsey, 322, 324
Guizot, François, 123, 143 *and* n

Habsburg Empire, 393 n
Haiti, 352 n
Ham, prison, 188, 257, 344 *and* n
Hannibal, 338
Hardouin, M., 46
Hasselt, André van, 323
Hauranne, Duvergier de, 42
Hazlitt, William, 99

Heine, Heinrich, 150 n; Marx, 122
Hegel, Georg, 117–18, 141; history, 121; Marx, 113, 120–21, 125; *Philosophy of Law*, 114, 125
Hegelianism, 211, 212, 232, 403
Henry V, King of France, 174, 265 *and* n, 291, 348
Henry VIII, King of England, 338
Heroes (of history), 70
Herr, Richard, 30
Hess, Moses, 117
High Court of Justice, 13, 154, 378; decree against Louis Napoleon, 45–46
Himmelfarb, Gertrude, 58 n
History, 264, 265; conception-reality distinction, 160; Hegel, 141; heroes, 70; Marx's law of, 112–13 (*see* Marx); philosophies, 210, 403 ff.
Holy Alliance, 296, 297
Hook, Sidney, 134 n
Hugo, Victor, xii, 12 n, 15, 16, 29, 39 n, 171 n, 215, 232 n, 266 n; background, 311 ff.; beliefs, 325, 327–28; characteristics, 318, 321–22 *and* n, 326–27, 404, 408; *Coup*, 13 (*see* Louis Napoleon); exile, 311, 315, 321, 322–24, 399 *and* n; funeral, 325; honors, 312, 314; illusions, 60 n; Louis Napoleon, 317–19, 327, 372–75 (*see* Napoleon the Little *under* writings); Marx: assessment of, 406–7, comparison, 409–10; mistress, 321; moral judgment, 138; patriotism, 312, 323 n, 386, 394–95, 398–400; poetry, 311, 312, 321, 323, 324; politics, 311–18, 320 n, 324, 403, special function, 325; Prou-

5 5 8 9 5

December 2, 1851

Contemporary Writings on the Coup d'Etat
of Louis Napoleon

Edited with introductions by John B. Halsted

In this volume five leading thinkers comment on an important historical event just after it has taken place, revealing how much the interpretation of history rests on the preconceptions of the interpreter, and also how many illuminating interpretations of the same event are possible.

The fall of the Second French Republic in 1851 and the establishment of the Second Empire had important repercussions on the course of both French and world history. Of the five men included here, three—Tocqueville, Proudhon and Hugo—were Frenchmen whose own lives were immediately affected. Bagehot and Marx were foreigners who saw in the coup validations of their respective theories of politics and history.

The editor has provided introductory essays to each of the selections and a long introduction on the coup as it appears today.

Cover Design by Fred Troller

A Doubleday Anchor Original